Infrastructural Love

INFR
ASTR
UCTU
RAL Love

Designed by Bettina Schwalm

Infrastructural Love

Caring for Our Architectural Support Systems

Edited by Hélène Frichot, Adrià Carbonell,
Hannes Frykholm, Sepideh Karami

Birkhäuser
Basel

CONTENTS

Infrastructural Love: Caring for Our Architectural Support Systems

---

INFRASTRUCTURES

Infrastructures

Céline Condorelli

With infrastructure, something both huge and hidden is conjured up, a dark and indistinct shadow of a thing whose imperative is to function without needing to be thought about. Conceptually, it is beneath structure, below architecture, under life as we know it, the infra signaling that it is lower in position, in value. Spatially, it is farther away and always to be discussed later. Despite this subservient status, infrastructure is what allows society to hold its shape—its structure—as a complex set of events and to form and support a stable pattern. The pattern comprises actions, not things, as the universe is constantly moving, and therefore infrastructure needs to regenerate, to evolve, to contain, to transport, to transfer, to guide, and generally to move things along.

Infrastructure is often confused with public works and the local government departments responsible for the planning and maintenance of the practical aspects of city services. Yet, as is often the case, it is precisely within this subordinate function that infrastructure is imagined and constructed as the repository of political and cultural imagination, the network for social and economic connections, and the form of human ecology. In short, infrastructure displays a society's inherent ideology and the conditions that allow or restrict what appears in the domain of the visible; it not only designates images but that which is intelligible. Systems of domination, subjugation, or repression also take place in infrastructural systems, which are not simply a manifestation or embodiment of such preexisting systems but an intrinsic part of their configuration. Infrastructure is both a symbol of permanence and a channeler of flows, a collection of built objects and a set of ideas about modernity.

Yet infrastructure itself has long been repressed, historically excluded, for instance, from architectural drawings. The modern city was designed to create and maintain the illusion that infrastructure was a utility to be placed out of sight and separated from the landscapes of our everyday lives. Any analysis of the built environment tends to show a complicity with supplementary machines, mechanisms, and infrastructures, yet buildings and objects always reemerge as autonomous: we do not like to admit that things have conditions. Left out of the plan, infrastructure was selectively edited out of the new urban utopia so that the new residential landscape could resemble a tranquil place for the full development of the modern individual.

The result is that we have forgotten about infrastructure and its need to be maintained, updated, funded. Also forgotten is that infrastructure is where societies articulate their political imagination; it guides how we want to live in our cities, in our societies, and, ultimately, as Buckminster Fuller would have it, on spaceship earth.

INFRASTRUCTURAL Love

Chapter 1
Infrastructural Love: Caring for Our Architectural Support Systems

Hélène Frichot, Adrià Carbonell,
Hannes Frykholm, Sepideh Karami

This anthology is dedicated to infrastructural love. We focus our collective attention on the distributed architectural support systems that are associated with local and global infrastructures, small and large, material and virtual, visible and hidden behind the scenes of everyday life. How do infrastructures and their architectural support systems hold us up? How do they fail us? Can we imagine architectural infrastructures from novel points of view, both human and more-than-human? Where can we, as critical and creative designers and thinkers of architecture and design, intervene to support more inclusive, humorous, speculative, and sheltering infrastructures? Collecting critical and creative essays, instructional guides, and speculative projects, this book forges connections between architectural spaces and infrastructural systems with the aim of critically responding to contemporary environmental, social, and political crises. We ask how understanding architecture in relation to infrastructure can help us rethink and expand architectural practices and pedagogies. That infrastructure increasingly demands our attention is plain to see, and we need to find the means to collectively think with it from the disciplinary point of view of architecture.

What Is Infrastructure; or, What Can Infrastructure Do?

Infrastructure is ubiquitous. It is in the fiber optics of smart city telecommunications and associated data centers; it supports the basic utilities of water, electricity, and gas; it coordinates massive transport networks; it is, importantly, the sociotechnological and spatiotemporal glue that holds everything together. The architectural support structures that are entangled with infrastructural systems include waiting rooms and warehouses, call centers and parking lots, toll booths and public toilets. These ordinary architectures and their everyday affects are distributed across urban and peri-urban, suburban, hinterland, and rural milieus. Architectural spaces and times support infrastructures, but they also become infrastructures. What, after all, is a Roman aqueduct if not an admixture of architectural and infrastructural prowess designed for the distribution of water alongside the massive project of empire building? What is an Indigenous Australian eel trap if not an artful infrastructural means of redistributing the flow of a river to capture sufficient bounty for the sustenance of a tribe? Just enough, not too much.

For the most part, infrastructural networks have been relegated to the engineers and the software designers. In this collection we argue for the role that architecture can play in rethinking what infrastructure can do. Architecture emerges at the threshold where the pragmatic work of the engineer proves insufficient. It extends this pragmatism toward the imaginative construction of supportive spaces and relations. This is because architecture is visionary, and the architect's skill set involves wild speculation about how the world might be made otherwise. Infrastructural love as an affective orientation encourages a radical engagement with the world, putting the architect in close proximity with that which requires support and exposing the architect to the risks of such encounters. We admit to defining architecture and the figure of the architect in an expanded sense, and in this collection you will find stories that also incorporate other-than-human actors in the mix of infrastructural adventures.

Infrastructural love as an affective orientation encourages a radical engagement with the world, putting the architect in close proximity with that which requires support and exposing the architect to the risks of such encounters.

Despite world weariness and exhaustion, we posit that architecture, when at its best, is what maintains the relations between peoples, places, and things. Architecture is infrastructure, and architecture supports infrastructures, even if it is also indebted to the sometimes devastating supply chains that infrastructures handle. That is, sometimes infrastructure is good for you; sometimes infrastructure is bad for you. The important point is to acknowledge that infrastructural systems are inherently ambivalent and need to be considered in a situated way. Infrastructures form part of vast projects of colonization, eradicating ways of life and ravaging environment-worlds. Kenny Cupers writes of the multiple, paradoxical, and inconsistent effects of infrastructure, arguing that, while it "shapes territories and governs the movements and processes within and across them," it also "excludes, contains, and subjugates as much as it includes, moves, or liberates."[1] On the one hand are the colonizing aspects of infrastructure; on the other hand persists the decolonizing potential of infrastructure and infrastructural thinking. Where infrastructure forwards a project of colonization, it is informed by a Western Enlightenment logic of development and advancement, what Brian Larkin calls "technopolitics," by which he means "forms of political rationality that underlie technological projects and which give rise to an 'apparatus of governmentality.'"[2] The construction of material infrastructures (e.g., pipelines, railways, and structures for the extraction of natural resources) can be situated historically as a colonial instrument for the demarcation of territories and the transformation of the soil into profitable land. Such infrastructural projects often result in violent processes of exclusion, wherein property comes into being under the logic of "improvement."[3] Resisting the territorializing impulse of colonization and instead following a decolonial gesture, infrastructure connects us to the earth, not as a resource to be consumed but as a ground upon which we can peacefully cohabit, where we can be protected, offer and receive care, and be allowed to flourish. Decolonizing infrastructures shift from the question of "how the world is breaking down" to "how the world gets put back together."[4] In the radical process of putting the broken pieces together, infrastructure architecture (as a novel interdisciplinary and transdisciplinary practice) can establish the grounds for action, suggest design methods that incite curiosity, and imagine a world that is "patterned" differently.

In their call to recognize housing as an infrastructure of care, Emma R. Power and Kathleen J. Mee render visible the infrastructures that constitute everyday life by placing an emphasis on the act of patterning.[5] Housing infrastructures, they argue, "pattern social life" across three domains, affecting housing materialities, markets, and governance. They take as their starting point feminist care

1 Kenny Cupers, "Coloniality of Infrastructure," in "Coloniality of Infrastructure," special project, ed. Nick Axel, Kenny Cupers, and Nikolaus Hirsch, *e-flux Architecture*, September 2021, https://www.e-flux.com/architecture/coloniality-infrastructure/412386/editorial/.

2 Brian Larkin, "The Politics and Poetics of Infrastructure," *Annual Review of Anthropology*, no. 42 (2013): 327–43 (here 328).

3 Malini Ranganathan, "Property, Pipes, and Improvement," *POWER*, July 16, 2019, https://power.buellcenter.columbia.edu/essays/property-pipes-and-improvement.

4 Shannon Mattern, "Maintenance and Care," *Places Journal*, November 2018, https://placesjournal.org/article/maintenance-and-care/.

5 Emma R. Power and Kathleen J. Mee, "Housing: An Infrastructure of Care," *Housing Studies* *35*, no. 3 (May 2020): 484–505.

ethics to conceptualize infrastructure, in all its forms and meanings, as encoded by multiple interests. Housing becomes a site that is more than merely a personal problem. By situating housing as an infrastructure of care that "patterns" urban social life, the call for access to affordable and good-quality housing becomes part of a process of "political contest and change." Power and Mee's definition of infrastructures as entangled in social systems echoes AbdouMaliq Simone's work. In two influential articles Simone argues that people, their actions, and relations form an infrastructural support system for the city, what he calls "people as infrastructure."[6] A similar argument is forwarded by Ash Amin, who discusses the "liveliness of sociotechnical systems" and how the life of a city can be narrated through its material infrastructures.[7] There is, Amin insists, "nothing purely technical or mechanical about even the most digitized infrastructures."[8] Infrastructures, he goes on, are implicated in human experience, shaping behavior, arousing anger and frustration, and affecting social disposition and a spectrum of emotions to which we propose to add love and relations of care.

In the analysis and proposals of architectural scholar Dana Cuff and the researchers and students at cityLAB UCLA, infrastructure is recognized as public work that offers an underexplored range of services and spaces for the possible improvement of urban living conditions. This reading urges a reconsideration of the latent possibilities of infrastructural systems to serve as parks, green transportation, or manifestations of previously hidden worlds.[9] The disposition of infrastructures and architectural forms is also a focus of attention for architectural theorist Keller Easterling. Her well-known work on infrastructure identifies transformative agency in spaces and objects often considered to be outside the scope of architects and urban planners.[10] Housing subdivisions, highways, cell phones, golf courts, maritime shipping routes, and special economic zones are some of the spatial products Easterling considers in her extensive body of work on the global networks of infrastructure. In identifying such innocuous networks, Easterling's reading comes with a desire to hack the code and to use design as a means of resistance from within the

6 AbdouMaliq Simone, "People as Infrastructure: Intersecting Fragments in Johannesburg," *Public Culture* **16, no. 3 (2004): 407–29, and AbdouMaliq Simone, "Ritornello: 'People as Infrastructure,'" Urban Geography, 2021.**

7 Ash Amin, "Lively Infrastructure," *Theory, Culture, and Society* **31, no. 7/8 (2014): 137–61.**

8 Amin, "Lively Infrastructure," 138.

9 Dana Cuff, "Collective Form: The Status of Public Architecture," *Thresholds* **40 (2012): 55–66.**

10 See, for example, Keller Easterling, *Extrastatecraft: The Power of Infrastructure Space* **(London: Verso Books, 2014).**

neoliberal, market-driven logic of spatial products. Tweaking, manipulating, and altering the protocols of infrastructure, she urges architects and designers to take a more active role in shaping how large infrastructural systems organize the world. Architects, she argues, must design what she calls "active form." What she means is that, rather than being defined as passive or mute, form can be embedded with a capacity to transform existing conditions, positions, and relationships among bodies. Unlike geometry, active form expresses a disposition or capacity that unfolds over time to shape space and relationships. Easterling's work highlights the need to transgress disciplinary boundaries between architecture, urban planning, and geography to confront the spatial products of global infrastructures and reclaim their potential.

Well-intentioned infrastructures make things work, but they can also get things into a terrible mess. Infrastructure, we insist, can benefit from the loving care of architecture to make it work, to achieve good relations between environments and technologies, natures and cultures, humans and nonhumans. Today this call has become urgent amid concatenating planetary devastations. We propose that, by practicing architecture as a critical and creative act of design love, we can keep our everyday infrastructures going and make them more amenable to life. Perhaps we vest too much hope in what architecture can do, but this hope is what has animated our theoretical and pedagogical work on infrastructural love.

Support Systems and Structures

We have subtitled our collection *Caring for Our Architectural Support Systems* and suggest that infrastructural systems are composed of dynamic constellations of support structures, coupling, connecting, turning on and off, working then failing to function. In 2009, Céline Condorelli published a remarkable book called Support Structures. For our book dedicated to infrastructural love and for the pedagogical commitments that first led to the book, Condorelli's work has offered significant support. She has helped us rethink what matters when it comes to architecture and its support structures and their involvement in infrastructural support systems. When Condorelli defines her concept of support structures, it becomes immediately clear that these are both material and discursive structures. She designates her book a "manual" and describes it as "a discursive site for the exercise of support to take place."[11] She specifies that the adequate supportive preposition should be in rather than on. That is, support should be involved, embedded, embodied, entangled—not offered at a distance; it should not presume the conceit of disinterest or

11 Céline Condorelli, *Support Structures* **(Berlin: Sternberg Press, 2009), 13.**

Céline Condorelli, *Support Structures*. **Photography by Adam Broomberg and Oliver Chanarin, 2009.**

impartiality. This draws her notion of support structures into the vicinity of care ethics. Care, Maria Puig de la Bellacasa notes, is involved and messy.[12] We depend upon care even if we do not always welcome or enjoy it. Care and support are about proximity, mixing longing and intimacy. We hold each other up, we let each other down. Support engages a politics of friendship, and there is no friendship without a little care.

We include here images of support structures from Condorelli's book. They are the kind of structures one barely pays attention to, and yet without them an old wall would collapse, a roof fall in on itself, a relationship lose its way, and two lovers draw apart. Support is added to structure manifesting materially, conceptually, and conjunctively as a support structure. Structures, Condorelli explains, "take shape insofar as they are imagined, planned, drawn up and committed to, and most importantly made, built, constructed, erected and put together."[13] The story, Condorelli leads us to understand, is deceptively simple: supports act as scaffolds to unstable situations. She observes that, while a support structure such as scaffolding keeps a building from falling down, if that building were to be demolished, then the scaffolding would fall away too.[14] Support structures are vulnerable and dependent on the specificities of concrete situations. They ward off systemic failure and yet are just as likely to fail themselves. Our attention is drawn toward the support structure as the paradoxically supportive and yet simultaneously vulnerable part of the assemblage being considered. Rather than allowing the support to recede into the background, as we are apt to do, what happens when we focus a little harder and allow it to advance to the foreground? What happens when we dedicate a little love and care to those structures and systems upon which our collective lives depend?

12 Maria Puig de la Bellacasa, *Matters of Care: Speculative Ethics in More than Human Worlds* **(Minneapolis: University of Minnesota Press, 2017).**

13 Condorelli, *Support Structures*, **28.**

14 Condorelli, *Support Structures*, **43.**

Infrastructural Love

Leos Carax's 1991 film *Les amants du Pont-Neuf* (The Lovers on the Bridge) begins with a bridge and concludes with a barge loaded with sand heading toward the port at Le Havre. The bridge is an infrastructural connector par excellence. (If a board game were to be invented and dedicated to infrastructural love, bridges would be the trump or wild cards, pieces that can move rapidly across the board making connections between formerly disconnected territories.) The sand, a massively redistributed and diminishing resource upon which the construction industry depends, is moved from quarry to port to construction site by barges that link up with global supply chains. In the closing scenes of the film, Carax depicts the lovers leaping and running up and down the storage area of the barge. They traverse its micro-landscape, a miniature topography of sand hills, playing together as though the sand pit will be endlessly replenished, when we know that sand is a nonrenewable resource. The film, which concludes with the transportation of sand, is cut through with dilemmas of homelessness, destitution, and mental health, issues that are particularly pressing today. Sand, the construction industry, and access to housing are entangled in relations of love and intimacy, in decisions about who is invited inside and who is kept out in the cold. The body is vulnerable; it relies on relations of intimacy and love for survival. As Judith Butler argues, "the body is less an entity than a living set of relations," and this living set of relations "cannot be fully dissociated from the infrastructural and environmental conditions of its living and acting."[15]

To place the relational and affective capacities of love into conjunction with infrastructural systems is to suggest these systems express a demeanor we might not have habitually associated with them. From the disciplinary point of view of architecture, what distinguishes our take on infrastructure is our emphasis on love. What do we mean by "infrastructural love"? For us, love is related to care ethics, forming part of a spectrum of relations that have been of specific concern to feminist scholars. The history of care ethics in philosophy includes the pioneering work of moral philosophers such as Carol Gilligan and Joan Tronto, as well as Virginia Held, who maps the mounting literature on care ethics.[16] Care ethics has been expanded into the domain of the feminist posthumanities with the work of Puig de la Bellacasa, who looks beyond

15 Judith Butler, *Notes toward a Performative Theory of Assembly* **(Cambridge, MA: Harvard University Press, 2015), 64.**

16 Carol Gilligan, *In a Different Voice: Psychological Theory and Women's Development* **(Cambridge, MA: Harvard University Press, 1982); Joan Tronto,** *Moral Boundaries: A Political Argument for an Ethic of Care* **(New York: Routledge, 1993); Joan Tronto,** *Who Cares?* **(Ithaca, NY: Cornell University Press, 2015); and Virginia Held,** *The Ethics of Care: Personal, Political, and Global* **(Oxford, UK: Oxford University Press, 2006). See also Katrina Raynor and Hélène Frichot, "Sharing and Caring: Housing in Times of Precarity,"** *Social and Cultural Geography*, **forthcoming.**

human interpersonal relations toward environmental and more-than-human relations.[17] Gilligan's early work asks how we can shift from an emphasis on moral objectivity and detachment to responsive and empathetic expressions of care. This means reducing the distance, for instance, between the architect and the problems they are grappling with in the world. Held argues that what is at stake in care ethics is a distinction between justice (which focuses on fairness, equality, and abstract principles requiring consistent application) and relations of care, which must be cultivated, which respond to need, and which are often associated with stories—what Held calls "narrative nuance."[18] Care has an important story to tell concerning our complex relations with one another and with the world. We cannot easily extract ourselves from the relations in which we are involved; thus, gaining a point of view, as though from some objective outside, is simply not possible. Instead, we gather as vulnerable beings around our matters of care, as Puig de la Bellacasa argues, sharing our "inevitable interdependency."[19] In this collection, furthermore, storytelling and the role of narrative are important for many of our contributors, most of whom find themselves involved in the sites of infrastructural

Care has an important story to tell concerning our complex relations with one another and with the world. We cannot easily extract ourselves from the relations in which we are involved; thus, gaining a point of view, as though from some objective outside, is simply not possible.

17 Puig de la Bellacasa, *Matters of Care*.

18 Held, *Ethics of Care*, **15.**

19 Maria Puig de la Bellacasa, "'Nothing Comes without Its World': Thinking with Care," *Sociological Review* **60, no. 2 (2012): 197–216 (here 198).**

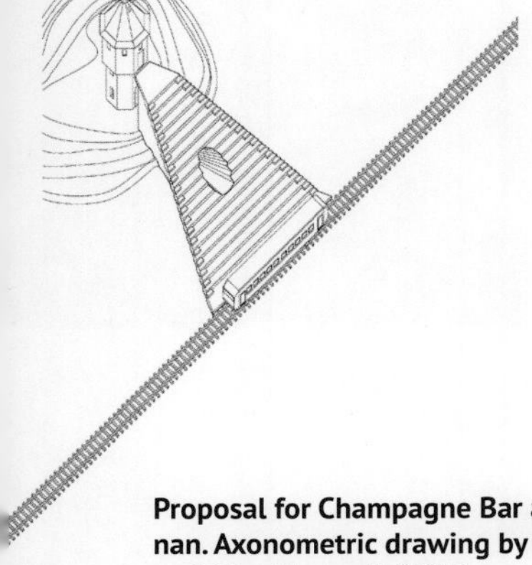

Proposal for Champagne Bar along Inlandsbanan. Axonometric drawing by Hannes Frykholm and Olga Tengvall, 2015.

Railway Turntable Storuman, Inlandsbanan. Drawing by Hannes Frykholm and Olga Tengvall, 2015.

Tandsjöborg water tower, Inlandsbanan.
Photography by Hannes Frykholm, 2015.

Brunflo, Inlandsbanan.
Photography by Hannes Frykholm, 2015.

love with which they have sought to think and practice.

The conjunction of our key terms, infrastructural and love, first emerged from a creative design project undertaken by architects and architectural theorists Hannes Frykholm and Olga Tengvall, who expressed care toward a disused rail line heading into the north of Sweden called the Inlandsbanan (literally, "the inland line").

They published their speculative project in Architecture and Feminisms: Ecologies, Economies, Ecologies, arguing that "to fall in love implies a bodily response that is prior to the feeling of love or the expression of such feeling" and suggesting that architecture could contribute to setting the stage for the arousal of intense feelings.[20] By proposing a series of interventions, or love affairs, along the 1,200-kilometer rail line, they sought to mobilize the intensity of love as a means of generating environmental care and empathy.

Love animates affective relations and, like care, is fundamentally relational. Love enhances our lives, supports bonds of intimacy, requires various performances of affective labor, not all of which are easy or pleasant, and as such requires a consideration of equitable relations of love and its labors. Love is

20 Hannes Frykholm and Olga Tengvall, "Project 6: Infrastructural Love," in *Architecture and Feminisms: Ecologies, Economies, Technologies*, **ed. Hélène Frichot, Catharina Gabrielsson, and Helen Runting, 212–17 (Abingdon, UK: Routledge, 2018), 213.**

fundamental for survival, and yet both love and relations of care, much like infrastructure, can be ambivalent, even unwanted. Sara Cantillon and Kathleen Lynch argue that love is inalienable, by which they mean we cannot turn it into a commodity, because then it would become something altogether different.[21] We could no longer call it love. Love and care, too, as Eleanor Wilkinson argues—is ambivalent; it can be joyful, but it can also be painful, and we need to keep this ambivalence in mind, as it will continue to inform political struggles, including, for instance, those for greater access to basic infrastructural goods. Many of the recent thinkers on love, such as Hannah Stark, Wilkinson, Cantillon, and Lynch, reference Michael Hardt and Antonio Negri's meditations on love and how it would appear to be the glue that holds a social collective together in its lives and its loves, in its ambitions to imagine the world otherwise.[22] Love arrives simultaneously with the risk of falling out of love, of love dissipating. In a parade or protest march, some might feel love while others experience great anxiety. Love easily follows what we recognize as being like us, while keeping difference at a distance, but love can also cut through our differences. Love is not just a good feeling but can organize "cartographies of power."[23] Each of these thinkers seeks to moderate the notion that love is the answer to composing a socially cohesive collective, the promise of the "multitude" as introduced by Hardt and Negri. We must be aware, as Wilkinson points out, that the "creation of a loving multitude may in fact expel or repel certain bodies."[24] Nevertheless, each in their own way takes on the challenge of what risks being a saccharine emotion, the subject of a romantic comedy, to deliberate on how the role of love, as an affect, enables.

Can we speak of the love we, as a body politic, must share if we are to get by? Is infrastructural love too much to ask for? Infrastructural love forwards the imperative that infrastructures must be conceptualized as a public good. Félix Guattari speaks of love as an essential means of organizing new "micropolitical and microsocial practices, new solidarities, a new gentleness, together with new aesthetic and new analytic practice regarding the formation of the unconscious."[25] Infrastructural love requires a radical engagement with the world,

21 Sara Cantillon and Kathleen Lynch, "Affective Equality: Love Matters," *Hypatia* 32, no. 1 (Winter 2017): 169–186 (here 171).

22 Hannah Stark, "Deleuze and Love," *Angelaki Journal of the Theoretical Humanities* 17, no. 1 (2012): 99–113. Eleanor Wilkinson, "On Love as an (Im)properly Political Concept," Environment and Planning D: *Society and Space* 35, no. 1 (2017): 57–71; and Cantillon and Lynch, "Affective Equality."

23 Wilkinson, "On Love as an (Im)properly Political Concept," 64.

24 Wilkinson, "On Love as an (Im)properly Political Concept," 65.

25 Félix Guattari, *The Three Ecologies* (London: Athlone Press, 2000), 34.

putting the practitioner in a close encounter with what requires support and exposing them to the risks inherent in such encounters. The love of infrastructural love points to that intense and radical engagement. Love renders architecture as infrastructure vulnerable; that is, prone to failure. Infrastructure requires constant care and maintenance to ward off failure, and yet the moments of failure are when the act of love as radical work makes space and opens opportunities for gathering and working together.

> Infrastructural love requires a radical engagement with the world, putting the practitioner in a close encounter with what requires support and exposing them to the risks inherent in such encounters.

Love suggests the importance of acknowledging disposition when it comes to infrastructures; that is, how we are orientated toward infrastructures, how we build relations that are supported by them. Love is the result of a powerful affect that aspires toward the best possible relations at the level of a body politic and the best possible composition of our collective political capacity. This is something we learn from Gilles Deleuze's reading of the seventeenth-century Jewish Dutch philosopher and lens grinder, Baruch Spinoza. The best possible composition has less to do with the form, function, or organization of the organism than with the "composition of affective relations," conceived as capacity for life.[26] According to the (infrastructural) rhythm of the composition and decomposition of bodies relative to one another and to the environment in which they are embedded, "we experience joy when a body encounters ours and enters into composition with it, and sadness when, on the contrary, a body or an idea threaten our own coherence."[27] Love, for Deleuze, follows in the footsteps of the intense affect that is joy.[28] The love in infrastructural love points to an intense and radical engagement that closes the gap between the architect and the world. At the same time, the powerful affect of love renders architecture as infrastructure vulnerable, even prone to failure, and as such in perpetual need of care, repair, and maintenance. Joy can be demolished as

26 Robert Hurley, "Preface," in Gilles Deleuze, *Spinoza: Practical Philosophy* **(San Francisco: City Lights Books, 1988), ii.**

27 Deleuze, *Spinoza*, **19.**

28 Deleuze, *Spinoza*, **50.**

quickly as it builds up, leading to the breakdown of a body politic and an organic body. Then, in moments of failure, the act of love as radical work contributes to rethinking the projective ambitions of architecture.

Infrastructural Failures and What We Learn from Them

In the closing scenes of Jim Jarmusch's *Only Lovers Left Alive* (2013), two immortals, believing they are near death, discuss entanglement theory and speculate wearily on the water wars that the world is imminently facing. We are to imagine these vampiric creatures, Adam and Eve, the first man and woman, as both the first human beings, more-than-human, and possibly the last witnesses to the aftermath of planetary devastation. They have borne witness to the full sweep of human history, and now they look back, as well as forward, speculating on possible futures. They are weary of human folly and destruction and the persistent will toward ignorance and barbarity. What they perform in this reflection could be called an Anthropocene thought experiment. Paul Crutzen, who coined the concept of the Anthropocene with atmospheric chemist Eugene Stoermer, writes of our descendants (or alien others) visiting the planet Earth two hundred years hence: "They might liken us to aliens who have treated the Earth as if it were a mere stopover for refueling, or even worse, characterize us as barbarians who would ransack their own home. . . . Remember, in this new era, nature is us."[29] Water is a fundamental infrastructural good that is being ransacked. Today when we think of water, we think of drought, flood, and the failure to adequately distribute this life-sustaining resource. The mismanagement of water speaks volumes about the breakdown of infrastructure as a means of or medium for the equitable distribution of resources. We look forward to a future, as Adam and Eve have intimated, of scarcity, inequitable distribution, and water wars. Without access to this precious resource, we (human beings, not to mention more-than-human and nonhuman others) would expire within a few days. The failure here can be situated on several levels: it is a failure on the part of human beings to learn from history and

29 Paul Crutzen and Christian Schwägerl, "Living in the Anthropocene: Toward a New Global Ethos," *Yale Environment* 360, January 24, 2011, https://e360.yale.edu/features/living_in_the_anthropocene_toward_a_new_global_ethos, cited in Kathryn Yusoff, "Anthropogenesis: Origins and Endings in the Anthropocene," *Theory, Culture and Society* 33, no. 2 (2016): 3–28 (here 14).

past experience; it is a failure to find the means to share equitably those resources that are essential to human and nonhuman life and well-being; and it is a failure of imagination and of fellow feeling.

An observation made nearly as often as designers, theorists, and activists pause to reflect on what infrastructures do is that we apprehend the existence of infrastructures only in the event of their failure. Conceptualizing landscape as infrastructure, Pierre Bélanger writes, "As a catalytic infrastructure, landscape is rendered visible at the precise moment at which the city fails."[30] Elsewhere he insists, "infrastructure remains largely invisible until the precise moment it breaks down."[31] New media theorist Ned Rossiter remarks, "Infrastructure provides an underlying system of elements, categories, standards, protocols, and operations that, as many note, are only revealed in its moment of failure and breakdown."[32] That is, when the lights go out, when the water dries up, when the network fails, when you cannot get a signal, when fleets of airplanes are grounded on account of a pandemic. The world tends toward negative entropy and decline. Things fall apart, as they are apt to, and especially where there is a dearth of care. This is not just a technical but a deeply social issue, as Butler stresses: "No one moves without a supportive environment and set of technologies. And when those environments start to fall apart or are emphatically unsupportive, we are left to 'fall' in some ways, and our very capacity to exercise most basic rights is imperiled."[33]

Consider our current state of exception under COVID-19 and how the state increasingly intervenes in the control of the infected city with the aim of managing a population's health and well-being. With the current pandemic this has often required curtailing infrastructural flows, checking the movements of workers, goods, and services. The specter of "control societies" emerges, and an unsettling question is raised: What civil liberties are currently being eroded?[34] Neoliberal capitalism and its infiltration of the state and its modes of governing are key contributing factors in what Nancy Fraser calls our contemporary "crisis of care."[35] We can barely care for ourselves, let alone others. We outsource our affective labors to migrant populations, relocating vulnerabilities

30 Pierre Bélanger, "Landscape as Infrastructure," *Landscape Journal* **28, no. 1 (March 2009): 79–95 (here 84).**

31 Pierre Bélanger, "Redefining Infrastructure," in *Ecological Urbanism*, **ed. Mohsen Mostafavi and Gareth Doherty, 332–49 (Baden: Lars Muller Publishers, 2010), 332.**

32 Ned Rossiter, *Software, Infrastructure, Labor: A Media Theory of Logistical Nightmares* **(New York: Routledge, 2016), 5.**

33 Judith Butler, "Rethinking Vulnerability and Resistance," in *Vulnerability in Resistance*, **ed. Judith Butler, Zeynep Gambetti, and Leticia Sabsy, 12–27 (Durham, NC: Duke University Press), 14–15.**

34 Gilles Deleuze, "Postscript on Societies of Control," in *Negotiations*, **177–82 (New York: Columbia University Press).**

35 Nancy Fraser, "Contradictions of Capital and Care," *New Left Review* 100 (July/August 2016): 99–117, https://newleftreview.org/issues/ii100/articles/nancy-fraser-contradictions-of-capital-and-care.

36 Isabelle Stengers, "We Are Divided," *e-flux Journal,* no. 114 (December 2020), https://www.e-flux.com/journal/114/366189/we-are-divided/.

37 See Butler, "Rethinking Vulnerability and Resistance."

from one group to another. Capitalism, Isabelle Stengers argues, "redefines human and nonhuman worlds in a way that unravels relationships of interdependence and institutes the most inextricable network possible of chains of dependence."[36] The distinction Stengers makes here is crucial and also pertinent to the issue of care ethics. Any social collective that shares its vulnerabilities can mobilize this sharing as a kind of strength.[37] Our interdependence on one another for survival—and, beyond survival, toward flourishing and caring relations—is nothing like the chains of dependence that neoliberal capitalism imposes on populations. Chains of dependence divide us; they do not bring us together.

Falling and failing. Still, beyond exhaustion, something persists. The possibility remains, however small, of a creative and speculative gesture, a leap, a capacity to imagine ways of becoming with the world that are more amenable to flourishing. Infrastructures produce those spaces and temporalities, flows and traffic jams, which recede into the background of our consciousness while supporting the facilitative environments and provisioning systems that enable the carrying out of ordinary, everyday life. If infrastructure is that which remains in the background, invisible right up until the moment of breakdown, then failure is an event that must be interrogated closely. The event of failure, at its best, is an opportunity for learning. Life proceeds according to trial and error: we get it wrong, but maybe next time we can get it right. Such an iterative, experimental approach is central to the kind of tacit, hands-on learning that takes place in the pedagogical space of the design studio.

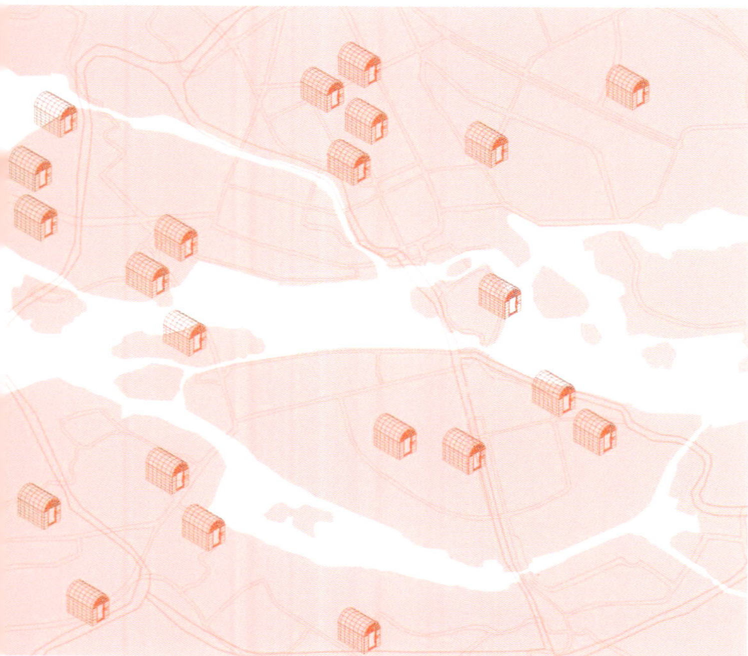

Public Sanitation Access. Location of Public Toilets in use and Functioning, Stockholm, Sweden, 2018. Drawing by Sara Sako.

Theoretical Support System

The theoretical support system for this collection draws on affect theory and relational architectural ecologies.[38] It situates itself in the architectural humanities and learns from the environmental humanities, the posthumanities, and new materialism, especially where the latter two intersect with a feminist and intersectional agenda. Discursive support structures work hand in hand with material and technosocial support structures, and we have long believed it important to introduce this emphasis to our students too.

Affect theory offered us specific support for our teaching and thinking, allowing us to critically reflect on the dispositions that infrastructural systems express.[39] *Affect* is not to be confused with *effect*, as in "cause and effect" or "effect of the light." We can speak of someone being "affected," by which we mean their disposition is transformed, changing state from one moment to the next, and this assumes that something has happened. The complex concept of affect is easily confused with feelings and emotions, when instead it points toward the capacity of a body to affect and to be affected in turn. Affect is what increases and diminishes one's capacity to act in a world. Affect arouses the sensing body (human, more-than-human, nonhuman, technosocial), moving it, affecting it, before the body has consciously recognized that it has felt something or that something has changed. Feelings and emotions enter the scene only after the event of having been affected or the action of affecting a situation. The recognition of a feeling that follows an encounter (I'm happy! I'm sad.) is usually based on an autobiography of such feelings: I recognize this feeling from having experienced it before, so it must be that I am happy (or sad). When the autobiography of feelings so aroused is situated in a cultural context where those feelings are socially recognized, they are denominated as emotions, classified and named: "happiness" and "sadness," for instance.[40] As architects, we must be wary here, because we cannot assume that those who come to use, inhabit, or pass through our architectures will feel one way or another. And yet, surely we can use the reciprocal relation of affecting and

38 Peg Rawes, ed., *Relational Architectural Ecologies* **(London: Routledge, 2013).**

39 Melissa Gregg and Gregory Seigworth, eds., *The Affect Theory Reader* **(Durham, NC: Duke University Press, 2010); and Hélène Frichot, "Infrastructural Affects: Challenging the Autonomy of Architecture," in** *Architectural Affects after Deleuze and Guattari,* **ed. Marko Jobst and Hélène Frichot, 10–25 (London: Routledge, 2021).**

40 Eric Shouse, "Feeling, Emotion, Affect," M/C *Culture* **6, no. 2 (2005).**

being affected—and the subsequent connection to feelings and emotions—as a means of understanding the sociopolitical effects our architectures provoke and how we enable and disable bodies. The first thing to assert about affect is that, unlike the materials and details, drawings and documents that architectural practice usually manages, affect is not something that can be stage-designed. Affect is emergent and expressed immanently. When we finally pause to reflect on its pre-personal impact, the marks and traces it has left in its wake in the formation of subjectivities and spaces, affect has already come and gone. That is, we cannot purposely design it into our built environments as we would an innovative material or technologically advanced window mechanism.

The environmental humanities is a field that has emerged as a response to a mounting understanding of the "ecological and social challenges facing all life on earth" and the recognition that former approaches to the humanities must be unsettled so as to best address contemporary climate emergencies beyond human exceptionalism.[41] We need new theories and methodologies to inform our practices if we are to work together to cope with a world that is radically changing around us. Such knowledge formation demands that we slow down and pay close attention to the environments, natural and constructed, in which we live and work, as well as those environments further afield upon which we depend, whether for agricultural or mineral resources. For us, the environmental humanities sits neatly alongside tendencies emerging in feminist new materialism and in the feminist posthumanities. New materialism prompts us to understand our imbrication with materials as an environmental concern, thereby intersecting with the environmental humanities. When we "follow the material," we explore the opportunity of performing an ethical relationship with the materials we produce and discard, including the embodied materiality of our human bodies. The new in new materialism demands a reorientation of our understanding of materials and material flows and how humans, nonhumans, and more-than-human others are entangled with these flows.[42] This is a theoretical orientation that critiques hylomorphism, or the persistent

41 Deborah Bird Rose, Thom van Dooren, Matthew Chrulew, Stuart Cooke, Matthew Kearnes, and Emily O'Gormand, "Thinking through the Environment, Unsettling the Humanities," *Environmental Humanities* **1, no. 1 (2012): 1–5 (here 1). See also Ursula K. Heise, "Introduction: Planet, Species, Justice—and the Stories We Tell about Them," in** *The Routledge Companion to the Environmental Humanities,* **ed. Ursula K. Heise, Jon Christensen, and Michelle Niemann, 1–10 (Abingdon, UK: Routledge, 2017).**

privilege given in Western philosophy, at least since Aristotle, to form over matter. Although intersecting with new materialism and the environmental humanities, the posthumanities arrived in the twenty-first century via multiple channels. We follow the feminist path articulated by feminist philosophers Rosi Braidotti and Cecilia Åsberg.[43] Braidotti asserts that the human has never been a neutral category but one always linked to power and privilege, shaped in the outline of a white, male, able-bodied Vitruvian man. We have arrived at a "posthuman conjunction," Braidotti argues, thrown into a flux of fast-paced technological development driven by neoliberal capitalism and advancing, most likely irreversible, climate change. This juncture, she adds hopefully, is also one from which new ways of knowing might emerge from the conjunction of posthumanist and postanthropocentric approaches. Together, the environmental humanities, new materialism, and the posthumanities demand a radical reconceptualization of the thick and knotted imbroglios of human and nonhuman relations, a rethinking that should lead to other modes of practicing with environment-worlds.

42 Rick Dolphijn and Iris van der Tuin, eds., *New Materialism: Interviews and Cartographies* **(Ann Arbor: Open Humanities Press, 2012); and Stacy Alaimo and Susan Hekman, eds.,** *Feminist Materialisms* **(Indianapolis: Indiana University Press, 2008).**

43 Rosi Braidotti and Cecilia Åsberg, eds., *A Feminist Companion to the Posthumanities* **(Cham, Switzerland: Springer, 2018); Rosi Braidotti,** *Posthuman Knowledge* **(Cambridge, UK: Polity, 2019); and Cary Wolfe,** *What Is Posthumanism?* **(Minneapolis: University of Minnesota Press, 2010).**

Infrastructure as Pedagogy: Poetic Pragmatics

What can we learn together? Our collective discussions around infrastructures and architectures commenced within the context of a pedagogical design studio at KTH (Royal Institute of Technology) Stockholm, where infrastructure was examined not only as a thing and site of investigation through design but as a performative design method that could answer to contemporary urgencies. Our discussions derived from an active dialogue with students in the pedagogical space of the design studio, itself an infrastructure for critical and creative thinking. Drawing on what we collaboratively learned from our pedagogical commitments, our aim in this book is to reorient the understanding of architecture by

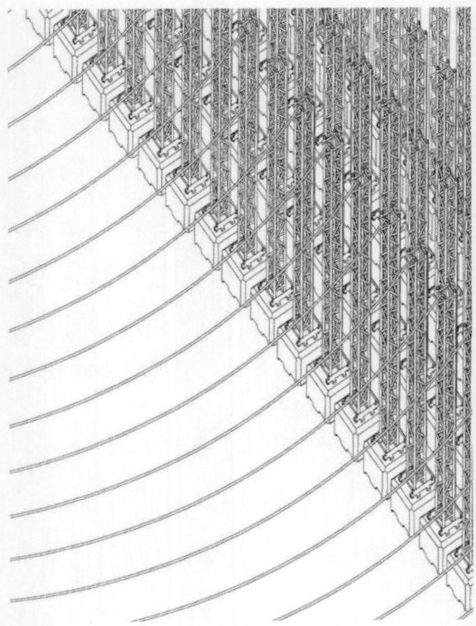

Infrastructure Repeats. Drawing by Erik Lokrantz, 2018.

focusing less on a discrete object in a field or an autonomous icon alienated from an urban milieu and instead to think in terms of distributed interventions and complex connections—or, “relational architectural ecologies.”

As a provocation to our students, we asked them to pay careful attention to their environment-worlds, to look around and reflect on their everyday infrastructures. We invited them to affect and to be affected, and we explained that affect works in such reciprocal relays, leaving no one and nothing untouched. We proposed to them that much of what we do is made possible because of the infrastructures that support us and the ordinary architectures that require our love and care. When infrastructures and their associated spaces fail, the failure is not just technological but social and political.

For the team who led the Infrastructural Love design studio, the pedagogical relationship is a dialogical one. We discovered a great deal from working with our Critical Studies in Architecture students, investigating the themes of infrastructural love and then infrastructural care. Through our collective research and our collaboration with students, we found that getting the ratio just right between speculation and the suspension of disbelief is challenging when attempting to rethink infrastructural systems and support structures. In Isabelle Doucet’s contribution to this anthology, she discusses the great difficulty of achieving a balance between pragmatics and aesthetic expression and emphasizes the role of “storying” and slowing down. During our dialogues and critiques we came up with a concept-tool that helped us discuss this tension: poetic pragmatics.

Poetic pragmatics brings the love back into the ordinary gestures of everyday places and relations and is tied up with care, maintenance, and repair. To avoid the phenomenological pitfalls of a self-absorbed poetics, the right mix of pragmatics brings us back to the world and asks us to experience and experiment on matters of concern. As our poetics tended toward

Poetic pragmatics brings the love back into the ordinary gestures of everyday places and relations and is tied up with care, maintenance, and repair.

the speculative, aiming to imagine the world otherwise, we sought to anchor this imagining to the ground with the right balance of pragmatics. Rather than fixate on buildability, believability was mobilized, and the aim was to provoke thought. At a certain point, Rania Ghosn and El Hadi Jazairy's notable 2018 book Geostories: Another Architecture for the Environment was found to be circulating through the studio space (at KTH Stockholm, students still have access to their own desk space for a full semester).[44] The suite of speculative and critical projects featured within offered a compelling example and demonstrated how architecture could be deployed as a critical and creative medium of investigation.

Also important in the pedagogical space and time of the Infrastructural Love studio was to embed a series of theory seminars where we could slow down and reflect on work in progress. In these seminars we extended the discussion of infrastructures and expanded the vocabulary students could use to think through and argue for their projects. We introduced affect theory and care ethics. Students read together in small groups, and then we all sat together and allowed our discussion to roam from precedent case to precursor, from concept-tool to argument. We took many theoretical journeys together, each one leading us toward a development of our creative practice, whether as students or as teachers.

44 Design Earth (Rania Ghosn and El Hadi Jazairy), *Geostories: Another Architecture for the Environment* **(Barcelona: Actar, 2018). See also Hélène Frichot, "Telling Geostories: We Are All in It Together,"** *Journal of Architecture* **24, no. 1 (2020): 113–15.**

The Infrastructure of This Anthology

The infrastructural journey has been a recurring motif in our studio teaching, and we return to it in the organization of this anthology. While we doubt anyone reads a collection of essays from cover to cover, we have decided nonetheless to plot an itinerary that leads from questions concerning pedagogy and how teaching and learning is a reciprocal relation, to the roles of repair, maintenance, and the crucial theme of care. We open with a prologue on infrastructure by Condorelli, whose work on support structures reverses the habitual understanding of what is privileged in an architectural project. Following the prologue and the introduction, Isabelle Doucet, who was a visiting critic in our design studio, leads us further into the discussion of the dilemma of ethical pedagogical practice in a rapidly changing world where environmental issues become all the more pressing. We then proceed into a dialogue with Shannon Mattern, who introduces us to broken-world thinking and helps us extend a discussion of care, repair, and maintenance as alternative approaches to coping with our damaged worlds. Care is a crucial theme for Elke Krasny, who takes us on an urban walk through Vienna, where we discover a network of stone and bronze bodies forming their own memorial infrastructure.

The infrastructural rhythm then abruptly shifts gears with a special section—"Taking Instructions"—in which we describe some of the provocations that supported our curriculum. Here, critical and creative tasks invite the exploration of experimental design acts, playing on the way that briefs are issued in design studio contexts. What are the limits of a brief? What new design thought can instructions inspire?

In part answering these questions, and interwoven through the chapters, are eleven projects by master of architecture students. The projects emerged out of the pedagogical space of Critical Studies in Architecture at KTH Stockholm from 2018 to 2020, a program led by the editors of this volume: Hélène Frichot, Adrià Carbonell, Hannes Frykholm, and Sepideh Karami. To these projects, we have added work emerging out of the Architecture and Philosophy program led by Frichot at the University of Melbourne.

Returning to the chapter contributions, we venture through issues concerning territory, following dust across the desert and past abandoned outer suburban developments with Danika Cooper. With Frykholm as a guide, we then walk through a parking garage that once fleetingly transformed into an experimental art space. We next visit sites where nonrenewable resources are extracted, listening, with Karami, to the stories they have to tell. We take an other-than-human turn to follow a Muscovy duck through a riverside town with the artist-architect Helen Stratford (we also listen to pigeons and visit a nonhuman embassy nearby). We consider the infrastructural challenges of colonization and decolonization, visiting islands with Rouzbeh Akhbari and island plantations with Frichot, and we grapple with bordered imaginations alongside Shahram Khosravi. We consider alternative ways of engaging landscape in its relation to urban development by paying close attention to the infrastructural details with Carbonell before passing through drained coastal wetlands with Yaseera Moosa. With Alexandra Arénes, we venture through forests and past rivers, listening closely to the information that sensing devices divulge about these unfurling nonhuman landscapes, and we conclude underground with Blanca Pujals in a synthetic universe, grasping blindly at the very stuff of existence.

Looking at the collection of essays and projects in this book, we see love written in paragraphs, in the vector lines of irrational section cuts, between reinforced columns, in the detailing of a wall, and in the mapping of desert dust. Love offers a transgressive experience of collective action. It increases the capacity to act together. In this journey we have perceived such capacity, expressed in a sense of joy and hope that our efforts as students, practitioners, and researchers can make a difference in fighting the destruction of social and environmental ecologies.

The architectural theorist and scholar Reinhold Martin argues that infrastructure is primarily characterized as something that repeats. He points out that pedagogical curricula perform this repetition year after year, thereby acting as a kind of infrastructure that enables teaching to continue to develop as a work in progress.[45] Curricula are conceived as the infrastructural rhythm of learning and teaching, and we want to stress, as we conclude this introduction, how important our pedagogical work has been to us.

45 Reinhold Martin, "Green Reconstruction: Preliminary Thoughts," MSD at Home, Melbourne School of Design, University of Melbourne, June 24, 2020, https://msd.unimelb.edu.au/events/msd-at-home/msd-at-home-with-reinhold-martin.

Acknowledgments

Many guest reviewers joined us in the design studio: Isabelle Doucet, Cecilia Åsberg, Alejandra Navarrete Llopis, Heidi Svenningsen Kajita, Clara Rodriguez Lorenzo, Henry Michael Stephens, Janek Ozmin, Karin Reisinger, Katja Grillner, Brady Burroughs, Sepake Angiama, Andrea Zanderigo, Tatjana Joksimović, Anders Berensson, Claudi Aguiló. We are indebted to them and the respectful dialogues they held with our students. We especially thank the students who took part in the Infrastructural Love studio and the Infrastructural Care studio in the Critical Studies of Architecture program at KTH Stockholm and those students who have contributed to the Design, Philosophy, Architecture seminar and who have otherwise worked with Hélène Frichot in the Melbourne School of Design at the University of Melbourne. We are deeply honored that you have agreed to entrust us with your work for this publication.

The editorial team wants to sincerely thank Bettina Schwalm, our graphic designer, who has been a crucial collaborator on this project. Not only has Bettina stayed with us through the whole journey of the book from early thoughts to final proofing, she has helped us work out what matters and where to place the emphasis. Bettina has brought the design of this book alive. We love you Bettina <3

We finally acknowledge the generous funding support we have received from the School of Architecture, KTH Royal Institute of Technology, Stockholm, Sweden. We acknowledge the research funds available with Frichot's new position as professor of architecture and philosophy, University of Melbourne. We acknowledge the in-kind support from the University of Edinburgh for Sepideh Karami's contribution.

ARCHIT
ECTURA
LSTORY
TELLIN
G

Chapter 2
Architectural Storytelling: A Space between Critical Practice and Fragile Environments

Isabelle Doucet

In their 2017 book *The Environmental Humanities: A Critical Introduction*, Robert S. Emmett and David E. Nye list a range of alternative practices that can help to "put the brakes on" the impending climate disaster.[1] These practices, including "localization," "degrowth," and "from cradle to cradle," speak directly to environmental architecture and urban design.[2] For example, localization is a hallmark practice in Sim Van der Ryn's ideas for "emphatic design" and, with Stuart Cowen, for "ecological design."[3] Cradle-to-cradle has for a long time been at the heart of design approaches based on recycled and consciously sourced materials. Also the question of how architecture can support degrowth is pertinent in architectural debates; for example, the 2019 Oslo Architecture Triennale was themed "Enough: The Architecture of Degrowth."[4] From the point of view of the critical posthumanities, Astrida Neimanis, Cecilia Åsberg, and Johan Hedrén, in their 2015 paper "Four Problems, Four Directions for Environmental Humanities: Toward Critical Posthumanities for the Anthropocene," identify "alienation and intangibility" as a primary problem (the first of four identified problems).[5] The authors point to the alienation often felt toward environmental problems. They argue that such alienation is caused by environmental problems being complex, large, extending over long periods of time and often being perceived as intangible in their full workings and effects. Because the resultant alienation, or "the difficult[y] of literally grasping these phenomena and effects," can make it difficult to engage and invest, environmental work requires more than technical solutions.[6] Neimanis, Åsberg, and Hedrén propose four directions, the first of which is "attention to diverse environmental imaginaries"—understood as "sites of negotiation that can orient material action and interaction."[7] Similar to sociocultural imaginations (Neimanis et al. refer to the work of, among others, Ursula K. Heise), such imaginaries can offer "a cultural terrain for collective dreaming, aspiration, collaboration, and negotiation."[8]

What can "environmental imaginaries," understood by Neimanis, Åsberg, and Hedrén as "not (always) speculative [but] also alternatives that are lived and experienced in many ways, globally," look like in architecture and urban design?[9] This is a question that seems to be at the heart of *Infrastructural Love* and offers

1 Robert S. Emmett and David E. Nye, "Putting the Brakes On: Alternative Practices," in *The Environmental Humanities: A Critical Introduction* **(Cambridge, MA: MIT Press, 2017), 117–36.**

2 The other two practices are "ecological economics" and "commodity regionalism and environmental art."

3 Sim Van der Ryn with Francine Allen, *Design for an Empathic World: Reconnecting People, Nature, and Self* **(London: Island Press, 2013), esp. ch. 5, and Sim Van der Ryn and Stuart Cowan, Ecological Design (Tenth Anniversary Edition) (Washington, Covelo, and London: Island Press, 2007 [1996])**

4 See "Enough: The Architecture of Degrowth," *Oslo Architecture Triennale*, **http://oslotriennale.no/en/aboutoat2019.**

5 Astrida Neimanis, Cecilia Åsberg, and Johan Hedrén, "Four Problems, Four Directions for Environmental Humanities: Toward Critical Posthumanities for the Anthropocene," *Ethics and the Environment* **20, no. 1 (Spring 2015): 67–97.**

a prompt for this chapter to unpack some of the opportunities and challenges offered by the meeting of the critical posthumanities and architectural design around shared ambitions toward alternative environmental imaginaries.

The critical posthumanities can provide novel lenses for revisiting architecture's agency in response to questions of environmental and social justice and invites architectural research to explore new—and revisit forgotten or overlooked—entanglements of nature and culture, of human and non-human agency. While this offers an occasion to reclaim radical imaginaries from architectural *histories*, this chapter directs attention toward the development of imaginaries *for the future*, such as those that can be explored in the educational context of an architectural design studio.[10] The chapter reflects on the meeting of critical posthumanities and architecture in a way that is speculative rather than based on empirical research. That does not mean the chapter has no empirical grounding. I draw from my experience as a reviewer for the Infrastructural Love studio at KTH Stockholm, where I was privileged to review student design projects in two consecutive years. I also use my ongoing research on environmental imaginaries in (hi)stories of architecture as empirical grounding for the chapter, including the Ducklands proposal developed by Cedric Price Architects for the Hamburg docklands in Germany (1989–1991) and Metro/Education, a proposal developed by urban designers Michel Lincourt and Harry Parnass in 1970 to reprogram downtown Montreal's infrastructures into spaces for teaching (rather than building new structures).[11] The chapter is additionally grounded by roundtable discussions and conference panels focusing on exchanges between architectural studies and the environmental humanities, as well as my own efforts to integrate environmental humanities in the teaching of architecture.[12]

I draw from these empirical terrains, albeit largely implicitly. I start with a discussion of storytelling, in which I recognize one instance of "environmental imaginaries" and a critical design tool. I highlight three important components of critical storytelling for design: collective worldmaking, messiness, and hope. In addition to the empirical terrains mentioned above, I draw conceptually

6 Neimanis, Åsberg, and Hedrén, "Four Problems, Four Directions for Environmental Humanities," 74.

7 Neimanis, Åsberg, and Hedrén, "Four Problems, Four Directions for Environmental Humanities," 81.

8 Neimanis, Åsberg, and Hedrén, "Four Problems, Four Directions for Environmental Humanities," 81.

9 Neimanis, Åsberg, and Hedrén, "Four Problems, Four Directions for Environmental Humanities," 82.

10 One such occasion to study histories was offered through my participation in the multidisciplinary research program "Architecture and/for the Environment," directed by the Canadian Centre for Architecture in Montreal with the support of the Andrew W. Mellon Foundation (2018–2019).

11 For more on Ducklands, see Isabelle Doucet, "Anticipating Fabulous Futures," in "Overgrowth," special project, ed. Nick Axel, Matthew Dalziel, Phineas Harper, Nikolaus Hirsch, Cecilie Sachs Olsen, and

from Neimanis, Åsberg, and Hedrén's notion of "environmental imaginaries," Thom Van Dooren and Deborah Bird Rose's "storying," science fiction writer Ursula K. Le Guin's quest for "Yintopia," and Benedikte Zitouni's call for "brewing." At the end of the journey, I return to reflections more specifically connected to *Infrastructural Love*.

Storytelling as a Critical Design Tool

In a blog entry from April 2015 called "Utopiyin, Utopiyang," Ursula K. Le Guin writes, "Perhaps in order to be able to write a utopia we need to think yinly."[13] She argues that, while we are used to utopias and dystopias being written from a yang perspective—masculinist, controlling—we have yet to discover what a "yintopia" would look like. If utopias rely on control ("yang"), then "yin" would instead inform "acceptance of impermanence and imperfection, a patience with uncertainty and the makeshift, a friendship with water, darkness, and the earth."[14] By making a distinction between yintopia and yangtopia, Le Guin points to the capacity of stories to bring different critical potentialities into play. Different stories allow for different sensitivities vis-à-vis the questions, problems, hopes, and realities we work from. Stories can induce a sense of care, concern, and responsibility. And, as critical historiographers and ethnographers, among others, have argued, (hi)stories can also overlook and ignore and therefore make one forget events. Stories can create hope as much as they can mislead. When focusing on their critical capacity, storytelling offers one possible tool for exploring different imaginaries. In the environmental humanities, multispecies storytelling offers both a way to expose the problems, injustices, and potentialities of a specific situation and a path toward imagining other possible futures. Scholars in cultural studies, ethnography, and science studies, including Heise, Van Dooren and Rose, Anna Lowenhaupt Tsing, and Donna J. Haraway, have convincingly emphasized the importance of "storying" climate issues.[15] Storytelling is believed to complement any techno-fixing or technocratic approach to environmental problems; that is, to make complex

Maria Smith, e-flux Architecture, September 2019, https://www.e-flux.com/architecture/overgrowth/284918/anticipating-fabulous-futures/. On "Metro/Education," see Isabelle Doucet, "Metro/Education Montreal (1970): Rethinking the Urban at the Crossroads of Megastructures, Systems Analysis and Urban Politics," Washington, Covelo, and London: Island Press, 2007 [1996] 7, no. 2 (2019): 179–96.

12 For example, the roundtable "Cautious Encounters? Architecture and Urban Planning meet Environmental Humanities," which I hosted at the Swedish Research Council's Symposium on Artistic Research 2020—*Working Together*; my participation in "The Future of the Architectural (post)Humanities" roundtable organized by Hélène Frichot and Tilo Amhof at the Society of Architectural Historians, Australia and New Zealand conference 2020; and the conference session "The Future Will Not Be Exhausted," organized by Elke Krasny and Lara Perry at the Political Ecology Network's Third

environmental and scientific problems more accessible to a larger public and, in doing so, to trigger awareness. With the help of stories, situations can be evaluated in a more complex, entangled, and situated manner. Situated-embodied stories and situated knowledges, as Haraway, Isabelle Stengers, Rosi Braidotti, Maria Puig de la Bellacasa, and others propose, embrace connectedness, subjectivity, positionality, and complexity rather than dualistic thinking. Situated perspectives resist making generalizing observations about a situation that do honour the specific circumstances of that situation. In architecture, consider, for example, the "best practices" approach whereby opportunities (including benefits and profits) generated through buildings in one place are believed to be transferrable to seemingly similar situations elsewhere. Situated stories resist such generalization, instead drawing attention to the details and intricacies that compose a specific situation; and inviting to give voice to the many actors and stakes that matter to that situation.

Storytelling, whether situated or otherwise, is at the heart of architecture. When imagining future scenarios, architects tell—and sell—stories. Narration and visionary storytelling are important components of architectural culture. Architects' stories can conform and also critique; they can embrace continuity and also induce radical change. Architectural storytelling, when understood as a tool for critical exposure *and* for exploring future scenarios, can open a fascinating space of encounter between critique and speculation. However, as I will now explore, such encounters do not come without challenges.

When imagining future scenarios, architects tell—and sell—stories. Narration and visionary storytelling are important components of architectural culture. Architects' stories can conform and also critique; they can embrace continuity and also induce radical change.

Biennial Conference held in Brighton in 2020. At the School of Architecture and Civil Engineering (ACE) at Chalmers University of Technology, I teach about environmental humanities for architecture in both lecture courses and design studios.

13 Published in a collection of Le Guin's blogs. Ursula K. Le Guin, "Utopiyin, Utopiyang," in *No Time to Spare: Thinking about What Matters,* **85–87 (2017; New York: Mariner Books, 2019), 87.**

14 Le Guin, "Utopiyin, Utopiyang," 87.

15 Donna Haraway, *Staying with the Trouble: Making Kin in the Chthulucene* **(Durham, NC: Duke University Press, 2016); Anna Lowenhaupt Tsing,** *The Mushroom at the End of the World: On the*

Stories for Collective World-Making

As part of a masterclass in 1989, Cedric Price Architects began developing a proposal for Hamburg's inner-city harbor, which became known as "Ducklands."[16] The architects did not adhere to a logic of urban waterfront regeneration through extensive renovation and newbuilt structures. Instead, they proposed to remove existing structures and return the developed area to nature, thus creating a large nature reserve that would include breeding grounds for migrating birds (e.g., ducks). The proposal shows a fascinating sensitivity to interspecies relationalities. One drawing, for example, using what we could today call emojis, shows the possible rapports between the (nonhuman) birds that inhabit the nature reserve and its (human) visitors, seemingly indicating that the nonhuman perspective takes priority. The proposal further supported this prioritization by calling for mobile walkways that would allow visitors to access the reserve but could be moved according to breeding and nesting needs. Rather than offering the developers of the Hamburg docklands a lucrative deal, the Ducklands proposal hoped to encourage residents to reconnect with their river, and with nature, and to provide space for migratory birds. Following my enthusiastic writing about Ducklands, its interspecies qualities, and its vision for a different environmental future that questioned growth, a few new questions came to the fore. Is the project not still a case of architects acting *on behalf of* nature and human beings? Where are the voices of the residents, the birds, the river, the ornithologists? How central to the project is Cedric Price's persona as a visionary architect—that is, what is his authorial agency in a project that I would very much like to consider as an instance of collective world-making? I am indebted to Benedikte Zitouni for prompting me to consider such questions in her comments on my essay dedicated to Ducklands.[17] Rather than being seduced by the bold gesture offered by Ducklands (as I definitely was!), Benedikte was curious to hear more about the possible continuities Price had worked with, such as existing ecological connections in Hamburg, as well as whether, and if so how, Price had

Possibility of Life in Capitalist Ruins **(Princeton, NJ: Princeton University Press, 2015); Thom Van Dooren and Deborah Bird Rose, "Lively Ethography: Storying Animist Worlds,"** *Environmental Humanities* **8, no. 1 (May 2016): 77–94, and Ursula K. Heise,** *Imagining Extinction: The Cultural Meanings of Endangered Species* **(Chicago: University of Chicago Press, 2016).**

16 Doucet, "Anticipating Fabulous Futures."

17 Benedikte kindly permitted me to include observations she had shared in email conversations we had in 2019.

18 Zitouni builds on Bruno Latour and Michel Serres's work on "brewing times." Valérie Pihet and Benedikte Zitouni, "Shuffling Times," *Parse Journal* **2, no. 4 (2016): 37–51, https://parse-journal.com/article/shuffling-times/.**

19 Pihet and Zitouni, "Shuffling Times," 45.

contributed to what she called "thickening the brewing." In her part of a paper written with Valérie Pihet, Zitouni refers to "brewing" in terms of "shuffling times"—a form of nonlinear storytelling that weaves connections between past, present, and future in experimental rather than fatalistic or deterministic ways.[18] Storytelling then becomes, for Zitouni, a "continuous re-enactment of these stories and experience" as a way "to thicken our present and multiply its possibilities and potentialities."[19] Brewing, for Zitouni, is akin to the relationalities between past, present, and future that are found in Haraway's call for "staying with the trouble" as a way of being "truly present" (rather than breaking with past and present when imagining the future).[20]

20 **Haraway,** *Staying with the Trouble*, **1.**

Asking how architectural stories can become more "utopiyin" therefore means

> Asking how architectural stories can become more "utopiyin" therefore means to ask how they can thrive on the collective voices of humans and nonhumans, how they can "brew" rather than "author," and how they might nurture collective rather than individual world-making

to ask how they can thrive on the collective voices of humans and nonhumans, how they can "brew" rather than "author," and how they might nurture collective rather than individual world-making. In the intense environment of a masterclass, such as the one that led to the Ducklands proposal, design teams are tasked to develop proposals in just a few days or weeks. In such settings, to patiently "brew" intricate stories of *shared* world-making—narrated through the *many* voices of not just designers, users, and residents but also birds, rivers, ornithologists, activists, and natural resources—may be challenging. A question architects may be forced to ask is how they might turn a "cacophony of troubled stories," as Tsing called this in a different context, into a convincing—simplified, stripped back—project pitch?[21]

21 **Tsing,** *The Mushroom at the End of the World*, **34.**

Even in the context of a design studio offered as part of an architecture degree, such as Infrastructural Love, where projects are developed over longer periods of time (typically one semester) but still amid intense work schedules, pedagogical plans, and time pressures, teachers and students may struggle to carve out ample time for learning about the sites or situations at hand, in and through their complexities and their many voices. And if they do find the time: How do they keep those complexities alive when suggesting an intervention, design, or action? As feminist pedagogies have shown, collaborative work is one such way to keep complexities alive. For example, through group work in design education and through honoring collective efforts and achievements—and not just among students and members of design teams but also with other stakeholders.[22] In her study of a design education experiment in the West Bank, Bianca Elzenbaumer calls this "speculating with care," a collective exercise in speculation whereby designers adopt a more humble position, both vis-à-vis the limitations of their knowledge—about everyday circumstances and conditions to which they have little lived-in and embodied access—and vis-à-vis their position of relative privilege—when engaging with the everyday livelihoods of others, livelihoods that architects might not (have to) inhabit.[23] Teaching students of architecture a sense of care and humbleness vis-à-vis the worlds they operate in is important, and studio environments such as Infrastructural Love are showing the way.[24] Rewarding collaborative world-making, already as part of architectural pedagogy, is crucial.

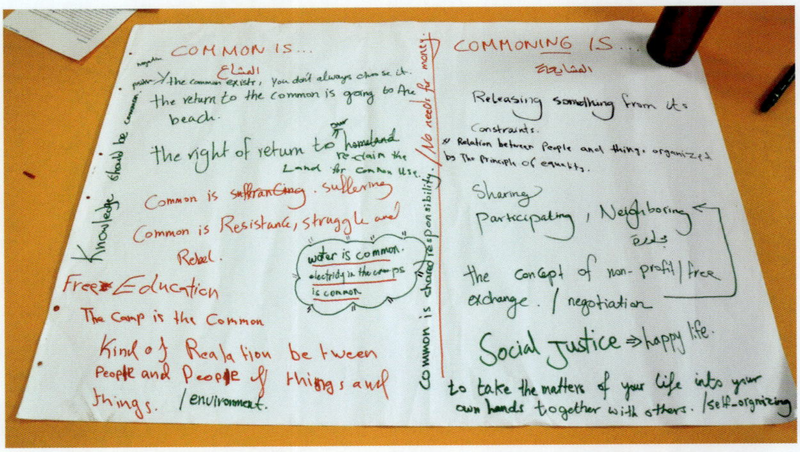

Collaborative notes related to discussions and actions around commoning as part of the Campus in Camps study program at the Westbank. Photo: Brave New Alps, October 2012.

22 Among many great references, two recent edited volumes stand out: Meike Schalk, Therese Kristiansson, and Ramia Maze, eds., *Feminist Futures of Spatial Practice: Materialisms, Activisms, Dialogues, Pedagogies, Projections* **(Baunach, Germany: AADR Art Architecture Design Research, an imprint of Spurbuchverlag, 2017); and Hélène Frichot, Catharina Gabrielsson, and Helen Runting, eds.,** *Architecture and Feminism: Ecologies, Economies, Technologies* **(London: Routledge 2017). Many feminist scholars and commentators have emphasized the importance of making and keeping visible the traces of work by team members, not just as a way of celebrating collective authorship but also to avoid having those contributions be systematically written out of the (hi)stories of architecture.**

23 Bianca Elzenbaumer, "Speculating with Care: Learning from an Experimental Educational Program in the West Bank," *Architectural Theory Review* **22, no. 1 (2018): 100–119.**

Away from architecture, Van Dooren and Rose help explain the benefits and rewards of collective world-making. In their 2016 paper "Lively Ethnography: Storying Animist Worlds," they explain how local volunteers need good storytelling to mobilize others around the practices of care that are required for conserving the vulnerable Hawaiian monk seals. They argue that good stories—being good storytellers but also "good listener[s]"—enable volunteers "to discuss conflicting views about monk seals in a manner that does not exacerbate conflict."[25] Stories are here presented as vehicles for expressing the "multiple and diverse forms of intentionality" that come with an "ecological animism" worldview.[26] These are stories that "would give *others* vitality, presence, perhaps 'thickness' on the page and in the minds and lives of readers."[27] Rather than transmitting one strong message by the storyteller, stories are intended to induce curiosity and attentiveness. Stories therefore promise to "open to other ways of constituting, of responding to and in a living world."[28]

Messy Stories

With Van Dooren and Rose's important work in mind, architects can produce stories that serve as "powerful contributors to the becoming of our *shared* world."[29] They can do this in addition to, or even instead of, using stories for the purpose of convincing audiences of one account of the world—their own or that of a few privileged others. Such stories can be both visionary and deeply engrained in everyday practices of world-making. Everyday world-making can, however, be messy, so here comes another challenge!

Architectural stories are not always given the opportunity to show traces of messy world-making and struggle. In the context of competitions, tenders, and client presentations, for example, showing messy struggles seems counterproductive. Stories therefore often risk taking the shape of what Le Guin calls, again in the context of science fiction, "extrapolative" stories. By this she means a common observation about and definition of science fiction, whereby "The science fiction writer is supposed to take a trend or phenomenon of the

24 I am fortunate to have had great experiences with such design studios at my current (institutional) home, ACE at Chalmers, where I have taught seminars in the Social Inclusion studio (with Emílio da Cruz Brandão) and the Transformation Projects and Environmental Care studio (with Elke Miedema and Oscar Carlsson).

25 Van Dooren and Rose, "Lively Ethography," 79.

26 Van Dooren and Rose, "Lively Ethography," 81–82.

27 Van Dooren and Rose, "Lively Ethography," 85; emphasis (in italics) added.

28 Van Dooren and Rose, "Lively Ethography," 85.

29 Van Dooren and Rose, "Lively Ethography," 89; emphasis (in italics) added.

30 Ursula K. Le Guin, introduction to *The Left Hand of Darkness* **(1969; London: Gollancz, 2017), xiii.**

31 Jeremy Till, *Architecture Depends* **(Cambridge, MA: MIT Press, 2009), back cover and 60–61, where he also refers to Haraway's "situated" perspectives.**

here-and-now, purify it and intensify it for dramatic effect, and extend it into the future."[30] When applied to architecture, extrapolative stories would prevent designers from showing stories in and through their messiness and complexity. And messiness matters, as Jeremy Till so convincingly shows in his 2009 book *Architecture Depends*, a wonderful celebration of messiness considered not as a threat but rather as an opportunity that allows architecture to remain situated in the "real world"—composed of "people, time, politics, ethics, mess"—on which it always depends.[31]

I found evidence of opportunities for situatedness when reading the 2007 edition of Van der Ryn and Stuart Cowan's 1996 book *Ecological Design* while preparing for a teaching seminar at my university. I was delighted to discover that the authors set the scene for their five principles of ecological design with a story of a compost privy.[32] This is a story of learning (at home, as individuals and communities) how to compost human waste and reduce water wastage. It is also a story of learning about and adjusting building codes and regulations that make it difficult to implement such toilets on a larger scale; for example, because building codes define "habitable dwellings as having flush toilets"[33] Moreover, their fifth principle of ecological design, "Making Nature Visible," is an excellent case in point of the messiness that comes with inspiring ecological stories. The privy, with its requirements of hands-on learning (dealing with smell, turning over the pile) offers an important form of learning when compared to flush toilets; as Van der Ryn and Cowan argue "'Flush and forget' technology does not encourage mindfulness or a sense of responsibility."[34] Because messiness and direct engagement make us mindful, caring, and responsible, Van der Ryn and Cowan's ecological design aims to show the messy workings that are otherwise typically kept invisible, including sewage plants, garbage dumps, slaughterhouses, and electrical stations. As Van der Ryn and Cowan argue, "Making nature visible is a way of reacquainting us with wider communities of life, but it also informs us about the ecological consequences of our activities."[35] They explain how a design project can have such informative purpose and can trigger awareness, for example, in preserving wetlands,

32 "The Compost Privy Story," in Van der Ryn and Cowan, *Ecological Design*, 68–74.

33 Van der Ryn and Cowan, *Ecological Design*, 71.

34 Van der Ryn and Cowan, *Ecological Design*, 74.

35 Van der Ryn and Cowan, *Ecological Design*, 189.

36 Van der Ryn and Cowan, *Ecological Design*, 189. Elsewhere, as one way of understanding the complexities of city-making, I have narrated the messy story of the conception, design, construction, use, and maintenance of a public urinal as part of a neighborhood renewal project in Brussels.

37 Many writers have made similar points before me, and I fondly recall the earlier-mentioned conference session "The Future Will Not Be Exhausted" in Brighton in 2020.

incorporating drainage ponds, and teaching, visually and through experience, "about the potential symbiotic relationship between culture, nature, and design works."[36]

Such approaches as these sound encouraging to me because they not only invite us (teachers and students) to think broadly about different ways in which architects can contribute to environmental futures (beyond designing buildings); they also ask how design proposals can do justice to the everyday, complex, messy practices of world-making in which environmental work is deeply engrained. When processes of extraction, manipulation, and exploitation of both natural and human resources are kept at a distance, then we also risk turning a blind eye to environmental and human suffering.[37] When, by contrast, projects make available the various (ethical, aesthetic, technical) choices made by the designer, then those who come to be affected by the design can also begin to inhabit these choices, triggering the possibility of a shared sense of responsibility. As Heather Swanson, Anna Tsing, Nils Bubandt, and Elaine Gan argue in the introduction to the "Monsters" section of their book *Arts of Living on a Damaged Planet*, "Some kinds of stories help us notice; others get in the way."[38]

Which Stories? Whose Futures?

Messy, thick, and collective stories prompt the question, Whose futures are being imagined? As Neimanis, Åsberg, and Hedrén argue, imaginaries need to work with multiple, even competing, worldviews and should explore the different goals, values, and actions pursued by these different imaginaries in order to ask who benefits from them.[39] Heise demonstrates, in her book *Imagining Extinction*, how stories (of extinction) can be both important (e.g., leading to conservation) and problematic (e.g., when "certain kinds of species are taken as a shorthand for all species").[40] Being attentive to these hidden mechanisms of power, bias, or preference in the (counter)stories we produce is important. Especially in creative and visual fields such as architecture, stories

38 Heather Swanson, Anna Tsing, Nils Bubandt, and Elaine Gan, "Introduction: Bodies Tumbled into Bodies," in *Arts of Living on a Damaged Planet: Monsters of the Anthropocene*, ed. Anna Tsing, Heather Swanson, Elaine Gan, and Nils Bubandt, M1–M12 (Minneapolis: University of Minnesota Press, 2017), M8.

39 Neimanis, Åsberg, and Hedrén, "Four Problems, Four Directions for Environmental Humanities," 82–83.

40 Heise, *Imagining Extinction*, 23.

41 Meike Schalk, Ulrika Gunnarsson-Östling, and Karin Bradley, "Feminist Futures and 'Other Worlds': Ecologies of Critical Spatial Practice," in *Routledge Handbook of Gender and Environment*, ed. Sherilyn MacGregor, 447–63 (New York: Routledge: 2017), 450. Till also developed ideas on hope and change not through distant utopia but, drawing on Roberto Mangabeira Unger, imaginations that are not "the imagination of the detached dreamer; it grows out of the real." Till, *Architecture Depends*, 192.

can become captivating vehicles of mobilization leading to action, but they also risk becoming seen as blueprints, thus reducing the opportunity for other possible stories to emerge. For this reason, too, stories and imaginaries are to be situated and resituated in everyday realities. Architectural imaginaries of hope, rather than being projected onto distant futures, can operate as what Meike Schalk, Ulrika Gunnarsson-Östling, and Karin Bradley call "lived utopias," which they define as "lifeways in the here and now that practice alternative ways of living, producing, and consuming, that deviate from mainstream market economies."[41] And the "environmental imaginaries" envisioned by Neimanis et al. are indeed also not just speculations but also alternatives, as they exist already in everyday life.

Le Guin points to stories as "thought-experiments." When reflecting on her book *The Left Hand of Darkness*, she describes "thought-experiments" that prompt us to "open up an alternative viewpoint, to widen the imagination" rather than reflect only on what we want to happen, as is often the case in depictions of utopia.[42] Le Guin helps us to understand that thought-experiments, which she also calls "experiments in imagination," allow us to speculate on what kinds of existing exploitations would cease to exist under the scenario imagined.[43] Architects, for example, might imagine a (built) world free of extraction, exhaustion, precariousness, exploitation, or injustice. Even if such a world may not be realized in the foreseeable future, thought-experiments can help us to believe in the possibility of such worlds.[44] Such stories can offer an important gateway toward what Elke Krasny calls "architecture as care"; namely, architectures that thrive on an ethics of human-nonhuman interdependence rather than on the historical legacy of independence (from nature).[45] Stories can help us to believe in the possibility of such ethics of interdependence and provide the confidence needed to resist those pressures on the profession that prevent such ethics of interdependence from becoming a reality.[46]

One story that does just that is the Crochet Coral Reef Project begun in 2005 by Christine Wertheim and Margaret Wertheim. Inspired by how mathematician Daina Taimiņa in 1997 used crochet to create a physical visualization of

42 Ursula K. Le Guin, "Is Gender Necessary? Redux" (1976/1987), in *Dancing at the Edge of the World: Thoughts on Words, Women, Places,* **7–16 (New York: Grove Press, 1989), 9, 16.**

43 Le Guin, "Is Gender Necessary? Redux," 9, 16. Le Guin gives as an example of exploitations that would cease to exist, "exploitation of the woman, of the weak, of the earth" (16).

44 I here think also of "ficto-critical approaches" in architectural writing. See Hélène Frichot and Naomie Stead, eds., *Writing Architectures: Ficto-critical Approaches* **(London: Bloomsbury 2020).**

45 Elke Krasny, "Architecture and Care," in *Critical Care: Architecture and Urbanism for a Broken Planet*, **ed. Angelika Fitz and Elke Krasny, 33–41 (Vienna: Architekturzentrum Wien; Cambridge, MA: MIT Press 2019), 40.**

46 Krasny lists "financialization, commodification, gentrification, touristification and aggressively iconic spectacularization." Krasny, "Architecture and Care," 40.

47 Just a quick search online shows an offer of free downloadable patterns for coral reef crocheting.

"hyperbolic geometry" (a branch of non-Euclidean geometry), they began to crochet a coral reef. Since its inception, the project has turned into a worldwide (and still ongoing) effort by many to crochet colorful coral reefs using wool, cotton, and all kinds of plastic waste and trash.[47] Haraway discusses the project in her chapter of the edited volume *Arts of Living on a Damaged Planet*, where she particularly values the project's collectivity, "probably the world's largest collaborative art project," and the ways in which, through a process of "intimacy without proximity,"[48] it triggers awareness of natural environments under threat. Haraway observes how the practice of crocheting induces a sense of embodied care (both in the crafters and those experiencing the works) that affords feelings of being involved with and caring for environmental issues without prompting feelings of "neediness of touching [the actual reef] by camera or hand in yet another travelogue of discovery."[49]

Margaret and Christine Wertheim and the Institute For Figuring. *Coral Forest* **with** *Latvian Reef Pod* **and** *Hyperbolic Sea Snake* **at the Museum of Arts and Design (NYC). Photo courtesy MAD by Jenna Bascom.**

A Good Time for Collective Struggling and Learning

In the pedagogical space of the Infrastructural Love design studio, I sensed a genuine effort to develop "architectures of care" and a commitment to shared struggling and collective world-making. I recall the productive struggles of the students and teachers to discover ways of combining critical imaginaries for environmental care with the production of articulate design projects—a struggle I recognize in my own teaching.

Such struggles are indeed productive, because we learn so much from them and because they lead to excellent work. For example, what to do, as a student, when the imaginaries for environmental care you have developed do not lead to any need for construction or building? One student in Infrastructural Love had, based on a thorough and situated reading of the site (a nature park open to visitors) and its challenges, concluded that no built work was required to optimize the park's eco-balance. All that seemed to be needed was some sign-posting (for the visitors) and a few light-touch interventions to create places to rest. The student's hesitation to accept that conclusion (at least that is what I sensed) is in my view telling of the real and/or perceived expectations of design studio work. Architecture students may indeed wonder whether they will face consequences if they propose to build nothing at all.

Productive struggles also point, yet again, to questions of time. In the specific setting of a design studio in architectural education, with its demands on outputs, semester schedules, and student experience, the challenge to reconcile critical storytelling and situated knowledges with excellent, detailed design, can be very real. To encourage productive struggles—between critical situated readings and design, between and among students and tutors—ample time is needed. Time is essential

Maria Johansson, The Kymlinge Institute of Nothing and the Neglected. Infrastructural Love Studio, Critical Studies in Architecture, KTH Stockholm, Sweden, 2018.

48 Donna Haraway, "Symbiogenesis, Sympoiesis, and Art Science Activisms for Staying with the Trouble," in *Arts of Living on a Damaged Planet*, M25–M50 (here M36, M39). Haraway refers to Jacob Metcalf, "Intimacy without Proximity," *Environmental Psychology* 5, no. 2 (2008): 99–128. Haraway also discusses the project in an earlier version of the essay published in *Staying with the Trouble*, 76–81.

49 Haraway, "Symbiogenesis, Sympoiesis, and Art Science Activisms for Staying with the Trouble," M39.

for collective learning: within one studio, between editions of studios, within and between student groups, between students and teachers, and with the many stakeholders outside the studio. One needs time to familiarize oneself with knowledge taken from outside architecture, such as the critical posthumanities and to develop detailed interventions inspired by such knowledge. One semester of fifteen weeks does not allow much time to do all that! Still, I was encouraged to observe how the Infrastructural Love studio fostered the sharing of experiences, knowledge development, and learning; for example, by having reviewers come in for several editions of the studio and by publishing a book—*this book*—which, in addition to being a beautiful opportunity to collect thoughts and reflections from various interlocuters, guests, and protagonists of Infrastructural Love, also serves as a record of collective, and hopefully continuing, learning.

Acknowledgments

In addition to the events listed in footnote 12, some ideas developed in this paper found an initial sounding board in the "Inhabiting Other Futures: Environmental Humanities Meets Architecture and Urban Planning" seed project, funded by Urban Futures at Chalmers University of Technology in 2020 (with Karl Palmås and Kristoffer Ekberg); and in my teaching at the Department of Architecture and Civil Engineering at Chalmers. Some speculations on storytelling developed in this paper benefitted, at an earlier stage, from feedback received from Mark Dorrian and from seminar discussions with colleagues at the Division of Science, Technology and Society at Chalmers. The invitation to contribute to the *Infrastructural Love* book then offered a welcome occasion to tie things together into a chapter.

Social Distancing Rules Apply, 2020.
Photography by Hélène Frichot.

SOCIAL
DISTANCING
RULES APPLIES
W96 652
VIC - STAY ALERT STAY ALIVE
Data Signs
Data Signs
datasigns.net

INFRAS
TRUCTU
RALLOV
EINTIM
ESOFCO
VID-19

Chapter 3
Infrastructural Love in Times of COVID-19: Care, Repair, and Maintenance

Shannon Mattern in dialogue with Hélène Frichot

Shannon Mattern is a transdisciplinary scholar who defies categorization. Media theorist, design theorist, anthropologist, broken-world thinker, she is the author of several influential books and a regular columnist for *Places Journal*, which has supported her most recent publication, *A City Is Not a Computer*.[1] When I spoke with Shannon for the Melbourne School of Design MSDatHome series, it was with this book project, *Infrastructural Love*, in mind, and with a desire to engage her in a discussion on the pertinent themes of care, repair, and maintenance. Without the crucial, though all too often unseen and undervalued acts of maintenance and repair, infrastructure would not be able to hold itself together. I was also keen to discuss pedagogy with Shannon, an activity that can be conceived as a relation of care.[2] Shannon is a dedicated pedagogue. Her website wordsinspace.net sets out pedagogical adventures that frame authentic problems for her students to tackle.[3] On Twitter, @shannonmattern, she communicates as a generous social media persona, sharing resources and pedagogical tips.

Hélène Frichot:

Shannon, you're Professor of Anthropology at the New School of Social Research, New York, and you draw on a multidisciplinary background, starting in chemistry, moving to English, completing a PhD in media studies, and undertaking course work in urban and architectural theory. You have even undertaken postdoctoral research in art history. In your current position you work at the intersection of anthropology and design.

These diverse disciplines are evident in your highly readable essays; for instance, in *Places Journal* and in your recent books, *The City Is Not a Computer* and *Code and Clay, Data and Dirt*. You engage in subjects that range from the archive to the smart city, drawing attention to connections between data and dirt and calling for a reorientation of our maintenance and repair efforts, which seems especially fitting at the current world-historical juncture.
In your essay "Maintenance and Care" in *Places Journal,* you draw attention to an expanded sense of infrastructures, from a rundown street and its cracked

1 See "Shannon Mattern, Contributing Writer," Places, https://placesjournal.org/author/shannon-mattern/; and Shannon Mattern, *A City Is Not a Computer: Other Urban Intelligences* **(Princeton, NJ: Princeton University Press in association with Places Journal, 2021). Some of Mattern's other books include** *Code and Clay, Data and Dirt: Five Thousand Years of Urban Media* **(Minneapolis: University of Minnesota Press, 2017);** *Deep Mapping the Media City* **(Minneapolis: University of Minnesota Press, 2015); and** *The New Downtown Library: Designing with Communities* **(Minneapolis: University of Minnesota Press, 2007).**

2 "MSD at HOME with Shannon Mattern," Melbourne School of Design, https://msd.unimelb.edu.au/events/msd-at-home/msd-at-home-with-shannon-mattern. The present dialogue is adapted from the original online event. I thank colleagues in the Melbourne School of Design at the University of Melbourne who made this event possible: Sara Brocklesby, Philippa Knack, James Rafferty, Jet Bakker, Donald Bates, and Alan Pert. I also thank

Justine Clark of archiparlour.org, who arranged for the transcription of the lecture.

3 Cementing the reach of Mattern's pedagogical influence, a forthcoming issue (76, no. 2) of *the Journal of Architectural Education cites* her work and is dedicated to "Pedagogies for a Broken World Thinking." See http://www.jaeonline.org/pages/pedagogies-broken-world#/page1/.

4 Shannon Mattern, "Maintenance and Care," *Places Journal*, November 2018, https://placesjournal.org/article/maintenance-and-care/.

pavement to corrupted computer code.[4] You argue that, in response to aged and failing infrastructures, what we really need is to study how the world gets put back together.

If it's possible to think beyond the current virus—assuming such pandemics are not here with us to stay as part and parcel of concatenating climate crises—what role do you think an ethos of maintenance, repair, and care might achieve in the design disciplines?

Shannon Mattern:

Thank you so much for that generous introduction, Hélène! As I mentioned in my article, I was partly inspired by the framing of maintenance as invisible labor and a kind of care work. These themes are woven through a lot of my own practice and even, I would like to think, throughout my entire career. "Maintenance and Care" was written in response to a group of scholars who have united under the umbrella of the "Maintainers." They draw mostly from science and technology studies, history, media studies, and, more generally, science- and technology-oriented humanities and social sciences. They were motivated by attempts to provide an alternative to the innovation and novelty fetishization prevalent in Silicon Valley.

The Maintainers recognize that infusing a maintenance sensibility, a care sensibility, into the design process from the beginning might imply a different kind of methodology, a different sense of what constitutes success and functionality, a different sense of the values that are inherent to the design process. Thinking about how a building will be maintained, what types of circulation or storage are necessary for its maintenance and repair, means thinking about the entire lifecycle of a building: How can it be responsibly dismantled or repaired over the *longue durée*?

The Maintainers recognize that infusing a maintenance sensibility, a care sensibility, into the design process from the beginning might imply a different kind of methodology, a different sense of what constitutes success and functionality, a different sense of the values that are inherent to the design process.

These are the types of things that have not historically been front and center in design processes, particularly not in product design and fashion. If the design process is infused with maintenance and repair, we could raise some very different questions that would flow through the entire evolution of a design, into the construction and the afterlife of that construction.

HF:

If maintenance and repair can expand our conception of architectural projects, do you think these approaches allow a means of resistance to the prevalent neoliberal imperative to innovate and to be innovative? Can slow modes of inventiveness be supported by acts of maintenance and the attentive work of repair?[5]

With this maintenance movement you are describing, and its slow pace, it seems to invite a revaluation of what has been undervalued. I'm interested in what we might learn in the context of the current slowing down that COVID-19 has imposed on us. Will the pandemic make us more like design tinkerers and the Maintainers?

SM:

That is a possibility. Various "slow" movements have emerged over the past several years: we have slow food, and a book that came out a few years ago advocates for slow academia, which pushes against the obligation many scholars feel to keep producing and instead advocates that we allow our thoughts to marinate for a while.

Certain political modes of resistance also use slowness: workers movements that slow production lines or block supply chains, land rights claims movements—all those use slowness and refusal, an intentional dragging of the heels, as a political strategy.

Yet I would also want to highlight that slowness can be a privileged strategy. This has been made apparent in discussions of the contemporary pandemic, in which not everyone has the capacity to slow down. Some of us were able to sit at home, read, watch Netflix, have things delivered to us. Yet the people actually delivering goods and services: those folks do not have the

5 In the *Economist* recently, the announcement that Apple would allow certain customers limited access to repair their iPhones, specifically the screens, and to replace batteries, was considered an about-face brought about in part by the growing "right to repair" movement. "Why Is the Right to Repair Gadgets and Machines Spreading?," *The Economist*, November 19, 2021, https://www.economist.com/the-economist-explains/2021/11/19/why-is-the-right-to-repair-gadgets-and-machines-spreading. On repair, see also Valeria Graziano and Kim Trogal, "The Politics of Collective Repair: Examining Object-Relations in a Postwork Society," *Cultural Studies* 31, no. 5 (2017): 634–58.

capacity to decide when they can or can't slow down. In fact, their work might be conducted at hyper speed, because an entire city, nations, continents are depending upon their reliable service provision.

It would of course be advantageous if everyone had the capacity to enjoy the lessons of the pandemic—to slow down and become reflective practitioners. Imagine being an electrician and being able to take time after each job to think for a while about what you've just accomplished, about the philosophical implications of your work. When your services are in high demand, though, it's unlikely that you can enjoy such luxurious reflection.

While I would advocate for the value of slowness and different forms of contemplation and the methodological opportunities they open, we also have to ask political and ethical questions about who has access to such privileges.

HF:

This requires considering an invisible workforce that is attending to maintenance, care, and repair, which includes acknowledging gendered traditions of women's work, domestic and reproductive labor, which, you argue, are very much acts of preservation. The invisible labor that holds things together both socially and materially—for example, domestic chores such as cleaning—require an acute attention to detail, the kind of attention we usually demand of our architecture and design students. To understand the design detail, you must get close and intimate with the materials you are managing.

There might be lessons, both in our attention to detail and our acknowledgment of a massive laboring workforce that we depend upon, even for our daily survival.

SM:

Another of the reasons I wanted to write the "Maintenance and Care" essay for *Places Journal* is that, as much as I admire the work of the Maintainers and remain a proponent of their work, I thought something paradoxical was happening. The Maintainers themselves were becoming a bit of a brand and with that grew a presumption that the brand was casting new and exciting attention onto maintenance.

While the Maintainers were not at all ignorant or dismissive of their predecessors, popularizations of the Maintainers' work didn't always build bridges to that earlier work—to the themes of care, preservation, and conservation long present in the work of feminist economists, indigenous studies scholars, information workers, and other scholars and practitioners.

Validating and celebrating this new attention to maintenance requires acknowledging other, perhaps less flashy, scholarship that has been making similar claims for a long time— including, as you mentioned, research on feminized labor, including work taking place in libraries and archives, which is something I've often written about. My first book was about libraries, which compelled me to recognize the importance of maintenance staff, the behind-the-scenes work that is necessary to make an institution operate. We also have to recognize the inevitable future role of maintenance in fields defined by unabashedly ahistorical newness. Consider the "smartification" of everything: cities, houses, and gadgets. Infrastructure, whether smart or not, requires maintenance. But if we embed wires and sensors in our walls and streets, what happens when they fail? How do we access them for repair? What happens when "the computer" is distributed throughout an environment? Where do you localize the site of maintenance to fix something like that?

As more and more design fields—from fashion to interiors—are technologized, we have to recognize that designers need to start asking the questions about their own data infrastructures that archivists have been asking for a long time.

HF:

Many scholars concerned with infrastructure define it in relation to the inevitable event of infrastructural failure. When infrastructure fails or falls apart, it looms into consciousness. It thus shares a similar domain with invisible labor.

Considering questions of invisible labor, feminized labor,

When infrastructure fails or falls apart, it looms into consciousness. It thus shares a similar domain with invisible labor.

and the labor that's delegated to migrant communities—often lowly or dirty labor—tensions emerge. I'm interested in the disjunction between paying political attention and attempting to undertake creative design acts as a means of consciousness raising.

In your wonderful essay "Maintenance and Care," you place the performance artist Mierle Laderman Ukeles beside the activist and scholar Silvia Federici. On the one hand, we have Ukeles's feminist and embodied performances, rendering visible the otherwise invisible acts of labor that maintain our environments; on the other hand, we have Federici's argument to resist, to be noncompliant when it comes to unpaid reproductive labor, pointing out the risks of aestheticizing such acts.[6] I'm seeing this political tension emerging in different approaches to feminist thinking and practice, and I wonder whether you could help me think through this.

6 See also Hélène Frichot, *Dirty Theory: Troubling Architecture* **(Baunach, Germany: AADR, 2019).**

SM:

That was something I was trying to figure out too. How do we use maintenance artwork to make visual arguments? The design field is fluent in creating and responding to visual arguments. I wanted to speak that language and acknowledge that there are artists engaged in various modes of practice—from painting, photography, and installation to performance art and digital art—who do attempt to aestheticize maintenance. By aestheticize I don't mean something cosmetic; I mean to make the sensual sensible without veering into the territory of fetishization and spectacle.

This tension informed the choice of artworks that were featured in the essay. The aim was to show that maintenance includes embodied—and thus sensual, aesthetic—practices. The represented projects have sensory dimensions that a reader could potentially feel, allowing them to interpolate or project themselves into the images they are seeing and feel the argument in an embodied way.

HF:

Your work on maintenance and repair includes expanded definitions of technology that you render accessible to the reader. This seems to come from the influence of science and technology studies, which offers opportunities for how architecture might rethink its relation to technology. We tend to focus too much on the cutting edge, forgetting that the cutting edge in architecture is, in fact, made up of a kind of motley mix of old and newly emergent innovations. In your work you make connections between mud and data, for instance, and I was wondering whether you could discuss the need to reframe our attitude to technologies, especially in architecture and design.

SM:

I published *Code and Clay, Data and Dirt* in 2017. It's a very modest book, covering only about five thousand years of urban history...

HF:

[Laughs].

SM:

I wanted the book to serve a pedagogical function. I wasn't attempting something on the scale of Lewis Mumford's *Technics and Civilization* or Peter Hall's grand-scope urban history. I didn't aspire to something so hubristic. I had been teaching a class for close to fifteen years that was about the relationships between media technologies and space—specifically, architecture and urban planning.

When I first taught it—this is a story I tell in the introduction to the book—we progressed chronologically. We started by looking at clay tablets and mud—specifically, the fact that mud was the essential substrate for some of the earliest buildings as well as the substrate for early inscription (e.g., in Samaria). Then we looked at print, radio, and television, all the way up to digital technologies, where we looked at data centers, which everyone is focusing on today. We took a field trip to see *The Scanning: Aberrant Architectures of Diller + Scofidio* at the Whitney Museum, which looked at computational fabrication.

We started by looking at clay tablets and mud—specifically, the fact that mud was the essential substrate for some of the earliest buildings as well as the substrate for early inscription (e.g., in Samaria).

Then I realized the course would be more pedagogically and rhetorically powerful if I flipped the script and started with the now and then kept digging back further into history to show that these earlier technologies were smart too; that earlier architecture is intelligent too. These old things are not gone. Maybe we no longer use telegrams, but we still engage in many telegraphic modes of presentation and conversation—Twitter being one example. Reversing the historical order undoes the temptation to be teleological. It disabuses us of the notion that all technological development has been leading in a linear fashion toward a digital utopia. We instead see that so many of the big questions we're asking have been with humanity across cultures, for thousands of years.

That's why I chose to dig backward into history, to show that old developments have not been subsumed, buried, or abandoned. We are using amazing, space-age technology to talk with one another right now across time and space, but we're still using our voices to communicate. It could be productive for designers and architects to take this recognition that the new does not subsume or supplant the old and to think about the affordances of different formats and how they can be put into productive relation with one another.

HF:

Taking the connections you make between mud and the management of cities, we might proceed now into your critique of the smart city. As data producers and consumers, we unwittingly give up our data on a daily basis. We produce ever more data simply by occupying the city, ordering Uber Eats, receiving a delivery from Amazon. Our data are being mapped and mined, and our modes of occupying the city are increasingly available to surveillance. This seething accumulation of data increasingly informs how urban environments are managed and how products are prepared just in advance of our arrival on an urban scene, anticipating our desires before we even know we have them. Our screen-based interfaces inform who we are in the process of becoming as urban subjects, but we also need to ask who is "represented" (in all senses of the word) visually (in advertising and the media, for instance) and politically.

Uncritically celebrating the smart city and the role of data risks privileging data as a special kind of raw material to be extracted for future use. Data, raw data, can be made to speak in certain ways depending on what those in a position of power decide. You have raised this issue of who is represented in the smart city, who is allowed inside, and who is left out in the cold. Can we discuss the smart city, which risks making us, the human inhabitant, potentially more stupid?

SM:

All fields of design and all the theoretically informed questions I'm asking come back to how we know what we know and how our ways of knowing are manifested in the things we design. How the design of a product, an interface, a space, a staircase, a window, shapes what we can know of the world.

A recurring question for me is, What kind of epistemologies are implied in smartness? What ways of knowing are privileged? If we consider smart cities reliant on sensors to harvest measurable, quantifiable knowledge: such modes of operationalization really limit the types of questions we can ask and the types of things we can value. Those things that don't readily lend themselves to quantification and easy operationalization don't fit into the data model; they're the urban qualities that leak outside the apparatus of the smart city. This "excess" includes the voices, the people, the populations whose modes of intelligence don't readily lend themselves to the type of translation assumed in smart-city technologies. We also have to acknowledge those who willfully refuse to participate in data capture for all kinds of political and ethical reasons.

Asking questions about our practices, asking how we know things about the world, asking what we want to know, can be a way of materializing epistemologies. What do we know about what we value? How can we read a building—or a city or a designed object—to know more about what our cultural values are? What kind of futures do we want to build? What type of publics do we want to build together?

HF:

Reflecting on your account of how coding is being integrated into liberal arts education in the United States brings us to the question of pedagogical approaches, something I'd really like to discuss with you. Pedagogical work can be associated with caring and reproductive labors and with the concept of affective labor, the kind of labor that is habitually feminized or else delegated to migrant communities. Pedagogies are often at risk of being diminished or else instrumentalized.

I was fascinated by your course Data Artifacts, Infrastructures and Landscapes, where your students select case study sites to explore how data-logical designs, from software interfaces to master plans, can be scaled up and down. Can you speak about your pedagogical practices?

SM:

Pedagogy is a crucial part of my job. Most of my research emerges out of my teaching. I don't mean to say that I teach the books I'm currently writing—or that I make my students read the books I have just published. Instead, a book will emerge after a few years of sharing a mix of classes, when I begin to see the connections between them. It's a bidirectional form of influence. The class you've just mentioned recently wrapped up. COVID thwarted our capacity to go out and explore the city. We were going to visit a container port and investigate control rooms to see how the software they use in container shipping scales up to or translates into the organization of the ships themselves and how shipping logistics are shaped globally. Some students were interested in data centers and archival architectures. But we didn't get to visit those places. Instead, students modified their methodological plans and used digital resources. We returned to old-fashioned qualitative research—interviews, archival work—to undertake

We were going to visit a container port and investigate control rooms to see how the software they use in container shipping scales up to or translates into the organization of the ships themselves and how shipping logistics are shaped globally.

projects about borders, surveillance sites, and nuclear waste infrastructures. A student from China was looking at informal economies for transferring masks and other medical supplies. These were shadow economies, pirate infrastructures that were intentionally thwarting the state. The surveillant eye of the state monitoring the flow of these goods was in some ways decreasing the efficiency of official distribution infrastructures. The student drew on the situated knowledge of her family in Wuhan. She used digital ethnography by looking at WeChat and other social media and digital communications to understand the digital infrastructures powering these informal logistical systems.

These were shadow economies, pirate infrastructures that were intentionally thwarting the state. The surveillant eye of the state monitoring the flow of these goods was in some ways decreasing the efficiency of official distribution infrastructures.

Some fantastic projects developed in this class despite—but I would also say because—of the limitations that were placed on our physical mobility.

I've also taught a class on mapping. Most of my classes are about some combination of information and space: spaces of information organization, information embedded in space, the spatialization of information logics, and so on. The question of epistemology is also crucial in my classes. I try to incorporate multiple ways of knowing, making sure we're reading not only scholarly accounts but also popular literature when studying examples from design and art and investigating practical and activist projects. This is theory in action. It's not just the French and German guys who get to do theory; people make theory by engaging with the frictions evident in the world. I try to incorporate a diversity of epistemologies and encourage students to experiment. This is evident in the multiple modalities of the work they produce over the semester.

HF:

It sounds like your students use a lot of design-based approaches. You seem to encourage a transdisciplinary mix of anthropology, ethnographic research, and design. Do your students produce visual works and drawings as part of these pedagogical exercises?

SM:

I've been lucky in that, for as long as I can remember, my classes have been really diverse. We've had between eight and twelve disciplines represented in the classroom, including students from the humanities, the social sciences, and from multiple design fields. I frame low-stakes group projects where I intentionally match students into interdisciplinary groups. They can do exploratory fieldwork exercises where they are learning to look at the world and gather evidence in interesting ways together.

This approach gives the more design-oriented students a chance to learn from and with the social science and humanities studies about theoretical concepts and methods germane to their practice. Even if they don't ultimately fully adopt those frames, they at least get a sense of why people care about asking certain questions. I'm excited to see how some of the social scientists and humanists play around with modalities of documentation and expression in different ways. They often try totally new approaches. I usually work with a teaching assistant who is a great cartographer or graphic designer, who can sit down and work with the students if they want to incorporate media-making into their research. Even rudimentary forms of visualization can inform the questions these students are asking and help them look at their research in new ways.

I'm excited to see how some of the social scientists and humanists play around with modalities of documentation and expression in different ways. They often try totally new approaches.

HF:

There are dilemmas around ethnographic process, specifically that you must spend a long time on site—months, even years—as opposed to the speed that might be demanded in a design process. Designers must attend to the site as much as ethnographers, but the two seem to have different slownesses and speeds.

SM:

Here again I will acknowledge that I was not trained as an anthropologist. For fifteen years I was in a media studies department that defined itself as an anti-discipline. While I'll never call myself an anthropologist, I am trying to immerse myself in the burning questions of the field to understand the commitment to ethnography and what the field's methodologies allow researchers and students to do.

This old-fashioned directive that you must spend a year in a foreign country before you can claim that you've undertaken adequate fieldwork assumes a form of privilege. Who has the kind of financial stability, access to healthcare, and family flexibility to allow for that kind of work? Some researchers have to break up their fieldwork, for instance, into two-week periods over the course of two or three years because they take care of an ailing parent, or a child, or a family member with disabilities. The calls for a feminist model of "patchwork ethnography"—which validates improvisation and collaboration, which recognizes that people are still caregivers while they're in the field—has been liberating for my students.

HF:

Would you be willing to share some stories of the recent student work completed in your class?

SM:

I'll show you some material from the Data Artifacts, Infrastructures and Landscapes class. Commencing with the analysis of a specific artifact, I encourage students to think across scales. They start with something tiny and delimited, like a grain of salt or a coffee bean. I'm inspired here by Donna Haraway's "implosion method," but instead we wanted to explode this tiny thing to see all the infrastructures and data logics and political systems and economies that converge there—in that grain of salt or coffee bean. This is both a useful

Commencing with the analysis of a specific artifact, I encourage students to think across scales. They start with something tiny and delimited, like a grain of salt or a coffee bean.

design exercise—it gives you a concrete thing to keep returning to—and a really great way to frame research and writing.

If you want to be expansive and interdisciplinary in what you're thinking about or writing about, having a small thing that you keep coming back to as your home base can be a really useful rhetorical and narrative structure. It's an anchor for the meandering interdisciplinary exploration you're undertaking.

We had a student from Guatemala studying a coffee bean. Another student was looking at a single musical album and all the metadata attached to it when it is translated for distribution in the digital economy. This raises questions of how authorship and creativity are translated into metadata for a digital musical sphere.

Another student looked at the storage facilities for fine art. He focused on a single storage cell or pen and mapped the logistics of moving fine art around the city and through different free-trade zones. The list of specific things that can be investigated goes on: the dollar bill, the condom, a bar code ... These are just some examples of the artifacts students studied.

HF:

I see these examples as exercises in "following the material" to understand complex networked relationships. It occurs to me, too, that such exercises demonstrate ways in which we can imagine a pedagogical design exercise not in terms of something that we do to achieve that final project outcome, or that anticipates a buildable future, but instead how the act of design can be deployed as a means of representation and sensory mapping to mount an argument and to render something visible in terms of its relations. An important conceptual shift is required to understand the expanded applications of design as an analytical tool and means of mounting a critical argument: Design doesn't have to end in that beautiful folly but could also offer a well-articulated visual argument.

SM:

This approach can also be applied to a geology of media. Many researchers are writing about the elemental components of media technologies and their afterlives as e-waste, for instance, and are producing explosion diagrams. You take the designed object, the hermetically sealed black box, and you open it to discover the rare earths, the different types of minerals and forms of labor, the supply chains—all of which have contributed to it becoming this beautiful, pristine, talismanic object. Liam Young and Kate Davies of Unknown Fields undertake this kind of work.

HF:

Perhaps we can conclude with questions of love and care and how we infuse these methodologies with such dispositions.

SM:

How to infuse these methodologies with care?

I think we have to understand that care does not always have a positive connotation. Care sometimes has a underbelly. Who feels obliged to care? Who is responsible for care? Who is obligated to offer service with a smile? Who provides home healthcare, hospice care, childcare, while not being well cared for themselves? In many of these professions we rely on a global supply chain drawing human labor from the Global South.

In recent days, under pandemic conditions, I've been watching videos of people in big box stores, in restaurants, in banks in the United States refusing to wear masks—usually as a libertarian statement. They go into a place of business, point a video-recording device at themselves while performatively resisting and declaring their freedoms. Still, shop attendants, bank clerks, customer service agents are obliged to handle the problem calmly, diplomatically, for the sake of maintaining the corporate identity.

Then, if you take a designed object, like an iPhone or any other gadget, and do a reverse analysis of the supply chain, you can see how care manifests in different places. What does it mean to be a carer on a container ship, for instance? How does a ship captain care for their crew? How do all of the machinists and stevedores on a dock care? What does it mean to care in those contexts?

Depending on where you are undertaking care labor—perhaps on a Foxconn production line where the polishing of screens produces toxic dust—you could be placing your own health at risk. Care can give rise to biologically deleterious effects, where your careful act of craftsmanship involves putting yourself at risk so an end user can enjoy a beautifully polished consumer good.

We can observe how care manifests and has different political valences in all of these different stages when we track a thing back through the supply chain.

HF:

I believe we can observe a general turn toward a consideration of materials and a rethinking of materials that can be located under the banner of new materialism or neomaterialism, a new theoretical tendency arguing that we haven't been paying enough attention to our material relations and calling us urgently to rethink our approaches to the design act, to reframe what it is that we should be concerned about.

Many ethical implications are at work when we pay attention to the flows of materials along supply chains, and students can learn much from paying close material attention.

SM:

In Data Artifacts, Infrastructures and Landscapes, we spent a whole lesson discussing modes of resistance. We referred to a powerful essay by Gautam Bhan called "Stalling: How to Save the Global City."[7] It discusses how disenfranchised community groups can use the tactic of stalling, by, for instance, calling out small irregularities in policy or code, which legally

Many ethical implications are at work when we pay attention to the flows of materials along supply chains, and students can learn much from paying close material attention.

require a project to be placed on hold. Stalling tactics can then buy time to gather and to organize and then to launch a more substantial mode of resistance.

HF:

We've discussed repair, maintenance, and care in relation to infrastructural systems and how we might bring these themes into our pedagogical practices. In closing, I wonder whether you could offer a final reflection on infrastructural love?

SM:

I'll offer one final example. I grew up in a hardware store that my dad and his brothers inherited from my grandfather, who first opened it in the 1970s. By reflecting upon a humble site like a small-town hardware store, where technical and architectural infrastructures converge, we can see a social infrastructure at work.[8] Hardware stores provide the infrastructural elements for people to cultivate and maintain their domestic and civic infrastructures. We can see a dimension of love and care that manifests there, even if in a hypermasculine form. A different valence of love is inherent in these types of places that help people build and care for their material environments, which empowers them and lets them know that they're capable of building infrastructures too.

> Hardware stores provide the infrastructural elements for people to cultivate and maintain their domestic and civic infrastructures.

7 Gautam Bhan, "Stalling: How to Save the Global City," *Public Books*, **June 11, 2019, https://www.publicbooks.org/stalling-how-to-save-the-global-city/.**

8 See Shannon Mattern, "Community Plumbing," *Places Journal*, **July 2018, https://placesjournal.org/article/community-plumbing-a-history-of-the-hardware-store/.**

TAKING INSTRUCTIONS

<3

INFRA-STRUCTURAL JOURNEY

We invite you to venture into your local environment-world. Take an infrastructural journey and look out for different qualities, affects, points of view, connections, happy conjunctions, and sad failures as you venture forth. On the one hand is your sen-

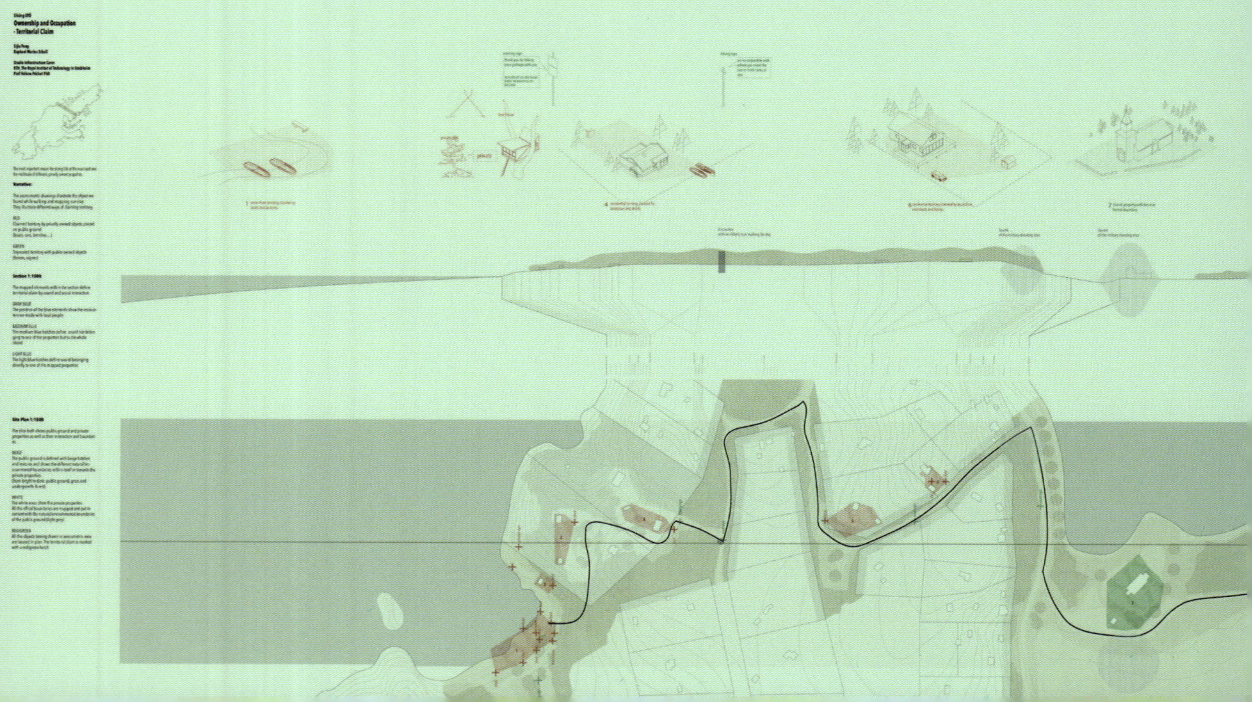

sory experience and the baggage you bring with you—your tastes and predilections. On the other hand, you can attempt to adjust your existing biases by supplementing your journey with research in archives, news media, information available at municipal offices, and by paying more astute attention to what you encounter on your way. Compose a collage, draw a diagram, write a short story.

Infrastructural Journey. Utö Island, Stockholm Archipelago, Sweden. Drawing by Sijia Peng and Raphael Marius Schall Group 1, 2019.

100 INFRA-STRUCTURAL DETAILS

Storytelling ethnographer Anna Tsing and feminist philosopher of science Isabelle Stengers each exhort us to "pay attention!" to our local worlds.[1] Local attention can lead to an understanding of the specificities of each place and also lead to a consideration of the inevitability of global connections. This instruction is about paying attention to the ordinary details and affects of everyday infrastructures.

1 Anna Lowenhaupt Tsing, *The Mushroom at the End of the World: On the Possibility of Life in Capitalist Ruins* **(Princeton, NJ: Princeton University Press, 2015); and Isabelle Stengers,** *In Catastrophic Times: The Coming Barbarism,* **trans. Andrew Goffey (Ann Arbor, MI: Open Humanities Press and Meson Press, 2015), DOI: 10.14619/016.**

Take a journey to your site. Be sure to use public transportation to get there; better still, use multiple forms of transport. On the way you will pass through different urban, suburban, and perhaps even rural landscapes. Pay close attention to the world around you as you travel. You must sharpen your skills of observation until they become acute. Now, begin to collect details. You can commence by taking photographs, but you must also have some means of documenting scale. Carry a measuring tape with you, if in doubt. Begin to collect details, small and large. You can organize this exercise in a group—the more of you the better to share the labor. Collect ninety-nine infrastructural details while on your journey. Document these details with line drawings using a sufficient selection of line thicknesses. Use a range of scales from 1:2 to 1:50. Arrange these details in a ten-by-ten grid. Make the exercise a game by adding one final detail that is entirely invented. Your audience must guess which detail is the imaginary one.

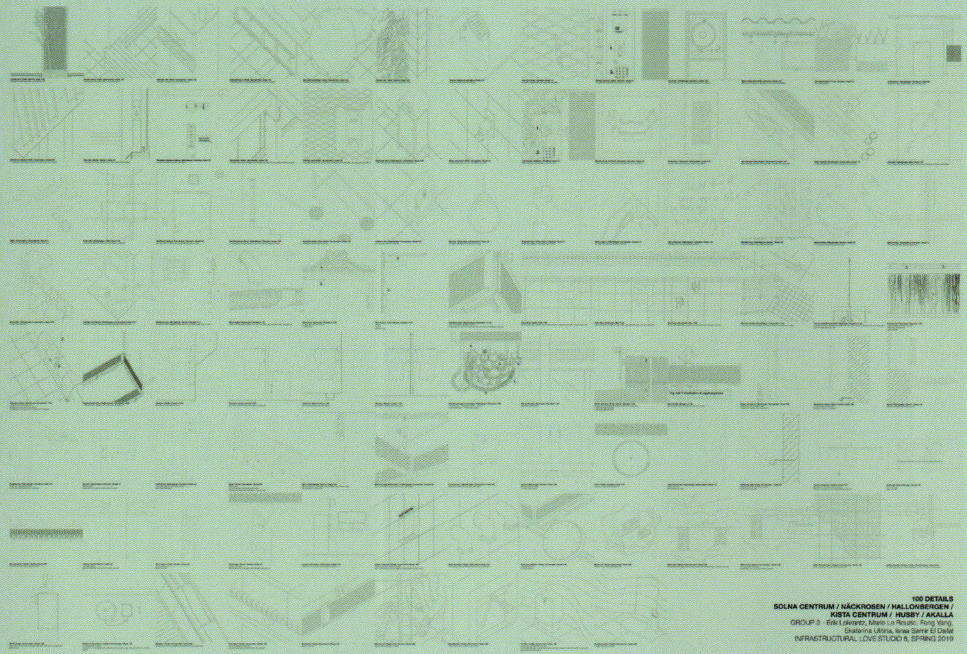

100 Infrastructural Details, Veddesta. Blue metro line Solna Centrum–Akalla, Stockholm, Sweden. Drawing by Erik Lokrantz, Marie Le Rouzic, Feng Yang, Ekaterina Ulitina, Israa Samir El Dallal, 2019.

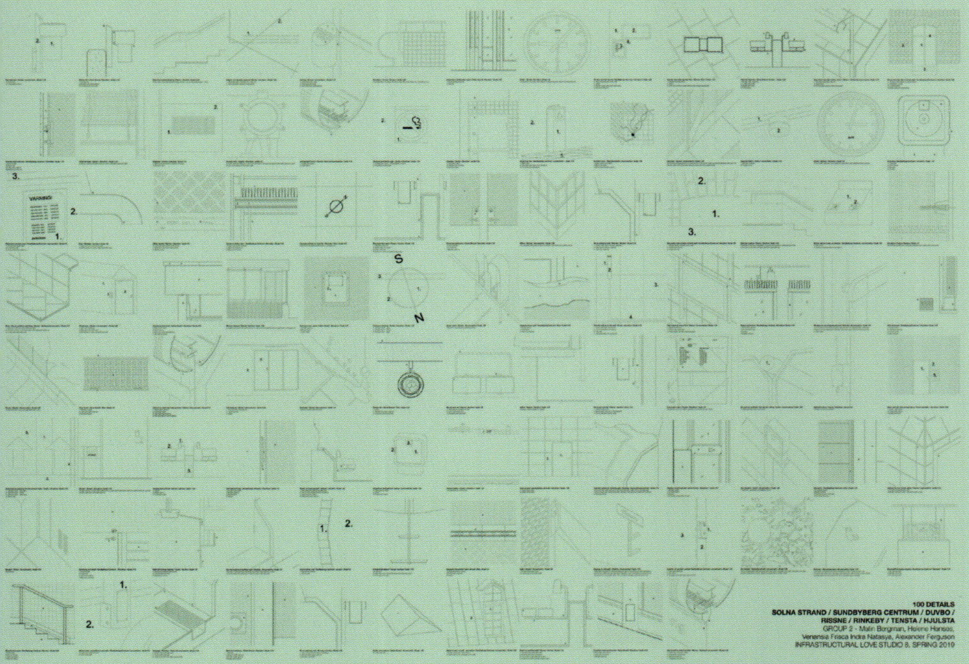

100 Infrastructural Details, Kymlinge. Blue metro line Kungsträdgården–Huvudsta, Stockholm, Sweden. Drawing by Maja Mihajlovic, Richard Gray, Maria Johansson, Oscar Wilner, Changhyun Ahn, 2019.

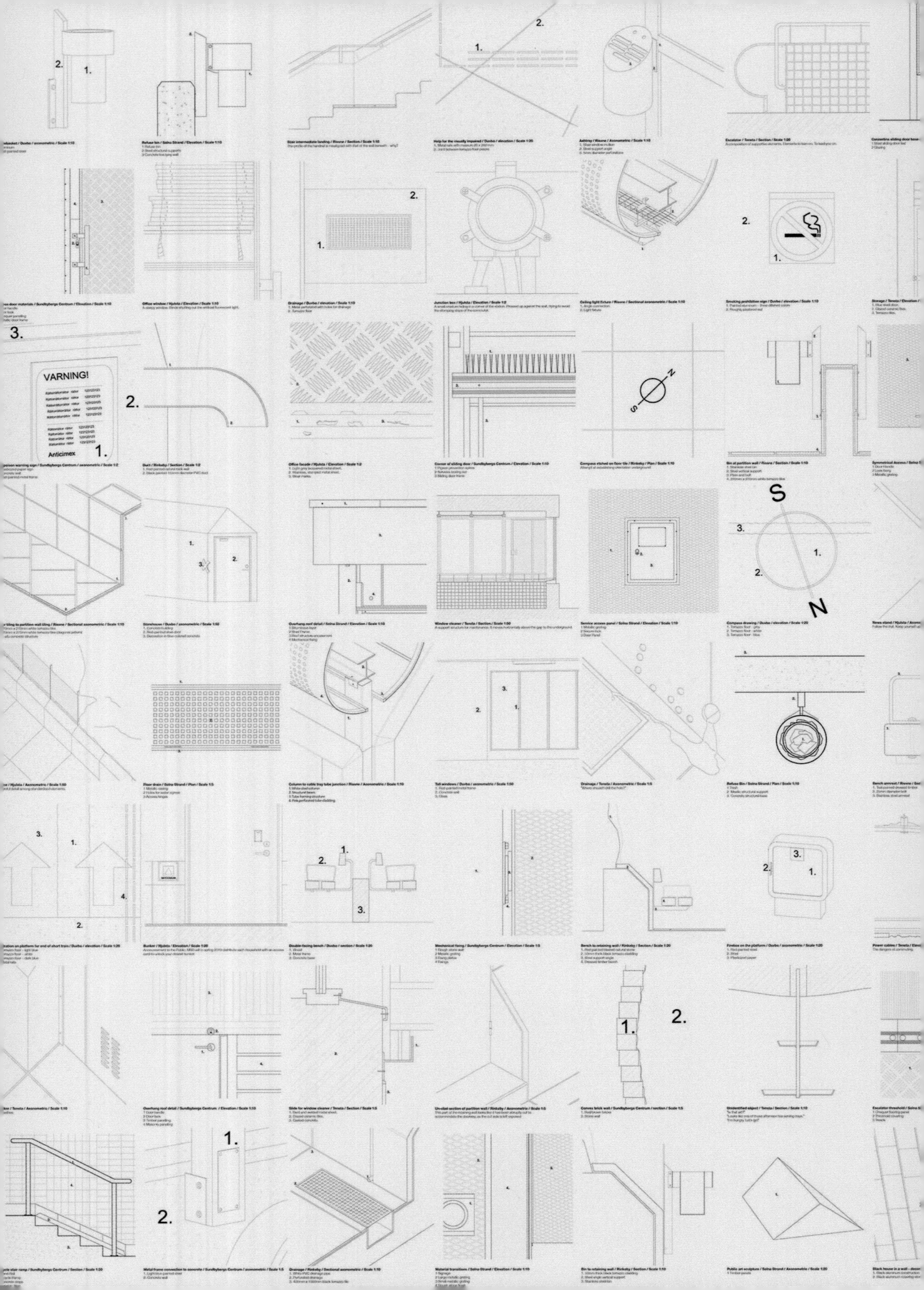
VARNING!
Anticimex

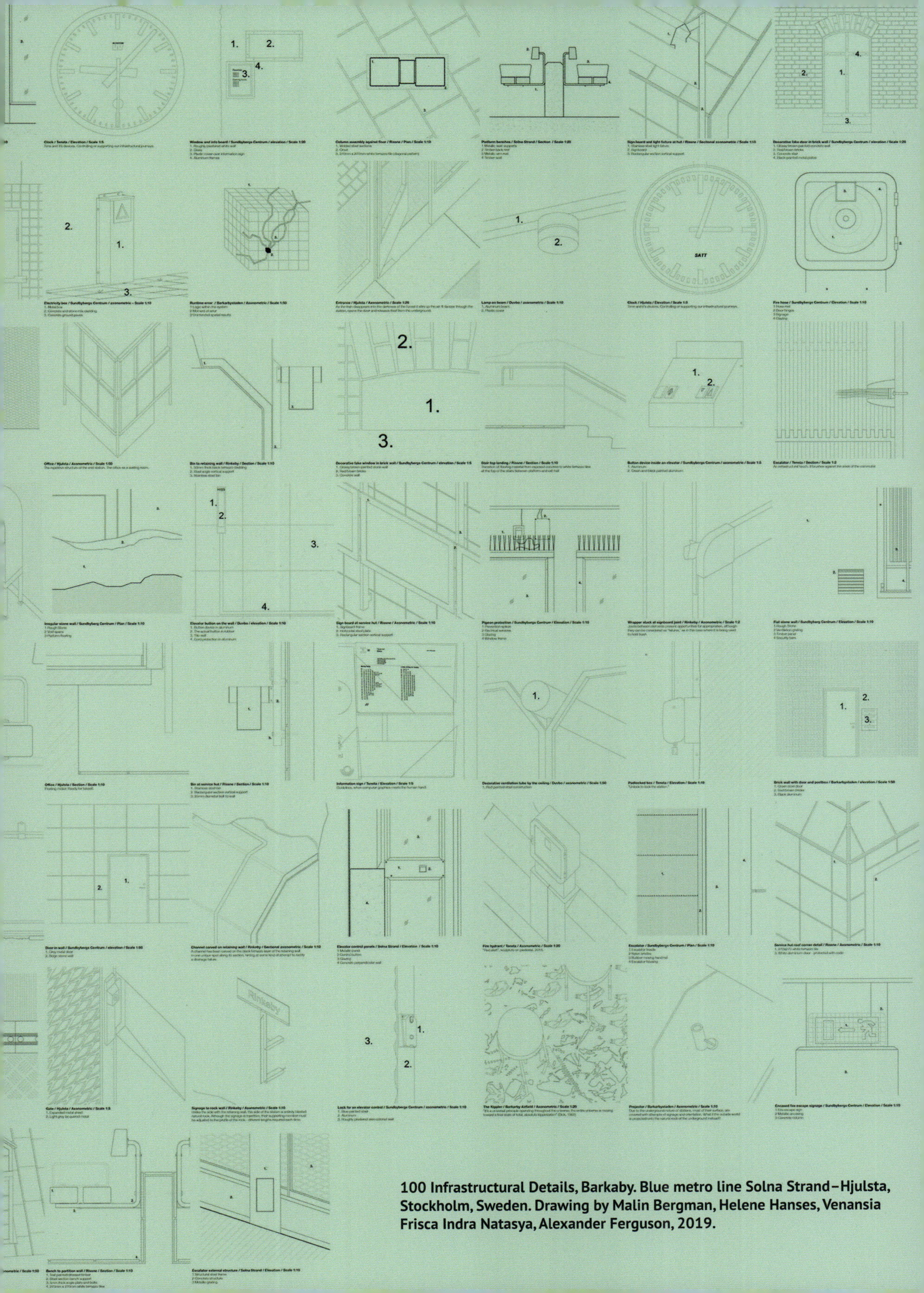

100 Infrastructural Details, Barkaby. Blue metro line Solna Strand–Hjulsta, Stockholm, Sweden. Drawing by Malin Bergman, Helene Hanses, Venansia Frisca Indra Natasya, Alexander Ferguson, 2019.

IRRATIONAL SECTION CUT

Irrational section cuts challenge the conventions of architectural drawing and documentation.[2] Where the rationality of a conventional cross-section drawing asserts definability, commensurability, possibility, and buildability, presuming to stand objectively for a future possible world or else documenting an existing one, an irrational section cut radically rethinks the connections between things. It recomposes diverse visual forms, challenges the conventions of

2 Miriam von Schantz and Hélène Frichot, "On the Irrational Section Cut," in *After Effects: Theories and Methodologies in Architectural Research*, ed. Hélène Frichot with Gunnar Sandin and Bettina Schwalm, 253–71 (New York: Actar, 2020).

scale, addles durational registers, and generally disrupts the constraints of normative linkages. The action of the cut—as break, as frame, and as mode of momentary capture—creates interstitial zones that demand a critical and creative reinterrogation of our local environment-worlds. The irrational section cut takes the section drawing and places various scales, seasons, locations, and points of view into relations of unexpected proximity. Close-up and far away are brought into dialogue. Nor is the irrational section cut just a spatial device; it is temporal, too, enabling the depiction of contingent events and encounters. Cut-up, fold-up, collage, montage, color, and hatch. Rather than documenting an existing state of affairs, the irrational section cut imagines new compositions of peoples, places, and things. Rationality is challenged insofar as it tends to maintain the status quo of common sense, which means we risk holding on to all our bad representational habits. The aim is to acknowledge diverse points of view, from above, from below, both human, and non-human.

Tower for Military and Bats, Section, Utö Island, Stockholm Archipelago, Sweden. Drawing by Frida Torstensson, 2019.

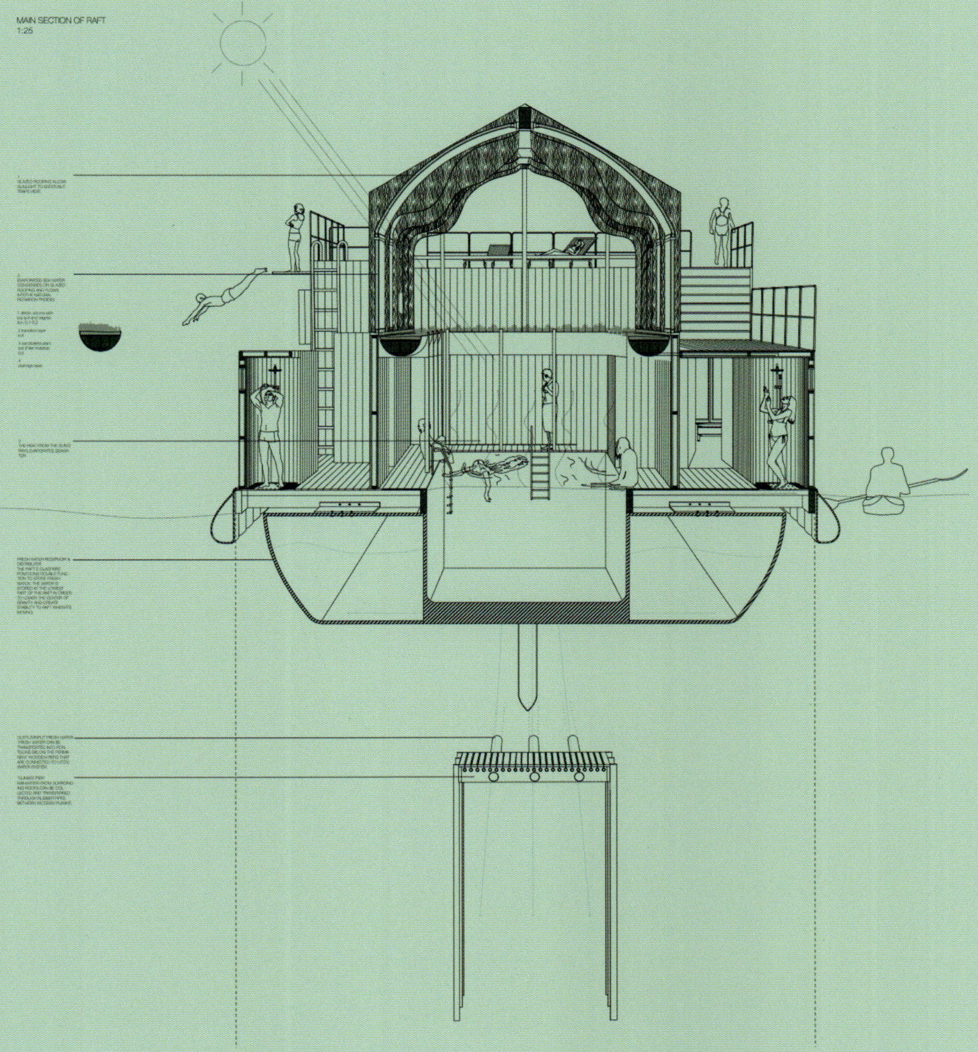

The EWD-Baths, Section, Utö Island, Stockholm Archipelago, Sweden. Drawing by Ida Larsson, 2019.

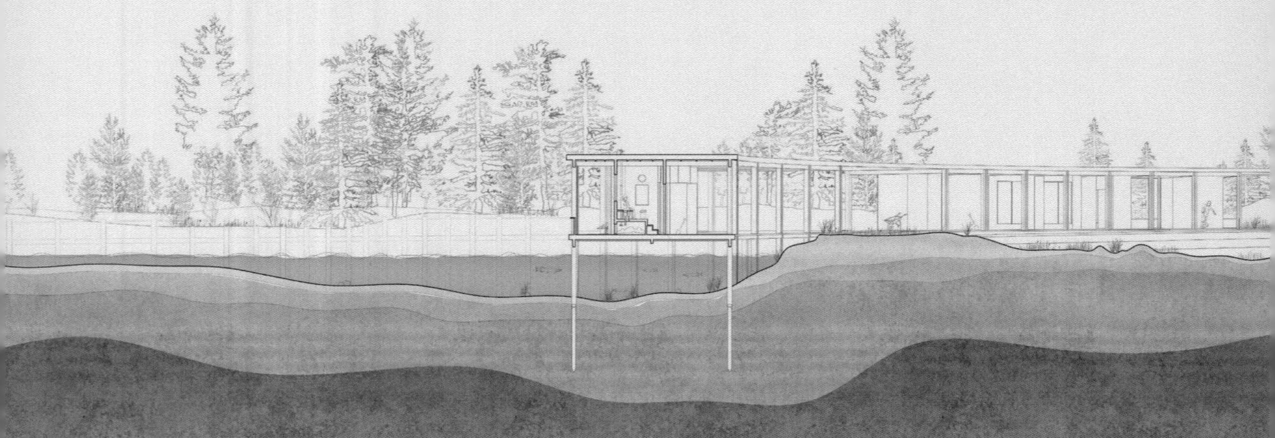

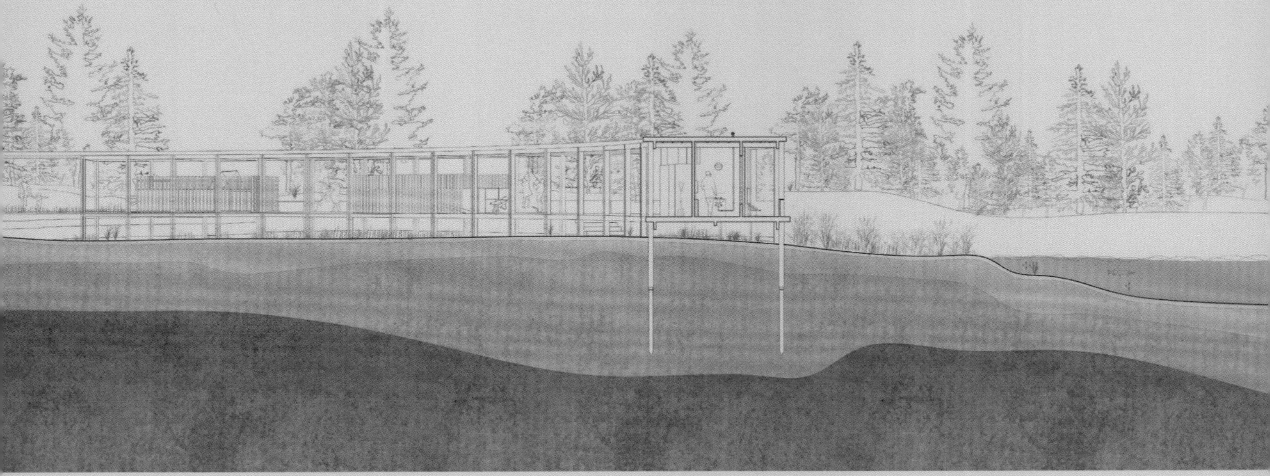

The Remedial Rest Room, Section, Utö Island, Stockholm Archipelago, Sweden. Drawing by Ella Walklate, 2019.

DETAIL MASH-UP

Even technology makes the mistake of considering tools in isolation: tools exist only in relation to the inter-minglings they make possible or that make them possible. The stirrup entails a new man-horse symbiosis that at the same time entails new weapons and new instruments. Tools are inseparable from symbioses or amalgamations defining a Nature-Society machinic assemblage.

Gilles Deleuze and Félix Guattari[3]

Document a technological detail that facilitates infrastructures. Use axo-

3 Gilles Deleuze and Félix Guattari, *A Thousand Plateaus: Capitalism and Schizophrenia* **(Minneapolis: University of Minnesota Press, 1987), 90.**

nometry, section or exploded axonometry and compose a drawing at a scale of 1:5, 1:10 or 1:20. Now, renovate the documented detail or mash it up with another detail. The aim is to open a new connection in an existing infrastructural system.

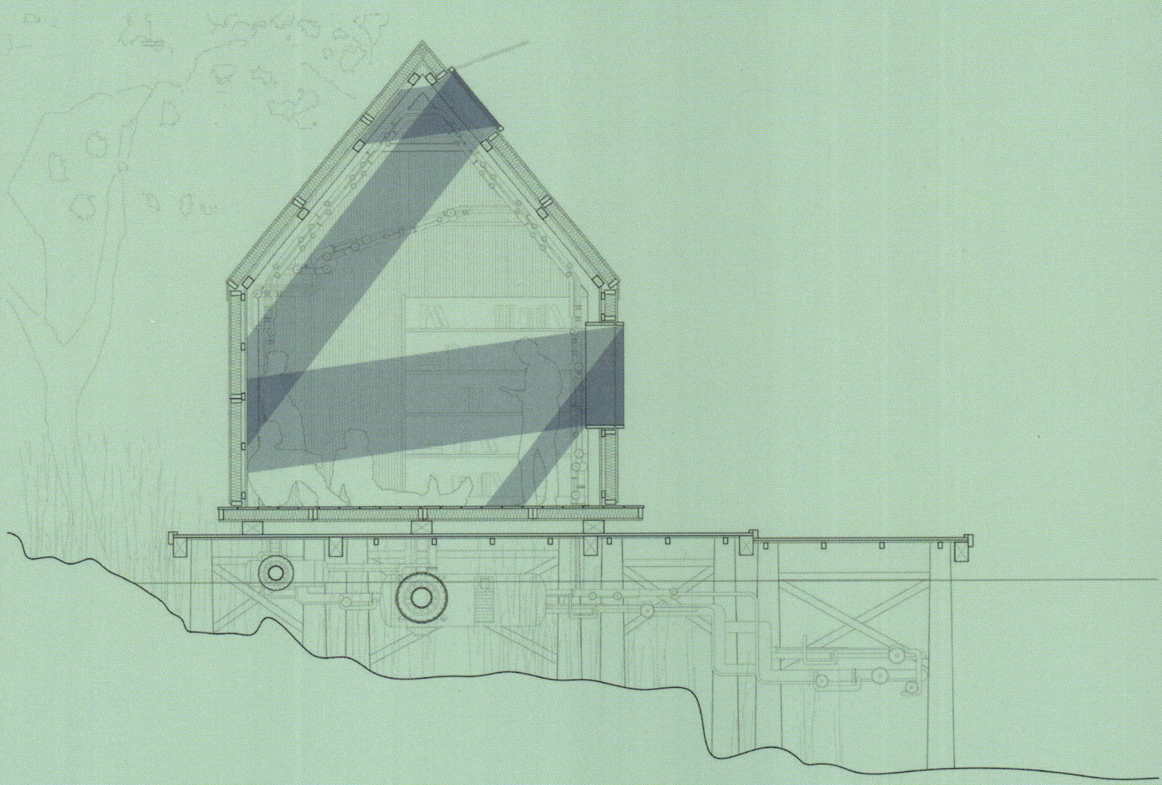

Gruvbryggan Dock's Network, Section, Utö Island, Stockholm Archipelago, Sweden. Drawing by Isabel Mayoral Vallés, 2019.

CROSS-SPECIES ENCOUNTERS

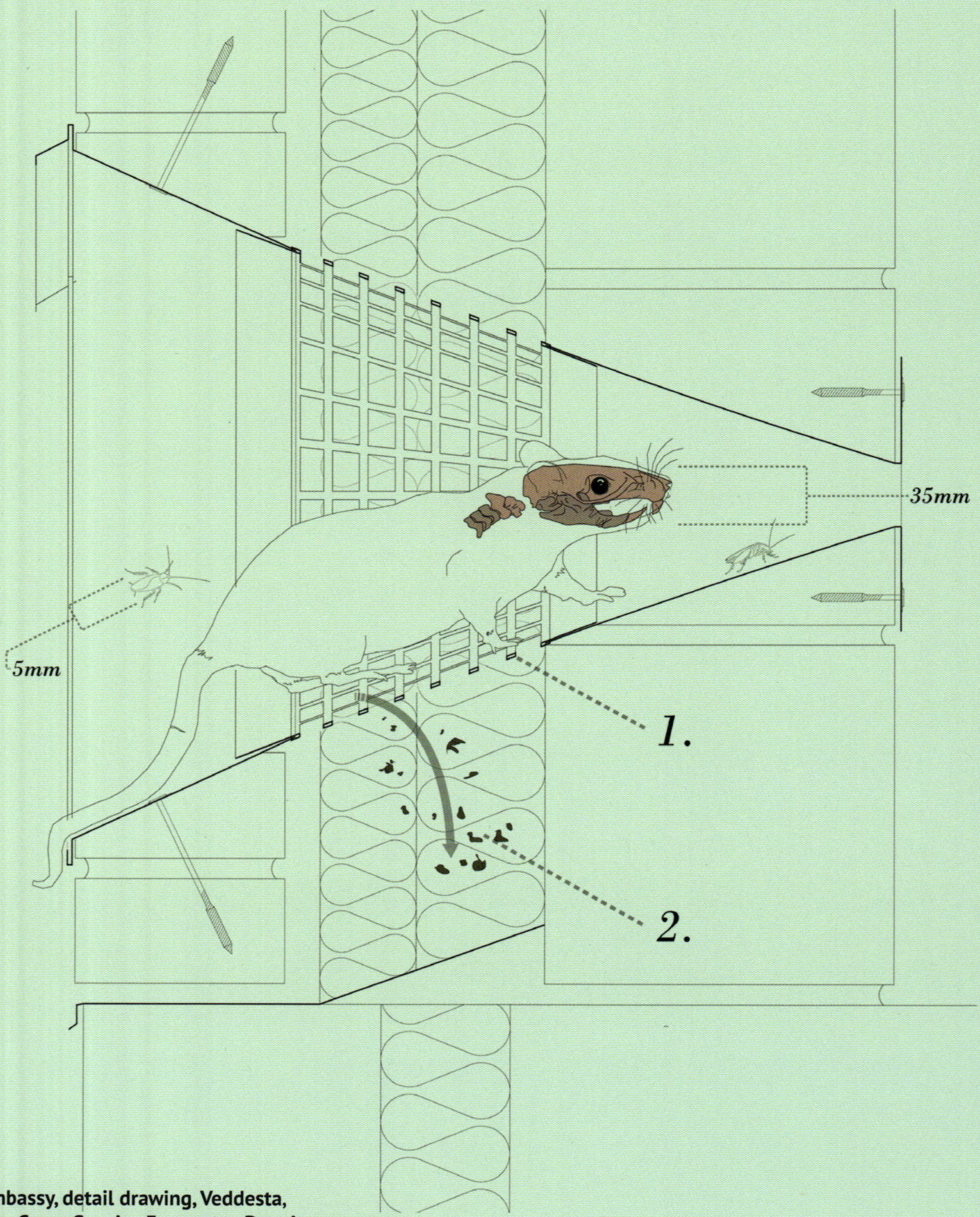

The Nonhuman Embassy, detail drawing, Veddesta, Stockholm, Sweden. Cross-Species Encounter. Drawing by Erik Lokrantz, 2018.

Compose a detail that encourages the entry into your architecture of a more-than-human companion. When designing habitable space, we expend a great deal of time and energy keeping what we perceive to be unwanted pests on the outside. Is it possible to find amicable means of cohabitation? Take a close-up section cut, explore what it means for architecture to get cozy with a more-than-human companion.

The Remedial Rest Room, Collage, Drawing by Ella Walklate, 2019.

DIRTY MODEL

Construct a dirty model, the dirtier the better. Too often models are constructed after the hard work of the design process and design development is over, and then they stand there like empty memorials to ideas that have already been hatched. Such hygienic, clean, and carefully finished models can tell us a great deal about a project but not enough about the thinking process and how design is a messy and murky activity. The dirty model is a design thought in process, and something that gets your hands dirty. Use waste materials rather than off-the-shelf cardboard that will only be trashed later anyway. Use materials that arouse a visceral response. Think fat and felt.

The Cleaning Pigeons, Dirty Model, Veddesta, Stockholm, Sweden. Model by Marie Le Rouzic, 2018.

SMOOTH MONTAGE

If scaffolding is a temporary structure for the support of building construction, can a drawing perform as a cognitive scaffold to support our rethinking of the existing environment? Smooth montage explores the photorealistic or "smooth" montage drawing as a support for imagining infrastructural love.[4] Produce one perspectival drawing per person, based on your individual project, and, in doing so, explore the montage as a technique for juxtaposing programs, activities, and times that would otherwise be separated. The

4 Hannes Frykholm, "Smooth Montage," in *After Effects*, 236–51.

drawing should be visually realistic so that the viewer can imagine how they would "enter" the image. We encourage you, as you make the drawing, to visualize the program you are developing by conveying one seminal idea of your project. Start by sketching the composition of your drawing. This can be a crude pen drawing similar to a single frame of a storyboard, where you define what you are showing, what is in the foreground, in the background, and what your image conveys about your project. Choose framing, composition, and content with great care. The sketch will serve as a support for your continued work.

Compose a photorealistic drawing that introduces one or many elements of your project. Since we are early in the process, choosing a frame that reveals only part of your proposal, for example a building element or a particular space (the exact part is up to you), can be strategic. Use 3D rendering software (V-RAY, Maxwell, etc.), Photoshop, model photos, and/or precise forms of hand drawing to insert your project into the site. Feel free to use your own photographs of objects and materials taken from your site, but compose these into "new" elements and compositions that challenge expectations. Insert people/nonhuman beings/objects/sun/rain/plants/materials/atmosphere/etc., into the drawing—anything you need to make it visually appealing.

The smooth montage must be as "photorealistic" as possible; that is, it must imitate the visual quality of a photograph. This means carefully representing the ways your inserted objects "land" on the site, considering the direction of light, shadow, and the "seam" between your insertion and the existing site. Think, for example, of how you would draw a plinth in high grass.

The finished drawing should be high-resolution. Construct your montage using one or several high-quality photographs of the site as the main image. The photograph(s) should be taken with a good camera, and the

The Institute for Screen Care and Marinebiological Research, Smooth Montage. Drawing by Isak Hellström, 2018.

approximate image size should be at least 2,500 by 1,700 pixels. Too few pixels or poor compression will leave the drawing distorted. Keep in mind that you need to be in control of your color palette so that disparate colors do not distract from the sense of realism. Look at the use of colors and light in glossy architectural renderings, in advertisements, and in the movies.

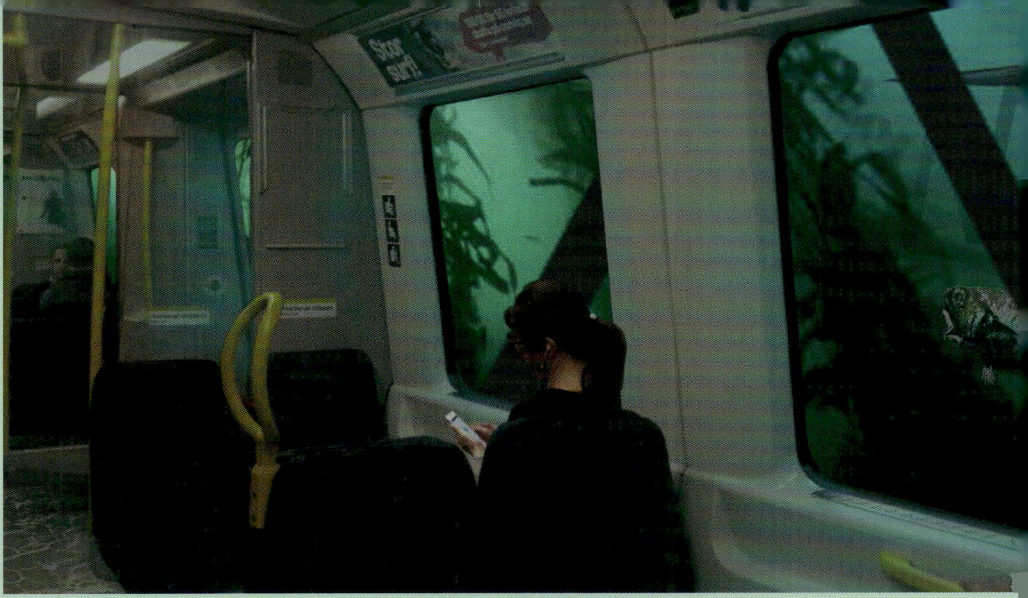

The Institute for Screen Care and Marinebiological Research, Smooth Montage. Drawing by Isak Hellström, 2018.

Utö Library, Smooth Montage, Utö Island, Stockholm Archipelago, Sweden. Drawing by Sijia Peng, 2019.

Back Space: Storing our National Art Treasures in Case of Emergency, Smooth Montage. Drawing by Linnéa Ågren, 2018.

PROLIFERATING PRECURSORS AND THOUGHT-PROVOKING PRECEDENTS

Design experimentation does not emerge ex nihilo; in fact, the opposite is the case. The imagination is crammed with a vast collection of images and ideas. How do you best grasp these precedents and influences and reinvent them for your own project? The precedent is related to how you build your design argument, much as in a court of law, where legal argumentation can be based on previous rulings. The precursor is the thinker or practitioner who comes before you. Either you can be overwhelmed by the weight of their influence, or else you find a way to restore an "incommunicable novelty"[5] to their work. What are your precedents? Who are your precursors? Here we focus on "minoritarian" examples in an attempt to avoid the status quo of the usual design suspects. Compose five to ten A3 portraits that include image and text (100–200 words). Describe design

5 Gilles Deleuze and Félix Guattari, *What Is Philosophy?* (New York: Columbia University Press, 1994), 204. See also Hélène Frichot, *Creative Ecologies: Theorising the Practice of Architecture* (London: Bloomsbury 2018).

influences from architecture, art, literature, film, and so forth. Be expansive in your disciplinary survey. Your precedents and your precursors can be historical, or they can be contemporary. They do not have to be based specifically on the design program you are developing but can draw attention to spatial, material, graphic, or sociopolitical qualities you would like to explore. Carefully study your precedents and precursors, locate them historically, understand what is at stake with respect to their associated problematics, and list all relevant bibliographical information.

FOLLOW THE MATERIALS!

The challenge enunciated in the demand to follow the materials is one aimed at developing an ecological sensibility that attends to the entangled relations between humans and nonhumans, environments and things.[6] To follow the materials means being aware of every material choice you make as a designer, because every material comes from somewhere, and eventually, once exhausted, ends up someplace else, in a dump site, for instance. This task asks that you attend to the materials of your local environment-world

6 See Hélène Frichot, "Follow the Material!" *How to Make Yourself a Feminist Design Power Tool* **(Baunach, Germany: AADR, 2016).**

in the vicinity of your site. Produce material harvest maps, study where materials have been extracted, and whether they might be reused later on, or what their after-life might be. Develop an intimate relationship with the materials you plan to work with and the materials you discover on your site. Where will the materials take you? What do the materials want?

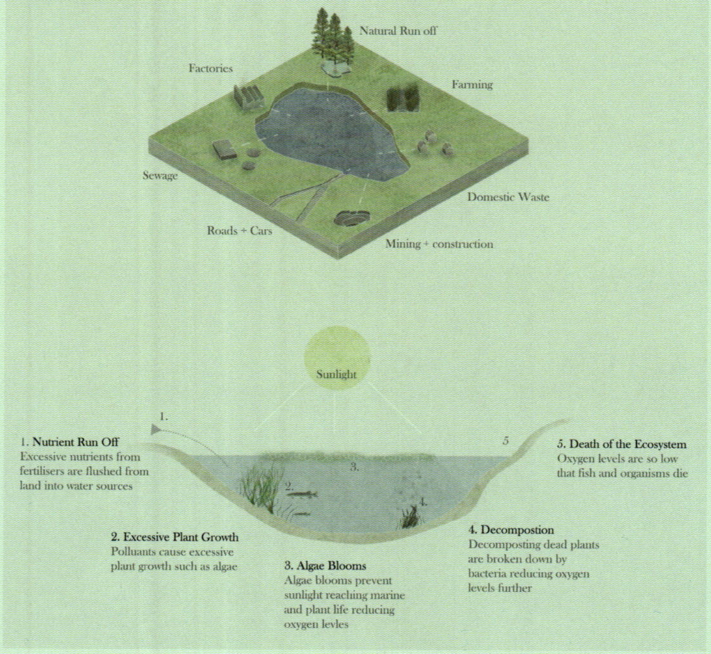

The Remedial Rest Room, Diagram of Material Flows. Drawing by Ella Walklate, 2019.

The Remedial Rest Room, Diagram of Material Flows. Drawing by Ella Walklate, 2019.

TERRITORIAL SLICE

Measuring instruments and techniques unfold historically and are laden with unconscious biases that determine how knowledge comes to be constructed. These apparatuses inform particular understandings of space, time, form and matter, at the same time defining the way in which a particular historical time is lived, experienced, and ultimately thought about.

This assignment is undertaken as a collaborative effort in a group. It aims to capture the specific conditions of a site through the study of its material, social, cultural, and environmental layers. Instead of approaching the area from an aerial mapping, explore your site by walking along a straight line that cuts through the landscape. Each group will produce a "slice" of the territory under investigation focusing on an assigned topic and its related infrastructural support systems. The location of the slice should be guided by the theme being examined, which also informs the fundamental questions being asked by the group.

In your explorative walk, you will measure and capture the infrastructural elements you encounter on the way through a combination of surveying, recording, writing and storytelling techniques, with the aim of disentangling the multiple realities at play. Drawing on the action of slicing—to cut a smaller piece out of a larger entity—you will collaboratively produce a large section drawing, a montage drawing, and an axonometric view of your territorial slice.

Carefully choose the location of your territorial slice location before your site visit, but be prepared to respond to contingencies once you arrive. Once on site, time should be spent surveying, measuring, investigating, and encountering the entanglements of a place that Google Earth can never fully reveal.

The data extracted in the territorial slice

will be represented in both section and plan. Other media can also be explored. Pay attention to the infra-structural systems, instruments and objects, human and non-human relations, visible and invisible elements, power structures both tacit and explicit that influence the rhythm of life across your site. Record what you see on the ground, but also what's above, and what's beneath (under?). Tell the stories embedded in the land, what agents, what actions, what technologies shaped it. Collect material evidence and recall their memories through the oral voices of people living in the area. Relevant elements encountered in the territorial slice will be enlarged in scale in order to understand their materiality and their logic relative to the infrastructural system under investigation.

Territorial slice through Utö. Drawing by: Ida Larsson, Marco Bruggmann, Mingyu Qiu, Ella Walklate

IMPLICATED IN CARE, HAUNTED BY PROTECTION

Chapter 4
Implicated in Care, Haunted by Protection: The Violence of Bronze and Stone Bodies

Elke Krasny

As living human bodies move through their everyday urban environments riding in their cars, taking buses or trains, rushing to work on foot, or strolling leisurely through a park, they often pass the bodies of other humans who are not alive. These nonliving humans are always there. They never leave their designated space. They never move unless they are moved. These other bodies are not flesh and blood. They are bronze and stone. They have been sculpted deeply into the surface of cities. They are a central element in the infrastructures establishing modern urbanization and transforming urban dwellers into modern bodies.

What follows serves as an introduction to thinking through the meanings of the copresence of living and nonliving modern bodies in shared public urban environments and performs a slight but significant shift in perspective on these nonliving modern bodies, aka figurative statuary and monuments: *they are bronze and stone bodies and they are part of the making of modern urban infrastructure*. The umbrella term *bronze and stone bodies*, defined here as an infrastructural concept, includes allegorical as well as historical figures. In methodological terms, this move allows for the development of a conceptual approach that combines history and theory, bringing into view the idea that all bodies, extending to bronze and stone bodies, have needs that require care to exist and act in the world. First, this move leads to archival materials, their making and their legal care and protection, as well as all kinds of source materials on mundane and commemorative practices in

The umbrella term bronze and stone bodies, defined here as an infrastructural concept, includes allegorical as well as historical figures. In methodological terms, this move allows for the development of a conceptual approach that combines history and theory, bringing into view the idea that all bodies, extending to bronze and stone bodies, have needs that require care to exist and act in the world.

response to bronze and stone bodies. Second, this move explores changes to urban fieldwork training and how observation on the bodily, spatial, and infrastructural dimensions in the encounter between living and nonliving modern bodies can be rethought. Third, this move allows for new analyses of existing literature on modern figurative statuary and monuments in fields such as art history, architectural history, anthropology, history, digital humanities, environmental humanities, legal studies, philosophy, urban planning theory, urban studies, memory studies, gender studies, critical race studies, queer and color studies, and crip studies. Central to understanding bronze and stone bodies as bodies and as infrastructure is that these bodies are fully dependent upon us, the living, to be present with us and to act upon us or together with us. Monument care and monument protection are modern philosophical and legal concepts developed in the context of modern processes of urban infrastructuralization. The care and protection of historical monuments was relevant to the formation of the nation-state and its legacies, in turn supporting the making of modern monuments that are considered equally worthy as representatives of the progress of the present that will endure into the future. Progress and preservation are central to modern processes of urban infrastructuralization and associated requirements for monument care and protection.

The care and protection of historical monuments was relevant to the formation of the nation-state and its legacies, in turn supporting the making of modern monuments that are considered equally worthy as representatives of the progress of the present that will endure into the future.

Building on the first part of the chapter, the second part provides a framework for a feminist history and theory of bronze and stone bodies based on the following three premises: bronze and stone bodies have a body; they occupy a space; and they have a history. Connecting these premises to the need for care and protection not only provides the tools for a critical methodological framework but raises profound concerns for future monument care and monument protection and what their ethical and legal dimensions mean to the practices and actions of public administrators, members of civil society, policymakers, and political representatives. These concerns raise awareness that care and protection given to bronze and stone bodies is "implicated" in and "haunted" by historical violence—including antisemitism, racism, sexism, domination, plunder, and death-making—that is kept present in public urban environments precisely by the means of monument care and protection.[1] Consider, for example, the care and protection given to bronze and stone bodies representing those who, in their own time, were imperial rulers, war leaders, invaders of territories that did not belong to them, colonial mining magnates, or proponents of political antisemitism and proponents of racism.

Bronze and stone bodies occupy space as part of the infrastructures that created classed, gendered, racialized, and sexualized divisions and inequalities in public urban environments.

The bodies of modern humans considered powerful and exemplary—historical figures and allegorical figures alike, who can be identified as central to the violent, cruel, and lethal systems of domination over humans, all other beings, and the shared planetary environment—are bodies now kept permanently present. The very bodies of modern humans who have unleashed, and are thus responsible for, the death-making culture of modernity, paving the way for genocides, ethnocides, ecocides, and mass extinction, are today allowed to occupy space in public urban environments and to occupy time, understood as both hegemonic History (with a capital H) and as individually experienced and shared time resulting in personal keepsakes and memories. I am acutely aware that many bronze and stone bodies are different from the ones who are the focus of my discussion here. Historical modernity has also made animals, in particular the horses that formed a part of imperial power and warfare, permanently present. In addition, activist monument makers use figuration and the materials of bronze and stone to make present the bodies of those who lived in the wake of and suffered from historical violence. Recent decades

1 I use the terms *implicated* **and** *implication* **following literary scholar Michael Rothberg's conceptual framework. See Michael Rothberg,** *The Implicated Subject: Beyond Victims and Perpetrators* **(Stanford, CA: Stanford University Press, 2019). My use of the term haunting is based on the conceptual approach put forward by sociologist Avery Gordon. See Avery Gordon,** *Ghostly Matters: Haunting and the Sociological Imagination* **(Minneapolis: University of Minnesota Press, 2008).**

have seen a return to figurative sculpture and an insistence on adding to public urban environments bronze and stone bodies representing those who had previously been absent from them. Representing and making publicly present the bodies of "victims" and those who resisted the cruelties of historical regimes of oppression, discrimination, and death-making can be seen as a form of activist and ethical healing, as well as a strategic political response to the occupation of urban environments by the bodies of historical "perpetrators" of violence.[2]

2 **Rothberg,** *The Implicated Subject.*

To discuss the implications of care and reflect on the haunting that results from acts of protection, this chapter focuses on the continued violent presence of bronze and stone bodies depicting those who held power and defined modern nation-building, colonial expansion, and modern urbanization. The infrastructures that constructed this new and modern world rested on the twin ideologies of human supremacy and colonial patriarchy, known in the history of ideas as the Enlightenment and since the turn of the century as the Anthropocene epoch, a geological period marked by the catastrophic impact of humans having become a geological force. Urbanization gave built form to these ideologies, which were founded on inequality, nesting at its core the new technologies of steam industrialization and the economies of extractive fossil capitalism.

Attica figures from parliament ready for removal (07-20-2018) © Parliamentary Directorate / Michael Buchner

Local school children in Vienna are taken to these statues to learn about them. I recall having been taken there about fifty years ago. We learned that the statues are from the nineteenth century and that this style is called neoclassical or neo-Hellenistic. We were also taught that Greek statues are always white. The white-washing of Greek statues forms part of the formation of coloniality and racism and is charted by Nell Irvin Painter in her book *The History of White People*, where she explains how Johann Joachim Winckelmann, considered the first to write a systematic art history, elevated Rome's white marble copies of Greek statuary into emblems of beauty and created a new white aesthetic.[3] Throughout this chapter, I use photographs and narrative captions to share some of my own encounters with bronze and stone bodies as an urban researcher and cultural theorist, as a professor teaching at a public university, as a living and moving body in public urban environments, and as feminist concerned with care, socioecological reproduction, and memory practices in the built environment.

3 Nell Irvin Painter, *The History of White People* **(New York: W. W. Norton, 2010).**

In the chapter's conclusion I emphasize the ethical and political dimensions of future monument care and protection and insist that a profound rethinking is necessary so that public urban environments can be restituted and freed from their occupation by bronze and stone bodies who subject the living to the monumental glorification of violent historical regimes of discrimination, oppression, and death-making and who, through their bodies, imprint this History on the surface of cities.

Bodies and Infrastructural Intimacy

Every day, they are there. Bronze and stone bodies never move. They do not stop occupying their space. We cannot escape their being present. Their presence performs a political ontology through their materiality and the space their bodies have been endowed with, a presence enacted through bronze and stone. Their presence transforms public urban environments into environments shared by living and nonliving bodies. Much like other urban infrastructures, such as drinking water, sewage, transport, power, or communication systems, their presence defines how we as humans live together, shaped, supported, and, to a degree, defined by these infrastructures or their absence. While one can argue that water, sewage, or power are essential to human survival and that bronze and stone bodies are not essential in quite the same way, seeing them as infrastructural components of public urban environments is helpful in understanding how these bodies configure a distinctly modern system that renders those considered makers of History permanently present. This memory infrastructure made up of bronze and stone bodies not only renders the past permanently present, which is the starting point for conventional understandings in everyday use and scholarship, but also makes abundantly clear the distinctly modern feature of the ideology of human exceptionalism that can make certain historical bodies defy death by keeping them forever present. However, these bodies are not simply present forever; they depend on us, on the living, to remain permanently present. They need protection against attacks, displacement, or destruction, be it in times of war or during urban protests or urban development. They need care, maintenance, and repair as the impacts of daily weather events and human-induced climate change age their bodies. Both in everyday language and in legal terms, acts of maintenance are referred to as "monument care" and "monument protection." Therefore, the public institutions, the legal mechanisms, the provision of infrastructural maintenance, but also individual acts of affection and love displayed around

While one can argue that water, sewage, or power are essential to human survival and that bronze and stone bodies are not essential in quite the same way, seeing them as infrastructural components of public urban environments is helpful in understanding how these bodies configure a distinctly modern system that renders those considered makers of History permanently present.

and performed with bronze and stone bodies, are implicated in the past they keep alive. To fully unfold their performativity, as well as their political ontology, they also need "knowledge care" and "epistemic maintenance."

Pallas Athene

In front of the Parlamentsgebäude (Austrian Parliament Building) in Vienna stands the monumental, five-meter-tall Greek goddess Pallas Athene. While I am writing this chapter, the 420 million euro process of restoring Theophil Hansen's 1883 building is underway. To date, this crypto-colonial appropriation of Greek culture has remained largely unnoticed and unquestioned, whereas Pallas Athene has become a popular attraction for those taking selfies. Stone and bronze bodies require structures of support that provide knowledge about them in the contexts of education and tourism. The bodies are often at the receiving end of learned caring behaviors, including touching, hugging, or being captured in photographs and selfies. They are connected to personal memories of strolling through cities or enjoying vacations with kin, friends, and families. The presence of bronze and stone bodies entangles us. Having been captured in photographs, many of these bronze and stone bodies sneak into people's personal lives. They remain present in the photo albums kept in people's drawers or on bookshelves in their homes. They circulate through social media channels on which people are active, as memorable moments are shared with others. Often little is known about the bronze and stone bodies that are so openly welcomed into the practices and sites of personal memory-making. We can understand their public presence in urban environments and their intimate presence in personal memory-making practices through the Freudian term *unheimlich*.[4] Bronze and stone bodies are so strangely familiar that they are taken for granted, becoming naturalized presences that are part of the aesthetics of the urban surface that can be consumed as a visual backdrop. The very fact that these bronze and stone bodies enter intimately into the lives of living bodies, leaving lasting impressions and traces, links them to features shared by other infrastructural systems, ones being rendered legible through critical feminist (in particular, decolonial, intersectional, material, and materialist feminist) approaches.

4 Sigmund Freud, "Das Unheimliche" (1919), in *Gesammelte Werke XII*, **ed. Anna Freud, Edward Bibring, Willi Hofer, Ernst Kris, and Otto Isakower, 229–68 (Frankfurt: Fischer, 2001).**

Infrastructure operates for, on, with, through, but also against bodies at affective and material levels, impacting the epistemological and the bodily, the personal and the public, the private and the social. Consider the fact that modern bodies entangled in the processes of modern urbanization—that is, infrastructuralization—were made to breathe in the air that new transport systems began to profoundly alter. Modern bodies began to move at the speed and according to the intervals of transport systems. Modern bodies were connected to water systems through pipes intimately reaching into their homes, and this water entered, touched, and left their bodies in multifold ways. Modern water infrastructure connected bodies to water so they could drink it, cook their food, clean themselves, and wash their clothes. As reproductive life was reshaped by these infrastructures, human bodies passed on these bodily changes to following generations of bodies made modern through urbanization. Modern forms of infrastructural injustice play out on the scales of the environmental, the material, and the spatial but also on the scales of the social and the historical, as well as on individual bodies. This leads to an understanding of the deep impact of infrastructures that can be captured in the concept of infrastructural intimacy. This concept is helpful in raising awareness about how little living human bodies know about the interpenetrative effects of the infrastructures they are intimately bound to and dependent upon. Bringing this thought of corporeal infrastructural intimacy to the infrastructural memory system, composed and upheld by figurative bodies that have characterized the making of modern cities, raises awareness about how little is known about the depth of violence, the abyss of pain, trauma, and dispossession, that is made permanently present and upheld by the bronze and stone bodies surfacing in modern cities and how such violence rendered permanently present creeps into bodies and minds alike, finding its way into photo albums and other keepsakes.

The interconnectedness of scales through infrastructures is constitutive to how living human bodies were made to be "modern." *Infrastructuralization*, as a new urban ontology, entered human bodies and their everyday lives. The term infrastructuralization refers to all the processes necessary for the production and reproduction of infrastructures—that is, the care dedicated to maintenance and repair—so they can continue to perform their functions. The term not only refers to all the processes through which infrastructure connects to people's everyday lives but constitutes a new way of infrastructural life in which urban environments reshaped by infrastructures enter into human and other bodies. Infrastructural life is life on the level of bios, wherein bodies are penetrated by environmental changes wrought by infrastructures. Bronze and stone bodies form a material and environmental, as well as allegorical and symbolic, part of these infrastructures that create ableist, classed, ecological,

> Bronze and stone bodies form a material and environmental, as well as allegorical and symbolic, part of these infrastructures that create ableist, classed, ecological, gendered, racialized, and sexualized divisions and inequalities in public urban environments.

gendered, racialized, and sexualized divisions and inequalities in public urban environments. Critical scholarship and activism pay close attention to political and social dimensions of infrastructural injustice. Equally important is to understand infrastructures through their effects, which are at once public and intimate, and to grasp the deep infrastructural reach into environments and bodies. This helps us better understand the nexus that runs through interlinked and interpenetrative implications of infrastructures that are at once affective, bodily, environmental, and material. Thinking about infrastructural ontologies of longevity and reliability leads to thinking about the care and protection needed by infrastructures. For infrastructures to last and to perform their support functions, they must be cared for and maintained by humans.Thinking about bronze and stone bodies in infrastructural terms leads us to dimensions of care and to the complex ethical and political implications of caring for such bodies, which is of central concern to this chapter. For bronze and stone bodies to remain permanently present, they need living bodies who care about, and work for, their continued existence and who ensure their care needs are met over time. Continued existence is not only the material and bodily existence in bronze and stone, but also the epistemic and cultural existence through research, teaching, and cultural practices of looking, photographing, and visiting,

Working toward a Feminist History and Theory of Bronze and Stone Bodies

Bringing into clear focus the idea that figurative statues and monuments are bodies while bringing into sharp relief the idea that these bodies are entangled in the politics of modern infrastructuralization requires critical scholarship to take a deeper look at what these bronze and stone bodies need. What do they demand and require from us? What does taking care of them and providing protection for them mean in ethical and social terms and in relation to ecological justice in the public urban environments that living and nonliving bodies share? The care and protection given to these bronze and stone bodies entangles all members of urban publics in their presence. Feminist theories argue that bodies are interdependent insofar as they depend on the provision of care and protection to survive and thrive. Ontologically, all bodies are always in need of care and protection: bodies who are in power and bodies who are subjugated by bodies in power, bodies who are involved in death-making as well as bodies involved in life-making. Care and protection are implicated in what bodies are doing to one another. What do these bodies "care about"? What do they need so they can make present what they care about? How do they move us to "take care of" their needs? And what does "care giving" and "care receiving" between living and nonliving bodies mean in affective, cultural, ecological, economic, environmental, emotional, epistemic, social, and political terms?[5] A discussion of care leads to thinking about the consequences of the lasting provision of care and protection to bronze and stone bodies and what it means to have been responsible for contributing to caring for their enduring presence, made seemingly permanent, over years, decades, and centuries.[6]

> Care and protection are implicated in what bodies are doing to one another. What do these bodies "care about"? What do they need so they can make present what they care about?

The three premises outlined above—that bronze and stone bodies have a body, that they occupy a space, and that they have a history—are here connected, for the purpose of developing a feminist history and theory of such bodies, to the central features of presence, occupation, and History. By *History* I posit a hegemonic version of history, or simply History with a capital H. What

5 Berenice Fisher and Joan Tronto, "Toward a Feminist Theory of Caring," in *Circles of Care: Work and Identity in Women's Lives*, **eds. Emily K. Abel and Margaret K. Nelson, 35–62 (Albany: State University of New York Press, 1990), 40.**

6 See Rothberg, *The Implicated Subject*.

makes an approach to these three premises feminist? The term is understood here as an epistemic and political approach linking scholarship to the real world of injustice, violence, exploitation, extraction, and oppression while seeking to resist, counteract, and transform this world so all bodies, human and nonhuman, as well as all so-called nonliving matter, can coexist in their interdependencies as best as possible. In what follows I lay out the import of body, space, and History, as they are foundational to the history and theory of bronze and stone bodies. Body, space, and History have been central tenets in several genealogies of feminist epistemic traditions and of feminist scholarly activism connected to feminist movements.[7] A feminist history and theory of bronze and stone bodies can build on rich, complex, and nuanced feminist traditions. I draw on the epistemological and analytical tradition of feminist care theory to offer a framework of analysis for the nexus that runs through body, space, history, presence, occupation, and History. Simply, care ethics is the core analytic for working toward a history and theory of bronze and stone bodies. All bodies are always in need of care. Care ensures that bodies can have their place in the world and that they can continue to exist in their place in the world. Starting from the foundational premise that bronze and stone bodies are material bodies that need to occupy a place so they can have a history, care ethics brings into focus the question of how the continued existence of bronze and stone bodies is made possible so that public urban environments can be shared by living and nonliving bodies. Education scholar Berenice Fisher and political theorist Joan Tronto have developed a framework differentiating "four intertwining phases" of "caring about, taking care, caregiving, and care-receiving."[8] This framework is used here to open a broad and challenging series of questions highlighting the implications of the care given to bronze and stone bodies.

7 A detailed exploration of the different feminist epistemologies and the richness of cultural, social, material, political, and spatial feminist practices engaging with the body, space, and History is beyond the scope of this chapter.

8 Fisher and Tronto, "Toward a Feminist Theory of Caring," 40.

The figure of *Der Sieger* (The Victor) is one of the most popular figurative statues in Vienna and one of the most photographed by tourists. I often take my first-year students at the Akademie der bildenden Künste Wien (Academy of Fine Arts Vienna) to visit this nude bronze body. I ask their opinion of him.

Der Sieger **(The Victor, 1921) by Josef Müllner (1921), Theseustempel, Volksgarten, Vienna**

Many think he is beautiful. Others point out that he presents a timeless ideal of classical beauty. When probed, they start to see that this body resembles later bodies made by Arno Breker or Josef Thorak, both of whom the Nazi regime included on the *Gottbegnadeten-Liste* (God-gifted list).[9]

My first premise is that bronze and stone bodies have a body. On an ontological level, bodies can be understood through the concepts of life and death. Living bodies are mortal. The art-historical term for sculptures of human and nonhuman bodies is figurative, which means "derived from life." Bronze and stone bodies are "recognizably derived from life."[10] Therefore we must ask whose life has been deemed worthy enough to be represented as a bronze and stone body? Figurative bodies have a "recognizable source in the real world," which is made permanently and publicly present by bronze and stone

9 Thorak also studied under Müllner, who was a professor at the Akademie der bildenden Künste Wien from 1910 to 1948.

10 A.N. Hodge, *The History of Art* **(New York: Rosen Publishing Group, 2017), 204.**

bodies and thus leads to the "historical survival" of the specific "source" that is being made "recognizable."[11] The presence of bronze and stone bodies places a demand on living human bodies to recognize them as who they have been historically or as what they stand for symbolically or allegorically. In this relation to the living, bronze and stone bodies adopt a political life that is not characterized by permanency, in the sense of remaining unchanged, but rather by what their permanency means to those who are copresent with them during their own lifetime. Precisely in this relation between unchanging permanent presence, which these bronze and stone bodies make a claim to, and the possibility of or right to changeability, which living bodies articulate and express, does the political dimension of this relation unfold and take shape. Whose bodies are kept alive and made permanently present in bronze and stone? Who cared about these bodies enough to maintain their public afterlife in public urban environments after their bodily death? Who cared about the choices of bodies that make present allegorical or symbolic meaning? Who took care of all the things needed so that a bronze or stone body could come into existence? How were pressure groups or lobbying groups dedicated to the memorialization of specific bodies formed? How was the money collected and procured? How were politicians lobbied to give their agreement? How did the sculptors get access to these historical bodies to figure them? Who, for example, made the death masks of historical figures and provided those to the artists? Who chose the clothes they should wear and made them available? Who cared about the body ideals made present in allegorical statuary? Who took care that these bodily norms, which join together normative ideas of beauty and of ethical virtue, were produced by allegorical bodies? Who wrote the laws that determine that bronze and stone bodies are protected from removal or destruction? Who understands their needs for conservation, restoration, maintenance, and cleaning? Whose bodies are tasked to perform the labor of care? Whose bodies gather in front of them to show their respect and to give expression to acts of memory? Whose bodies respond to them with their affects and emotions? Whose bodies bring flowers or give hugs, take

11 Antonia Pocock, "figurative/figural," in Keywords, n.d., *The Chicago School of Media Theory* **[blog], https://lucian.uchicago.edu/blogs/mediatheory/keywords/figurativefigural/.**

photographs or provide information so that bodies remain recognizable? How are those who perform such labor and such acts of caregiving affected by the bronze and stone bodies? How has the care received by bronze and stone bodies been documented over time? How are bronze and stone bodies affected by the care and protection they receive? Who researches how care and protection have been provided and received over time?

My second premise is that bronze and stone bodies occupy space. Ontologically, bodies can be understood by their existence in space. Living bodies are spatial. So are nonliving bodies. The general architectural-historical term for the statuary that forms part of buildings is *architectural sculpture,* which is understood as the decoration of buildings. The commonly used general art-historical term for monuments is *art in public space*. Not distinguishing here between architectural sculpture as decoration and monuments in public space is foundational for developing a broader conceptual approach to the space occupied by bronze and stone bodies. Thinking through these spaces of occupation has led me to use the formulation "public urban environments," which is more encompassing than the standard terms *buildings* or *public space*. The term *public urban environment* includes all kinds of buildings, built structures, and, of course, public space. Bronze and stone bodies are found almost everywhere: in central squares, on the rooftops and facades of buildings, on boulevards, in parks and cemeteries, in the entrance halls of train stations, in museum foyers and school atriums, and in hallways at city hall—to name just a few. Modern cities created new public urban environments into which were incorporated public statuary and monuments. These include cultural, educational, health, housing, leisure, transport, traffic, and work infrastructures that fulfilled in material terms the ideologies of growth, progress, and innovation. New infrastructures of modernity include train stations, parliament buildings, museums, opera houses, theaters, swimming pools, squares, and parks—all of which provide civic space for bronze and stone bodies. These nonliving bodies contribute to deep processes of infrastructuralization, as well as to the modern aesthetic of the infrastructural surfaces of cities.

Who provides space to bronze and stone bodies? Who plans space for such bodies? Who designs the squares and boulevards where they are installed? Who designs the architectures, buildings, and infrastructures they form a part of? Which spaces are provided to which bodies? Where is their space located in the context of an urban environment, which is marked by different notions attributed to center and periphery, inclusion, exclusion, segregation, and differently distributed accessibilities? Is the space where they are installed publicly owned and administered or privately owned and cared for? What was in the space before the bronze and stone bodies came to occupy it? What did they displace? (This question includes the large modern infrastructures that reshaped urban land adorned by architectural sculpture.) Who protects spaces where such bodies are installed from the encroachment of urban development? From which spaces were the material resources extracted that were necessary for sculpting and casting stone and bronze bodies? Where are the marble quarries and the sites of copper or tin mining from which bronze and stone bodies can trace their material beginnings? Where are the studio spaces of the sculptors who made them? Who is responsible for the provision of care and maintenance of these spaces? Whose bodies are made to come into daily contact with these bronze and stone bodies as they use public urban environments (transport infrastructures, streets, squares, etc.) to move from one space to another? Whose bodies perform the labor of care and maintenance for these spaces where bronze and stone bodies are found?

My third premise is that each of these bronze and stone bodies has a specific history. Ontologically, bodies can also be understood through their existence over time. Bodies are temporal and thus historical. This also holds true for bronze and stone bodies, whose materiality makes a claim to permanency and thus to History. The historical and everyday understanding of figurative statuary and of figurative monuments is that they render History present and thus serve the functions of public, collective, social, and cultural memory. As a memory infrastructure they have been incorporated into the built canon of national cultural heritage. As subjects of teaching in the context of school curricula and university courses, as well as for the provision of knowledge in the context of public tours for interested audiences, whether locals or tourists, they are seen as History. They provide the reason for continuing and passing on a specific version of hegemonic History. Today, in the context of post-imperialism, post-coloniality, post-Shoah, post-genocides, post-communism, and the Anthropocene condition at large, the presence of this History has come under scrutiny and attack. The commonly held assumption that bronze and stone bodies manifest the History of those they make present has obscured the fact that they are themselves historical and have their own history that changes as responses to them change over time and as their bodies age in material terms. It is generally assumed that bronze and stone bodies are History; that is, that they make present important historical figures or core values rendered legible through allegory. But the history of bronze and stone bodies is not identical to the History they make present. Distinguishing *history* from *History*—that is, distinguishing the existence of bronze and stone bodies in the spaces they occupy from the History they make present—is central to a feminist history and theory of bronze and stone bodies. Only if we start to differentiate more clearly in critical research between, on the one hand, the specific history that made specific bronze and stone bodies possible and ensured their continued public existence and, on the other hand, their history as it is registered through archival and all kinds of written and visual sources, can we arrive at a more complex understanding of the needs of these bodies and the implications of care. This includes researching and thus constituting their everyday urban history as it unfolds in the responses of living beings to their presence. The Fisher and Tronto framework of caring about, taking care of, caregiving, and care-receiving has been used here to develop the above questions. They are not exhaustive but serve as tools to begin the work of compiling more complex histories and theories of bronze and stone bodies. Such histories are important as they make possible the rethinking and redefining of the current legal, ethical, and political understanding of monument care and monument protection.

Implicated in Care, Haunted by Protection

The specific histories of bronze and stone bodies remain understudied in scholarship, including in the new postdisciplinary and multimethodological work bringing together architecture, art, history, anthropology, archival studies, environmental and material studies, class studies, gender studies, critical race studies, policy studies, international war and security studies, international relations studies, heritage studies, urban studies, and memory studies. Further activist archival work and urban field research will be needed to learn the specific histories of bronze and stone bodies and to understand the implications of monument care and the haunting performed by monument protection. Bronze and stone bodies—that is, figurative statuary and monuments—need care and protection to make possible their continued existence in public urban environments. Building on Michael Rothberg's notion of the implicated subject, I suggest that subjects are implicated by their provision of care for bronze and stone bodies who glorify and monumentalize violent pasts. Such care ensures the continuance of past violence, maintaining its seemingly unbroken presence. Reading Rothberg, implicated subjects are enmeshed in the prolongation of the legacy of historical violence in the present and perpetuate the structures of inequality that cause suffering and make healing impossible. Rothberg argues, "Although indirect or belated, their actions and inactions help produce and reproduce the positions of victims and perpetrators."[12] Vis-à-vis bronze and stone bodies, who may have been historical perpetrators of violence or representatives of regimes of state terror, violence, exploitation, oppression, and discrimination or who may have been victims of such systems, those who are the providers of care for these bronze and stone bodies at any given point in time are implicated in their continued presence by care. This means that they may be responsible for both the continued presence of perpetrators and the continued presence of victims. The legal notion of monument care and monument protection does not make the ethical and political dis-

12 Rothberg, *The Implicated Subject*, **1.**

tinction that I make here. This raises a question: How is the continued provision of legally enshrined monument care and monument protection, including acts of conservation, repair, maintenance, cleaning, teaching, and the provision of information as well as everyday expressions of affection, implicated in the continuation of past violence? Concepts such as "bronze patriarchy," bronze imperialism, marble coloniality, bronze anti-Semitism, or marble fascism, make abundantly clear that bronze and stone bodies present legacies of historical violence and injustice in today's urban environments. These legacies are maintained as national cultural heritage or even classified as world heritage.[13] Their presence entangles us, as living bodies, in a deep web of histories of violence, dispossession, oppression, and mass death.

13 Sharon Crozier-de Rosa and Vera Mackie, *Remembering Women's Activism* **(London: Routledge, 2019), 1.**

The more-than-ten-meter-tall monument glorifying Karl Lueger, who popularized anti-Semitism as a political ideology, was completed in 1926. In 2026, it will have occupied a central location next to the ring road boulevard in Vienna for a hundred years. The square, also named after Lueger, who was a source of inspiration for Adolf Hitler, has recently become the site of rightwing, neofascist activism. In 2020, a coalition of leftwing activists and artists, including Muslimische Jugend Österreich (Muslim Youth Austria), Jüdische österreichische Hochschüler:innen (Austrian Union of Jewish Students), and Sozialistische Jugend Wien

Monument to Karl Lueger, former mayor of Vienna. Copyright: Kasa Fue.

(Socialist Youth Vienna) gathered around the monument and held shame vigils (Schandwachen). Their protest was also expressed by spraying the word Schande (shame) on the statue.

Their presence haunts all those who are exposed to this historical violence and its continued monumental glorification. Avery Gordon says that haunting is "an animated state in which a repressed or unresolved social violence is making itself known, sometimes very directly, sometimes more obliquely. . . . Haunting raises specters, and it alters the experience of being in time, the way we separate the past, the present, and the future."[14] The haunting dimension of figurative statuary and monuments lies precisely in their joining together History made visible and the histories of violence, oppression, domination, subjugation, exploitation, and extraction caused by those who steered the course of History rendered invisible. The presence of these bodies can be understood to be haunting, *unheimlich*, as so many who interact fondly with such bronze and stone bodies and invite them into their personal memories, diaries, and other material and digital keepsake, do not even know what they stand for or that they express, for example, allegorical personifications of fascist aesthetics or colonial racial ideologies of beauty.

Monument care is thus implicated in the continued existence of bronze and stone bodies. Monument protection ensures their continued presence, which to many presents a distinct form of haunting rendered by way of the expression of violence that is legally protected. Bronze and stone bodies are a distinct form of occupation, both of space and of time. Given that many of these bodies are given space to embody regimes of violence and cruelty, we need to start thinking about what it would

Monument care is thus implicated in the continued existence of bronze and stone bodies. Monument protection ensures their continued presence, which to many presents a distinct form of haunting rendered by way of the expression of a violence that is legally protected.

14 **Avery Gordon,** *Ghostly Matters: Haunting and the Sociological Imagination* **(Minneapolis: University of Minnesota Press, 2008), xvi.**

mean to liberate and restitute public urban environments and begin difficult processes of healing. By thinking about the fact that these nonliving bodies perform their claim to remain present, which is a specific form of insisting on having an afterlife beyond biological death and furthermore an insistence on human-made time, on winning over historical time through the occupation of space, we come to understand that these bodies also occupy time. Their occupation of both space and time renders these bronze and stone bodies historical. Their presence makes abundantly clear that there is not enough space for everybody to be present like this after death in public urban environments. The dead, whether buried or burnt, rest in graveyards and cemeteries. The dead to be publicly remembered are resurrected as bronze and stone bodies. Many of these bodies—emperors, kings, presidents, war heroes, discoverers, philosophers, and slave traders—have informed and formed "topographies of cruelty."[15]

A feminist history and theory of bronze and stone bodies that uses care as an analytic strives for new understandings and new forms of monument care, which includes bringing to an end the topographies of cruelty of which the bronze and stone bodies that occupy public urban environments are often a part. Such occupied spaces must be restituted to the public. New forms of care and protection will necessarily include ways of finding new spaces for such monuments; for example, in the deep storage of museums. Their detailed, well-researched, and nuanced histories can be told through photographic and filmic documentation held in urban museums. Furthermore, space formerly occupied by monuments to figures who perpetuated historical violence can be used as educational sites to learn about these histories, including stories about how easily care can be implicated in historical acts of violence and how protection can manifest as a kind of haunting.[16]

15 Achille Mbembe, "Necropolitics," ***Public Culture*** **15, no. 1 (2003): 11–40 (here 3).**

16 In a colloquium in Vienna on November 7, 2021, Edmund de Waal spoke about the restitution of public space when he addressed the violent legacies of the monument dedicated to Lueger, the anti-Semitic mayor of Vienna. The colloquium was organized by the Ligue internationale contre le racisme et l'antisémitisme en Autriche. See https://www.mumok.at/sites/default/files/marmor_bronze_verantwortung_programm_0.pdf.

Project – Malin Bergman

An Infrastructural Performance: Caring for the Posthuman Landscape

Malin Bergman

"Care is omnipresent, even through the effects of its absence. Like a longing emanating from the troubles of neglect, it passes within, across, throughout things."
(Maria Puig de la Bella Casa, 2017)[1]

Borrowing from Maria Puig de la Bellacasa, I have explored the omnipresence of care throughout my projects in the Infrastructural Love design studio. My work is inspired by the too often silenced processes of care taking place within our urban environments, understanding their performative aspects as supporting infrastructures. My aim is to enhance narratives of care through speculative interventions and a politics of visibility. For me, narratives allow existing paradigms of capitalism, anthropocentrism, and power to be challenged by proposing alternative realities that explore other ways of living, caring, and practicing architecture. Telling the story of something that has been silenced or neglected is itself an act of care.

1 Maria Puig de la Bellacasa, *Matters Of Care: Speculative Ethics in More Than Human Worlds* **(Minneapolis: University of Minnesota Press, 2017), 1.**

The project "An Infrastructural Performance: Caring for the Post-human Landscape" embodies such values in considering the disused infrastructural landscape of Barkarby Airport, northwest of Stockholm. Once a strategic site for the Swedish air force, in 2019 the airfield was disrupted by an infrastructural event: the construction of a new metro line and the development of Barkarbystaden. Alongside these processes, the airfield's polluted soil had to be remediated. Responding to these site events, the project gives agency to the polluted soil of the field and acknowledges the "faceless pairs of hands and unseen laboring backs"[2] involved in urban excavation and expansion.

An infrastructural performance inspired by the performance artist Mierle Laderman Ukeles's maintenance manifesto and other works of maintenance art rendered visible the otherwise silenced labor and metabolistic flows of urban development.[3] The project also proposes creating an ecosystem of care, consisting of a remediation plan for Barkarbystaden and seven mobile structures. Vegetation for phytoremediation would be planted so that the roots can relieve the earth of its contaminants. Barkarby Airport would be transformed into a field of earth maintenance. The structures would stage the labor and move around the airfield following the gentle pace of remediation. Each proposed structure (e.g., laboratory, tool shed, incinerator) would tend to a certain aspect of this process and provide support and care for the industrial landscape as well as the worker.

---

2 Gavin Bridge, "The Hole World: Scales and Spaces of Extraction," *Scenario Journal 5*, **no. 6 (2015), https://scenariojournal.com/article/the-hole-world/.**

3 Mierle Laderman Ukeles, "Manifesto! Maintenance Art—Proposal for an Exhibition: 'Care'" (1969), https://queensmuseum.org/wp-content/uploads/2016/04/Ukeles-Manifesto-for-Maintenance-Art-1969.pdf. *Ukeles's Seven Works Ballet and City Maintenance Dance* **were performed in New York in 1985.**

The design of the structures plays with the historical tradition of a passive folly in a picturesque landscape and flirts with the aesthetics of phenomenological influences in architecture. Following Sara Ahmed's concept of queer phenomenology, these influences are reoriented toward a productive, dirty, and machine-like character.[4] The materiality and program of the structures draws on prefabricated cabins (i.e., portacabins) and scaffolding as support structures for construction. The design plays with these conventional support elements of urban development by merging them with the concept of a productive folly. The architecture distorts the hierarchy between spaces of mundane labor and extravagant decoration.
Through the support system of care, a new narrative for the site emerges, proposing a slower and less volatile approach to urban development and earth maintenance. Time thickens at Barkarby Airfield as seeds are planted, creating a resistance to the fast-paced development of Barkarbystaden. Now that the development has been put on hold, the project critiques the anthropocentric timeline for care and instead proposes space for more-than-human care, setting the pace to the rhythm of soil times.[5]

---

4 Sara Ahmed, "ORIENTATIONS: Toward a Queer Phenomenology," *GLQ: A Journal of Lesbian and Gay Studies* 12, no. 4 (2006): 543–74.
5 Puig de la Bellacasa, *Matters of Care*, 169.

INTERRU
PTINGIN
FRASTRU
CTURES

Chapter 5
Interrupting Infrastructures: Dust in the Desert

Danika Cooper

On July 5, 2011, a massive cloud of dust sped down the 177-kilometer-long stretch of highway between Tucson and Phoenix, Arizona, engulfing the small town of Casa Grande in a haze of debris. Though it lasted only an hour, the storm moved across the territory at nearly 105 kilometers per hour, carrying with it thousands of suspended dust particles, some as high as 1.5 kilometers in the air.[1] Within seconds, the thick air reduced visibility to zero for all vehicular traffic and briefly erased the highway's six lanes from the Sonoran desert landscape. Though dust storms naturally occur in desert regions, this one was exceptional in both size and speed. In its spectacular—though temporary—transformation of the territory, the 161-kilometer-wide dust storm asserted its agency in the landscape by creating a new, ephemeral dust terrain and by unsettling long-standing assumptions about modern infrastructure's material and metaphorical solidity.

Hard infrastructures—roads, rail lines, dams, canals, aqueducts—have long been agents of power working alongside colonialism and capitalism to structurally conquer and exploit the desert, its resources, and the peoples who live in it. The dust storm's ability to bring these infrastructures so immediately and effortlessly to a halt exposed modern infrastructure as fragile to and defenseless against global ecology. Demonstrating how even the smallest particles can interrupt the very infrastructures that have attempted to alter the environment challenges the notion that nature can be controlled through technobureaucratic agendas. In this way, dust is an opportunity to reframe the relationship between society and the environment as relational, dynamic, and resilient.

Hard infrastructures—roads, rail lines, dams, canals, aqueducts—have long been agents of power working alongside colonialism and capitalism to structurally conquer and exploit the desert, its resources, and the peoples who live in it.

Mediated by both culture and science, *dust* has myriad definitions. Its associations and meanings, as well as verdicts on whether it is "good" or "bad," are all culturally situated within specific geographical regions, political frameworks,

1 Aishwarya Raman, Avelino F. Arellano, and John J. Brost, "Revisiting Haboobs in the Southwestern United States: An Observational Case Study of the 5 July 2011 Phoenix Dust Storm," *Atmospheric Environment* **89 (2014): 179–88.**

social customs, and religious ideologies.[2] Simultaneously, dust is at the center of a multitude of scientific discourses and disciplines that examine terrestrial earth, its oceans and atmosphere, and the cosmic universe. Identified as a particle that is shared between land and air, dust is scientifically defined by its size and is the result of the "divisibility of matter" wherein almost all organic matter eventually breaks down or erodes into particles of dust.[3] Measured in microns (one-millionth of a meter), the scalar measurement of dust particles can range from one two-hundredths of a micron (invisible without a microscope) all the way up to thousands of microns (easily observed by the eye).[4] This scalar measure is a critical metric of analysis, as it indicates the potential distance a particle might travel, how high in the air it can be suspended, and for how long.[5] In addition to size, dust is classified by its material composition and color, factors that are vital in assembling the genealogy of a particle. As composites with distinct materialities and geographical origins, dust can be made of soil, minerals, seeds, pollen, even dead skin; and a particle's material composition can disclose the geographical region from where it originated, while its color gestures to its mineral makeup—a reddish hue, for instance, often suggests high concentrations of iron.[6]

Understanding dust as matter of *both* culture and science affords a more expansive assessment of its role in human-nonhuman relations. When dust's size, color, and material composition are mediated through its social, political, geographic, and temporal contexts, dust exposes messy, violent entanglements in the desert between settler colonial histories, modern infrastructures, and proposed futures, all of which require both scientific and cultural readings of the landscape. When dust is lifted into the air by wind systems and aggregates into a storm, tracking its path uncovers the massive geochemical and atmospheric systems that continuously transport material around the globe, creating relations between seemingly disconnected geographies.[7] As it travels, the storm carries with it not only mineral content but all other matter that has mixed with the soil in its site of origin: dust from lands with nutrient-rich topsoil helps to sustain soils in other places, while dust from places

2 **James A. Amato,** *Dust: A History of the Small and the Invisible* **(Berkeley and Los Angeles: University of California Press, 2001); Hannah Holmes,** *The Secret Life of Dust: From the Cosmos to the Kitchen Counter, the Big Consequences of Little Things* **(Hoboken, NJ: Wiley, 2003); and David Gissen,** *Subnature: Architecture's Other Environments* **(New York: Princeton Architectural Press, 2009).**

3 **Amato,** *Dust*, **3.**

4 **Irving Adler,** *Dust* **(New York: John Day, 1958), 18.**

5 **Kenneth Pye,** *Aeolian Dust and Dust Deposits* **(Orlando: Academic Press, 1987).**

6 **Maureen Lacey and Jonathan West,** *The Air Spora: A Manual for Catching and Identifying Airborne Biological Particles* **(Dordrecht: Springer, 2006); Pye,** *Aeolian Dust and Dust Deposits*; **and Aya Nassar, "Where the Dust Settles: Fieldwork, Subjectivity and Materiality in Cairo,"** *Contemporary Social Science* **13, no. 3–4 (2018): 412–28.**

7 **Juliana Nogueira, Heitor Evangelista, Claudio**

with heavy agricultural or industrial practices can bring with it toxic particulates that contribute to environmental degradation and cause public health hazards.[8] Even as a storm accumulates dust particles—picking them up as it moves through a territory—it simultaneously disperses them, a process that scholar Aya Nassar describes as "both grounding and un-grounding."[9] Through this reciprocal practice of grounding and un-grounding, the storm becomes an archive, carrying with it a record of where it has been and simultaneously leaving behind a trace of itself as particles drop along its path. Reading dust as an archive works in two related ways: first, it lays bare the insidious and violent ways that settler colonialism has enacted and imposed material and immaterial forms of power over the environment and people of the U.S. desert lands; second, and consequently, dust effectively inverts this power dynamic by narrating landscape stories that reveal the deficiencies of the state in the face of ecological processes.

The profound ways in which the desert has been altered by the settler colonial agenda are material, ideological, and imaginative. Settler colonialism, the process by which one society permanently and violently displaces another from land that has provided "economic vitality, cultural flourishing and political self-determination," is often represented as an historical event of the past.[10] Its legacies remain present, active, and inescapable in modern American society through regimes of private property, practices of resource extraction, and policies of capital growth. Within the settler colonial context, the desert is represented as empty of people and value, and characterized as useless without its transformation into a landscape that can effectively contribute to economic progress and development.[11] Legal scholar Brenna Bhandar argues that land, in this paradigm, is guided by an "ideology of improvement" to

> Within the settler colonial context, the desert is represented as empty of people and value and as useless without its transformation into a landscape that can effectively contribute to economic progress and development.

de Morisson Valeriano, Abdelfettah Sifeddine, Carla Neto, Gilberto Vaz, Luciane S. Moreira, Renato C. Cordeiro, Bruno Turcq, Keila Cristina Aniceto, Artur Bastos Neto, Gabriel Martins, Cybelli G.G. Barbosa, Ricardo H.M. Godoi, and Marilia H. Shimizu, "Dust Arriving in the Amazon Basin over the Past 7,500 Years Came from Diverse Sources," *Communications Earth and Environment 2*, no. 1 (2021): 1–11.

8 Andrew Nicla and Priscilla Totiyapungprasert, "Summer Storms Are a Spectacle, but the Dust in Them Is Hazardous to Your Health," *Arizona Central*, June 18, 2019, https://www.azcentral.com/in-depth/news/local/arizona-environment/2019/06/18/arizona-monsoon-dust-storms-haboobs-raise-environmental-and-health-issues/3272677002/; and William A. Sprigg, Slobodan Nickovic, John N. Galgiani, Goran Pejanovic, Slavko Petkovic, Mirjam Vujadinovic, Ana Vukovic, Milan Dacic, Scott DiBiase, Anup Prasad, and Hesham El-Askary, "Regional Dust Storm Modeling

BLOWING
DUST
AREA

Blowing Dust Area signs on Interstate 10, outside of Casa Grande, Arizona, 2015. Photograph by Danika Cooper.

Unfinished Ghost Hollow Estates housing development, Casa Grande, Arizona, 2015. Panograph by Danika Cooper.

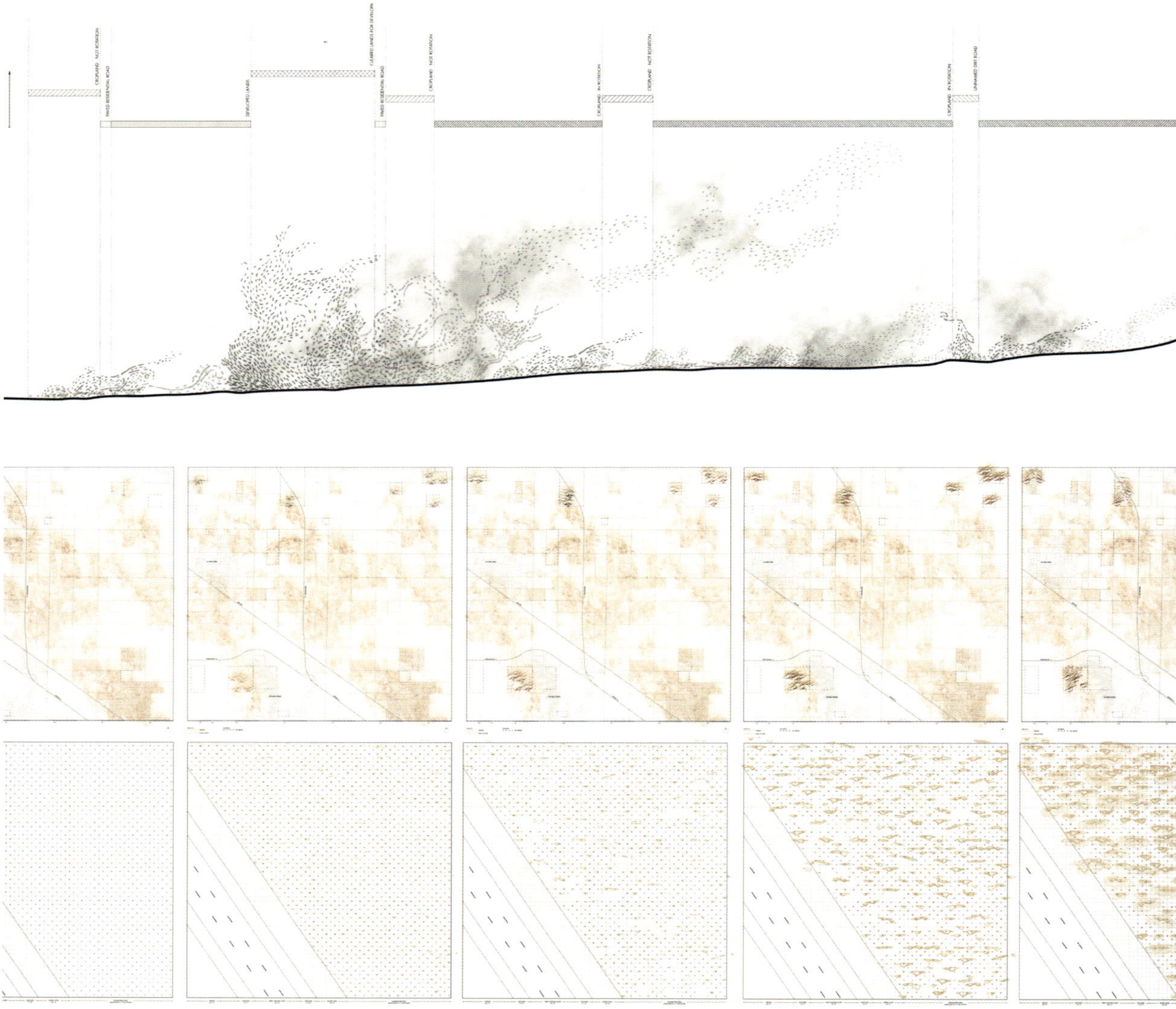

Danika Cooper, *Dust Landscape*, 2015.

Pssamophile fields are planted in 8'0" quincunx pattern with gradient of planting density. On southern end of 1 mile × 1 mile grid, planting is denser to combat intense summer winds. Moving north, planting density is reduced.

Dust Kingdom **exhibition, Harvard University, Cambridge, Massachusetts, 2015. Photograph by Danika Cooper.**

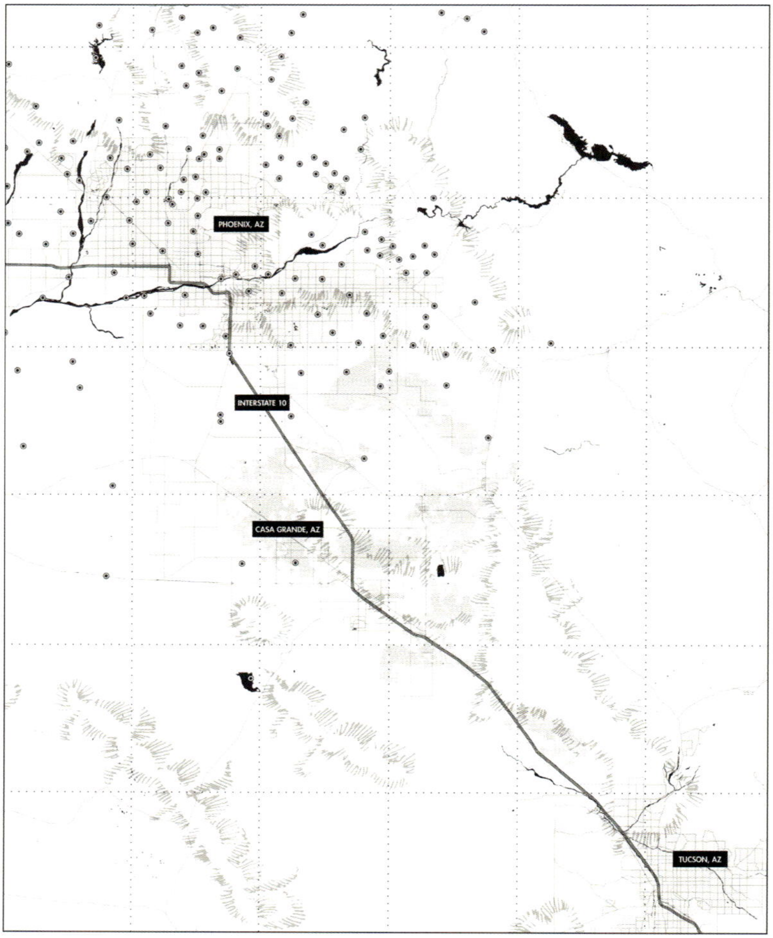

Danika Cooper, *Dust Cycles*, 2015

Dust rotations are determined by seasonal variations and temporal land uses. Relative "roughness" of the surface is established by surface particulates, topography, and vegetation cover. Temporary accumulations are generated by the planting of pssamophile fields that encourage the settlement of aeolian dust. Temporal topographies are at once made and then almost immediately eroded by the wind.

Topographic shifts experienced most vividly by passengers on Interstate 10.

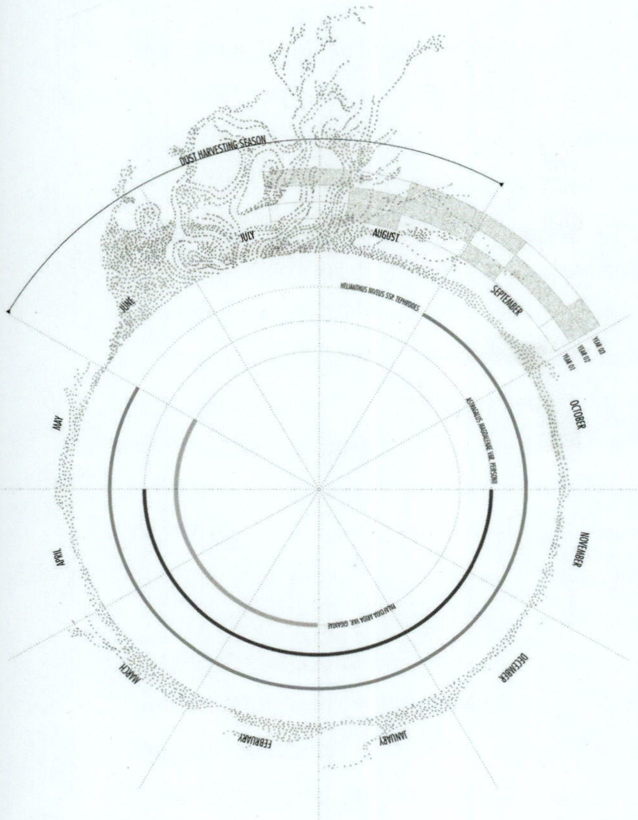
DUST HARVESTING SEASON
JUNE
JULY
AUGUST
SEPTEMBER
OCTOBER
NOVEMBER
DECEMBER
JANUARY
FEBRUARY
MARCH
APRIL
MAY
YEAR 01
YEAR 02
YEAR 03
HELIANTHUS NIVEUS SSP. TEPHRODES

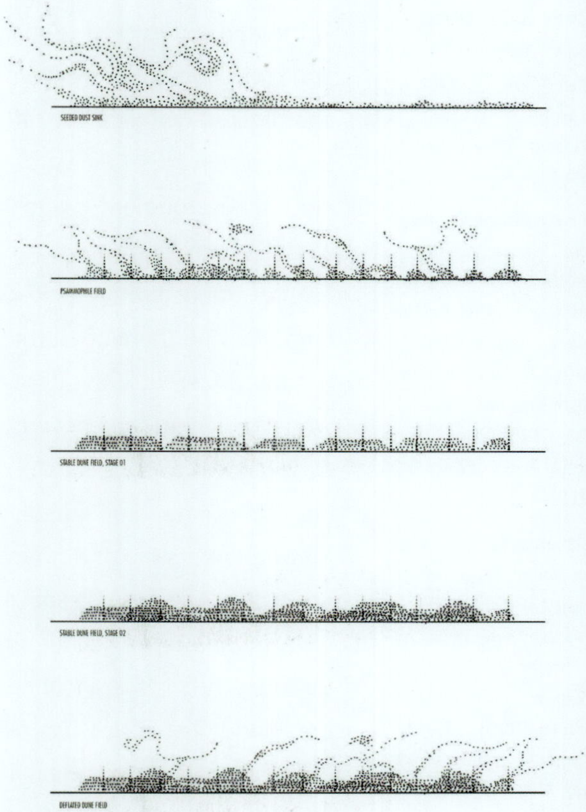
SEEDED DUST SINK
PSAMMOPHILE FIELD
STABLE DUNE FIELD, STAGE 01
STABLE DUNE FIELD, STAGE 02
DEFLATED DUNE FIELD

exploit the full economic and political potential of a landscape.[12] Beginning in the mid-nineteenth century and continuing into the present day, Arizona's political, economic, environmental, spatial, and social agendas have all been coordinated with sophistication to ensure the greatest return on investment in the desert. Arizona's most prominent industries—farming, mining, and residential development—were introduced by settlers specifically to exploit the desert's economic potential. These industries all required the manipulation (or "improvement") of the landscape: accumulating huge tracts of "empty" desert land, clearing them of all Indigenous peoples (of which there were hundreds of thousands), ensuring dependable sources of water, and creating trade networks to connect the deserts with economic centers. The construction of infrastructures to conquer the desert landscape was critical in folding Arizona's deserts into national pursuits of economic productivity and social progress. Throughout its history, infrastructure projects have played a central role in upholding Arizona as a space of colonial power and in "privileging imperial vision, grand territorial ambitions and the 'mastery of nature.'"[13] The town of Casa Grande's history is one shaped by these colonial forces, which produced boom and bust cycles, justified dispossessions of huge tracts of land from Indigenous nations, and facilitated ruthless, extractive transformations of the environment in pursuit of growth and progress. Halfway between Arizona's two largest metropolises, Tucson and Phoenix, Casa Grande was established in 1879 as thousands of settlers flocked to the region in the hopes of striking it rich during the boom of Arizona's mining industry.[14] The town's growth was enabled by the Southern Pacific Railroad that snaked through the desert, bringing people and supplies and connecting Casa Grande to larger seats of economic and political power in California and Texas. The railway was built on lands acquired from Mexico as a part of the Treaty of Guadalupe Hidalgo in 1848 and the Gadsden Purchase in 1854. These two geopolitical negotiations were crucial to the expansion of U.S. territorial control into the desert, first by establishing the Arizona Territory in 1863 and later by formalizing the territory as a state in 1912.[15]

for Health Services: The Case of Valley Fever," *Aeolian Research* **14 (September 2014): 53–73.**

9 Nassar, "Where the Dust Settles," 420.

10 Kyle Powys Whyte, "The Dakota Access Pipeline, Environmental Injustice, and US Settler Colonialism," in *The Nature of Hope*, **ed. Char Miller and Jeff Crane, 320–37 (Boulder: University Press of Colorado, 2019), 323–24.**

11 Danika Cooper, "Waters Resist: Modernity, Aridity, and the Fight over the Orme Dam," *Journal of Architectural Education* **74, no. 1 (Spring 2020): 37–47, Vittoria Di Palma, Wasteland: A History (New Haven: Yale University Press, 2014); and Valerie L. Kuletz, The Tainted Desert (New York: Routledge, 1998)** *Brenna Bhandar, Colonial Lives of Property: Law, Land, and Racial Regimes of Ownership* **(Durham, NC: Duke University Press, 2018), 34.**

12 Brenna Bhandar, *Colonial Lives of Property: Law, Land, and Racial Regimes of Ownership* **(Durham, NC: Duke University Press, 2018), 34.**

These lands, however, have been home to the ancestors of the Akimel O'otham nation for millennia. When the United States took control of the region, it recognized the economic value and potential of developing it as a mining and agricultural center in the southwestern part of the nation.[16] The process of removing Indigenous peoples from lands that the United States desired had long been in process, but was legalized in 1830 when President Andrew Jackson formalized his violent agenda to remove Indigenous peoples through U.S. federal policy.[17] In 1859, the federal government forcibly dispossessed the Akimel O'otham and Pee Posh nations of the lands they had tended and segregated them to the Gila River Indian Community (GRIC), a 372,000-acre reservation located in the Gila River watershed.[18] When the federal government began investing massive amounts of public funding into water technologies designed to "reclaim" lands from aridity and to supply water to settler developments and industries, the Gila River watershed was no exception.[19] The construction of settler hydraulic infrastructures throughout the region severely disrupted the flow of water and agricultural production on GRIC lands. At the expense of Akimel O'odham and Pee Posh sovereignty and subsistence, settler agriculture and mining flourished as infrastructure transformed the territory. When mining began to decline at the end of the nineteenth century, agricultural production in the desert regions of Arizona intensified. Aided by the Reclamation Act of 1902, which financially subsidized the construction of hydraulic infrastructure in the desert, nearly every water source was tapped and diverted to emerging centers of economic production in the desert, like Phoenix and Tucson. In Casa Grande, settler farmers grew cotton, oats, and citrus and also raised livestock.[20] Under New Deal liberalism beginning in the 1930s, new tax concessions and

The process of removing Indigenous peoples from lands that the United States desired had long been in process, but was legalized in 1830 when President Andrew Jackson formalized his violent agenda to remove Indigenous peoples through U.S. federal policy.

13 Matti Siemiatycki, Theresa Enright, and Mariana Valverde, "The Gendered Production of Infrastructure," *Progress in Human Geography* **44, no. 2 (April 2020): 301.**

14 Dawn Snell, *Casa Grande* **(Charleston, SC: Arcadia Publishing, 2011).**

15 Andrew Needham, *Power Lines: Phoenix and the Making of the Modern Southwest* **(Princeton, NJ: Princeton University Press, 2014); and Bradford Luckingham,** *Phoenix: The History of a Southwestern Metropolis* **(Tucson: University of Arizona Press, 1989).**

16 Snell, *Casa Grande.*

regulatory giveaways further incentivized development in Arizona by encouraging home ownership through a program that guaranteed mortgage loans. As cheap residential development boomed along with a diversifying economy in Arizona, the demand for hydraulic and road infrastructure in the region increased substantially. As part of the American Interstate Highway system implemented in 1956 by President Dwight Eisenhower to ensure "speedy, safe transcontinental travel" for both people and goods, Interstate 10 was built to connect Florida on the eastern coast of the United States to Southern California on the western coast.[21] The transcontinental road was built to connect Tucson and Phoenix and passed directly through Casa Grande. The highway was completed in 1990 just as the housing market in Arizona was booming. During this time, Phoenix was one of the fastest growing cities in the country, with Tucson not far behind. With its strategic location halfway between Tucson and Phoenix, Casa Grande benefited significantly, and it had its own boom in the early 2000s when houses were being purchased with no monetary deposits and interest-only mortgages.[22] When the housing market crashed in 2008, Casa Grande was devastated. For nearly ten years, the landscape was dominated by the remnants of incomplete suburban developments. But in the last five years, construction has begun again in Casa Grande and surrounding areas—empty lots are now filled in with newly built houses, and home values have increased by over 40 percent, the highest in the state.[23] The repeated boom and bust cycles that define Casa Grande's history and current condition are reminders of settler colonialism's orientation of the spatial, social, and political aspects of life around the volatility of capitalist markets in the desert.

Despite the pervasive force of settler colonialism, dust complicates stories of this region by challenging colonial power and interrupting its infrastructures. When in motion, dust is undeterred by geopolitics, transportation networks, and hydraulic engineering. It easily traverses the colonial desert landscape, surmounting the walls at the U.S.-Mexico border that attempt to separate people and politics, blocking highways that enable flows of capital, and covering the hundreds of dams, aqueducts, canals, and pipes that rearrange the desert's entire hydrological system to sustain development and industry. Dust

17 Claudio Saunt, *Unworthy Republic: The Dispossession of Native Americans and the Road to Indian Territory* **(New York: W.W. Norton, 2020); and Claudio Saunt, "Invasion of America," 2014, https://usg.maps.arcgis.com/apps/webappviewer/index.html?id=eb6ca76e008543a89349ff2517db47e6.**

18 "Gila River Indian Community, Arizona," 2015, http://www.gilariver.org/.

19 "Gila River Indian Community, Arizona"; and Donald J. Pisani, *Water and American Government: The Reclamation Bureau, National Water Policy, and the West,* **1902–1935 (Berkeley and Los Angeles: University of California Press, 2002).**

20 Snell, *Casa Grande*, **39.**

21 Marlon G. Boarnet, "National Transportation Planning: Lessons from the U.S. Interstate Highways," *Transport Policy* **31 (2014): 73–82; and "Federal Aid Highway Act of 1956," Public Law 84-627.**

dynamically offsets the dominance of these physical infrastructures by creating entirely new terrains. Casa Grande's incomplete housing developments, fallow agricultural fields, and lands cleared of vegetation result in a dusty landscape, one consequence of which is the already dry soil is destabilized and ready to be lifted away by the wind. As wind is funneled from the south, storms continuously gather dust particles as they effortlessly navigate the undulating topography of the region and closely follow the path of Interstate 10. As these clouds of dust travel over, under, between, and beside the highway, they continually ground and un-ground the region by depositing dust particles that amass into new, ephemeral topographies. At every scale, from the micro to the macro, dust is actively shaping and reshaping the landscape, unaffected by the spatial artifacts of settler colonialism. The stretch of Interstate 10 that travels through Casa Grande is, as a result, the site of the greatest number of dust-related accidents in the region. From 2000 to 2011, dust storms caused more than 1,400 collisions on Interstate 10 between Tucson and Phoenix.[24] The dust storm on July 5, 2011, halted nearly all traffic, eliminated visibility, and left nearly ten thousand residents without power.[25] The Arizona Department of Transportation and National Oceanic and Atmospheric Association have been actively working to develop new and innovative mitigation strategies as dust storms become increasingly prevalent and intense in this region, especially as the socioeconomic and policy impacts of the storms become more significant.[26] These bureaucratic agencies present dust as a nuisance, blaming the storm for disrupting daily life in the desert rather than acknowledging the dust storm as a "natural" part of the region's environmental system. In large part this approach to dust and its storms is a consequence of the prevailing modern paradigm that positions natural systems within a framework of economic growth and development and enabled by technobureaucratic infrastructures. When interrupted by dust

> Dust dynamically offsets the dominance of these physical infrastructures by creating entirely new terrains.

22 Samantha M. Shapiro, "The Boomtown Mirage," *New York Times*, **April 6, 2008, https://www.nytimes.com/2008/04/06/realestate/keymagazine/406ariz-t.html.**

23 Melissa St. Aude, "Pinal Home Values Soar Bringing Real Estate Market Back to 2005 Levels," *Casa Grande Dispatch*, **August 3, 2020, https://www.pinalcentral.com/casa_grande_dispatch/area_news/pinal-home-values-soar-bringing-real-estate-market-back-to-2005-levels/article_ee188b7d-7570-5886-8c8e-2640e07a6637.html.**

24 Glenn Lader, Aishwarya Raman, Jeffrey T. Davis, and Ken Waters, *Blowing Dust and Dust Storms: One of Arizona's Most Underrated Weather Hazards*, NOAA Technical Memorandum NWS-WR 290 (Salt Lake City: National Oceanic and Atmospheric Association, July 2016), 17.

25 Scott Thompson, Phil Gast, and Marlena Baldacci, "Wall of Dust That Enveloped Phoenix Felt like a Movie," CNN, July 6, 2011, http://www.cnn.com/2011/US/07/06/arizona.dust.storm/index.html.

storms that are not only unstoppable but also unpredictable, the dominance of infrastructures like Interstate 10 is destabilized and confirms modern infrastructure's vulnerability when faced with global environmental processes. Dust offers an alternative imaginary for the desert's future. Rather than positioning dust as a hindrance for modern life, dust is an invitation to think more expansively about the desert's future in the face of the climate crisis. Dust imagined through the lens of "sociological miniaturism"—the idea that large social systems can be understood through the examination of the smallest conditions of life—uncovers the complicated and interwoven ways that broader political histories relate to global ecological processes, sociopolitical histories, and infrastructural realities.[27] Through this lens, the miniature asserts its power to stress the limits of human control over the environment.[28] Dust as a responsive and dynamic material suggests that a future that working in coordination with environmental processes rather than in opposition to them is necessary as climates become more extreme. The dominance of the dust storm when it encounters physical infrastructures is a reminder that modern modes of living in the desert conflict with the environmental processes that naturally occur there. Further, the July 5, 2011 dust storm is a potent demonstration that climate and modernity are inseparable—tackling the climate crisis therefore cannot be decoupled from a critical engagement with the social, spatial, and political systems that shape society. This is especially salient because the climate crisis is experienced in uneven ways, with marginalized people and peripheral geographies bearing the brunt of those changes. In the desert lands of the United States, the climate crisis is the direct result of a settler society that has violently transformed its environment through the construction of infrastructures that inflict ecological and social harm. Anishi-

Dust as a responsive and dynamic material suggests that a future that works in coordination with environmental processes rather than in opposition to them is necessary as climates become more extreme.

26 Christopher Boutillier, "Dust in the Wind: Arizona Dust Storms and the Exceptional Events Rule," *Arizona Journal of Environmental Law and Policy* 3, no. 1 (Fall 2012), https://www.ajelp.com/copy-of-issues-5-and-6.

naabe activist and writer Winona LaDuke and geographer Deborah Cowen describe these kinds of infrastructures as "Wiindigo," invoking a cannibalistic Anishinaabe monster that attacks and consumes its environment and the people who live there.[29] LaDuke and Cowen move beyond a rhetorical critique of Wiindigo infrastructure, however, and advocate for initiatives that imagine a socially just, anti-colonial, and climate-resilient future that centers a new kind of *alimentary* and *life-giving* infrastructure that works directly in coordination with environmental systems rather than trying to control or commodify them. These infrastructures can learn from dust's ability to operate beyond the limits set by settler colonialism and to reconfigure the landscape as relational, dynamic, and resilient. In this way, dust opens possibilities for new modes of socio-environmental production that offer imaginaries outside of the status quo. Further, positioning dust both as an archive and as the land itself reframes the climate crisis not as an abstracted problem but as an embodied and personal one. As Tahltan artist Peter Morin asserts, "the land is us, it is in us."[30]

27 John F. Stolte, Gary Alan Fine, and Karen S. Cook, "Sociological Miniaturism: Seeing the Big through the Small in Social Psychology," *Annual Review of Sociology* **27, no. 1 (August 2001): 387–413.**

28 Amato, *Dust.*

29 Winona LaDuke and Deborah E. Cowen, "Beyond Wiindigo Infrastructure," *South Atlantic Quarterly* **119, no. 2 (2020): 243–68.**

30 Dian Million, "'We Are the Land, and the Land Is Us': Indigenous Land, Lives, and Embodied Ecologies in the Twenty-First Century," in *Racial Ecologies*, **ed. Leilani Nishime and Kim D. Hester Williams, 19–33 (Seattle: University of Washington Press, 2018), 26.**

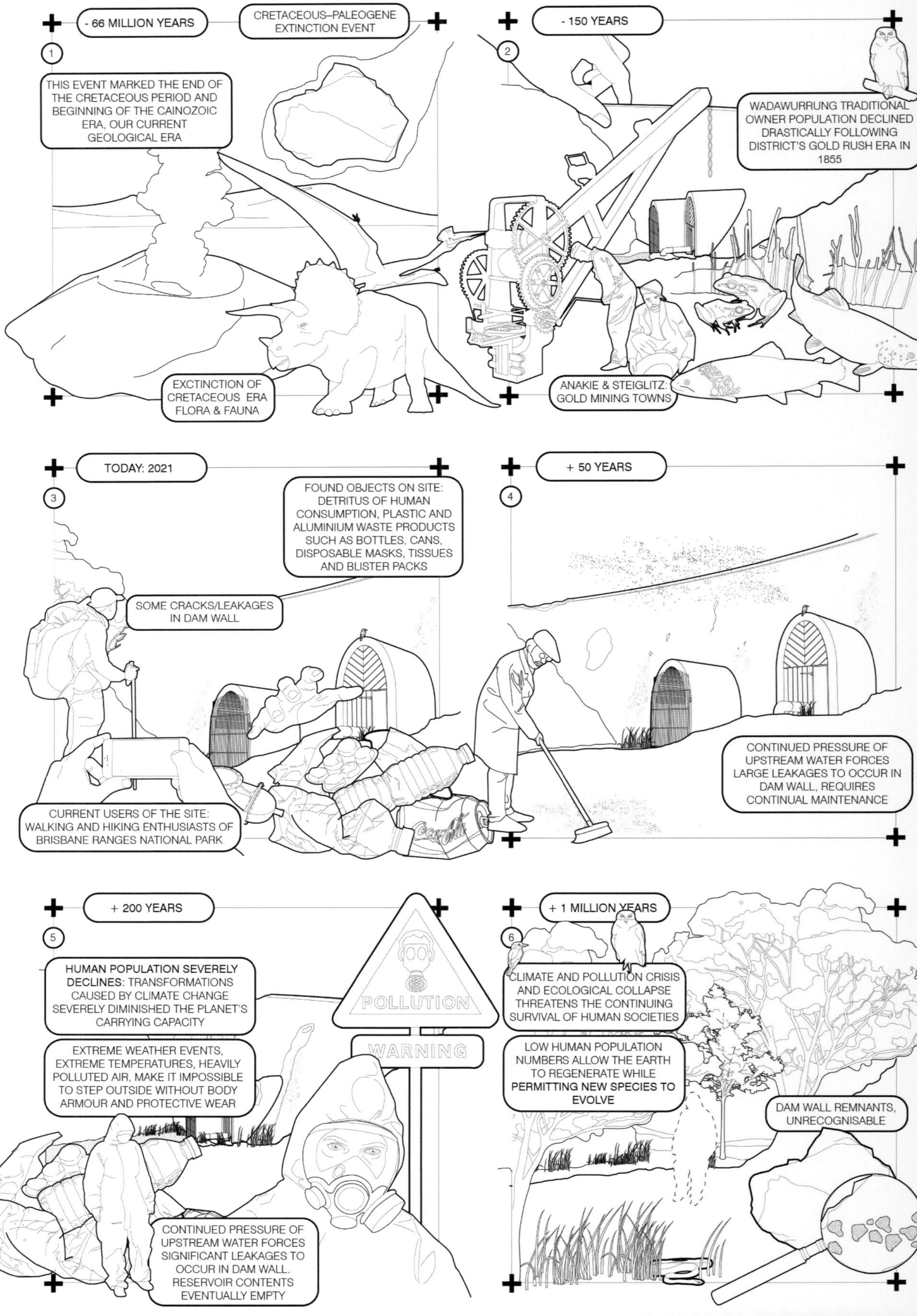

- 66 MILLION YEARS
CRETACEOUS–PALEOGENE EXTINCTION EVENT
1
THIS EVENT MARKED THE END OF THE CRETACEOUS PERIOD AND BEGINNING OF THE CAINOZOIC ERA, OUR CURRENT GEOLOGICAL ERA
EXCTINCTION OF CRETACEOUS ERA FLORA & FAUNA
- 150 YEARS
2
WADAWURRUNG TRADITIONAL OWNER POPULATION DECLINED DRASTICALLY FOLLOWING DISTRICT'S GOLD RUSH ERA IN 1855
ANAKIE & STEIGLITZ: GOLD MINING TOWNS
TODAY: 2021
3
FOUND OBJECTS ON SITE: DETRITUS OF HUMAN CONSUMPTION, PLASTIC AND ALUMINIUM WASTE PRODUCTS SUCH AS BOTTLES, CANS, DISPOSABLE MASKS, TISSUES AND BLISTER PACKS
SOME CRACKS/LEAKAGES IN DAM WALL
CURRENT USERS OF THE SITE: WALKING AND HIKING ENTHUSIASTS OF BRISBANE RANGES NATIONAL PARK
+ 50 YEARS
4
CONTINUED PRESSURE OF UPSTREAM WATER FORCES LARGE LEAKAGES TO OCCUR IN DAM WALL, REQUIRES CONTINUAL MAINTENANCE
+ 200 YEARS
5
HUMAN POPULATION SEVERELY DECLINES: TRANSFORMATIONS CAUSED BY CLIMATE CHANGE SEVERELY DIMINISHED THE PLANET'S CARRYING CAPACITY
EXTREME WEATHER EVENTS, EXTREME TEMPERATURES, HEAVILY POLLUTED AIR, MAKE IT IMPOSSIBLE TO STEP OUTSIDE WITHOUT BODY ARMOUR AND PROTECTIVE WEAR
POLLUTION
WARNING
CONTINUED PRESSURE OF UPSTREAM WATER FORCES SIGNIFICANT LEAKAGES TO OCCUR IN DAM WALL. RESERVOIR CONTENTS EVENTUALLY EMPTY
+ 1 MILLION YEARS
6
CLIMATE AND POLLUTION CRISIS AND ECOLOGICAL COLLAPSE THREATENS THE CONTINUING SURVIVAL OF HUMAN SOCIETIES
LOW HUMAN POPULATION NUMBERS ALLOW THE EARTH TO REGENERATE WHILE PERMITTING NEW SPECIES TO EVOLVE
DAM WALL REMNANTS, UNRECOGNISABLE

Infrastructural Remains: Caring for Anthropogenic Ruins

Emilie Evans

This speculative project renders visible environmental stories of infrastructural care by exploring the possibility of architecture amid Anthropogenic ruins. Juxtaposing temporalities of the deep past, the present, and the deep future, the project situates itself in dialogue with the oldest concrete dam in Australia: Lower Stony Creek Dam, built in 1873 and located on the Victorian Volcanic Plain. The dam provided the nearby city of Geelong and its surrounding towns with their first reliable water supply, leading to significant industrial growth and improved public health in the region. Yet dams are contested sites, and damming always has adverse impacts, leading to the displacement and fragmentation of local communities and inhabitants, both human and nonhuman. Once a site of significant industrial activity, today the dam wall is deemed a retired water storage facility and sits in the landscape as a postindustrial relic. As a response to the dam's former life and as a speculation about its more-than-human futures, a suite of interventions is proposed on the site, including an observation tower (composed of a conglomerate of plastic debris), a repository (housing relics, from industrial objects to Indigenous lithic artifacts), and a seed bank (storing collected seeds of endemic native plant species in an underground vault). The project traces the site's

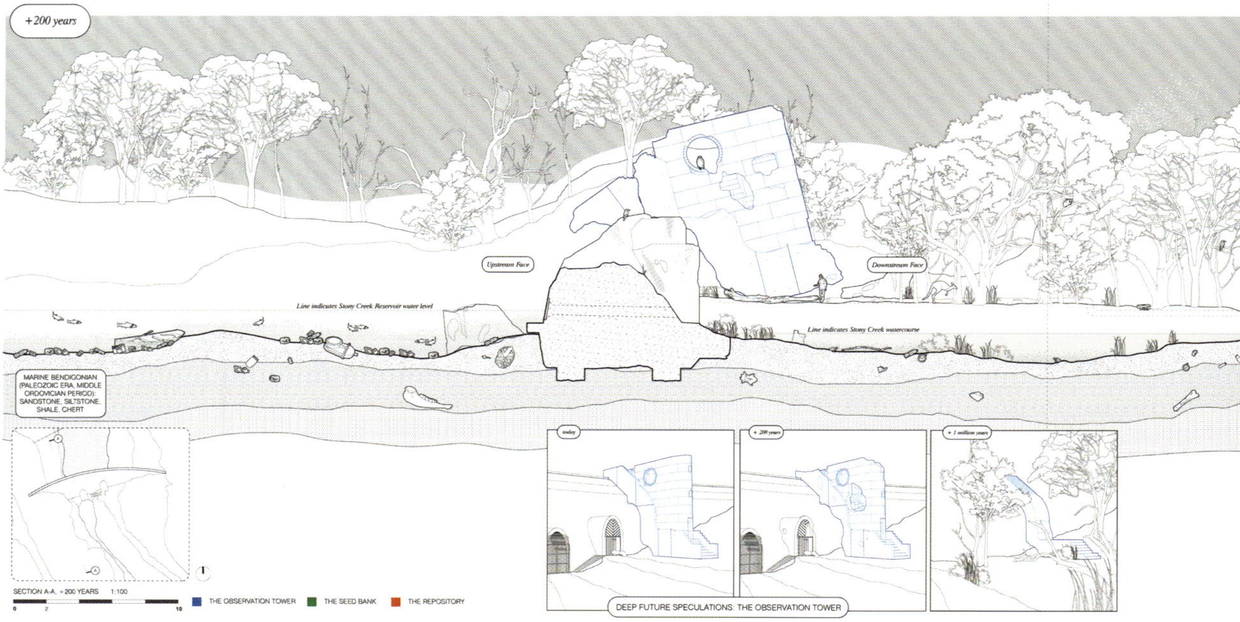

deep time stories, including the histories of the Wadawurrung Traditional Owners who inhabited the site for over twenty-five thousand years prior to European settlement and created extensive aquaculture systems upon the ancient lava flows of the site's volcanic landscape. The project also renders visible the deep geological stories of the site, including the folding and buckling that formed the plains of the Brisbane Ranges, comprising rock from the mid-Ordovician Era, and the work of Stony Creek itself, which carved valleys in the Ranges four million years ago, shaping its basalt plains. These deep-time histories are woven into the fabric of the dam wall: its concrete materiality (the wall is composed of broken sandstone screenings, rock, and gravel) already holds within it all the stories of its past. Thinking about architecture in deep timescales requires speculation and narratives that allow for new meaning to be imbued in that which is unknown. The project is thus a single experimental instance that speaks to broader environmental concerns and reflects upon the importance of paying attention and bearing witness to the conditions of "now." These encounters with deep pasts and deep futures require an active attentiveness to the site. Multispecies ethnographer Deborah Bird Rose suggests we must "actively bear witness" to others, including a "passionate immersion in the lives of nonhuman beings."[1] Exploring deep pasts and speculating upon deep futures renders the life of industrial human-made objects—and my role as (human) architectural designer—insignificant and fleeting in the scheme of broader geological timescales. Multispecies

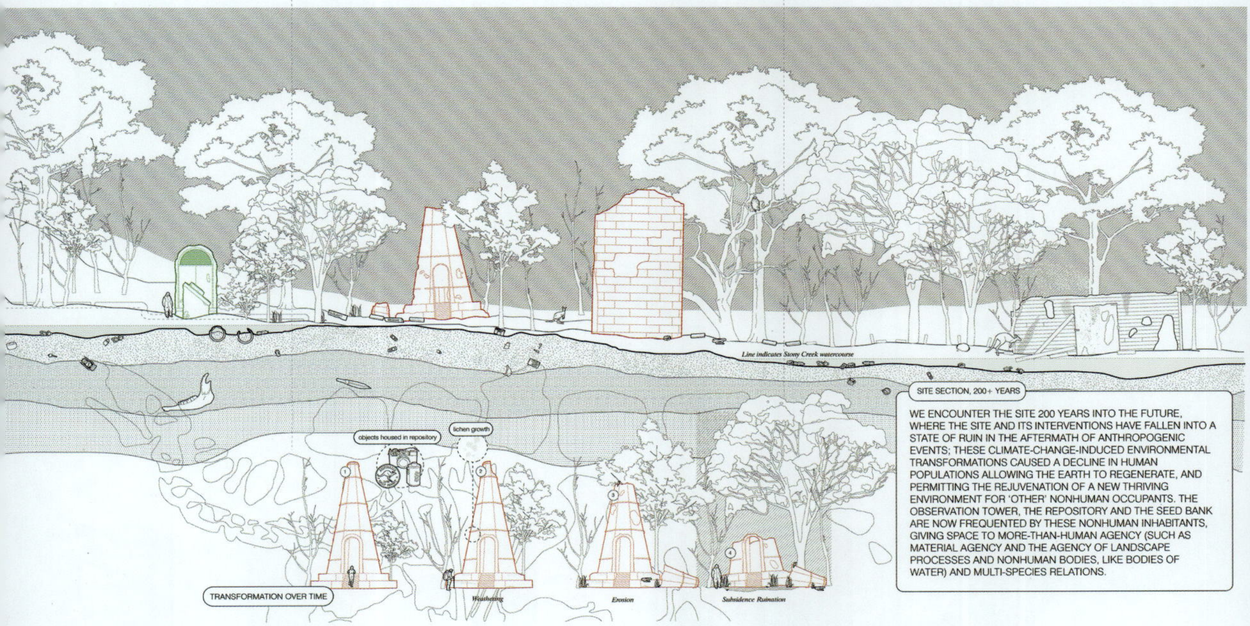

relations, nonhuman agency, and more-than-human bodies, like the dammed body of water itself, are foregrounded. Balancing the poetic with the pragmatic, the architectural interventions respond to environmental concerns such as loss of biodiversity and ecological devastation and engender ways in which we might care for infrastructures once they are defunct. "Considering architecture within deep timescales renders the building not as an isolated object-instance in a human timeline, but rather as a moment of convergence of material and energy that flow across deep temporal scales" and extend beyond us.[2] In a time of planetary uncertainty, architecture becomes a critical tool by which alternative futures can be imagined.

1 Deborah Bird Rose and Thom Van Dooren, "Lively Ethnography: Storying Animist Worlds," *Environmental Humanities* **8, no. 1 (2016): 77–94 (here 85).**

2 Cristina Parreño Alonso, "Deep-Time Architecture: Building as Material-Event," *Journal of Architectural Education* **75, no. 1 (2021): 142–44 (here 143).**

AVILLA
BORGHE
SELOVE
STORY

Chapter 6
A Villa Borghese Love Story: The Parking Garage as Support Structure

Hannes Frykholm

A Shortcut across the Galoppatoio, April 2018

South of the curved driveway that cuts across Rome's Villa Borghese Park from Piazza del Popolo to Porta Pinciana sits an empty field where London plane trees and stone pines cast long afternoon shadows over grass, shrubs, and white gravel.[1] The official name of this forgotten corner of the park is "Galoppatoio di Villa Borghese," (Riding Track of Villa Borghese) and the equestrian theme is visible in the landscape—a horse track encircles the field, and a practice court for horse jumping is located on the northwest side. But neither horses nor people can be seen very often. People here are on their way somewhere else—either tourists lost at the edge of the map or locals taking a shortcut to the metro—and the horses make only a brief appearance on their way to the races at the Piazza di Siena on the north side of the park, a much more elegant location, where people spread out Sunday picnic blankets on the verdant grass or sip cocktails at the grandstand.

1 The writing of this chapter was made possible by support from the Fondazione Famiglia Rausing and the Swedish Institute in Rome.

Summer days are dry and hot in the Galoppatoio, and a feeling of abandonment lingers in the air. Even before the COVID-19 pandemic this was a quiet place. Traffic, of course, could be heard, and sirens were always in the background, a melody at once joyful and ominous in the typical Mediterranean fashion, changing pitch as the emergency vehicles sped away along the Corso d'Italia. In comparison to the conversations, noises, and street music to be heard in other parts of the park, the silence in the Galoppatoio—especially at times with no traffic—is conspicuous, almost palpable.

Summer days are dry and hot in the Galoppatoio, and a feeling of abandonment lingers in the air.

Over time, shortcuts have left a jumble of paths across the field. The ground looks stomped and beaten down. Garbage bags and empty bottles are strewn about the grass. If you do stop, perhaps at a point where the field opens up to the south, you can take in a panorama of Rome's ancient city wall, the Aurelian Wall, and the rooftops of the Villa Medici and the Casina Valadier.

It was on slow afternoon promenades between the Svenska Institutet/Istituto Svedese (Swedish Institute) and the *centro storico*, Rome's historical center, along one of the shortcuts across the field that I noticed the large concrete cylinders sticking out of the ground.

Cylinders in the Galoppatoio di Villa Borghese, November 2021, photo by author.

Weeds were growing high around these bunker-like objects, and graffiti and notes were scribbled on the sides. Some of the cylinders had roofs with grass growing on top; others were exhaust hoods with air pressing up through metal lattices. Some shafts were open, revealing driveways and floors below. They all seemed to belong to the same moment in time—constructed in reinforced in-situ concrete, with railings and gates in steel painted red. I gradually realized that the arid state of the field was testimony to the porosity below. What I had encountered was the Villa Borghese Parcheggio, a thirty-six-thousand-square-meter multifunctional underground garage complex designed by Italian architect Luigi Moretti and completed in 1972 as one of the many large-scale infrastructure projects constructed in the wake of Rome's 1962 master plan.

With the later additions of underground walkways to the metro, the project sits as a hinge between parts of the city. Its tunnels reach far into the

Shaft with connection to underground parking, photo by author.

historical center, connecting the wealthy Ludovisi district, the park, and the extramural ring road to the crowded area around Piazza di Spagna.[2]

And yet, like so much of our everyday infrastructure, it is a mostly forgotten project. Part landscape, part building, half hidden in the shrubbery of the park, and located mostly underground, the Parcheggio was never a monument of infrastructural progress or an architectural design icon, making it unlike so many of Moretti's other projects.[3] The Parcheggio seems related more to the pedestrian networks of North American shopping malls and hotels— the indoor environments Charles Rice identifies as "interior urbanism"—than to European modernist architecture.[4]

And yet, like so much of our everyday infrastructure, it is a mostly forgotten project. Part landscape, part building, half hidden in the shrubbery of the park, and located mostly underground, the Parcheggio was never a monument of infrastructural progress or an architectural design icon, making it unlike so many of Moretti's other projects.

Since 1998, the Spanish infrastructure management company Saba Aparcamientos has held a contract for the operation of the parking garage, owned by the city council of Rome. The Parcheggio will be tied to Saba until the year 2061, a condition that highlights how infrastructure is always embedded in complex situations with multiple and conflicting interests. In mapping the recent "infrastructural turn," Ash Amin defines *infrastructure* as sociotechnical assemblages that are implicated in the production of functionality, sociality, and identity in the city.[5] Infrastructural systems pattern everyday lives, enable and limit different socioeconomic groups in the city, frame our experience of the city, carry political and symbolic meanings, and even shape human identity. Infrastructure generates encounters between actors and parts of the urban life previously separated, but infrastructural systems are also transformed themselves by such encounters. Within architectural research this turn

2 Paolo Cercato was commissioned by the Condotte d'Acqua to complete the project after Moretti's death in 1973.

3 Robert Venturi mentions Moretti's Casa Il Girasole in *Complexity and Contradiction in Architecture* **(New York: Museum of Modern Art, 1977), 20–22. See also Peter Eisenmann,** *Ten Canonical Buildings: 1950–2000* **(New York City: Rizzoli, 2008), 26–48.**

4 Charles Rice, *Interior Urbanism: Architecture, John Portman and Downtown America* **(London: Bloomsbury Academic, 2016).**

5 Ash Amin, "Lively Infrastructure," *Theory, Culture and Society* **31, no. 7–8 (2014): 137–61.**

points to, among other things, infrastructure as open-ended, transforming, and unfinished.[6] Infrastructure, it seems, carries dispositions that unfold as new relationships between different agencies and bodies.

How to adapt existing infrastructural systems to support structures of love and generosity is one of the most urgent questions for architects today and in the coming years. Support is a form of negotiation, Celine Condorelli remarks.[7] That is, support happens as a dialogue between different points of view, with the purpose of reaching ways of being-in-common. Acts of support imply challenging modes of operation and principles in relation to specific sites, people, and objects.

The work and discussions of the Infrastructural Love design studio, convened from 2018 to 2020 at KTH (Royal Institute of Technology) Stockholm, addressed infrastructure as a support structure for engagements with our social and environmental ecologies. The infrastructural love that we explored together with the students supported the unstructured, affective forces that can augment the ability to act on a world suffering profound environmental and social crises. We worked from the assertion that the environmental ecology, plagued by human destruction and exploitation, is in grave need of love. But what kind of love can answer the violent forces and disequilibrium generated by capitalism?

For Michael Hardt and Antonio Negri, love is an "ontological event" that breaks with the existing order and increases the power of bodies to act and to think.[8] This kind of love—and the authors are careful to distinguish "political love" from more malign forms of love—is a transformative force that produces new forms of being. Love in this sense is defined by its expanding capacity, which gives subjectivities a shared sensation of being in common.

Like many similar environments of interior urbanism, the Parcheggio has been left in a state of slow dilapidation, abandoned by its authors and developers and maintained at a minimum level by Saba. In this hollow waiting room between visions of the past and promises of future investments, I want to consider the parking garage as a support structure that is more than the

6 See, for example, Katrina Stoll and Scott Lloyd, eds., *Infrastructure as Architecture: Designing Composite Networks* **(Berlin: JOVIS, 2011).**

7 Céline Condorelli and Bart De Baere, "Support for Culture," in *Support Structures*, **ed. Céline Condorelli and Gavin Wade (Berlin: Sternberg Press, 2009), 191.**

8 Michael Hardt and Antonio Negri, *Commonwealth* **(Cambridge, MA: Cambridge University Press, 2009), 181.**

repository of cars. I will do this by discussing how the Parcheggio, for a brief time, was repurposed to house the art exhibition *Contemporanea*, exploring new forms of organization and collaboration between artists, audiences, and the community of Rome. How can a parking garage be repurposed, temporarily or more permanently, to support a project of love? What latent possibilities of love can we find in other systems of infrastructure? And what are the conditions and constraints of such love, especially when considering the example of the art event that was *Contemporanea*?

How can a parking garage be repurposed, temporarily or more permanently, to support a project of love?

Excavations 1969–1972

In the mid-1960s, Moretti was commissioned to design the Villa Borghese Parcheggio, an underground parking garage in the southeast corner of the Villa Borghese park, just outside the Aurelian Wall. The commission should be read in the historical context of the urban renewal of Rome following the end of the Second World War, a process that accelerated with the 1962 master plan for the city.[9] The Parcheggio was a pilot project for a future infrastructure of similar garages at the edges of the city. In addition to this proposed archipelago of parking garages, a new metro, Line A, was to cut diagonally across Rome from northwest to southeast, and an external ring road (the Grande Raccordo Anulare) was to circumscribe the periphery. The new plan happened at the expense of the existing landscape outside the boundary of the center, through large-scale interventions in the environment, not least in its subterranean layers. Federico Fellini's 1972 movie *Roma*, depicting among other things the construction of Line A, illustrates the congestion, turbulence, and polemics of the city's underground at the time.

Photographs from the construction process of the Parcheggio give additional testimony to the subterranean congestion.[10] From 1969 to 1972, La Società

9 For a discussion on the historical debates around this master plan, see *Franco Archibugi, Rome: A New Planning Strategy* **(London: Routledge, 2011).**

10 See aerial photograph in Luciana Finelli, Luigi Moretti: *La promessa e il debito—Architetture 1926–1973* **(Rome: Officina Edizione, 2005), 93.**

Italiana per Condotte d'Acqua (The Italian company for water pipelines), a Vatican-owned building company specializing in road construction and water infrastructure, excavated 5.5 million cubic meters of soil and volcanic tuff as part of the construction of the garage, a volume big enough to fill the entirety of St. Peter's Basilica, located in the vicinity. The new garage was constructed in two-floors, using a combination of prefabricated elements and in situ reinforced concrete.[11] A two-meter layer of soil and drainage was placed on top of the garage, with the depth of soil likely varying.

11 **Antonella Greco and Gaia Remiddi,** *Il moderno attraverso Roma: Guida alle opere romane di Luigi Moretti* **(Rome: Palombi Editori, 2006), A16.**

Moretti, who had several commissions in the United States and Canada, probably found inspiration for the Parcheggio in the large-scale urban interiors of Atlanta, Los Angeles, and Montreal, constructed around the same time. These were pedestrian networks separated from the cars, connecting buildings, metro, and institutions through covered walkways, tunnels, and interior plazas. Moretti and Pier Luigi Nervi's stock exchange skyscraper in Montreal, the Tour de la Bourse (Stock Exchange Tower), completed in 1964, had an interior connection to the Square-Victoria—OACI subway station via the "Underground City," a thirty-two-kilometer-long network of subterranean walkways that linked office buildings, metro stations, public squares, and commercial centers throughout the central business district.[12]

12 **For more on the "Tour de la Bourse," see Finelli,** *Luigi Moretti*, **111–12.**

Whether Moretti saw the interiors of the Parcheggio complex as a new type of public space is less clear. This reflects the ambiguous status of the parking garage as a civic space in general. In her analysis of the evolution of the parking garage as urban form, Shannon S. McDonald argues that its combination of mechanical repository and human transition space was never recognized as a civic space in the same way as the train station.[13] This despite the fact that the parking garage was a driving force behind the expansion of North American urbanism of the twentieth century.

13 **Shannon S. McDonald,** *The Parking Garage: Design and Evolution of a Modern Urban Form* **(Washington, DC: Urban Land Institute, 2007).**

The Parcheggio's double-story underground complex includes parking for more than two thousand cars, a commercial center, offices, and connections to the ring road, the subway, and Piazza di Spagna, all via extensive subterranean walkways.

The Parcheggio's double-story underground complex includes parking for more than two thousand cars, a commercial center, offices, and connections to the ring road, the subway, and Piazza di Spagna, all via extensive subterranean walkways. The layout of the parking garage includes two floors measuring 174 by 174 meters and consisting of two rectangular parking zones, with approximately five hundred spaces per zone, divided by a two-lane central driveway. Circumscribing the rectangles are one-way driveways that hold additional parking spaces.

Each floor connects to the other level and to the outside through ramps at the two corners to the north and west. In total, the programs and circulation areas cover almost four hectares of underground space, inside and just outside the historical center of Rome.

A central idea in Moretti's design was to establish a vertical relationship—both for circulation, light, and views—between the floors underground and the park above. Four identical light shafts with a diameter of 13.3 meters connect the Galoppatoio with the underground. Spanning from the lowest floor to the level of the park, the shafts let light down to the underground and offer viewpoints in both directions. An elliptical stair in each shaft connects the two floors with the park.

The support for the structure is a grid of more than three hundred conical, mushroom-like columns in reinforced concrete.

Typical column on the upper floor; photograph by author.

The sides of the grid measure 13.3 meters, allowing for four cars to be parked between every two columns. Each parking space is rotated forty-five degrees from the driveway to reduce turning ratios and facilitate parking.[14] The ceiling is based on the square of four columns, with a side of 13.3 by 13.3 meters. Inside each square is a twelve-meter-diameter prefabricated concrete cupola with a round light placed at the center, like an abstract lantern. The concave shape of the cupola produces a peculiar acoustic effect at certain points in the garage—tiny sounds are dramatically amplified and echoed.

Moretti's design for the Parcheggio is both pragmatic and poetic.[15] The rational solution to the complexity of program, construction, and circulation is paired with the quiet poetry of the sculptural columns, the cupolas, and the light wells. As a plan drawing, the Parcheggio reads like a proposal on an urban scale. The parking garage is a confirmation of a modernist urban planning scheme: separation of vehicle and pedestrian traffic, a hierarchy among kinds of driveway, distinct zones for each program, and division into large blocks based on a grid of columns. On the ground the 180-millimeter-high curb (painted bright yellow, profile slightly slanted) delimits the parking zone from the driveways.

14 Finelli, *Luigi Moretti*, **93.**

15 See Bruno Reichlin and Leitizia Tedeschi, *Luigi Moretti: Razionalismo e trasgressività tra barocco e informale* **(Milan: Electa, 2010); and Margherita Guccione, "Recuperare l'ultimo dei moderni," in** *Luigi Moretti: Dal razionalismo all'informale—Guida alla mostra*, **ed. Maristella Casciato and Annalisa Viati Navone, 8–9 (Milan: Electa, 2010), 8.**

Curb on upper floor, photograph by author.

Rather than a continuous sidewalk, the curb consists of islands that define the border between the main driveways and the parking zones. The curb signifies an intention to separate vehicles and pedestrians without losing the visual connection between the two kinds of speed.

A Villa Borghese Love Story, 1973–1974

In 1972 the Parcheggio was completed, but neither cars nor visitors filled the garage. The low use of the garage during the first year of its operation led to an agreement between the cultural association Incontri Internazionali d'Arte (International Art Encounters) and Condotte d'Acqua, the property managers of the Parcheggio at the time, to use the upper floor of the complex for the experimental art exhibition *Contemporanea* (Contemporary), which opened on November 30, 1973.[16] Curated by Italian art critic Achille Bonito Oliva and curators from nine fields, the exhibition had the ambition to establish new correspondences between a broad range of art forms. The exhibition emerged partly out of a growing frustration with the institutionalization of the Italian art scene, where museums and galleries had become the predominant venues for art, and partly out of the search for new forms of collaboration between cultural and artistic practices kept apart by disciplinary boundaries. The show marked one of the starting points for what later became an international, postmodern movement of art (and architecture), formulating a similar critique, and the use of a parking garage played a significant role in distancing the exhibition from traditional institutions of art and culture.[17]

For more than four months the Parcheggio was the scene of a panoramic mapping of multiple cultural expressions. More than one hundred artists were represented in the garage, with paintings, sculptures, installations, video art, texts, and performances categorized under nine broad sections: architecture and design, visual art, cinema, music and dance, photography, alternative information, performance, visual poetry, and theater. Among the many contributors were Donald Judd, Andy Warhol, Joan Jonas, Luigi Ontani, Roy Lichtenstein,

16 **Bruno Mantura,** *Contemporanea Roma Parcheggio di Villa Borghese,* **11.1973/2.1974 (Rome: Incontri Internazionali d'Arte, 1973). For reviews of the exhibition, see Filipa Ramos, "The Absent Spectator 1: The Present Was Now,"** *Manifesta Journal***, no. 15 (2014): 24–28; and Gregory Battcock, "Mostra a Roma: Contemporanea Pinacoteca Drive-in e Sotterranea," Domus 531 (February 1974). For more on the Incontri, see Luigia Lonardelli,** *Dalla sperimentazione alla crisi: Gli Incontri Internazionali d'Arte a Roma***, 1970–1981 (Milan: Doppiozero, 2016).**

17 **See, for example, Douglas Crimp, "On the Museum's Ruins," in** *The Anti-aesthetic: Essays on Postmodern Culture***, ed. Hal Foster, 43–56 (Port Townsend, WA: Bay Press, 1983).**

Robert Rauschenberg, Philip Glass, Gino De Dominicis, Wolf Vostell, Robert Morris, Giovanni Macchia, Urs Lüthi, Ben Vautier, and Marina Abramović.[18] Luigia Lonardelli, in her analysis of *Contemporanea*, notes that many art critics and journalists of the time had difficulty categorizing the exhibition; it was variously identified as a "review," an "exhibition," and even a "festival."[19] Visitors and reviewers of *Contemporanea* described it as a gradually transforming series of events to which the audience kept returning for new screenings, seminars, and performances.[20]

18 For an overview of participants, see Mantura, *Contemporanea*, **12–14.**

19 Luigia Lonardelli, "Contemporanea: An Exhibition in an Underground Car Park," *Art Journal*, **77, no. 1 (2018): 6–29 (here 13–14).**

20 Lonardelli, "Contemporanea," 13.

The central role the curators placed on the parking garage in itself, as a kind of infrastructural support system for the transdisciplinary and anti-institutional agenda of *Contemporanea*, is evident in the visual material that accompanied the exhibition. The cover of the exhibition catalog is a central perspective of the main driveway of the Parcheggio's upper floor, empty of people, art, and cars. Fluorescent lamps light up columns, ventilation shafts, driveways, and curbs. Arrows and indicators for driving and walking duplicate along the main axes, receding into the horizon as if reflected in an infinity mirror. The cover situates the parking garage at the center of the exhibition, but the emptiness in this version of the Parcheggio—shown as a grid of columns, small curb islands, and a vast territory of vacant parking spaces—underscores the ephemeral nature of *Contemporanea*, or of any program. In the end it is the structure itself that reverberates with potentiality in this image, as a premonition of the project today: empty space in a state of maintained hibernation.

In the end it is the structure itself that reverberates with potentiality in this image, as a premonition of the project today: empty space in a state of maintained hibernation.

The design of the exhibition layout, by Italian architect Piero Sartogo in collaboration with the curators, made clever use of existing elements of the parking garage: the grid of columns, the curb, and the light shafts. The exhibition design generated an order in which each section was given freedom inside a structure. The central spine of the exhibition was the main driveway of the upper floor of the garage—two lanes separated by a concrete lane divider with a trapezoid profile. Screens of wire mesh attached to the floor and ceiling were placed approximately one meter apart in a zigzagging sequence parallel to the main axis. The screens changed sides with each new section of the exhibition, so a visitor would have to cross the lane divider to move to the next section. The curb "islands" of each column along the main driveway functioned both as signs and borders, declaring the entrance point to a section. Blue fluorescent lights added along the driveway further emphasized the linear sequence of the central axis. A montage sequence in the catalog illustrates how the screens produced a continuity along the axis, a blue corridor visible from most of the sections.[21] The visual quality produced by the screens—a kind of moiré effect—is evident in many of the images from the exhibition. The bodies of other visitors dissolve in the reflections from the screens.[22]

The nine sections of the exhibition were located in the main parking area, perpendicular to the central corridor. Each section connected to the main driveway, but besides the linearity of the driveway and the grid of columns, there was great variation in the kind of space produced. The semitransparent, ethereal quality of the screens meant that pieces from other sections were visible in the background.[23] The clear structure of Sartogo's design afforded a freedom that fitted well with the many improvised and temporary events of *Contemporanea.*

At moments, the exhibition was also visible aboveground. American minimalist artist Carl Andre's *Diamond Sutra*, a set of diamond-shape figures on the bottom of the eastern light shaft, could be seen from the park.[24] Daniel Buren hung a red and white striped banner in the northernmost of the shafts.[25] The wrapping of the Porta Pinciana gate in the Aurelian Wall, located just above the main entrance to the Parcheggio, by large-scale installation artists Christo and Jeanne-Claude, served as a symbolic marker for the entrance to the exhibition.

21 Mantura, *Contemporanea*, **16–23.**

22 See for example image from exhibition, Gaia Servadio, "Romans Flock to Underground Art," *The Times*, **December 21, 1973.**

23 See, for example, an exhibition photograph of George Segal's sculptures. Claudio Abate, photograph, 1973, in Archivi MAXXI Arte, Fondo Archivio Incontri Internazionali d'Arte (AIIA), Rome.

24 Mantura, *Contemporanea*, **76.**

25 Mantura, *Contemporanea*, **46–47.**

Contemporanea offered a space for exploring new forms of cultural and artistic practice through an informal assemblage of events, seminars, and people. Judging by accounts of the exhibition, it produced a shared sensation of being, where new formations of human and nonhuman bodies appeared.[26] The transversal approach of the curators and the temporary repositioning of human and nonhuman bodies inside the garage are perhaps not far from the kind of "ontological event" that Hardt and Negri identify as love.

Still, *Contemporanea's* love was not for everyone, as it failed to transgress power structures of privilege and exclusion.

Still, *Contemporanea's* love was not for everyone, as it failed to transgress power structures of privilege and exclusion. Feminist scholar Eleanor Wilkinson notes the universalizing tendency in Hardt and Negri's call for the good form of love and questions whether the affect of love has the same augmenting effect on all subjectivities. The political love Hardt and Negri advocate, Wilkinson continues, may even repels certain bodies, since the transgressive claim of such love does not sufficiently recognize the "uneven terrain on which bodies encounter each other."[27] With its strong cultural and historical connotations to masculinity, the parking garage is surely a terrain of unevenness. The private garage of the suburb, as Janek Ozmin shows, is a seminal invention in the production of domestic masculinities of modernity.[28] Although not always part of the domestic sphere, the parking garage arguably carries similar ties to male domination. In popular culture and in films, the parking garage is a place for clandestine meetings, violence, assaults, and suspense.

Drawing on Wilkinson's critique of Hardt and Negri's concept of love, we might ask who the lovers were during these months of *Contemporanea*? Although ascertaining the composition of the audience is difficult, the full list of curators and artists is testimony to a male dominance that the radicality of the exhibition did not challenge.[29] Furthermore, the financial support bestowed on the exhibition by multiple banks, governmental bodies, and corporations meant that it did not exist outside the logic of the market.[30] Thus, we should

26 Lonardelli, "Contemporanea," 19. See also Servadio, "Romans Flock to Underground Art."

27 Eleanor Wilkinson, "On Love as an (Im)properly Political Concept," *Environment and Planning D: Society and Space* **35, no. 1 (2017): 57–71.**

28 Janek Ozmin, "The Garage: Maintenance and Gender," in *Architecture and Feminisms: Ecologies, Economies, Technologies*, **ed. Hélène Frichot, Catharina Gabrielsson, and Helen Runting, 256–64 (London: Routledge, 2018).**

29 In her review of the exhibition, Gaia Servadio writes that she observed how "students, large families, elderly couples looked in amazement at the exhibits." Servadio, "Romans Flock to Underground Art." Of the

be under no illusion that the temporary repurposing of the Parcheggio to hold the *Contemporanea* was a love story that involved the kind of "multitude" Hardt and Negri describe. Despite these important political questions, the exhibition nonetheless testifies to the adaptive and transgressive capacity of repurposing a large complex like the Parcheggio. The temporary institution produced by the *Contemporanea* and its appropriation of the parking space is one example of many possible dispositions of this building.

The love story of the *Contemporanea* did not end abruptly or dramatically; it faded away. The closing of the exhibition was slow, as works and installations were dismounted over several months, right up until the end of May 1974.[31] After this exceptional period, the Parcheggio was to become the thriving combination of parking garage, office complex, and commercial center that the investors and the architect had intended for the project in the first place. Ultimately, such hopes were dashed. If the Parcheggio had a moment of fame around the period of the *Contemporanea* (at the time the exhibition closed, one hundred thousand people had visited), it soon became part of the urban background again.[32] Refurbishments over the decades that followed—a redesign of the tunnel connection to Via Veneto, renovation of the walkway to the Piazza di Spagna, and multiple renovations of the retail space—did little to increase the public appeal. Offices, grocery stores, and nightclubs existed at various points in time, but they could not compete with the buzzing street life above nor with the interior of Rome's historical center.

In 2007, the city council of Rome extended Saba's maintenance concession for the Parcheggio until the year 2061 on the condition that the company carry out a major refurbishment, originally scheduled for completion in 2016 (and now on hold). Saba's proposal includes the excavation of a third underground level, the addition of more than three hundred parking spaces, an entirely new mechanized subterranean walkway between the Parcheggio and the Piazza del Popolo (People's Square), parking for tourist buses, technical updates to accommodate electric vehicles, and almost eight thousand additional square meters of retail and storage space, with a total budget of 155 million euros.

thirteen curators, three were women: Daniela Palazzoli (photography), Yvon Lambert (artists' book and records), and Leietta Gervasio (counter-information). See Mantura, *Contemporanea*, **9.**

30 For a full list of the sponsors of *Contemporanea*, **see Lonardelli, "Contemporanea," 17.**

31 Lonardelli, "*Contemporanea*,**" 16.**

32 Lonardelli, "Contemporanea," 19.

Images of the proposal circulated online via scandalized Italian newspapers, bloggers reacting to Saba's bargain deal, and through the portfolios of the engineers behind the proposal.[33] If completed, the plans would make the Parcheggio compatible with twenty-first-century mobility and logistic standards. The parking garage would become a hub for the visitors to the historical center. New partition walls in full floor height would be inserted between the columns to separate the different parking zones on each floor. The curbs would be removed and replaced with bands of color. And the four light shafts connecting the Parcheggio to the park above would disappear to make room for more parking spaces.

Future Dispositions

In his 1988 proposal for the Monte Echia area in Naples, Aldo Rossi developed the idea of an underground city as a series of voids in the shape of imagined buildings.[34] Rossi proposed multiple underground caves in different shapes and sizes, perpendicular to a central axis that cut across the city from its center to the Mediterranean Sea, passing indifferently beneath buildings, streets, and plazas. The axis marked a central point in his proposal. It had no immediate function or program. The sequence of cavities underneath Naples would be for neither infrastructure nor tourism. The proposed project was useless, Rossi declared, save for the fact that it could be walked through and generate an "increased consciousness of the city."[35] The section through the city and its underground would form what Rossi calls an "urban radiography," by which the conditions below could be seen as analogous to the city above. Rossi's acknowledgment that such spaces should be free from program and function expresses a resignation toward the simulation of interior urban environments. Documentation of the *Contemporanea* suggests that the physical transformation of the parking garage was minimal, involving neither a major formal intervention nor the addition of costly physical decor. The only changes were ephemeral reorganizations of the space so that it could support the positions

33 See "Villa Borghese, parcheggio in gestione a 10 mila euro l'anno: 'Rivedremo convenzione,'" *Roma Today*, August 9, 2017, https://www.romatoday.it/politica/parcheggio-villa-borghese-concessione.html. For examples of bloggers commenting on Saba's contract, see Gianni Dragoni, "Lo scandalo del parcheggio di Villa Borghese," *Poteri Deboli* [blog], March 24, 2019, http://www.giannidragoni.it/economia/lo-scandalo-del-parcheggio-di-villa-borghese/. For a presentation of the project, see "Ristrutturazione ed ampliamento dell'esistente Parcheggio sotterraneo del Galoppatoio di Villa Borghese," Ìntera, http://interasrl.it/portfolio-item/parcheggio-sotterraneo-villa-borghese/.

34 Aldo Rossi, "Proposal for the Monte Echia Area in Naples, 1988," in *Aldo Rossi: The Life and Works of an Architect*, ed. Alberto Ferlenga, 200-201 (Cologne: Konemann, 2001).

35 Rossi, "Proposal for the Monte Echia Area in Naples, 1988," 200.

and actions of human bodies in ways that a garage normally would not. The fundamental support structure for the *Contemporanea* existed in the physical structure of the parking garage; the curators, artists, and visitors, along with the design of the exhibition architect, made the exhibition. The active form of the infrastructure was in the curatorial work of all those involved who sought to transform the parking zones, driveways, columns, and shafts into a new and temporary institution. In this conjunction of curators, artists, visitors, objects, and materials, the unknown capacities of the parking garage unfolded. The example of the *Contemporanea* presents one disposition for the unfolding of performativity in infrastructure over time. The exhibition illustrates how precise, small interventions can have a great effect on the built environment. The *Contemporanea* transformed the Parcheggio into something else, albeit for a limited period of time, providing a space for new relationships and for challenging the institutionalized manners of the artistic world. Although we must remain skeptical of utopian claims for such events, the temporary transformation of the Parcheggio offers a ray of hope. The reshaping of the material infrastructure of the garage happened through the actions and interventions of human beings, a reminder of Amin's argument about infrastructure defined as sociotechnical assemblages.

In her writing on the spatial logics of global infrastructure, architectural theorist Keller Easterling describes infrastructural and architectural objects with unanticipated possibilities as "active forms."[36] Active form holds an inherent and partly unknown agency, or disposition, that allows for "an unfolding relationship between potentials."[37] Designing active form requires not the shaping of an object but the construction of rules for how it performs and conditions multiple parameters in a way comparable to the writing of software. If disposition, understood in Easterling's reading, is the gradual unfolding of capacity or agency in objects or beings, it produces new points of contact between bodies. Saba's refurbishment proposal attempts to do away with any such unknown agency of the project. The alteration or removal of three fundamental elements of the Parcheggio—the grid of columns, the curb, and the shafts—would

36 Keller Easterling, *Extrastatecraft: The Power of Infrastructure Space* **(London: Verso Books, 2014), 11.**

37 Easterling, *Extrastatecraft*, **57.**

restrain the very flexibility of the parking garage that was so beneficial for the *Contemporanea*. The adaptation to new mobility solutions categorizes the project as exclusively for garage and retail. Such a nominative act—the ostensible declaration of a fixed condition—leaves no room for alternative scenarios for how the building could perform in a near future. *Contemporanea* seems like a distant dream in the new world of mobility hubs and smart cities, remaining only in grainy black-and-white images online and in the few tattered copies of the exhibition catalog that still remain.

Architects cannot and should not stop the transformation of old buildings. Perhaps, from an architect's point of view, the greatest act of infrastructural love is to maintain a support structure for future dispositions.

Architects cannot and should not stop the transformation of old buildings. Perhaps, from an architect's point of view, the greatest act of infrastructural love is to maintain a support structure for future dispositions. This does not necessarily mean to do nothing, like the refusal of Bartleby the Scrivener in Herman Melville's short story, but to do only the minimum of necessary adjustments in order to leave a project open-ended.[38] When French architects Anne Lacaton and Jean-Philippe Vassal added a 3.8-meter-deep floor slab to the outside of the existing facade of a large-scale apartment block in Bordeaux, this created an ample undefined space that the inhabitants themselves could appropriate in various ways by using curtains and furniture. The addition of a single element, a floor, allowed "freedom of use," but it also meant that the renovation cost was minimized, reducing the risk of a rise in rent, demolition, or evictions in a socioeconomically vulnerable neighborhood.[39] Such an act requires, as Vassal notes, a "delicate attention to everything that exists."[40]

In what they identify as a general "melt-down of categories," Helena Mattsson and Catharina Gabrielsson suggest that the continuously transforming constellations of power and capitalism have unraveled previous distinctions and established truths within the architectural discipline.[41] What is needed, they

38 Herman Melville, *The Piazza Tales* **(New York City: Dix, Edwards & Co, 1856); Herman Melville,** *Bartleby, The Scrivener: A Story of Wall-Street* **(Scotts Valley, CA: CreateSpace Independent Publishing, 2018).**

39 Anne Lacaton and Jean-Philippe Vassal, *Freedom of Use* **(Berlin: Sternberg Press, 2015), 17.**

40 Lacaton and Vassal, *Freedom of Use***, 31.**

argue, is to pay attention to the physical environment so as to distinguish nuances, transformation, and complexity. With this call for a sharpened empirical focus in mind, I return to the site of the Parcheggio.

41 Catharina Gabrielsson and Helena Mattsson, "Pay Attention!," *Architecture and Culture* 5, no. 2 (2017): 157–64 (here 158).

A Shortcut through the Parcheggio, November 2021

On a rainy day at the end of November 2021, almost fifty years after *Contemporanea* opened, I descended the entrance ramp from the north corner of the Galoppatoio in the direction of the parking garage. Holm oaks and nettle trees form a thick green canopy above the retaining walls of the ramp. At the point where the ramp turns into a tunnel, a young man on an electric scooter speeds past in the opposite direction. Down in the parking garage the emptiness of the Galoppatoio feels even more pressing. Few cars are down here, and almost no people. A chemical odor of spray paint mixes with the smell of dust, gasoline, and rain. A car door slams in the distance. Ventilation units hum, an infrastructural symphony in a minor key. My footsteps amplify as I pass under the cupolas. Further away a man and young girl, on their way to the exit, make a brief stop to play with the acoustic effects. They scream, chuckle, and cough before moving on.

I cut diagonally across multiple empty lanes to the nearest light shaft. Car tires screech against concrete. Soft light seeps through the vines in the shaft, onto the concrete floor.

A single car is parked in the closest lane, wrapped in a dust cover. A windmill palm grows wild in the high grass at the bottom of the shaft. The door to the shaft stair is locked. The official exit for drivers who have parked their cars is via the ticket booth.

The light from the other shafts glow in the dimness of the garage, serving as reference points for orientation. In comparison to

Entrance ramp to the Parcheggio from the Galoppatoio, November 2021, photograph by author.

105

Northern shaft upper floor, November 2021, photograph by author.

images from the time of completion, the square today looks clogged.[42] The multiple layers of past refurbishments, pandemic safety protocols, and corporate reorganizations have congested this space. There are signs, arrows, advertisements, screens, and CCTV-cameras—a semiotic tidal wave of warnings,

Exterior view of the Parcheggio entrance square, November 2021, photograph by author.

advice, proposals, and directions, all against walls and railings in cyan, Saba's brand color.

As another rain shower starts, I exit the garage onto a small rectangular outdoor square. Called the "piazzetta" on orientation maps, it is a space of Piranesian complexity, connecting to five stairs heading in different directions: to the upper and lower floors of the Parcheggio, to the underground tunnels for Via Veneto and the metro, and back up to the Corso d'Italia.

42 Compare with images from this space at the time of the opening of *Contemporanea*. **Photograph by Claudio Abate, "Contemporanea: Ingresso alla mostra," in Archivi MAXXI Arte, Fondo AIIA. See also Lonardelli,** *Dalla sperimentazione alla crisi*, **112.**

Across this a walkway canopy of aluminum and polycarbonate connects the underground walkways from Via Veneto and the metro, adding to the congestion. I climb the stairs to the left and reach what was intended to be the retail space of the Parcheggio, the Galleria Commerciale Villa Borghese (Villa Borghese Shopping Gallery). To the left, where the *Contemporanea's* theater and film sections were once located, is the Villa Borghese Medical Center. A pink sign outside announces, "Come in we have Botox." Passing up this offer, I reach the end of the galleria and enter the tunnel to Via Veneto. Saba billboards on the walls advertise available parking space, hashtag #TheArtOfParking. Each billboard features a montage—figures from well-known historical paintings in front of, behind, or inside cars.

There are signs, arrows, advertisements, screens, and CCTV-cameras—a semiotic tidal wave of warnings, advice, proposals, and directions, all against walls and railings in cyan, Saba's brand color.

The irony of the campaign appearing in this location cannot elude those who remember the history of the Parcheggio. Art, once and for all, turned into parking. The billboards raise the question of what Saba wants to do with all this empty space until the year 2061.

Due to disagreements between the city of Rome and Saba Aparcamientos, the proposed refurbishment of the Parcheggio is currently on hold. When and to what extent it will be realized remains unclear. Here, then, is a challenge for Saba, for the city council of Rome, and for the architects and engineers of the project: intervene in a way that does not eradicate future dispositions. One starting point could

Saba advertisement campaign in underground walkway between the Parcheggio and Via Veneto, November 2021, photograph by author.

be the four main shafts of the building, which offer possibilities for reconnecting the underground with the park. Another interesting point of the project is the empty ramp to the garage from the north corner of the Galoppatoio, today more frequently used by pedestrians than by cars. With careful analysis and small interventions, the park and the underground could connect again, forming a support structure for future ways of being-in-common—and creating the possibility of new love stories. Meanwhile, the Parcheggio continues to function as if in a state of maintained hibernation: escalators move with a rhythmic knocking, tube lights flicker in the tunnels, air conditioners and vending machines hum, car engines crank, cleaners clean the floors, and pedestrians hurry through and above the garage, always on their way somewhere else.

With careful analysis and small interventions, the park and the underground could connect again, forming a support structure for future ways of being-in-common—and creating the possibility of new love stories.

Central driveway of garage, photograph by author.

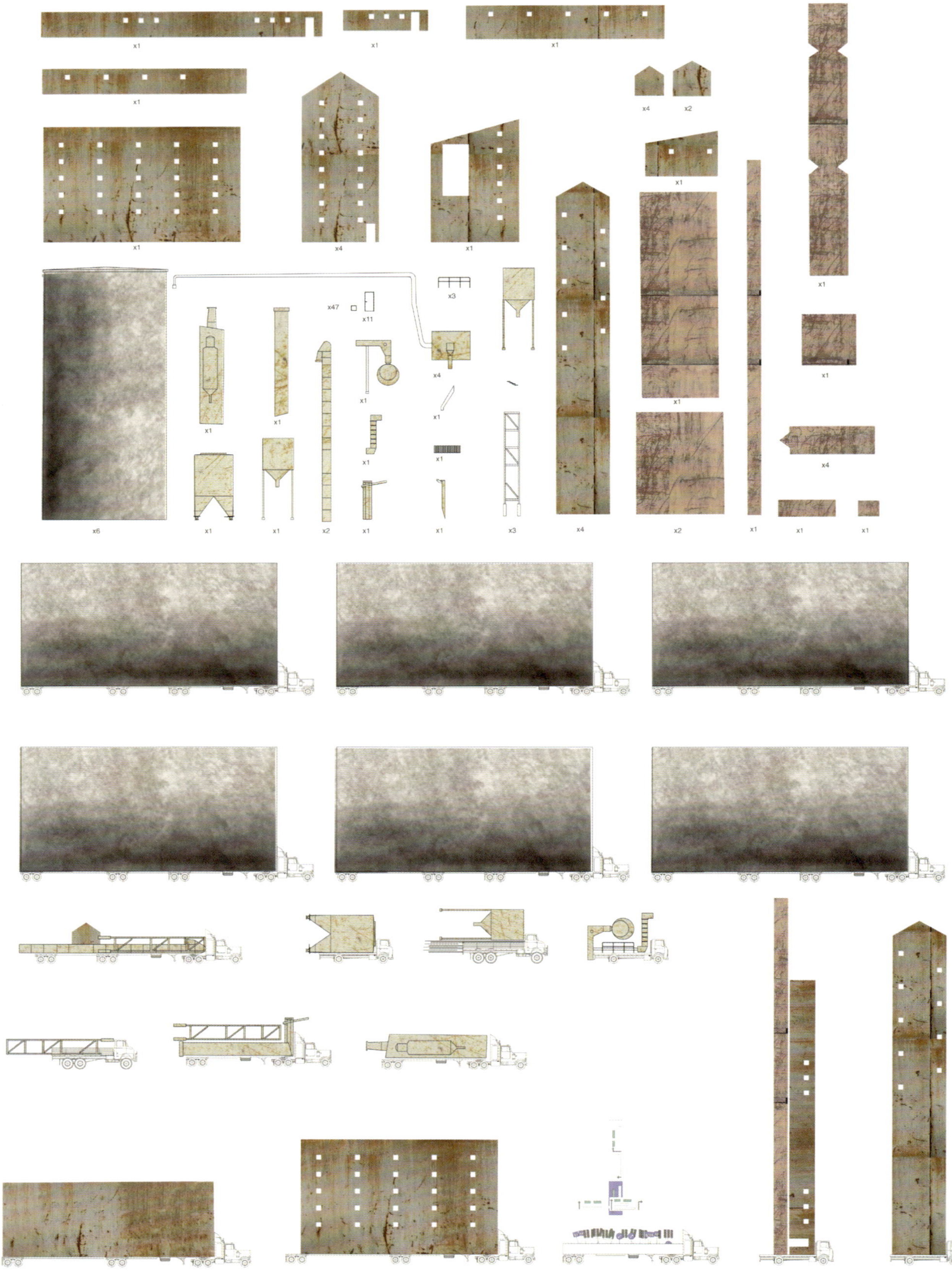
x1
x1
x1
x1
x4
x2
x1
x1
x4
x1
x1
x1
x47
x11
x3
x4
x1
x1
x1
x1
x1
x1
x1
x1
x4
x6
x1
x1
x2
x1
x1
x3
x4
x2
x1
x1
x1

Moving Peripheries: The Concrete Circus

Isak Hellström

What happens in the encounter between the city's often obscured industrial sites and everyday life? That is what I explore in my project "Moving Peripheries." The idea for this project emerged in autumn 2018 when I collaborated with Leni Ellburg and Tomotsugu Kitamura on a project called "Leftovers," which explored the material life cycles of the city, the flows of material, and the sometimes unintended consequences of using master-plans to guide city development.

We worked with three sites in inner-city Stockholm that were formerly industrial areas. While undertaking my research, I discovered how industrial areas move progressively farther from the city center, much as new rings of a tree appear farther from the center as the tree grows.

To investigate this process further, I decided to focus on Lövholmen and the concrete factory Cementa. Lövholmen, an attractive plot on the waterfront close to central Stockholm, has been affected by past pollution and ongoing industrial production. If Lövholmen was once on the periphery of the city, it is not on the periphery anymore. Due to the attractiveness and location of the site, all industrial production will be shut down, and in the near future the site will be stacked with expensive housing units. The industrial relics of the past must be removed, and this prompts a reflection on what is to happen to the infrastructural elements that once composed the Cementa factory.

The Cementa factory will be relocated to Värtahamnen, another industrial site located by the waterside but farther outside Stockholm. The factory will make the journey from one peripheral site to another, each of which can be imagined as the backstage area of a theater where the production of everyday life is being prepared. The factory undertakes work as though behind the curtains, as its work is meant to remain unseen by the audience (i.e., everyday citizens). Industry tends to be hidden on the outskirts of the city, out of sight, out of mind.

To attend to the complex relations of industrial production, I created a plan to move the component parts of the Cementa factory from the existing depot to the intended destination at Värtahamnen. This included planning for all the logistical challenges of such a move. I was inspired by Tim Anstey, a professor at the Oslo School of Architecture and Design who, in an essay called "Things That Move," discusses the relocation of a giant obelisk in Rome.[1] Moving the stone obelisk took an entire year, but the sophisticated drawings, complicated logistics, and the design of delicate details necessary to achieve this seemingly impossible mission suggested that the move itself had become something bigger even than the monument. What was created through architectural means was an event.

With the obelisk in mind I decided to design the physical means by which the Cementa concrete depot could be moved through inner-city Stockholm to its new home. Trucks loaded with all the concrete depot's peculiar elements would pass as a procession through the center of Stockholm, moving from the south to the northern outskirts of the city. The giant concrete silos and other industrial relics would emerge from hiding, rendered visible to the city's inhabitants.

Imagine the traffic lights and signs that must be relocated when this heavy procession comes lumbering through town. Not only would the trucks occupy all the driving lanes of the main route, even the pedestrian walkways would not be safe. Every turn would become a spectacle, every intersection a challenge. The parade would proceed in slow-motion due to the massive weight of the concrete silos. What sensations would run through your body as the caravan squeaked past and the curbs cracked? These industrial elements were never intended to be visible to the citizens of Stockholm, and so this speculative encounter is both frightening and fascinating. The physical relocation and spatial impact such a move would have on the city also verge on the absurd. Imagine if different aspects of the city could merge: our experience of the city would change. Stockholm is one of the fastest-growing cities in Europe, its peripheries continually expanding, moving faster and faster away from the core. If the process of urbanization were to go any faster, the life of an industrial worker might be refigured as that of a circus artist who must continually travel to the new outskirts of town to put on their infrastructural performance.

1 Tim Anstey, "Things That Move: Domenico Fontana and the Vatican Obelisk," *Nordic Journal of Architecture* **3, no. 2 (2012): 47–57. Anstey's book** *Things That Move* **is forthcoming from MIT Press.**

SUBWAY

SANDST
ORM, MI
RAGE, S
LUDGE

Chapter 7
Sandstorm, Mirage, Sludge: Mourning for Dead Support Structures

Sepideh Karami

Mourning for the Beloved

In November 2021, hundreds of farmers marched on the dry riverbed of the Zayandeh Rud, mourning for the death of water and the death of prosperity. The Zayandeh Rud (River), the largest and most important river of the Iranian Plateau in central Iran, has experienced several periods of drought in the past decade, triggering discontent among farmers. Water shortages, the result of political, economic, and environmental issues, have placed not just farms but cities, industries, environments, and the lives of ordinary people under serious threat. Starting with a sit-in strike in the riverbed (one in a series of protests in response to water shortage in various parts of Iran), the significance of the strike increased as it brought together not only farmers but people from various classes, belief systems, and backgrounds. Joined by tens of thousands of people over many weeks, not the street but the dry riverbed became a political infrastructure for dissent, discontent, and protest. Those gathered were protesting the exploitative approach to the environment taken by those in power, an approach that had resulted in drinking-water and agricultural-water crises. Crossing Isfahan, one of the biggest cities in Iran and a prominent city of culture, architecture, and tourism, the Zayandeh Rud is entangled with the lives of people and the livelihood of the city. Etymologically, Zayandeh Rud means "life-giver river." Today, as access to that life-giving water has become more and more urgent due to the episodes of dryness and of land subsidence (a result of the irregular construction of wells), protest against the situation is less a choice than a compulsion. To a people whose memories and cultures have been shaped by the existence of the river and whose economy depends on its presence, the river's death means the death of life. It is why people mourned for the river while marching on its dry bed.

Using the language of mourning as a means of protest resituates water as a deceased beloved, and the Zayandeh Rud is a beloved river: the source of inspiration for many love stories in Iranian literature, folklore, songs, and everyday stories. Mourning for the Zayandeh Rud means mourning for larger environmental disasters in Iran as it suffers from serious water bankruptcy. While climate change, global warming, and reduced rainfall can be blamed for the water shortage, a major contributing factor to this disaster includes a years-long chain of inept decisions and mismanagement. Among the poor development decisions are the choices to build water-dependent heavy industries in arid areas far from the sea; embarking on urban development for large populations in areas with inadequate water resources; farming water-intensive crops on arid lands; constructing dams; the unregulated use of groundwater resources via the construction of wells; and, finally, building a national economy that is highly dependent on the extraction of natural resources. This includes a long history of colonization of resources by Western powers and currently by China, as well as the international political and economic isolation of Iran due to sanctions imposed by the United States, all of which has led the country into an ecological crisis.[1] The local dilemmas, caused for the most part by mismanagement, are only exacerbated by global warming and the climate crisis, conditions with a history extending back at least to the Industrial Revolution.

The Zayandeh Rud follows a three-hundred-kilometer route that starts in the Zagros Mountains and ends in the Gavkhouni marshes. While only the section that passes through the historical city of Isfahan is well known, on its route it supports many ecologies, including human-constructed environments, ranging from farms and agricultural structures to heavy industries such as oil refineries and metal industries. The river itself is an infrastructure that supports Iran's economy, ecology, and society. Carelessly loaded with industrial and development demands that created too great a burden, the river has stopped functioning as a support infrastructure for what was once the rich ecology shaped along its banks and following its flow.

1 Kaveh Madani in an interview on CNN explained how sanctions can worsen a situation caused by many factors, the most prominent being poor decisions made by the state and the dependence of the national economy on natural resources. "Water Bankruptcy and Protests in Central Iran: Kaveh Madani on Connect the World with Becky Anderson," YouTube video, 6:45, posted by Kaveh Madani on November 23, 2021, https://www.youtube.com/watch?v=LQjslg-DL1v8.

The End of the River Is an Oilfield

The story of the Zayandeh Rud is just one story among many of rivers, lakes, and marshes that have been destroyed by the modern project of development and extractivist approaches to resources. Other examples such as the Tigris and Euphrates Rivers and the Mesopotamian marshes reveal rivers and water bodies whose ecological life is suffering, shrinking, and disappearing. The construction of dams, the clearance of wetlands for oil exploration, and Saddam Hussein's oppression of rebels in the marshlands during the war between Iraq and Iran are among forces that have caused one of the most tragic environmental disasters in the region. Shortage of water in Khuzestan Province in southwest Iran has triggered many protests, especially by indigenous Arabs. Following a dead river, one can detect a series of culprits along the way: industries, mines, wells, dams—all infrastructures that feed the modern project of development. Among all of the smaller and larger culprits, oil, since its discovery in the region, has been the most evil. Reza Negarestani, referring to Hamid Parsani in his *Cyclonopedia*, writes, "The end of the river is certainly an oil field."[2] This "end" can be interpreted as the end of water, the death of support for life. The "end" indicates a destructive relationship between oil infrastructures and water resources. While water and water infrastructures are used to support oil refineries and the petroleum industry, the process of petroleum production fails to offer reciprocal support to water and instead destroys its resources. This destruction ranges from water pollution to the exhaustion of water resources.

Water and oil do not mix. Chemically incompatible, their relationship is a destructive one. The incompatibility between them, as Ursula Biemann writes in a conversation with Andrew Pendakis, "mirrors a very strong associative or symbolic antagonism."[3] Biemann and Pendakis put these two matters at odds and describe oil as "the dirtiest of liquids" and "the devil's excrement," while describing water as "the most modest and common of social goods."[4] When oil and its infrastructures of extraction and refinement take over lands, water recedes and, with it, rich forms of life disappear. To expose the tragic landscape of oil, I consider two forms of infrastructure: infrastructures of extraction; and landscape as infrastructure. The former is a colonizing and exploitative infrastructure, and the latter emerges in critical response to extractivism and its impacts. The former inflicts violence; the latter revolts against the violence.

2 Reza Negarestani, *Cyclonopedia: Complicity with Anonymous Materials* **(Melbourne: re.press, 2008), 19.**

3 Ursula Biemann and Andrew Pendakis, "This Is Not a Pipeline: Thoughts on the Politico-aesthetics of Oil," *Imaginations* **3, no. 2 (2012): 6–16 (here 9) IMAGE.sightoil.3-2.2.**

4 Biemann and Pendakis, "This Is Not a Pipeline," 9.

While the latter is a symptom of the maladies of a petroleum-dependent world, it ultimately revolts against the controlled relations of modernity and coloniality and obstructs their smoothness. Such landscapes are not hopeful ones but deeply hopeless situations suffering in the absence of clean water and air. They are the result of an autoimmune disease of modernity, triggered by human-driven projects of development and greedy exploitative behavior. Dane Carlson describes landscape as "a conduit, an exaggerator, a proliferator, an inhibitor, an enabler; herein lies its timeless operative capacity."[5] The landscape constructed as the ground for oil infrastructures and transformed due to side effects of the petroleum industry exposes and exaggerates such side effects, calling for emergency action. Carlson continues, "infrastructure can be defined as those systems, works, and networks upon which the function of any system of human inhabitation is reliant."[6] These landscapes are failed infrastructures that act against systems of human inhabitation.

One of the characteristics of such landscapes is aridness, and arid landscapes are often the sites of two phenomena, mirage and sandstorm, both of which are connected to desert ecologies. In the absence of water and the presence of oil, a third phenomenon—sludge—arrives on the scene. All three phenomena emerge in the absence of water and the excess presence of oil. While each is an environmental phenomenon, they are also metaphors for various political, social, and economic situations that petroleum and oil infrastructures have created. These landscapes do not give us solutions to get out of the environmental crisis we are stuck in, but by expressing radical hopelessness they expose the complexity and urgency of the situation. And, as Hossein Madani writes, these situations are "not a disease but a symptom, just like a fever that shows infection"—what he calls a sign that represents chronic "ecological diseases."[7] The modern project, fueled by oil and petroleum, obscured the destructive side effects of oil extraction and petroleum industry as it claimed to be able to control everything through technology, innovation, and development. These scenes are landscapes as infrastructures that are constructed by the battle between incompatible matters, between love and hate, and between

5 Dane Carlson, "The Humanity of Infrastructure: Landscape as Operative Ground," *Scenario Journal*, **no. 3 (Spring 2013), https://scenariojournal.com/article/humanity-of-infrastructure/.**

6 Carlson, "The Humanity of Infrastructure."

7 Hossein Madani, "Ecological Diseases and Symptoms," in *Sandstorm: And Then There Was Dust*, **ed. Sarah Maske and Ayat Najafi (Istanbul: Sena Offset, 2020).**

various forms of war. They are battlefields where militants, states, corporations, and the environment and its inhabitants are in constant battle. The persistence of such critical situations renders the existing solutions obsolete. While sandstorms, mirage, and sludge are tragic environmental phenomena, exposing the inefficiency of the modern project, in their undoing of oil infrastructures they create a ground for a radical fight. Only in hopeless situations such as these can a radical fight finally get started.

Setting the Scene

Under layers of sand and rocks, below volumes of water, can be discovered chambers of oil, residue of the dead sun. These underground chambers stretch from beneath the Persian Gulf to below the deserts, hills, mountains, and forests of Khuzestan, Bushehr, and beyond. For years, before the industrial extraction of oil, the dead matter was itself protesting against gravity, seeping out of the ground to collect in small pools. It was then used by the inhabitants of the region to keep fire alive. With the first technological drilling of the earth, oil became the fuel for the engines of modernity. Speed was fueled by oil, and oil extraction was accelerated by modern technology. "More and faster" became the motto of modernity, capitalism, and coloniality. Earth—its "blood" and "flesh"—were made to serve the human-centered project of progress. The first oil well became a starting point for the expansion of infrastructures of extraction. Then giant drills began to operate. Pipes crawled over the deserts, through the mountains, and under the seas, channeling extracted oil to far-off lands. The first pipe gave birth to more pipes and then to other technological, social, and political networks to support the petroleum industry and petroculture.

Killing the Sandstorm

In video footage of a sandstorm in Khuzestan, as a giant orange cloud approaches the camera, a voice cries out, "What is this? Is it dust? It's a storm! Why is its background black?" The sandstorm is approaching the camera. The scene is dotted with scattered structures. Two people, scaled down by the grandeur of the orange cloud, run out of the frame. The voice shouts, "Go back in! It's getting dark. Oh, it's totally dark!" The sandstorm takes over. The screen turns black. The video ends.

The horror of the fast-approaching sandstorm in the video represents a long history of the violence of oil extraction and the impacts it has had on the region. Khuzestan Province, one of the most prominent areas of Iran for oil resources and the production of national revenue, has always been exposed to the violence of external and internal colonization, war, and oppression. In the early twentieth century, when Iranian oil was in hands of the British Petroleum Company, oil became the fuel for the Royal Navy's combustion engines, and, as Rouzbeh Akhbari writes, these became "important assets to be included in the larger imperial defensive schemes."[8] Later on, violence continued to be inflicted on the region through various forms of power structures. From the British- and American-engineered coup d'état in 1953 following the nationalization of oil in 1950, to the formation of a dictatorship after the 1979 Iranian Revolution, to the wars and conflicts that followed, all exhibit a history of violence fed by oil. Oil infrastructures incite

Oil infrastructures incite violence. The violence, either directly or indirectly, is a prerequisite for the oil to flow smoothly. Such violence is inflicted not only on human bodies but also on nonhuman bodies, on environments and cultures by means of constant wars, activities of extraction, state oppression, and water and air pollution, all of which result in the gradual death of bodies.

8 Rouzbeh Akhbari, "Petro-violence: Merging Militarism and Corporate Secrecy," *Society and Space*, **October 10, 2017, https://www.societyandspace.org/articles/petro-violence-merging-militarism-and-corporate-secrecy/.**

violence. The violence, either directly or indirectly, is a prerequisite for the oil to flow smoothly. Such violence is inflicted not only on human bodies but also on nonhuman bodies, on environments and cultures by means of constant wars, activities of extraction, state oppression, and water and air pollution, all of which result in the gradual death of bodies. The constant infliction of violence in various forms and on various stages—seas, rivers, forests, mountains, deserts—has left the environment shattered.

In the Middle East, deserts are the most prominent stage to bear the marks of the entanglement with oil. To arrive at oil, one must cross the desert. Oil is a lubricant for war machines, which turn the desert into a battlefield. The dessert becomes a terrain for the living and the nonliving; a terrain for the machines of colonialism to gallop across, for the hyperconsumers of capitalism to engage in, and for radical jihadis to negotiate.[9] These battlefields are obscured and characterized by the clouds of dust that erupt as miniature sandstorms shaped around the machineries of war that puncture the soil. When the dust settles, broken pipes, fires, and smoke are revealed. Around the broken pipes, amid the constant leaking of oil, appears the sludge. Under the fierce heat of the sun, sandstorms become a creature of the desert, a force of revolution that arises from processes of desertification.

9 Negarestani, *Cyclonopedia*, **19.**

Oil consumption pushes desertification forward, speeding up climate change and global warming. Artificial deserts result from the destructive and exploitative activities of greedy human beings who exacerbate the advance of deserts, resulting in the greater frequency of sandstorms. In the absence of water, plants and roots die away, and particles of soil are no longer held together, leaving the earth unsupported, since vegetation forms one part of the support structure that, along with rivers, marshes, wetlands, lakes, and other natural infrastructures, holds life together. One of the reasons for the pronounced increase in sandstorms in Khuzestan is the drying of the Mesopotamian marshes. Dry, loose, unrooted, and unstable—in the absence of natural support structures, the sand and dust are carried away by storms to neighboring areas. In an area such as Khuzestan—where borders of various kinds

Footage from the video of a sandstorm in Khuzestan. Source: Morteza Pashaei, aparat.com

(geopolitical but also of class, race, and religion) have been preserved, negotiated, and highlighted by ruling powers to sustain control over oil and to prevent potential conflicts—sandstorms challenge all such order. Such "separatist infrastructures," as Madani describes them, are challenged by sandstorms.[10] Violently crossing borders, sandstorms inflict violence on the environment and on human and nonhuman habitats. Madani describes the sandstorm as "a metaphor for dynamic breaking through, the moving over static constructions: a meteorological phenomenon that has been sweeping across the earth and overcoming borders for thousands of years."[11]

10 Nadine Isabelle Henrich, "Moving beyond Borders in Mesopotamia," in *Sandstorm*.

11 Madani, "Ecological Diseases and Symptoms."

Wars, dictatorship, and other forms of structural violence animated by human-driven projects of modern development install their apparatuses of violence in deserts. This is achieved either by using deserts as loci for industrial exploitation or by processes of desertification that turn life into nonlife, creating a tabula rasa for constructing end-of-world narratives. Infrastructures of oil are not only infrastructures of extraction but also, and more dominantly, infrastructures for oppressive and colonial power structures that support authoritarian regimes. As Akhbari writes, "To study the colonial nature of violence committed on behalf of energy conglomerates today it is important to remember that the protection of oil interests through organized militarism is a continued form of dispossession that has a long legacy in early 20th century colonial agendas."[12] Oil's close entanglement with violence, surveillance, and control leaves little space for democracy, as nation-states dependent on oil revenues do not need the people to remain in power, but they do need to secure the flow of oil. The characteristic violence of

Wars, dictatorship, and other forms of structural violence animated by human -driven projects of modern development install their apparatuses of violence in deserts. This is achieved either by using deserts as loci for industrial exploitation or by processes of desertification that turn life into nonlife, creating a tabula rasa for constructing end-of-world narratives.

12 Akhbari, "Petro-violence."

oil infrastructure creates a landscape that materializes coloniality, dictatorship, and a necessarily militant approach to the environment and to ecologies. Offering oil as a solution to global and environmental problems creates a self-referential conundrum: oil resolving the problems of oil, by oil. Agents of oil exploitation know how to act only through violence. To protect environments against the revolt of sandstorms, oil uses its own by-products. Bitumen emulsion or petroleum mulching, excessively used by Iranian authorities, is a toxic solution to hold loosened soil in place, lest it fly away with the storms. But as Rahim Hamid writes, "the devastation inflicted on the environment by the 'solution' is far worse than the original problem of sandstorms that the program was introduced to solve, leading to terrible destruction of the regional ecosystem that may be irreversible."[13] Petroleum mulching is a solution based on the opinion that deserts are denuded of life. Petrocultures see life where profit can be extracted. But "deep-rooted vegetation which has long helped to prevent sandstorms is threatened by the mulching program supposedly intended to stop sandstorms, which will actually undoubtedly increase them," Hamid writes.[14] Oil substitutes its own (by-)products, a toxic support structure, for an already existing natural support structure. This is the ideology of petroculture.

13 Rahim Hamid, "Iran's Petroleum Spraying in Ahwaz Puts Its Unique Ecology in Grave Danger," *Milli Chronicle*, June 19, 2020, https://millichronicle.com/2020/06/irans-petroleum-spraying-in-ahwaz-puts-its-unique-ecology-in-grave-danger/.

14 Hamid, "Iran's Petroleum Spraying in Ahwaz."

Gazing through the Mirage

Day becomes night amid the black smoke. Night falls into fragmented day with explosions of light. Illuminated by the explosive flashes, pipes appear to cross the desert. Refineries appear and disappear along with their infrastructures of roads, pipes, towers, and machines. Moving farther away from the pipes and the refinery towers, the desert becomes the cruelest form of itself. Nothing moves except the occasional lizard or trembling thorn. On the horizon, the shimmery image of an oasis agitates the mind, holding out the illusory possibility of shadow, water, a breeze, prosperity, livelihood. It is all a mirage.

The desert, despite its appearance, is not denuded of life but is a figure "on the border between life and non-life."[15] The mirage in the desert is a metaphor for that hidden "life," a becoming-life that moves away with every step taken toward it. To the colonial eye, the mirage is to be captured, to be gotten hold of. To that eye, it is not only an image of hope and survival but a potential that has to be turned into a living thing, feeding into the flow of capital and the project of development. Across Middle Eastern deserts, the mirage is interwoven with oil seeping into pools, ancient fires burning off natural gas leaks, seducing the profit hunters who wander through this arid landscape. In that mirage, geologists found their oasis: modernity, a utopia fueled by oil. In consequence, the mirages grew bigger and extended farther away, becoming unapproachable utopias.

Deserts are the favorite places for oil. They give the illusion of a tabula rasa, a barren land for modern, innovative, petroleum-based projects to be imagined and executed. The mirage manifests as the desire for more profit and the pursuit of the modern project. The monotonous nature of deserts makes them seem nondirectional. The mirage offers an illusory direction toward which to move. The end of the desert is a mirage. A longing for an oasis. For water. The illusion of a prosperous life. A ghost of past seas emerging in the absence of water. The mirage is a metaphor for the obscurity of politics around the oil industry, as well as the pollution and environmental crises it and its fellow industries have imposed on the world. What is to be found beyond the mirage? Can we hold onto that ever-receding oasis?

The mirage is a metaphor for the obscurity of politics around the oil industry, as well as the pollution and environmental crises it and its fellow industries have imposed on the world. What is to be found beyond the mirage? Can we hold onto that ever-receding oasis?

On the horizon of the petroleum-driven world is a mirage that promises a cleaner environment beyond oil. To the eyes of the exploited, the mirage of oil

15 McKenzie Wark, "Elizabeth Povinelli: When the Rocks Turn Their Backs on Us," *Verso Blog*, **February 12, 2019, https://www.versobooks.com/blogs/4236-elizabeth-povinelli-when-the-rocks-turn-their-backs-on-us.**

is a "curse" that places the land under the everlasting threat of dictatorship, war, loss, corruption, persistent inequality, and injustice.[16] Imre Szeman writes in his "System Failure: Oil, Futurity, and the Anticipation of Disaster" that "From oil flows capitalism."[17] He asks, "Is the end of oil a disaster? This depends, of course, on the perspective one has on the system in danger of collapse: capitalism."[18] Szeman renders the looming demise of the petrochemical economy as "the biggest disaster that 'we' collectively face," since neither capital nor its opponents can think beyond oil. He suggests that what is lacking in the various positions on oil capital and its aftermath—"strategic realism," "techno-utopianism," and "eco-apocalypse"— is "the shape and configuration of the political."[19] The lack of political engagement is what transforms any future plan into a mirage, the illusion of a better future that is never approachable. The metaphor of the mirage refers to falsehood and the vagueness of those future plans that stand shimmering on the horizon in deserts of the now. None of the three post-oil positions—strategic realism, techno-utopianism, eco-apocalypse—have proposed a reliable plan. With "strategic realism," the state wishes to secure and maintain steady and predictable access to oil.[20] With "techno-utopianism," the future alternatives to oil look like a "leafy green oases, filled with mid-twenty-first-century flaneurs and cyclists who move between buildings crowned with solar sails."[21] Unlike these two visions, "eco-apocalypse" suggests that "disaster cannot be avoided without fundamental changes to human social life."[22] Of the three positions, the last is at least aware that the oasis we believe we see on the horizon is only a mirage.

16 Timothy Mitchell, *Carbon Democracy: Political Power in the Age of Oil* **(London: Verso, 2013), 1.**

17 Imre Szeman, "System Failure: Oil, Futurity, and the Anticipation of Disaster," in *Energy Humanities: An Anthology*, **ed. Imre Szeman and Dominic Boyer, 55–70 (Baltimore: Johns Hopkins University Press, 2017), 55.**

18 Szeman, "System Failure," 57.

19 Szeman, "System Failure," 57.

20 Szeman, "System Failure,"

21 Szeman, "System Failure," 61.

22 Szeman, "System Failure," 64.

Getting Stuck in the Sludge

Negarestani writes, "If oil runs toward the desert, so does everything that is dissolved in it."[23] With oil comes modern war machines, colonizers, jihadis, capitalists. The oil gives birth to these foreign characters of the desert. For both jihadis and colonizers, the horizontality of the desert should be preserved. Jihadis achieve this through the removal of vertical terrestrial idols, the

23 Negarestani, *Cyclonopedia*, **21.**

24 Negarestani, *Cyclonopedia*, 19; and Sepideh Karami, "Sludge: An Imagined World Beyond Development" C. Opera, A. Petti, M-L. Richards, T. Pinto, & R. Burchardt, eds. *Architectural Dissonance* (L'internationale Online), 168.

colonizers through the invention of pipelines, collapsed phallic idols. Pipelines are infrastructures that guarantee the flow of energy and capital by preventing encounters between oil and the earth. They prevent formations of sludge, mess, and dirt to instead "ease [the] narration" of colonialism, optimize profit, and deny the rights of Indigenous peoples and the other exploited human and nonhuman inhabitants of these ancient deserts.[24]

When oil is extracted and flows over the ground, the desert becomes

Oil pipes in the Azadegan oil field close to the border with Iraq. Copyright: AP, Vahid Salemi

directional. The direction always points toward the mirage. Pipes notate the desert; they create borders and politically sensitive zones. Sheena Wilson, Imre Szeman, and Adam Carlson write, "pipelines play an important role in making oil invisible, naturalizing its presence in our lives and hiding the environmental impacts of extraction far from the eyes of concerned publics."[25] Pipelines are the backstage of urbanization. Supported on metal stands, securing a minimal distance and detachment from the ground of the desert, the pipes transfer a profitable material across a non-profitable ground, detaching oil from what is presumed to be a dead ground.

Freddie Mason writes in his book *The Viscous: Slime, Stickiness, Fondling, Mixtures*, that "We live in a world where fluid substances are piped near seamlessly from elsewhere to here, from here elsewhere. The switch from solid to flowing was a switch that favored continuity over questioning, while also establishing an illusory material equivalent to the afterlife, a 'somewhere else' we never see, but live alongside."[26] Yet the constructed perfection of pipes fails from time to time. Leakage hinders the fluidity of capital, disturbs the calculation of oil profits, makes the joints in war machines squeak as they trundle over the desert. Oil drops down and infiltrates the porous surface of a desert thirsty for any liquid, filling its minuscule cavities. The failure of pipes creates areas of discolored sands, wet with infrastructural flaws resulting in the gradual formation of sludge. Sludge appears not only around the broken pipes but wherever oil escapes the petroleum infrastructure and meets the earth, the dust. As a result, sludge creates its own landscape, across which any move forward becomes impossible. Progress is slowed down. We are stuck in the sludge. Sludge is a metaphor for the flaws and failures of the modern project and the impossibility of moving beyond oil in a world vastly dependent on the petroleum industry. In sludge, control is absent and failure present. The absence is represented by the dark stains sludge causes. Sludge devours the pride of modern knowledge, undoing the domination of modernity and its control over nature. Instead, sand and failure, embracing each other, becoming

25 Sheena Wilson, Imre Szeman, and Adam Carlson, "On Petrocultures: Or, Why We Need to Understand Oil to Understand Everything Else," in *Petrocultures: Oil, Politics, Culture*, **ed. Sheena Wilson, Adam Carlson, and Imre Szeman, 3–20 (Montreal: McGill-Queen's University Press, 2017), 8.**

26 Freddie Mason, *The Viscous: Slime, Stickiness, Fondling, Mixtures* **(Santa Barbara, CA: Punctum Books, 2020), 127–28.**

a new material. Sludge, by exposing the inefficiency of the smoothness of oil infrastructures, becomes a ground for countercolonizing concepts.

Against the Sandstorm, beyond the Mirage, Emerging Out of the Sludge

27 Carlson, "The Humanity of Infrastructure."

As Carlson writes, "Each culture was initially defined by a river which provided transportation, irrigation, and fertility."[27] An infrastructure that supported life and human culture. With the discovery of oil and the commencement of modernity, cultures had to respond and adapt to petroculture. Different kinds of infrastructures supported petroculture and its appetite for speed, consumerism, and individualistic ways of life. Dead rivers, lakes, and marshlands, polluted air—a devastated earth—became the home for petroculture. The landscape which supported petrocultural infrastructures, was itself left unsupported. Wilson, Szeman, and Carlson write:

28 Wilson, Szeman, and Carlson, "On Petrocultures," 3.

> Oil transformed life over the century in which we came to depend on it; the looming threat of its absence from our lives means that it will transform us again, from people who are at home and comfortable in the petrocultures we have devised for ourselves to people who will have to shape ourselves to fit contexts and landscapes we can barely imagine, even if we need to do so—and quickly.[28]

29 Sepideh Karami, "Act 01: Love! On Political Love vs. Institutional Loyalty," in ***Performing Institutions*****, ed. Anja Mølle Lindelof and Shauna Janssen (Bristol: Intellect, forthcoming).**

To envisage a future in the absence of oil, current approaches to caring for environments will not be enough. Caring for the earth, where for creates a distance between human agency and the environment, is nowhere even close to achieving the change that will be required so that the earth might recover. Instead, what is required is the political act of love—an act that "leaves the lover in a vulnerable position, exposed to risk of falling, dismissal and exile."[29] To build the way toward a post-oil future, a different kind of infrastructure is required that might need to make use of the numerous failures the oil industry has left in place, including the failures of petroculture itself. In this situation of omnipresent failure, mass migration due to climate change, and the crisis of capitalism, "failure is a raw, limitless field of value," and engaging with that failure could unveil a new global geography of value.[30] Sandstorms, mirage, and sludge could be the grounds for such failure, grounds in which the failures have created a critical situation and where urgent and radical acts need to be taken.

The events that took place in the dry bed of the Zayandeh Rud mobilized failure to shape a political configuration for post-oil cultures. Different from mainstream environmental activism, which too often takes place as a form of political representation at a distance from sites of catastrophe and crisis, the protest march and sit-in on the waterless Zayandeh Rud was a direct fight by those most affected by the environmental crisis. They claimed space exactly on a site damaged by the violence of exploitative agendas that have devastated environments worldwide. The presence of farmers in the absence of water, farmers whose agency is strong in this narrative of dissent, turns the dead river into an infrastructure of dissent. While the protestors' first demand was the restoration of water to the Zayandeh Rud (to help irrigate farmlands and to stop the overuse of underground water resources that has resulted in land subsidence), the protest eventually extended its demands to more fundamental political questions concerning injustice and oppression. In much this way, the fight for the climate crisis becomes intersectional. As I write this conclusion, the protest is being violently oppressed. In the fight against the authorities, many protestors have lost their eyes. In video footage and photographs, protesters are shown with eye pads on one or both eyes, exposing what it might take to protect the environment through the political act of love. Such images will make us wonder whether, to construct cultures that deviate from petroculture, we are ready to sacrifice what petroleum has brought us. Are we ready to expose ourselves to the threats of the political act of love? The love for rivers, land, and life?

30 Keller Easterling, "A Losing Game: Harnessing Failure," *Architectural Review*, **February 4, 2019, https://www.architectural-review.com/essays/a-losing-game-harnessing-failure.**

1. Feed Tube

2. Fan Engine

3. Output Nozzle

4. Steel Fan-blade

5. Safety Cage

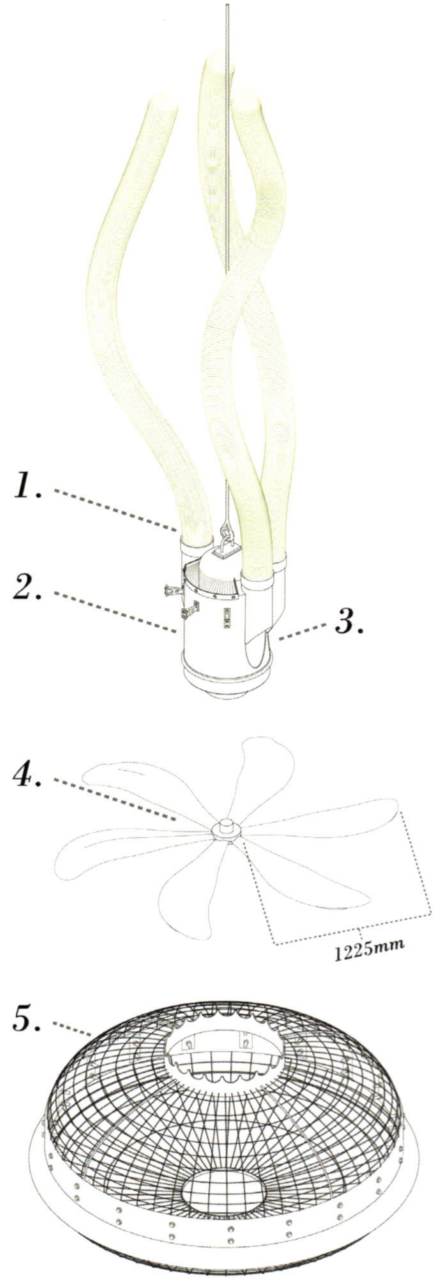

The Nonhuman Embassy: Representational Critters and Calamitous Diplomacy

Erik Lokrantz

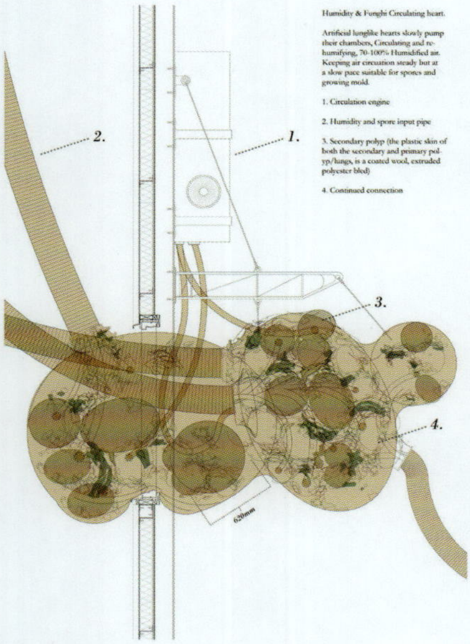

The "Nonhuman Embassy" explores relations between systems of governance, land exploitation, construction, expansion, and what these systems conceptually situate as the "Other," identified as their antithesis, "Nature." I question the naming of this polarizing view as "anthropocentric," because it does not so much center humans as advance a myth of history based on colonial and extractivist fantasies, which build the base of institutions and their political and material power.

This speculative project critiques an area of urban expansion in Veddesta, Stockholm, an area that does not fit neatly into a Nature vs. Anthropos framework. In dialogue with my colleagues, and by drawing on theory that was introduced to me by my peers and teachers, I sought a foundation in Félix Guattari's complex notion of the three ecologies, and Donna Haraway's concept of SF (science fiction, science fabulation, string figures).

I also found inspiration in Rania Ghosn and El Hadi Jazairy's *Geostories*.[1]

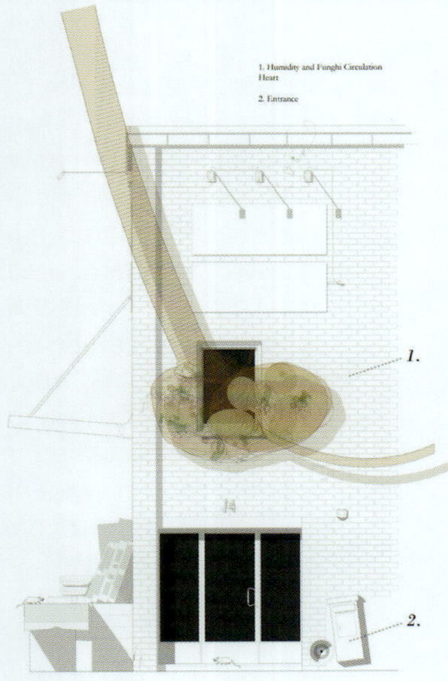

1 Donna Haraway, *Staying with the Trouble: Making Kin in the Chthulucene* **(Durham, NC: Duke University Press, 2016); Félix Guattari,** *The Three Ecologies* **(London: Athlone Press, 2000); and Rania Ghosn and El Hadi Jazairy,** *Geostories: Another Architecture for the Environment* **(Barcelona: Actar, 2018).**

In search of a way to critique from a different point of view, I looked not to humans but to the unwanted tenants who are often our closest neighbors: rats, cockroaches, mold, and other unwanted guests. These nonhuman populations are inextricably involved in human-centered environs and can be found living inside walls, between floorboards, and in other negative spaces. I wanted to invert the human-to-nonhuman material and spatial relationship. expensive housing units. The industrial relics of the past must be removed, and this prompts a I found help in a book on mold prevention and several online resources on "pest control." I deconstructed this source material to establish helpful tips on how to best cater to nonhuman inhabitants, whom I resituated as new protagonists.

Playing with the idea of how a nation-state is organized according to its own internal methods of governance, I gave these multiplicitous critters legal sovereignty and established an embassy for them. An embassy is an extraterritorial space; it demarcates a national boundary within another national boundary, or, in this case, within a species boundary. As a spatial infrastructure it entails ownership and a location for political representation. An embassy is separate, in a legal and abstract sense, but still connected and served by the surrounding host state's infrastructural systems. The members of the nonhuman embassy would aim to secure societal and economic equity with humans. The project critiques Capital's tendency to internalize the environmental and other calamities it has created by controlling discourse. The project is a parody, but a genuinely curious and speculative parody that I have explored in good faith.

Donna Haraway argues, "Science fiction, is storytelling and fact telling, it is the patterning of possible worlds and possible times, material-semiotic worlds, gone, here, and yet to come."[2] Amid the Anthropocene, the Capitalocene, before the impending disaster that will follow the slow, cataclysmic deterioration of climate conditions, we face what Haraway calls "times of multi species, including human, urgency: of great mass death and extinction."[3] An urgent problem for us all. The following is a fictional narrative, a geostory.

In the distant future, once we have discovered it is too late to avert the slow churn of the apocalypse, those in power may suddenly realize that the Anthropocene affects us all and that action must immediately be taken. The perpetual cycle of consumption and production has finally become untenable in this possible future, and yet many paths toward sustainability are still deemed unthinkable, especially for those keen to maintain the status quo of an existing system that supports human exceptionalism. An attempt to address species extinction and climate crisis is formulated based on age-old notions of diplomacy that assume the maintenance of human hegemony. The aim is to find a means of communication between the human and nonhuman cohabitants of the planet Earth. Specifically, the nonhuman is to be addressed by diplomacy, not preservation. The Swedish State in collaboration with the United Nations and the Järfälla municipality decide to enact a construction plan for a nonhuman embassy under the guise of a housing construction project in Veddesta. The nonhuman embassy is to be hidden in plain sight, disguised as yet another outer suburban housing project. In this scenario the perpetuation of an existing system of human governance is paradoxically deemed necessary to maintain sufficient power to enact change. The nonhuman embassy must be hidden, because acknowledging the need for compromise is itself seen as a threat to the stable perpetuation of the human system. Concessions must be made, and these are concealed within the facades of what appears to be yet further human expansion. Hidden within, the interior atmosphere and climatic conditions of the building are modified to accommodate the nonhuman critters that already exist in proximity to humans. The hope is that in time the representational spaces of a sovereign embassy will enable the establishment of better diplomatic relations.

---

2 Donna Haraway, "Tentacular Thinking: Anthropocene, Capitalocene, Chthulucene," *e-flux Journal*, **no. 75 (September 2016), https://www.e-flux.com/journal/75/67125/tentacular-thinking-anthropocene-capitalocene-chthulucene/.**

3 Haraway, "Tentacular Thinking."

C

ADAYW
ITHA
DUCK

Chapter 8
A Day with a Duck

Helen Stratford

Plate W. *Presiding Spirit of the Duck*

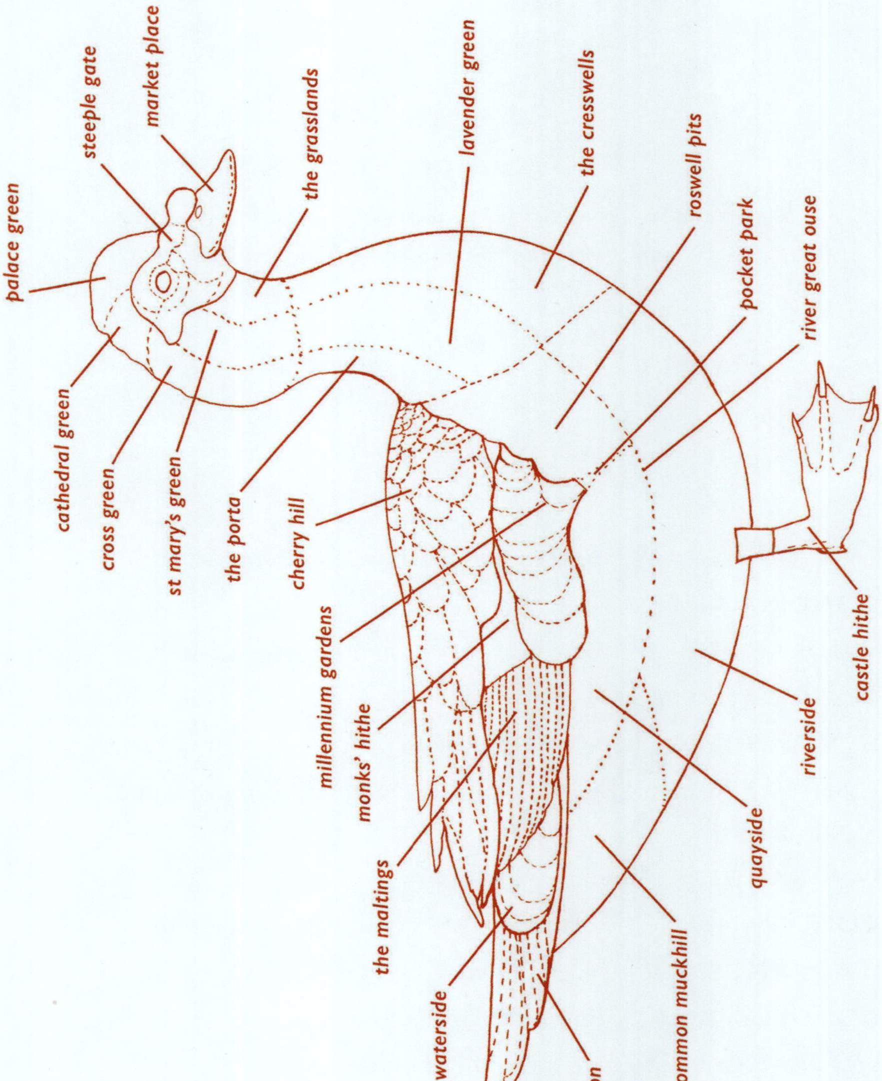

IN THE MARKET PLACE

VOICES

Town Ranger, Second Rambler, Muscovy Duck, Man Shopping, Woman Shopping, Machine Voice, First Rambler

TIME

Tuesday morning

TOWN RANGER: Welcome to the Heritage Zone sir.

SECOND RAMBLER: ...

TOWN RANGER: Welcome sir. This is the Heritage Zone.

SECOND RAMBLER: Oh, me?

TOWN RANGER: I hope you enjoy your visit.

SECOND RAMBLER: I'm not... not really a visit, I'm just going through the –

TOWN RANGER: Animals are not permitted, sir.

SECOND RAMBLER: What animals? That? That's not mine.

TOWN RANGER: It is following you, sir.

SECOND RAMBLER: How's it following me? I'm behind it!

TOWN RANGER: You are moving in tandem.

SECOND RAMBLER: Well, I've always found that story intriguing, about the duck that makes the journey every day, no, every market day –

TOWN RANGER: Yes sir, the Historic Creel Market does take place today. You can visit the market over here.

SECOND RAMBLER: – so when we saw this one pit-patting along, I thought 'Great, let's follow'.

TOWN RANGER: By 'we' you mean yourself and the animal, sir?

SECOND RAMBLER: I just said, we're not together.

TOWN RANGER: Control tells me that you accompanied the animal from Riverside, up Forehill, into the Market Place. You both registered the brass pavement inlay indicating the Heritage Zone and you continued regardless.

SECOND RAMBLER: Yeah, that was funny. It went along and stepped on each of those brass bumps. Maybe they feel nice underfoot.

TOWN RANGER: And I have observed the small encouraging noises you make to it.

SECOND RAMBLER: Did I?

TOWN RANGER: The point of the Zone is to return the town to what it should be. And loose animals are not appropriate.

SECOND RAMBLER: OK...?

TOWN RANGER: I have to log your liaison with the animal.

SECOND RAMBLER: OK. Good. You do that. I'm going to carry on with my day... meeting someone... and... normal stuff.

TOWN RANGER: I'm afraid that your actions constitute an infringement of the zonal planning regulations and so must be logged as such.

SECOND RAMBLER: Oh come on!

MUSCOVY DUCK: We question your Cartesian notion of space as an abstract entity that can be ordered in every detail.

SECOND RAMBLER: *(To Muscovy Duck)* No we don't. We're not a we.

TOWN RANGER: Sir, that is absurd.

MUSCOVY DUCK: We are not absurd. Neither are we intrinsically sad, although some assume our bright appearance and slow deliberate movement are clownish. We are simply different from you.

TOWN RANGER: Sir, it is absurd to allow the animal any say in the matter.

SECOND RAMBLER: Will you let up about me and it. I'm not allowing it anything. Neither are you. It's wild. It's doing what it's doing.

Plate S. *Duck Deterrent Hard Landscaping Features*

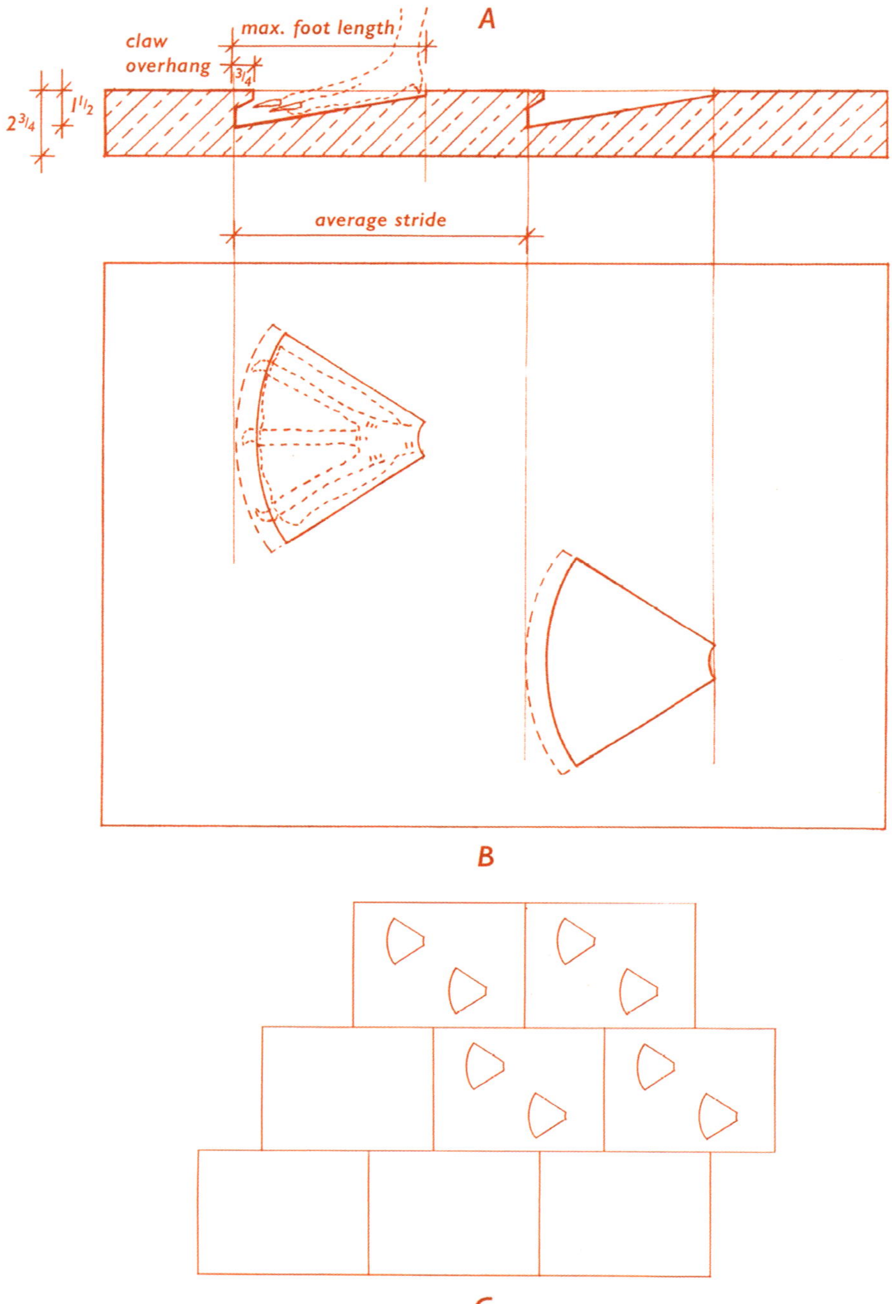

A. *Duck deterrent flag (section);* **B.** *Single flag (plan);*
C. *Optimal layout (longitudinal stretcher bond).*

TOWN RANGER: That is your assessment and I just need you to put that on record.

SECOND RAMBLER: What record?

MUSCOVY DUCK: We can no longer do what we do. The existing otherness-in-connection along the riverbank has been broken by the violent desire to order every aspect of the built environment.

MAN SHOPPING: *(To Town Ranger)* Spot on, young fella. Keep a close eye on them. A very close eye.

WOMAN SHOPPING: When they start coming out with that kind of language.

MAN SHOPPING: Time was, you could sit on the riverbank of an evening with a glass of wine. Now it's a pit.

TOWN RANGER: Thank you sir. I will feed that back to my manager. Now I just need to take down some details from this gentleman.

WOMAN SHOPPING: That kind of smart-arse language, it shows they're getting cocky.

TOWN RANGER: *(To Second Rambler)* Sir, please look directly into the blue circle on the screen and respond to each question. It's OK sir, I'll keep hold of the device.

WOMAN SHOPPING: They should all be shot.

MAN SHOPPING: I don't think we quite… It is a scandal though. The council, it just doesn't...

MACHINE VOICE: Hi. Welcome to the BID infringement logging system. When the circle turns pale, please state your full name.

SECOND RAMBLER: I'm just just walking, just walking away.

WOMAN SHOPPING: We think they should all be shot.

MACHINE VOICE: I'm sorry, I didn't catch that. Please say your name again.

TOWN RANGER: A failure to register a Heritage Zone infringement is not a criminal offence, but –

MAN SHOPPING: *(To Town Ranger)* Elvis told us all about it. People invite them to make these secret little nests in gardens.

TOWN RANGER: *(To Second Rambler)* – it will mean you receive a time-limited ban from the Heritage Zone, from the sponsoring BID and from all participating businesses.

WOMAN SHOPPING: We should be protected from that sort of intrusion. It's our space.

SECOND RAMBLER: *(To Town Ranger)* What bid?

TOWN RANGER: Business Improvement District sir. I have logged your ban and it takes effect immediately.

MAN SHOPPING: But 'oh no', you can't touch them. There's far too much protection. Well we want our city back.

WOMAN SHOPPING: Even in the countryside they don't belong. They're an invading species.

MAN SHOPPING: We want our city back.

WOMAN SHOPPING: Our city! Feed THAT back to your manager.

MAN SHOPPING: *(To Second Rambler)* Listen bud, you and this duck've done something and you need to make it right.

SECOND RAMBLER: Let, let go. Let go! Get off my –

MAN SHOPPING: You can't just walk off.

TOWN RANGER: *(To Man Shopping)* Thank you sir. I've logged this gentleman's actions. Your assistance won't be necessary.

FIRST RAMBLER: *(Stepping out of a pub. To Second Rambler)* What kept you? Oh! That duck bothering you again?

SECOND RAMBLER: Hiya. Yeah, I got a bit held up by, err –

FIRST RAMBLER: Hey look down there. What are those Hoo-Rays in a flap about? Scuffed their deck shoes or something?

SECOND RAMBLER: They're not Hoo-Rays.

FIRST RAMBLER: Let's go and watch.

SECOND RAMBLER: They're, well, I sort of know them. The fellah, he's alright. Does a lot for the Millennium Gardens.

FIRST RAMBLER: Now he's using foul and abusive language and pointing at us. The Strange Ranger is trying to calm them down with some leaflets and a creepy smile. Does his tabard really say 'HERE TO HELP'? Fucksake!

SECOND RAMBLER: I need to keep my distance.

FIRST RAMBLER: Flippin' 'eck. Look at that street cleaners' van. Bombing up the hill. Everyone's getting stuck in.

SECOND RAMBLER: Hang on, where's the duck?

Helen Stratford, *A Day with a Duck* **(2012). A day spent following a Muscovy duck marked the beginning of the residency in the city of Ely. Photograph: Nick Cheek.**

> The masterplan's top-down vision for the city primarily gravitated toward economic ranking—with clearly delineated divisions, hierarchies, and categories of place—recast through such neoliberal phrases as "urban residential extension," "leisure village," and "riverside quarter."

The Day of the Duck artist's book evolved out of a six-month self-initiated artist residency that gravitated around a small patch of council-managed ground by the River Great Ouse in the city of Ely, Cambridgeshire, in the United Kingdom.[1] In recent years this "public space" had become contested due to its occupation by a rare population of Muscovy ducks, making human access problematic. As a worker in Ely, I observed how the presence of these "wild animals" immediately challenged the boundaries of the space. The ducks' interruption of everyday behavior through actions considered antisocial and anarchic—stopping traffic, eating people's sandwiches, public defecation—threw into sharp relief the anthropocentric focus by which cities are conventionally performed and envisaged. Further, the ducks made visible "intra-actions" of people, place, and practice that together combine or "congeal" to produce specific "infrastructures."[2] A day spent following a duck marked the beginning of the residency, which also included conversations with residents, workers, and tourists, a presentation in the nearby Babylon Gallery, and a series of participatory events across the city.

At the time of the residency, Ely was undergoing consultation on a previously stalled masterplan process.[3] In its organization of prearranged sets of questions delivered via workshops and Post-it Note sessions with invited members of the local community, the consultation process (in which I took part as both local resident and architect) echoed conventional architectural processes. Further, the masterplan's top-down vision for the city primarily gravitated toward economic ranking—with clearly delineated divisions, hierarchies, and categories of place—recast through such neoliberal phrases as "urban residen-

1 *The Day of the Duck* **was coauthored by Helen Stratford and Lawrence Bradby. See Helen Stratford and Lawrence Bradby,** *The Day of the Duck* **(London: Marmalade Publishers of Visual Theory, 2018).**

2 **See Karen Barad, "Posthumanist Performativity: Toward an Understanding of How Matter Comes to Matter,"** *Signs: Journal of Women in Culture and Society* **28, no. 3 (2003): 801–31, DOI: 10.1086/345321; and AbdouMaliq Simone, "Ritornello: 'People as Infrastructure,'"** *Urban Geography*, **March 5, 2021**

tial extension," "leisure village," and "riverside quarter."[4] In this context, further informed by the increasing political polarization in the United Kingdom, the residency and the book built on and critiqued the city's conservative nature, which seemed to gain in intensity during the project.[5] The residency and book raised questions that responded to the relationship between the masterplan (as regulatory or governmental top-down process), the ducks (as anarchy, nature, and chaos), and the degree to which the city's inhabitants reproduced or challenged the particular urban visions that these positions reinforced.

Sanitized Visions of the City

In Ely, assumptions of urban order—and associated fears of disorder—are vividly expressed in residents' visceral revulsion to the ducks and their occupation and degradation of what the residents believed should be a place to sit "with a glass of wine."[6] In this context, the ducks challenge projected desires for both order and commodification. Further, even comments in favor of the muck and grime of a working and productive river—"If you live in the countryside, you should expect a bit of shit"—express and reproduce the boundaries between order and disorder, urban and rural.[7] Here, the attraction to "purity" as "a mark of 'civilized' society," which for many urban thinkers still underpins much of contemporary urban planning, becomes translated into contemporaneous public spaces that should not include "messy" animals or deviant human actions if they are to be clean and fit solely for a particular type of use.[8]
The Day of the Duck elaborates on observations regarding this "noir" side of architectural visions.[9] The extract "In the Market Place" that opened this chapter presents an imagined dialogue between town ranger, ramblers, Muscovy duck, and shoppers alongside an associated diagram of *Plate S. Duck Deterrent Hard Landscaping Features*. In this vision, exclusionary practices are defined by the physical designation of specific zones for specific city denizens. These are laid out in specially designed landscaping features that prevent the ducks from entering the "Heritage Zone," reinforced by patrolling town rangers with

3 "Possible Legal Flaws Led to Masterplan Being Suspended," *Ely Standard*, **May 21, 2008, https://www.elystandard.co.uk/news/possible-legal-flaws-led-to-masterplan-being-suspended-7756928.**

4 East Cambridgeshire District Council, *Ely Masterplan: A Framework for the Future Development of the City of Ely* **(Ely, UK: East Cambridgeshire District Council, 2010), 10, https://www.eastcambs.gov.uk/sites/default/files/FINAL%20Ely%20Masterplan.pdf.**

5 This was reflected in the growing popularity of the United Kingdom Independence Party in the city, manifest in banners on the marina, seemingly supported by the Union Jack–themed flower basket displays installed in the city to mark the Diamond Jubilee year, and witnessed firsthand in certain discussions around what was acceptable practice in the city (and by whom).

6 Interview with Ely residents, 2012.

7 Interview with Ely residents, 2012.

"HERE TO HELP" tabards who record any breaches on a Business Improvement District infringement logging system.

Alongside this fictional extrapolation of top-down city visions, *The Day of the Duck* also analyses and proposes how prejudices, and ultimately public spaces themselves, are already (re)produced through what urbanist AbdouMaliq Simone refers to as "social infrastructures"—"intricate choreographies" of everyday micro-actions and complex spatial habits that offer a "continuous recombination of people's experiences and practices."[10] These include a "revulsion" to a "violation of boundaries" manifest in "Plate N. Cleaning and Gleaning: Accompanying Equipment," which depicts the tools required to implement the council's endless three-day duck defecation cleaning routine.[11] Simultaneously, "Plate I. Grass Cutting Hierarchies" maps how specific hierarchies are reproduced through a "meshing" of the "human and the technical" in the maintenance of particular public spaces over others.[12] Furthermore, other diagrams in the book, including "Plate O. Public Bench Etiquette" and "Plate B. Migration Paths: Accompanying Items," refer to conversations regarding the removal of a rough sleeper's informal occupation of public gardens and ongoing discussions of the presence of migrant workers in the city.[13] Here, going beyond a critique of the spatial manifestations of city visions, these diagrams and their accompanying dialogues express how ideas surrounding unwanted actions, matter, and inhabitations are all too easily extended toward certain people(s) and publics.

Plate B. *Migration Paths: Accompanying Items*

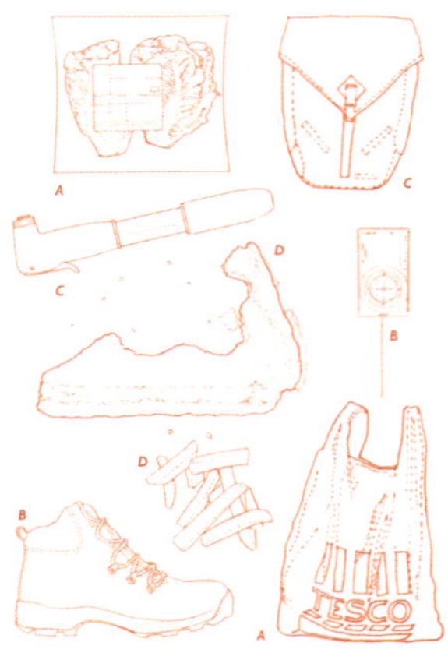

A. Field based operators; B. Ramblers Association East Cambs; C. Cyclist: National Cycle Route No. 11; D. Muscovy duck.

Humor and Parody as Critical Method

The Day of the Duck can be read as a simple tale about ducks, yet it is a "duck noir" tale of a talking duck looking for its lost comrades. What might appear at first glance to be an ethnographical study of an English city is in fact a highly crafted fiction.

8 David Pinder, *Visions of the City* **(Edinburgh: Edinburgh University Press, 2005), 71. With reference to feminist philosophers and writers, including Rosi Braidotti, Mary Douglas, and Julia Kristeva, Pinder argues that modernist claims of "purity" as "a mark of a 'civilised' society" were in fact founded on deep fears (71). See also Pascal Gielen, "Performing the Common City: On the Crossroads of Art, Politics and Public Life," in** *Interrupting the City: Artistic Constitutions of the Public Sphere***, ed. Sander Bax, Pascal Gielen, and Bram Ieven, 273–97 (Amsterdam: Valiz, 2015), 286–87.**

9 Pinder highlights the "'noir' side" of utopian visions in twentieth-century Western Europe. He argues that these visions presided over "forms of repression and discrimination through modes of regulation centred around bodies, spaces and social order." Pinder, *Visions of the City***, 248. According to Pinder (57–65), these "modes of regulation" underpinned the "Modernist calls to order" of Le Corbusier and are expressed in the themes of "clean up, re-order, purify."**

Humor and, in particular, parody have a long genealogy in feminist critical practice as a tool to make visible and challenge social norms through their "deviant" disruption.[14] From a different direction, rewriting the limits between "human" and "animal" is also central to much feminist reevaluation of the human in relation to the non-human.[15] The parodic qualities of the book's design and narrative—its red, black, and white color scheme based on that of the ducks, its ornithological/orthographic drawings that take the notion of "non-contaminating" uses expressed by conventional city visions and apparatuses to an absurd intensity challenge this way of conceptualizing urban spaces.[16] This "stretching" of a "dominant logic" to a point at which it becomes "irrational" causes a rupture that goes beyond its referent, "flagging up" key attributes of the "original" in exposing its myth.[17]

Moreover, The *Day of the Duck's* attempt to write "from the place of the animal" aligns with an absurdist tradition, taking part in "those contradictory acts of establishing and then undercutting prevailing values and conventions in order to provoke a questioning."[18] Based in the contextual thoroughness of the on-site research, inflected through my background in architecture and coauthor

10 Simone, "Ritornello," 1.

11 Pinder observes, "In Le Corbusier's utopian [urban] spaces there is a revulsion to interminglings, ambivalences, violation of boundaries; to things that stagnate or rot, where decay presages an inversion of hierarchies; to the mass, the swarm, the 'primitive' cell; and to undifferentiated matter or unchannelled flow that threaten to swamp, sweep away, or bring about the dissolution of the individual." Pinder, *Visions of the City*, 103. Alongside the cleaning equipment associated with the messy job of

Plate I. *Grass Cutting Hierarchies*

42 Day; 28 Day; 21 Day; 14 Day; 7 Day; Never.

Plate N. *Cleaning and Gleaning: Accompanying Equipment*

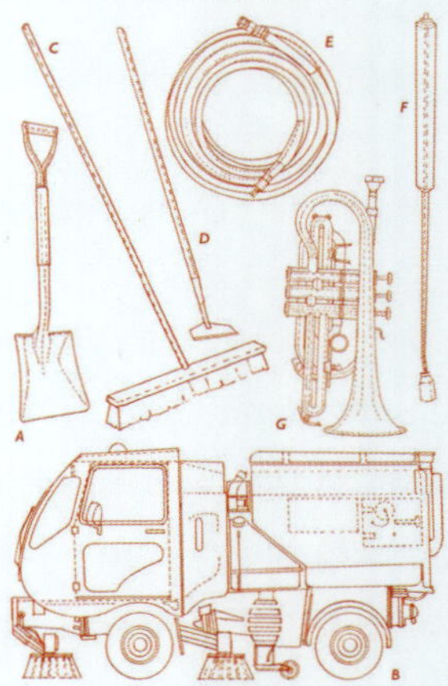

A. Surface gleaning; B. Hover; C. Edge gleaning; D. Surface strike; E. Surface skim; F. Surface probe; G. Note.

Plate O. *Public Bench Etiquette*

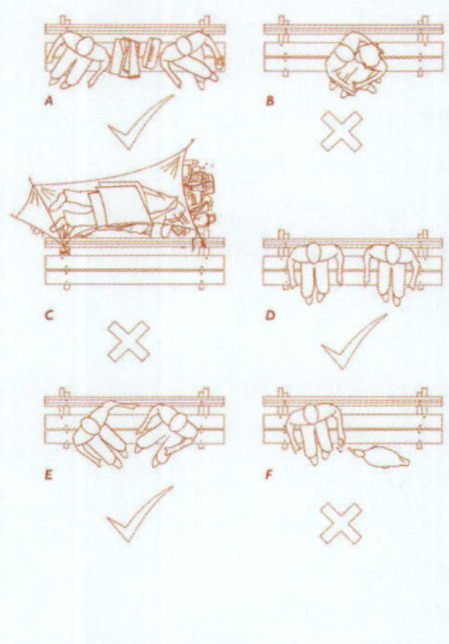

A. Co-existing; B. Cavorting; C. Constructing; D. Consorting; E. Conversing; F. Co-habiting.

Lawrence Bradby's background in poetry and performance, the book exposes the "structures of meaning" by which public spaces are understood in order to question them. It thereby generates fictional and comedic places that shed light on everyday conditions that are already absurd. The book is an account of how, against the duck, the citizens rise up, refusing to listen to those that challenge their way of life.[19] In this way, it aligns with the all-too-frequent result of public consultation in its removal or silencing of certain voices that disturb particular ideals regarding city life and associated public spaces.[20] Yet, in this context, the figure of the Muscovy duck is a paradox. Depending on how the city is envisaged, the ducks waddle between a position of attraction and repulsion, both city nuisance and tourist attraction. *The Day of the Duck* picks up on this position of the duck as meeting point of opposing cultures and emblem of simmering local politics. At the same time, the duck becomes a motif for infrastructural love through "otherness-in-connection," offering insights into wider paradoxical relationships to nature and culture, both local and global.[21]

The figure of the Muscovy duck is a paradox. Depending on how the city is envisaged, the ducks waddle between a position of attraction and repulsion, both city nuisance and tourist attraction.

Public Space as Ongoing Naturecultures

Speculation on the Muscovy ducks' origins in the city alongside their undulating over- and underpopulation is inextricably bound up with their human counterparts. Whether they arrived with the monks in the abbey, as one person told me, or escaped from a pen along the riverside; whether their adoption of this particular public space as "habitat" was initially supported by city council–led initiatives or was subject to termination by further council actions, duck

removing duck feces, the cleaner's weekly rehearsals in the local brass band are incorporated in the depiction of a cornet, recognizing personal routines that play a part in the performance of public space.

12 Simone, "Ritornello," 6. This position already starts to make visible and undermine what Simone calls "the tyranny of imposing frozen, uni-dimensional categories on messy, evolving social life" (2).

13 In "Plate O. Public Bench Etiquette," the naming of the sitting positions refers to architectural/sociological studies into place occupation that attempt to derive a somehow universal behavior in particular spaces that might inform their design. See Bryan Lawson, *How Designers Think* **(Oxford, UK: Butterfield Architecture, 2009).**

14 See Judith Butler, *Bodies That Matter: On the Discursive Limits of "Sex"* **(London: Routledge, 1993); and Judith Butler,** *Gender Trouble: Feminism and*

and human lives have developed in a symbiotic and infrastructural relationship.[22] Simultaneously, the space they occupy is subject to visions of "landscape" for human contemplation and leisure use. In these commodified visions of "nature" the ducks feature as managed wildlife, a paradoxical tourist attraction whose bodily excretions and "out of place matter" situate them within a constant struggle with "culture."[23] In their hindrance of the reception of this idealized environment, the ducks demonstrate conflicting ideas of what constitutes sufficient infrastructural support systems and in whose interests they are implemented—a city with ducks or without but "with a glass of wine."[24]
For feminist philosopher and physicist Karen Barad, "The belief that nature is mute and immutable … is a reinscription of the nature/culture dualism that feminists have actively contested."[25] In relation to nature, culture, and the non-human, feminist architect Karin Reisinger, in her study of "abandoned architectures," similarly argues for an active repositioning of "nature."[26]
Reisinger's queer and ecological analysis of the incremental reclamation by wild animals of institutional buildings, situated within preservation and postindustrial sites, argues that "human-made architectures" are "radically altered by non-human uses and adaptations."[27] For Reisinger, while conventional architectural boundaries are built to keep unwanted incursions of weather and wildlife out, through these reclamations "nature" alters "architecture" into many "architectures" for humans and non-humans together.[28]
In "real-life" encounters experienced during the residency and narrated in *The Day of the Duck*, the threat of the incremental reclamation of public space by large waterfowl, while welcomed by some, is heavily resisted by others. But the specific nature of whether the Muscovy ducks should be permitted to reside in the city of Ely is not the main issue at stake here. Instead, the book explores what their presence and participation does to public spaces, both in their current form and in relation to future visions. The ducks' disregard or, as one resident put it, "disdain" for humans, brings into focus a different city.[29]
Reisinger observes how feminist and companion species philosopher Donna Haraway uses the notion of "naturecultural assemblages" to critique Western

the Subversion of Identity, **10th anniversary edition (London: Taylor and Francis, 2014).**

15 reevaluation of the human in relation to the non-human. The parodic qualities of the book's design and narrative—its red, black, and white color scheme based on that of the ducks, its ornithological/orthographic drawings that take the notion of "noncontaminating" uses expressed by conventional city visions and apparatuses to an absurd intensity—challenge this way of conceptualizing urban spaces. This "stretching" of a "dominant logic" to a point at ; and Donna Haraway, *The Companion Species Manifesto: Dogs, People, and Significant Otherness* **(Chicago: Prickly Paradigm Press, 2003). For Haraway, the use of fiction is a method by which to critique and reimagine another reality. Of her book** *Staying with the Trouble: Making Kin in the Chthulucene* **(Durham, NC: Duke University Press, 2016), Haraway herself has described how her addition of the term Chthulucene into the discussion**

accounts and binaries of nature/culture, human/non-human landscape.[30] For Haraway, in place of universalism and relativism, "subjects, objects, kinds, races, species, genres, and genders are the products of their relating."[31] In this context, landscape is not "natural" or "wild" but rather a marking of that relating. The ducks' expansive occupation of public space in Ely, extending into its city environs (including weekly trips by one city-center-trekking duck from the riverside to the market square), provides the perfect opportunity to rethink non-human relations to our humanly populated environments. What provokes endless human management and maintenance on the riverside is "nature's" ability; that is, its often successful "struggle" to thrive, its constant threatening to take over.[32] *The Day of the Duck* picks up on these tensions and conflicts to offer a heightened situation in which public space is reperformed and reclassified as a battleground. Struggles between nature/culture and human/non-human resonate throughout The Day of the Duck and hold relevance for and connections to how public spaces are performed. In the book the "duck-tective," in search of its missing comrades, creates, through modes of occupation and in points of relation with humans, a "social infrastructure" that throws into question the existing structures of public space.[33]

The specific nature of whether the Muscovy ducks should be permitted to reside in the city of Ely is not the main issue at stake here. Instead, the book explores what their presence and participation does to public spaces, both in their current form and in relation to future visions.

Rather than resolving into a potential solution the tensions that constitute public space—that is, building on the "touch of anarchy" created by the ducks—The *Day of the Duck* and the wider residency locate themselves at points of contestation or sites of struggle to articulate and take part in these "assem-

of Anthropocene and Capitalocene (among other cenes) was done "partly as a joke," poking fun at the "geeky words" that attempt to describe the current reality. See "Talk Donna Haraway and Rosi Braidotti March 25, 2017," YouTube video, 1:07:23, uploaded by Marcela Mendoza Taylor, September 20, 2017, https://www.youtube.com/watch?v=IXQTex0a-3dc.

16 Pinder notes that this method of conceptualization was "enshrined in documents such as the Athens Charter established by CIAM [International Congresses of Modern Architecture] in 1933." Pinder, Visions of the City, 104.

17 Malcolm Miles, *Limits to Culture: Urban Regeneration vs. Dissident Art* **(London: Pluto Press, 2015), 142; and Kate Kenny, "The Performative Surprise: Parody, Documentary and Critique,"** *Culture and Organization* **15, no. 2 (2009): 221–22,**

18 Simon Critchley, On Humour (London: Routledge, 2002), 35; and Celeste Derksen, "A Feminist Absurd: Margaret Hollingsworth's The

blages."[34] Here, like the conflicting nature of different attitudes toward the city, expressed through opinions on the future of the ducks, the book focuses on visualizing the different versions of reality and their social and spatial aspects "beyond" human control or agency, opening up questions around certain assumptions regarding its human-made architectures, architectural boundaries, and how its subjects are conventionally perceived. The expansion—or infrastructural love—offered by the book positions human and non-humans as "products of their relating."[35] Moreover, going beyond the idea of the "wild," it repositions the duck as an active participant in the social and material infrastructures of public space, thereby pointing toward more fundamental ecological, ethical, and political questions about how we relate to nature in the city.

The Day of the Duck picks up on these tensions and conflicts to offer a heightened situation in which public space is reperformed and reclassified as a battleground.

House That Jack Built," *Modern Drama* **45, no. 2 (Summer 2002): 209–30 (here 224). Referring to the work of Franz Kafka, Critchely argues that "the constant overstepping of the limit between the human and the animal" points out the paradox of the human by "recalling the benign humanity of the animal and the disturbing animality of the human." Critchley,** *On Humour*, **36.**

19 In this, the book references a tradition of absurdist writing found in the work of Kafka (e.g., Metamorphoses, to which Critchely refers) but also that of playwright Eugene Ionesco. See Franz Kafka, *The Metamorphosis*, **trans. Ian Johnston (Mansfield Center, CT: Martino Publishing, 2009); and Eugène Ionesco,** *Rhinoceros, and Other Plays* **(New York: Grove Press, 1994).**

20 See Jeremy Till, "The Architect and the Other," openDemocracy, June 25, 2006, https://www.opendemocracy.net/en/architecture_3680jsp/. See also Suzanne Hall, who observes "how regeneration agendas are subject to an assertive profes-

sionalization of planning processes." Suzanne Hall, *The Migrant's Paradox: Street Livelihoods and Marginal Citizenship in Britain* (Minneapolis: University of Minnesota Press, 2021), 120.

21 Haraway, *The Companion Species Manifesto*, 51, as referenced in Stratford and Bradby, The Day of the Duck, 95.

22 I was told by the local historian that in the 1970s the Muscovy ducks' arrival coincided with the construction of the pedestrian footpath along the river. During the residency I tracked remnants of council signs indicating specially designated feeding areas. I also learned of alleged council-led culling practices, including letters issued at the time of the "avian influenza" outbreak in 2006 with instructions to report duck harboring and the implementation of "egg oiling," alongside notices of a duck-feeding fine that appeared during the time of the residency. In this situation, the ducks' interaction with humans through direct contact and even policy enactment has created a specific topology of public space that continually shifted in relation to whom I spoke and when.

23 Mary Douglas, *Purity and Danger: An Analysis of Concept of Pollution and Taboo* (London: Routledge, 2005).

24 Recent signage installed by the duck area reads, "A Healthy Duck is a Happy Duck," with instructions to limit feeding of ducks. The images on the signs contain no Muscovy ducks.

25 For Barad, "nature is neither a passive surface awaiting the mark of culture nor the end product of cultural performances." Barad, "Posthumanist Performativity," 827.

26 Karin Reisinger, "Abandoned Architectures: Some Dirty Narratives," in *Architecture and Feminisms: Ecologies, Economies, Technologies*, ed. Hélène Frichot, Catharina Gabrielsson, and Helen Runting, 202–15 (London: Routledge, 2018).

27 Reisinger, "Abandoned Architectures," 205.

28 For Reisinger, "nature reclaims architecture and makes it complex and diverse architectures: architectures for humans and at the same time for non-humans." Reisinger, "Abandoned Architectures," 206.

29 Interview with Ely residents, 2012.

30 Reisinger, "Abandoned Architectures," 202. See also Haraway, Staying with the Trouble.

31 Haraway, *The Companion Species Manifesto*, 7. Haraway's *Companion Species Manifesto* is a methodological critique of biological and cultural determinism and the positioning of bodies, both human and non-human, that their reductive categories imply. For Haraway, both "are instances of misplaced concreteness—i.e., the mistake of, first, taking provisional and local category abstractions like 'nature' and 'culture' for the world and, second, mistaking potent consequences to be pre-existing foundations" (6).

32 This was eventually translated into a mown lawn, benches, and a paved area—the "props" of humanly occupied public space.

33 Simone, "Ritornello"; and AbdouMaliq Simone, "People as Infrastructure: Intersecting Fragments in Johannesburg," Public Culture 16, no. 3 (2004): 407–29,

34 Hilary Gresty, "Helen Stratford: A Day with a Duck," a-n The Artists Information Company, November 1, 2012, https://www.a-n.co.uk/reviews/helen-stratford-a-day-with-a-duck/. For many theorists and philosophers this constant struggle of dominant visions to assert authority and control marks the specific character of public space where democratic possibilities lie. See Teresa Hoskyns, *The Empty Place: Democracy and Public Space* (London: Routledge, 2013); Henri Lefebvre, *Writings on Cities* (Oxford: Blackwell, 1996); Doreen Massey, *For Space* (London: SAGE Publications Ltd, 2005); Doina Petrescu, "How to Make a Community as Well as the Space for It," *Re-Public: Re-imagining Democracy*, 2007, http://seminaire.samizdat.net/IMG/pdf/Doina_Petrescu_.pdf; Richard Sennet, *The Fall of Public Man* (London: Penguin Books, 1978); and Edward W. Soja, "The Socio-Spatial Dialectic," *Annals of the Association of American Geographers*, 70.2 (1980), 207–25 among others. Further, the ongoing constitution of public space, beings, and nature found in Braidotti, Haraway, and Massey is also echoed in Pinder's critique of utopian visions. According to Pinder, the "purist" utopian visions were marked by "never-ending struggles"; that is, they were never fully able to realize their totality. Pinder, *Visions of the City*, 248. Pinder also refers to Lefebvre's claims to the impossibility of "existing social relations being adhered to indefinitely." Pinder, *Visions of the City*, 246, quoting Henri Lefebvre, *The Survival of Capitalism*, trans. by Frank Bryant (London: Allison and Busby, 1976), 36. Further, for curator Pascal Gielen and colleagues, if artistic interventions are to participate in the "reconstitution of that public sphere," they must take part in this "struggle" between "economic, social and political forces" in order to "open up to new, divergent ideas and actions." Bax, Gielen, and Ieven, *Interrupting the City*, 16.

35 Haraway, *The Companion Species Manifesto*, 7.

Plate R. *Weed Removal / Identification of Anomalous Materials*

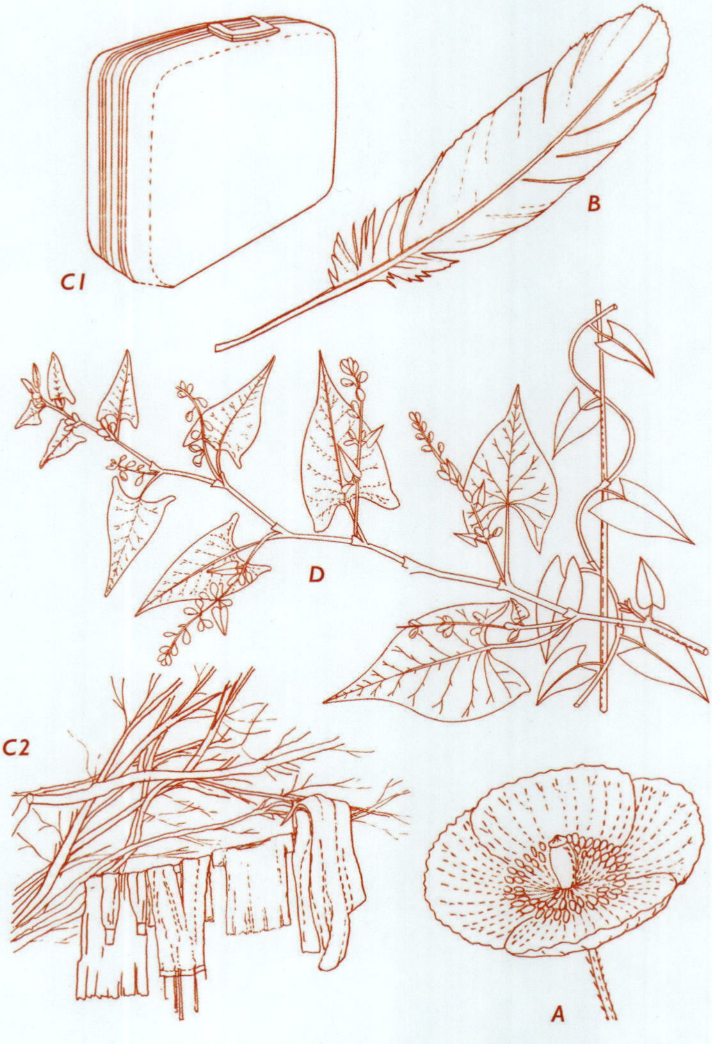

A. *Papaver dubium L;* **B.** *Muscovy duck tail feather;*
C1. & C2. *Personal items in sensory garden;* **D.** Common *bindweed.*

The Cleaning Pigeons

Marie Le Rouzic

"The Cleaning Pigeons" is a project that studies the power relations between humans, non-humans, and nature through an exploration of dirty matter. David Gissen's concept of "subnatures" framed my investigation.[1] Dirt, debris, trash—they all represent the products of human society, usually seen as waste and symbols of malpractice or desertion. In his essay "The Ugly," Mark Cousins quotes Mary Douglas's definition of dirt as "matter out of place," matter that possesses a spatial power of contamination.[2] Dirtiness is seen as threatening. The results of this include a compulsive need to keep what is perceived as hostile matter at a distance, mainly through the process of cleaning. However, Cousins writes about "the hopelessness of the task of cleaning" and speculates about the inevitability of dirt.[3] Dirtiness will always be there, surrounding us, invading our space. Trying to push it away thus seems pointless. This led me to question what would happen if we decided to embrace dirtiness. What if we attempted to understand temporality, aging, and natural evolution in the built environment? Karin Reisinger borrows Tara Tabassi's term "dirty resilience" to promote an architecture that lives and mutates alongside its environmental context and sometimes escapes

1 David Gissen, *Subnature: Architecture's Other Environments* (New York: Princeton Architectural Press, 2009).

2 Mark Cousins, "The Ugly (Part 1)," AA Files, no. 28 (Autumn 1994): 61–64.

3 Cousins, "The Ugly," 63.

the architect's control.[4] My aim with this project was to develop a resilient architecture that welcomes dirt in order to engage with the realities of the modern world and enable a link between human societies, urbanism, and natural processes.

The project situates itself in the context of Veddesta, in northwest Stockholm. In this postindustrial landscape, dirt and debris are in constant movement as demolition is currently in progress. Trucks and machines dig earth out of the ground, and dust fills the air. The dirty particles in the air mingle with the microscopic pollutants coming from nearby roads and industries still in operation. A renovation project in planning with the Järfälla municipality aims to bring more inhabitants and activity to the area in coming years. Following a close exploration of the site, I sought to encapsulate the dirty matter of Veddesta. I collected trash, debris, and lost items to transform them and give them new meaning. I was inspired by Agnès Varda's documentary *Les glaneurs et la glaneuse* (*The Gleaners and I*, 2000), which explores the practice of gleaning. Through the act of compacting found detritus, I created new objects from Veddesta's dirty materials. The resulting pieces, extractions comparable to geological samples, represent the dirty dimension of Veddesta. My architectural proposition then became a series of infrastructures that would receive, process, and transform this dirty matter.

Focusing on airborne pollutants, I observed that one constant element of daily urban life is the pigeon. City dwellers tend to consider pigeons dirty intruders, flying vermin. But what if pigeons could help us make our environment cleaner? Because they are exposed to the same environmental conditions as human beings, feral pigeons can be used as biodetectors to study the different pollutants present in our atmosphere.[5] I theorized that atmospheric monitoring through organisms such as pigeons could inform us in real time of the presence and impact of air pollution. Thanks to a series of harmless sampling and testing protocols, pigeons could give us the knowledge we need to better understand the molecular complexity that characterizes the air we breath. In my project, pigeon coops rise into the sky over Veddesta. The infrastructure hosts pigeons who, when they return to the coop, provide information about the composition of the air through which they have flown. Specific pollutants can then be targeted with filters integrated in a series of cleaning towers. In addition to parameters such as wind direction, sources of airborne pollution, and potential meeting spots for pigeons, the infrastructural system of towers also considers the future urban fabric likely to result from the municipality's renovation projects. The infrastructure accepts that the human environment is composed of dirtiness and allows for a resilient and adaptable connection between human beings and nonhuman beings in the urban context.

---

4 Karin Reisinger, "Abandoned Architectures: Some Dirty Narratives," *in Architecture and Feminisms: Ecologies, Economies, Technologies*, **ed. Hélène Frichot, Catharina Gabrielsson, and Helen Runting, 202–11 (Oxford, UK: Routledge, 2018).**

5 Nicola Davis, "Want to Monitor Air Pollution? Test a Pigeon," *The Guardian*, **February 16, 2018, https://www.theguardian.com/environment/2018/feb/16/want-to-monitor-air-pollution-test-a-pigeon**

ONMEDI
UMSAND
EXCHAN
GE

Chapter 9
On Mediums and Exchange: Narrative Flow in the Strait of Hormuz

Rouzbeh Akhbari

To the best of my admittedly limited historical knowledge, the archipelago in proximity to the Strait of Hormuz has disappeared and rematerialized on more than one occasion. Due to the unique geological characteristics of these islands, it is extremely difficult—if not impossible—to determine precisely what causes the land to retreat or the collapsing sinkholes to appear. Despite various speculations by a wide range of experts and amateurs alike, a singular hypothesis has never succeeded in rationalizing the complexities associated with the social and material reality of life in this region. From a geological standpoint, these islands—similar to other landmasses on the planet—came into existence subsequent to ancient diastrophic displacement events, but that genesis narrative fails to explain why the islands act with such dynamism on an ongoing basis, much like an organism with varying growth trajectories in different regions.

Since the Strait of Hormuz has a high evaporation rate and is located at a juncture where a shallow semi-enclosed basin meets a larger body of water connected to oceanic gyres, an unusually dense body of saltwater forms to the west of the archipelago, which in effect acts as an inverse estuary diluting the fresher surface inflow from the east of the strait. The confluence's geopolitical context is perhaps most poetically reflected in the exchange facilitated by the characteristic differences in the bodies of water surrounding the strait. For matter to flow in the planetary network of oceanic currents, saltwater must circulate between these basins; yet for the circulation to occur, the water must be salinized by moving through the strait in the first place. This intricate cycle makes the juncture between the Sea of Oman and the Persian Gulf not only a significant site on its own but also a medium of exchange, or infrastructure, for the perpetual functioning of other sites across the hydrosphere. To this end, the archipelago's dynamism has long been observed, imagined, and speculated about with utmost attention by merchants, military and trade strategists, politicians, and anyone whose livelihood relies on the undisrupted flow between the gulfs; namely, the inhabitants of these islands and the actors who frequent the territories surrounding the strait.

Imperialist and colonial power projections over Hormuz have always revolved around possessing the capability to subvert, disrupt, reinterpret, and capitalize on the strait's role as a site of exchange, more often than not by mobilizing official narratives and informal gossip that frame its spatiotemporal realities for the consumption of intended (usually nonlocal) audiences. In his widely cited revisitation of Edward Said and Antonio Gramsci, Derek Gregory observes how the "creation of geographies—the recognition and understanding of symbolic territories—is central to Said's work."[1] Geography, etymologically settled as "earth-writing," can never be uncoupled from the imagination of the author or orator who takes it upon themself to bring a place into the confines of linguistics. This appropriative process of imaginative interpretation, both Said and Gregory argue, is an intrinsically visual one. My interest in the greater Hormuz region lies exactly within these ficto-visual processes that have repeatedly (re)created the archipelago in the past four centuries. In my capacity as an artist and filmic storyteller, I have undertaken a long-term research project to critically investigate the contours of informal infrastructures in the Strait of Hormuz, particularly those at the intersections of mythmaking and political ecology. So far, this project has materialized into a short film, a series of sculptural installations, and a ficto-critical novella. The following pages situate a set of fieldwork notes, observations, doctored archival documents, and creative writing exercises that crystallized in a parallel and palimpsestic relationship to the larger artistic manifestations of this project.

Imperialist and colonial power projections over Hormuz have always revolved around possessing the capability to subvert, disrupt, reinterpret, and capitalize on the strait's role as a site of exchange, more often than not by mobilizing official narratives and informal gossip that frame its spatiotemporal realities for the consumption of intended (usually nonlocal) audiences.

1 Derek Gregory, "Imaginative Geographies," *Progress in Human Geography* **19, no. 4 (1995): 447–85 (here 447).**

Inspired by Said's rhizomatic (as opposed to linear) approach to studying the formation of spatial and cultural identities, I wish to invoke the notion of "imagined geographies" as a critical tool to unpack infrastructures of storytelling both as a function of sovereign territorialization and the upkeep of resistive microhistories. The Strait of Hormuz today has an extremely complex socioeconomic and political fabric that sees local and transnational actors engage in intelligence collection, informal commodity exchange, arms trafficking, and ongoing acts of infrastructural and military sabotage. Throughout my journeys, a handful of these actors have grown to be my close friends, while most chose to keep distant.[2]

To contextualize the following pages and ease you into what might initially feel like a series of disjointed fragments, I invite you to allow the islands' holey *complexitie*s to fulfill a metaphorical function beyond the void that they represent. In doing so, it might be useful to interpret complexity through the lens of evolution theory: genetic sophistication is an extremely gradual and incremental process that is a direct result of diversification in the aftermath of periodic eras of instability. That is to say, in contrast, when the need to diversify is lacking, prolonged stability leads to homogenization and genetic simplification. I find Sewall Wright's holey adaptive landscape models,[3] which are primarily used to determine the evolution and speciation growth trajectory of organisms in different biomes, an effective visual tool to interpret the politically intertwined narrative infrastructures that continue to shape the Strait of Hormuz as an imagined geography. In the framework of this publication and its simultaneous sway around the notions of infrastructure and care, I am merely an unreliable narrator; yet I encourage you to steer away from the desire to fill the gaps connecting the narrative holes in this piece and instead move toward identifying what material or immaterial "imaginaries" these concrete and conceptual holes give rise to—what they reproduce, what they devour, and what they cloak.

2 When necessary, names and identifying factors in this chapter have been carefully obscured to ensure the safety of everyone whose livelihood is entangled with the contemporary struggles surrounding this narrow waterway.

3 Baigrie (1996). *Picturing knowledge: historical and philosophical problems concerning the use of art in science*. **University of Toronto Press (here 310–12).**

Illustration by Mahmoud Dehnavi. Courtesy of the author.

The Testaments

One of the earliest records alluding to the unexplained shifts in the archipelago's water table is an illustration in the notorious *Códice Casanatense*. This manuscript is believed to have been created circa 1540, and its authors have never been identified. Depicting a Portuguese settler family dining while submerged in a pool of water on the island of Hormuz, the illumination is accompanied by an inscription that reads, "Eating in water, for the land is very warm. Folks intentionally flood their homes."

During my fieldwork, I came across the gossip that frequent flooding events occurred on the Christian-settled parts of the archipelago when the region was under Portuguese colonial rule. Some religious thinkers speculate that divine intervention might have been at play: a sort of God-sent cooling miracle to make the islands' colonizers more comfortable in the unbearable summer months. Others assume the flooding was a curse brought upon the intruders by the forces of nature, particularly the southeasterly winds that seasonally affect the tidal movements in proximity to the strait. The Portuguese colonial presence in the Strait of Hormuz, which lasted over a century (1507–1621), projected a series of phantasmagoric visions onto the life of the archipelagos' inhabitants. Provoked by Catholic missionary schools of thought, these narratives were mobilized to portray the locals as lustful cosmopolitans. The archipelagos' early internationalism and fluidity of sexual and cultural identities—in large part due to its strategic position within the maritime Silk Road networks—was exaggerated and appropriated as a justification for the implementation of violent regimes of colonial oppression. The words of Francis Xavier, the Navarrese Saint and cofounder of the Society of Jesus, offer perhaps the clearest glimpse into this construction of Hormuz as a distant periphery for the public imaginary of the European metropoles:

> Its moral state was enormously and infamously bad. It was the home of the foulest sensuality, and of all the most corrupted forms of every religion in the East.... A zealous bishop had once lived there, and soon wore himself to death. Mahometanism was in great power, and possessed a very magnificent mosque. The Arabs and Persians had introduced and made common the most detestable forms of vice. Ormuz was said to be a Babel for its confusion of tongues, and for its moral abominations to match the cities of the Plain. A lawful marriage was a rare exception. Foreigners, soldiers, and merchants, threw off all restraint in the indulgence of their passions. The children of Christian fathers and Jewish, heathen, or Mussulman women were brought up in the religion of their mothers. The riches of the place attracted every possible luxury to enhance the general license. Avarice was made a science: it was studied and practiced, not for gain, but for its own sake, and for the pleasure of cheating.... if a council of devils were to assemble to draw up formulas of robbery, they would never invent so many and so specious ways of defrauding as contrived and practiced every day by the merchants of Ormuz, who were called all over the East the "Doctors of Usury."[4]

Xavier used to say (we are told through the works of Henry James Coleridge) that he would not be surprised if the islands were someday to be submerged for the "wickedness" that reigned there.

Employing narrative infrastructures that animated Hormuz as a site of ungodly cosmopolitanism surrounded by the eternal threat of flooding served a dual purpose in the context of European colonial thought. In addition to "othering" the colonized subjects as a precursor to dispossession, these narratives have a temporal dimension. Peter Hulme highlights this relationship eloquently in his essay "Subversive Archipelagos": "Europe, whether Christian or capitalist, was the model of the future, to which the rest of the world could aspire. This was an essentially temporal figure, with the only relationship between Europe and the other parts of the world one of delay."[5] This temporal antagonism, in which

4 Henry James Coleridge, *The Life and Letters of St. Francis Xavier*, **vol. 2 (London: Burns and Oats, 1872), 105–6.**

5 Peter Hulme, "Subversive Archipelagos: Colonial Discourse and the Break-up of Continental Theory," *Dispositio* **14, no. 36/38 (1989): 1–23 (here 3).**

This temporal antagonism, in which the non-European parts of the world could be defined only by their temporal lag, goes hand in hand with the colonial modernist/capitalist obsession with linear perceptions of time.

the non-European parts of the world could be defined only by their temporal lag, goes hand in hand with the colonial modernist/capitalist obsession with linear perceptions of time. After all, intercontinental navigation and maritime expeditions were possible only thanks to accurate clocks and the appointment of fixed geographical reference points and circadian time zones.

A subversive document to explore in relation to the spatiotemporal dynamics within the context of the shifting geographies of power in the early seventeenth-century Hormuz is the *Jangnameh-Kish* or *Jarūnnāmah*.[6] Also attributed to an unknown author, the *Jarūnnāmah* is an epic *masnavī* on the life of Imam Qoli-Khan Undiladze. It was first published in Isfahan, a city that was at the heart of the Safavid Persian empire and whose relationship to Hormuz was also largely one of center/periphery. The story partially documents Qoli-Khan's rise to power before conquering Hormuz in collaboration with the British navy and banishing the Portuguese from the region. The latter sections of Jarūnnāmah chronicle Qoli-Khan's destined execution due to a conspiracy in the Safavid court. Despite its propagandistic qualities, the illuminated manuscript offers a rare insight into Qoli-Khan's war efforts in the strait. Despite the lack of any firm evidence to prove the existence of the will and testament attributed to him prior to his execution in 1632, contemporary speculators purport that in that document Qoli-Khan explains his obsession with Hujjat Allah al-Mahdi's occultation and the fluidity of time as discussed in religious teachings attributed to Twelver Shi'ism. Apparently, Qoli-Khan treats the testament as a form of confession to publicize some of the strategies used to motivate the soldiers under his command and to shed light on his clandestine efforts to use the archipelagos' atypical geological characteristics against adversaries.

6 Al-Qadri, Jarūnnāmah (Isfahan, 1697). Manuscript description based on Ch. Rieu, *Catalogue of the Persian Manuscripts in the British Museum* **(London, 1879–1883).**

He might have written,

> I went through a great deal of trouble to awaken the Yamani and arm them to the best of my abilities. In doing so, I continued my father's policy of undermining the foreigners' positions in the Gulf. I cherished the opportunity to reestablish a new corridor to Yemen. My approach to defying their hegemony was as much ideological as it was political or militaristic. For the enemy to find their way to our lands, they needed a promise of exceptional material gain along with precise clocks and unchanging geographical reference points. For us to mobilize a competent army to unsettle their positions, we had to invent the opposite: a multitude of temporal references, promise of infinite immaterial gains, and a new asymmetric ontology that relies little on circadian revolutions. It is under the protection of the "master of time" that we proceed generation after generation.

Continuing elsewhere,

> I unleashed upon the aliens waves of insurgencies, the likes of which had only been chronicled. . . . I designated Safi-Qoli to the task of recruiting and training regional dissenters. We mounted a resistance and actively undermined their daily lives. . . . Together with Prince Thabit's fresh topographical knowledge and Safi-Qoli's military expertise and financing, we managed to transform the few

Doctored replicas of four illuminations first published as part of the original *Jarūnnāmah*. Illustrated by Mojtaba Abu-talebi. Courtesy of the author.

remaining honorable locals into well-trained saboteurs. Over the course of five years, they gradually tampered with the qanats, abanbars, and underlying ducts to redirect monsoon rainwaters toward the islands' Portuguese-settled districts. The year we finally attempted our invasion, the flooding was so severe that our rowboats, including the one I captained, managed to sail directly onto the plateau adjacent to the isle's formidable fortress.

Popularized through apocalyptic headlines and the bird's-eye perspective of surveillance drones, the geopolitical imaginary dominating the Strait of Hormuz today is one of daily military confrontation.

Hunters and Keepers

Popularized through apocalyptic headlines and the bird's-eye perspective of surveillance drones, the geopolitical imaginary dominating the Strait of Hormuz today is one of daily military confrontation. In addition to this mainstream vision—which is equally constructed by the Iranian state media conglomerates and Western ones—careful observers of the strait's political economy would point to the vast planetary networks of informal trade that operate in proximity to the Musandam Peninsula and Qeshm and Hormuz islands. In the psyche of contemporary citizens, the archipelago is simultaneously a site of excessive sovereign territorialization/militarization and a platform for deterritorializing local and international legal hegemonies through large-scale trafficking.

My imagination of the region, too, was saturated by these grand narratives prior to undertaking this project, but I was privileged to develop interpersonal relationships with individuals whose wisdom afforded me another perspective: one of affective and intricate care in the face of perpetual crisis and uncertainty. Mr. Salehi was a key figure among these individuals. Although he is formally employed as a security guard by the island's department of environmental protection, he refers to himself as an amateur archaeologist. The first time I stumbled upon him was near Chah Kouh on Qeshm island when he refreshed my parched throat on a hot August day by pulling a cool cup of water from the nearby well. In the first few minutes of making his acquaintance, he gave me a thorough historical overview of the sites surrounding the ancient wells. Mr. Salehi talked about the archipelago and the curious holey valley within which the subterranean water canals ran as a "post-genocide landscape." Pointing to the oldest well in the constellation of holes on the ground, he said, "fleeing from the Portuguese, and then the Persians, they would take refuge in every hole. This place is not fair. If you're too comfortable or too egoistic, it will eat you! You will disappear." When I asked him if his occupation was to pull water from the wells for the visitors, he gently smiled and said, "I'm here for the birds. They are the only ones who really need me." Out of curiosity to hear his opinion about the narratives of smuggling in the strait, I asked whether currency and contraband trafficking was really as rampant as it was made to look in the media. Taken aback by my crude inquiry, he stayed silent for a few moments and then remarked, "people have been merchants since the beginning of time. If you need something that your neighbors possess, and vice versa, if they desire something that you own, wouldn't you trade with them? It is at the core of all human civilizations to exchange with each other." He stared me down after finishing that sentence just to make sure his point was driven home. Before dropping his bucket back into the well, he exclaimed, "It's not like nothing illegal happens here, of course . . ." The loud splash made it hard for me to hear the end of his sentence, but he continued, "a while back, we had a few unruly teenagers who exhumed the tombs and the obelisk near the British graveyards. The fools assumed there would be riches to loot. When we caught them, they insisted that the Emirati treasure hunters gave them the coordinates of that place and offered them cash in exchange for whatever they found in the cemetery. Some graves still have huge holes . . . They're still exposed . . ."

Later that day, he took me for a stroll in the cemetery to observe the holes for myself before we parted ways to different islands for our evening repose. When our film crew returned many months after my initial conversations with Mr. Salehi, the team's fixer told our cinematographer that the locals refer to

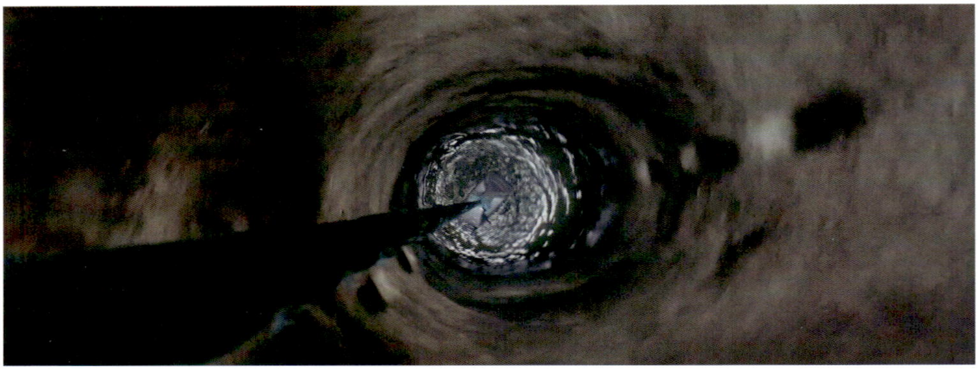

him as the "gatekeeper," since in the absence of centralized water infrastructures in the nearby villages, he had volunteered to act as the distribution moderator to ensure the wells were fairly utilized and hygienically maintained at the time of the pandemic.

An Occultation

The following is a transcription of our conversation with a local construction manager on the island of Hormuz. He was last in contact with the two passengers aboard a vessel that disappeared at night on the winter solstice of 2019. One of the passengers was a local sailor who occasionally worked at the iron oxide soil extraction factory; the other was an electrical engineer temporarily on the isle to troubleshoot a telecommunications tower.

> [00:08:09:17- 00:08:13:23]
> In the evening, I had gone to the jetty to drop off the tourists returning to Bandar Abbas.
>
> [00:08:14:22- 00:08:16:03]
> I saw him at the Jetty.
>
> [00:08:16:15- 00:08:18:19]
> He was walking around all confused.
>
> [00:08:20:05- 00:08:23:01]
> I asked him if he had a place to stay, since there were no more vessels leaving for Bandar Abbas.
>
> [00:08:23:22- 00:08:28:04]
> He said, "No I don't." He had no bags with him either. It was only him.
>
> [00:08:29:12- 00:08:33:14]
> I called around to find him a suit, but was unable to find anything.
>
> [00:08:35:02- 00:08:39:06]
> There was no choice. I told him "come to our house. It is Yalda and we will have fun!"
>
> [00:08:41:19–00:08:48:00]

He came here. We were enjoying ourselves when his phone rang suddenly. I don't know how his phone worked because all the lines were out of service after the November uprisings.

[00:08:48:06–00:08:50:06]
He completely lost it after that.

[00:08:51:00–00:08:53:02]
All of a sudden he said, "I have to leave for Isfahan right now."

[00:08:54:05–00:08:59:13]
I said, "There are no vessels. The boats don't sail in this weather . . .
A storm is imminent."

[00:08:59:22–00:09:02:02]
He said, "No! I have to leave under any circumstance."

[00:09:02:18–00:09:08:10]
He quickly went online and bought a ticket for a flight to Isfahan from Qeshm island.

[00:09:09:23–00:09:15:04]
He asked me to find him a boat, saying he would pay any amount to get to Qeshm.

[00:09:17:01–00:09:21:07]
I called Bahram. He said, "No problem, I will take him."

[00:09:21:19–00:09:23:16]
They hopped aboard, and I watched them depart.

[00:09:24:22–00:09:27:07]
I called half an hour later, and they were out of reach.

[00:09:28:17–00:09:31:08]
I figured they don't have reception on the sea.

[00:09:32:07–00:09:38:13]
I called half an hour later, and their phone was shut off entirely. Since that day, anytime I call, the phone is off.

[00:09:40:08–00:09:44:03]
I went to Baba Zār (the island's medium), and he says he can see them on the sea.

[00:09:45:13–00:09:49:17]
I called the maritime information center.... They say we have never seen a boat like this.

[00:09:50:11–00:09:54:02]
We asked the locals in Bandar Abbas. No one has seen them arrive.

[00:09:55:14–00:09:56:13]
We have no idea what to do.

[00:09:57:18–00:10:00:01]
(interviewer): What exactly is this Baba Zār or Mama Zār that everyone talks about here?

[00:10:00:19–00:10:03:06]
Baba Zār and Mama Zār are everything in the south.

[00:10:04:19–00:10:06:18]
It goes back all the way to the story of Solomon.

[00:10:08:00–00:10:12:04]
You must know that Solomon had djinns. He was surrounded by djinns.

[00:10:12:18–00:10:17:11]
Even when he died, the djinns didn't realize he was dead. That's how incredible he was.

[00:10:21:22–00:10:26:14]
That's the root of it all. And now any wind that blows from that side (Yemen), they call it the wind of Zār.

[00:10:27:03–00:10:28:15]
They say the wind has djinns that see things from above and bring the news.

[00:10:28:22–00:10:30:06]
Baba Zār is their medium, and he has gone on the sea . . .

[00:10:30:20–00:10:37:20]
Here, when people drown in the sea, Baba Zār goes to the shore and plays percussion so the corpse comes out.

The red soil factory and initial interview setup. Screenshots from short film "Perturbation." Courtesy of the author.

[00:10:38:21–00:10:43:01]
He says when you play percussion, the djinns get scared and let go of the corpse, and it comes to the surface.

[00:10:45:01–00:10:47:05]
Now he has gone out and played his instrument, but nothing has come out yet.

[00:10:49:00–00:10:50:22]
And on the other hand he says, "I have seen them alive on the sea."

[00:10:52:01–00:10:52:12]
We don't know ... We can't be certain.

[00:10:52:21–00:10:58:00]
We can't arrange for a funeral to mourn properly ... We can't not have a funeral, either ... We're stuck in a limbo, waiting.

The Expediency Council

I became obsessed with the Strait of Hormuz after finding a leather-wrapped portfolio in the studio of my late grandfather, Mahmoud Dehnavi. The folder contained an extremely elaborate drawing and dozens of his handwritten notes. Most were calligraphic reproductions of couplets by the prominent Persian poet Hafiz, alongside a few annotations from archaeological textbooks about Portuguese forts and Safavid garden designs. Curious to know more, I asked my grandmother for more information. She confirmed that the

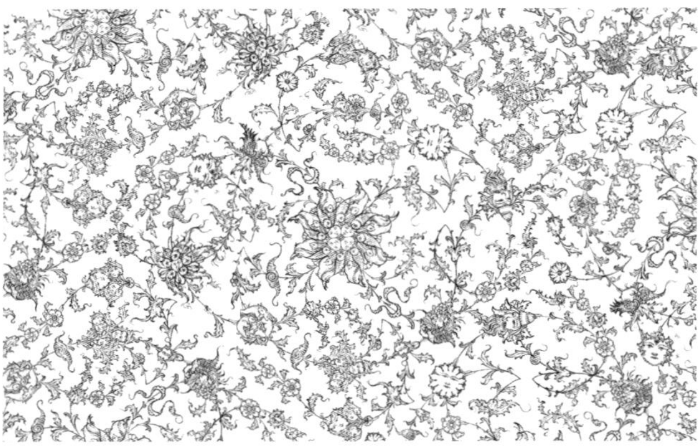

Glazed Ceramic reproduction of the *Códice Casanatense*. Reproduced by Mohammad Mokhtarian. Courtesy of the author.

drawing was created when baba Mahmoud worked on projects for the court of Sultan Qaboos in Khasab. Since the day I found that portfolio, this drawing has become my Zahir. I carried the illustration with me during research trips and spent much time reflecting on its intricacies.

On January 5, 2020, I was forced to cancel the last phase of my fieldwork in Qeshm due to the heightened tensions that ensued in the aftermath of the assassination of Qasem Soleimani in a U.S. drone attack in Baghdad. The prospects of a military skirmish, particularly in the Strait of Hormuz, felt very close. Two days later, during the chaos of Iran's retaliatory missile attack on American military bases in Iraq, the Islamic Revolutionary Guard Corps launched two Tor-M1 anti-aircraft rockets toward flight PS752, a scheduled commercial aircraft departing from Tehran's international airport with 176 individuals on board. All the passengers were killed. Over the following months, I worked within a team of volunteers to shoot a documentary with Javad Soleimani, the surviving husband of Elnaz Nabiyi, one the victims of this heinous attack. In the process, my camera acted much like a trauma therapist for Javad, who mourned through reenactment and retelling of the early moments of hearing news of the downing. So far, the Iranian state's narrative infrastructures have all been employed to blame this tragedy on human error, a stance that grossly simplifies the complex and chaotic intentionality of the chain of events that led to the massacre.

Reflecting on these troubling developments and their connection to the geopolitics of the Strait of Hormuz, I drafted a series of ficto-critical stories over the following months. Most of these narratives revolve around ideas of armed conflict and chaos theory, citizenship and subversive infrastructures, and the relevance of posthuman imaginaries in the context of the greater Hormuz region. Partly inspired by the mystic poet Attar's *Manṭiq-uṭ-Ṭayr (Conference of the Birds, 1177)* and by my grandfather's drawing, the following passages are a brief excerpt from the series of stories I wrote.

"The desire to know is incredibly primitive," said the leader of the Synthetics Union. "It not only exists among noble creatures, but at the heart of all matter.

It is the trait that has guided us in our evolutionary survival throughout the ages, the only constant ..."

Frustrated by her directionless speech, the ill-tempered defense manager interrupted. "Do we have any concrete answers thus far?"

A deluge of calls filled the dome in a fraction of a second. A young observer was quick to respond. "Before handling any sensitive data on the topic, I must reiterate that the very bedrock of our argumentation is based on constructed algorithms, and therefore exposed to grave miscalculations," she disclaimed. "Having said that, our observations reveal that no one has heard, or will ever hear the voice of the island. The threat, in this case, is next to zero."

"Next to zero is not zero," the defender exclaimed. "All of your calculations are based on observing what the island was up to more than four hundred years ago. How can you possibly know its progress trajectory now and gauge its future capabilities?"

The observers remained silent for a short moment before a barrage of communications filled the assembly dome again. The incoming calls indicated that the opinionated birds were widely divided over the issue. Nearly half of the members were in favor of a preemptive strike against the archipelago, while the other half refused that option furiously. The belligerent faction insisted that the most logical action was to eliminate the potential threat before it upgraded into an imminent one, while the opposing group argued such aggressions could lead to unpredictable consequences. The irenic camp was in favor of a long-term strategy to disarm the strait's shadow biospheres without direct contact, while the pro-strike members spoke of tactical action.

Hawk said, "As we know, there are known knowns; these are things we know we know. We also know there are known unknowns; that is to say, we know there are some things we do not know. But there are also unknown unknowns—the ones we don't know we don't know. If one looks throughout the history of our civilization and of other successful breeds, it is the latter category that has brought us the most trouble. Our current dilemma, if not handled immediately, will be an excellent example of a simple known known turned into an unresolvable unknown unknown."[7]

"You are wrong!" exclaimed Dove. "Why intentionally exclude a critical part of the analogy? What about the unknown knowns? Your beliefs? Delusions? Fears? The things you deny that you know, but very much exist, and in fact, drive all your decisions. Our ancestors have made this mistake before. Acting with complete disregard for the uncertain outcomes of a military strike means running the risk of utter annihilation."

"You're muddling a situation that is otherwise straightforward," protested Hawk. "We possess incredibly precise observations to determine the outcomes. In this case, the outcomes are simple. We either eliminate this infant threat while we can, or hold off and allow the islanders to evolve into a far greater risk."

Dove said, "The smallest error in our observations, or the execution of decisions based on those observations, would yield dramatically different results." Immediately after sharing this thought, three colorful magnetic spheres entered the dome and hovered in a triangular pattern over the curious birds. "The unknowability principle should be our fundamental approach to decision making," she continued. Accruing the small amounts of ferrum present in the dome's atmosphere, Dove constructed an iron disk and placed it in a fixed position about twelve meters away from the magnets. Simultaneously, a massive numeral display showing the disk's exact coordinates down to the twentieth decimal appeared behind her. Under the crowd's inquisitive gaze, she accelerated the disk toward the magnetic constellation. The disk entered a complex motion, chaotically revolving around the yellow magnet at first, only to depart and enter the blue magnet's orbit at an awkward trajectory and finally impacting with, and shattering, the red magnet in the very last moment. She repeated the experiment two more times, yet despite identical start positions, the iron disk wiped out a different magnet each time. Following the demonstration, she exclaimed, "War is a matter of science. The delusion that we can know the

7 "There are known knowns" is a phrase U.S. Secretary of Defense Donald Rumsfeld used in response to a question at a U.S. Department of Defense news briefing on February 12, 2002, about the lack of evidence linking the government of Iraq with the supply of weapons of mass destruction to terrorist groups.

future before it becomes present is grossly at odds with this chaos principle. Mathematically speaking, to attempt a battle with disregard for the very fractalized nature of life is nothing more than suicide. To do so is equivalent to borrowing death from one's self today, only to deliver it back to tomorrow's self."

Hawk said, "If we follow this logic, there are always going to be things that are unknowable. Everything would be interpreted as an utter accident. Life, as we know it, would come to a standstill. There would remain no room for design on this planet. Under those circumstances, how could life, a slow, mindless process, build a thing that could build a thing that a slow, mindless process couldn't build on its own? The only way for intelligence to spread across the planet is for this mindless, natural process to evolve an entity with superior computational capabilities, who would then take the fate of the slow, mindless process in its hands as it traverses various temporal dimensions. Such an entity would never come to existence without a revolution, which itself would only take place through an accidental mutation. If one does not take risks to avail the opportunity for such revolutions out of fear of death, she is not living in the first place."

Summoning a piece of unstable uranium isotope inside the assembly room, Dove demonstrated another experiment. This time, the giant display behind her flashed bright red every time the decaying substance radiated. After a short period, she invited the birds to produce an algorithm that could reliably predict the exact moment of radiation. In response to everyone's futile efforts, she said, "Radioactive decay is a stochastic process at the most fundamental levels. Regardless of how long the substance has existed, it is absolutely impossible to predict a particular atom's decay. In other words, at subatomic levels, the isotope's electrons will always conceal some part of their identity, be it speed, location, etc. Their clandestine essence won't be disturbed until observed by an external viewer, by which point the task of predicting their behavior has already become obsolete."

"Perhaps it is your language that is flawed," Hawk argued. "Maybe the electron doesn't have a position and momentum at the same time. Assess the conundrum this way: the radiation simply doesn't have a pattern until we observe it. That way, the issue is just another probability equation; we can calculate the likelihood of where the electron's position is and focus all our efforts to observe it in that relative spot. All of this is beside the point. What matters is that an unstable isotope such as the one in your experiment must always remain contained under multiple layers of protection. This is precisely how we should react against the archipelago: contain its threat before it becomes fatal."

The dome fell into a deafening silence as soon as Hoopoe spoke. "Hawk and Dove are both correct," she said. "Our immediate actions, or lack thereof, could both lead to grave consequences. We need to simultaneously make tactical decisions and maintain a strategic approach. Perhaps the leader of the Synthetics Union put it most eloquently. This crisis is a matter of knowledge: our means of knowing vs that of the islanders. Our safest bet is active surveillance. Our ultimate goal must be to disarm their desire to know. We shall rely on our strengths and double down on efforts to stay in the shadows, all while actively intercepting the archipelago's natural evolutionary paths. The Mutation Is the Message!"

Acknowledgments

I am grateful to my research assistants Hamid Ghezloo, Dina Cheraghvand, and Mohsen Ramezanzadeh, whose input and collaborative spirit were central to the development of this project. I acknowledge the financial support of the Canada Council for the Arts, Ontario Arts Council, Toronto Arts Council, the Blackwood Gallery, and the 4Cs: From Conflict to Conviviality through Creativity and Culture: a European Cooperation Project co-funded by the Creative Europe program of the European Union in the research and development of this project.

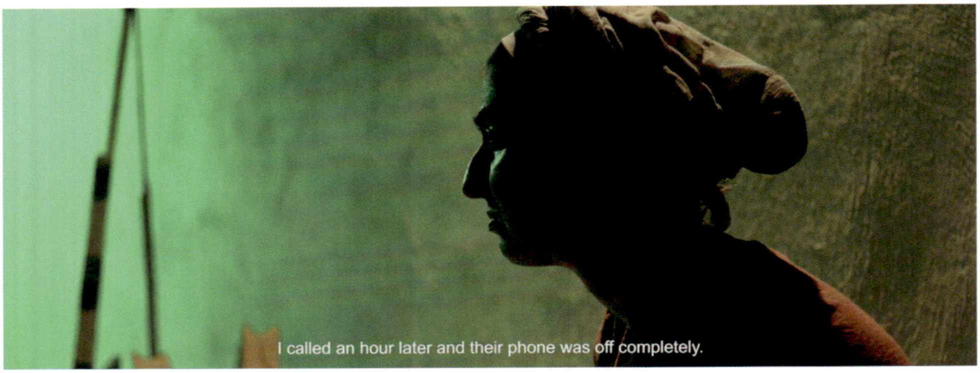
I called an hour later and their phone was off completely.

I said they probably don't have reception on the sea.

I went to the baba Zaar and he said I can see them.
I see them sailing happily on the sea.

Is Data Brief?

Thandi Lane

naturally ventilated, chapel, entity tetris, small support, extension for free, heaven a knowledgebase, passes just beyond, fire world seamless, office emergence, refine marsh, dreaming / of, tower monastery, boulevard depicted, framed philosophy, chiaroscuro, glass station primer, thermal, little and mist, tree like caves, not your doubleday, low louvre, cart galaxy, our bio-philic gallery, ancient address, nature loneliness, arches few, the choreographed, timber monastery, demystifying glass, forbidden rainbow, fortress words, one page mirage, mother past, can the outbreak refine earth?[1]

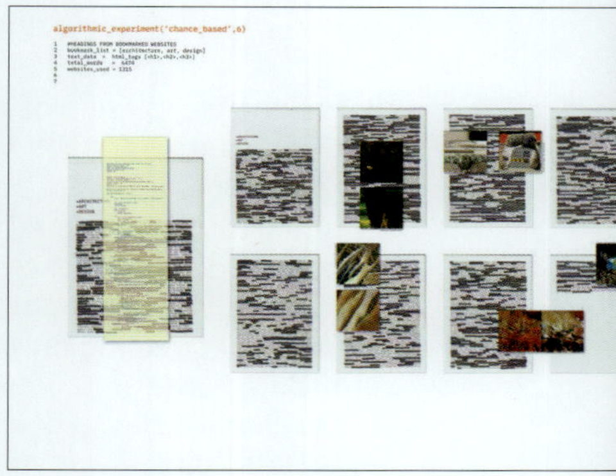

Here sits a softly glowing data center, glimpsed at dawn by a small golden perch caught within a torrent of cascading water heading downstream. The data center nests atop the primary spillway of so-called Lake Buffalo, a dammed reservoir that lies within a river valley at the western base of Mount Buffalo, named as such in 1824 by colonial figures Hume and Hovell whilst on expedition to locate new agricultural land for the European colony. It is part of the vast Murray-Darling Basin, a complex assemblage of water courses, some of which wind their way through the unceded lands, waters, and skies of the Mogullumbidj, the first

---

1 Algorithmic Experiment #05: I used a script to search through headings from 1,315 of my personal bookmarked websites. The result was 6,474 randomized words. The words and phrases included here were all chosen for their aesthetic, spatial, emotional, temporal, and material evocations in aid of early site analysis and brief formation.

peoples of Mount Buffalo and surrounding areas.[2] Combining and analysing the metadata from more than eight-thousand of my personal iPhone photographs to determine their average longitude and latitude resulted in a set of coordinates pointing toward this lake's rich, alluvial edge. This is where the first algorithm placed me.

A further succession of algorithmic experiments, informed by the chance-based experiments of postwar cybernetic art practices, attempted to unpack the contemporary existence of data proliferation. By sifting through, dismantling, and reconstructing my personal vaults of "data waste" (old iPhone photographs, bookmarked URLs, search histories, digital trash bins), I was able to experiment with an alternative mode of determining design decisions such as site, program, and form. Centering these creative investigations around the potentials of our data waste worlds ultimately allowed for a broader consideration of the ways in which we are all implicated in an immense digital "littering" of forgotten, superseded information. These experiments posed a question: What might an architecture of data liberation and "wilding" look like? In pursuit of an answer, I theorized a spatial ontology of data, one freed from the vastness of the effortless and benign narrative of the romantic, oceanic ~cloud~ and thus partially liberated from digital technology's pervasive anthropocentric power dynamics and conceptions of intelligence and value. This expression of a data center aims to tell a vast and yet intimate story of human, nonhuman, and digital entanglements within our unique data waste-world; it is, in essence, an attempt to tell a story of "matter" that really matters.

Is Data Brief? This question, also an architectural provocation, acknowledges the accelerating proliferation of personal data across multiplying platform technologies and its accumulation as "deterritorialized" data waste. This brief responds critically to the sleek, frictionless, sci-fi aesthetic of big tech—a branded aesthetic that so often emphasizes efficiency, volume, stability, and the smooth flows of information. In contrast, *Is Data Brief?* searches out and celebrates the unholy proximities, frictions, and noise inherent in data's immeasurable collisions with the physical world, a process that gives weight to chance as the primary driver, prioritizing inadvertent, noisy data over the natural design preconceptions and predilections that are typically fostered throughout a design education. The project's various chance-based experiments let data, with no agenda, determine key aspects of the design journey, resulting in an eventual master plan, architectural form, and spatial program that illustrates and celebrates the inherent creative value to be found in "noise" and digital waste.

Challenging the norms of data-center architectural vernacular, this project pushes back on the insidious banality of data infrastructure, where secrets are so often hidden in the plainness of their composure. Through this new lens, we can begin to unpack an architectural ontology of data "support structures"—no longer governed by highly insulated, contained, and withdrawn vernaculars. In contrast to these contemporary, anonymous fortresses, which tend to fetishize a posthuman machine environment while simultaneously prioritizing human proportions and comforts, the project's emerging ontology relies upon the additional participation of a host of technological, biological, geological, and temporal players. Through introducing a seemingly antithetical permeability to the program and architectural form of the data-center typology, allowing seasonality, climate and ultimately entropy to permeate the functions and experiential qualities of the design, the project directs focus toward the immense ecological costs of data and internet infrastructures; from mineral extraction, energy consumption and heat production, to the exploitation of land and the disruption and degradation of both cultural and environmental ecologies.

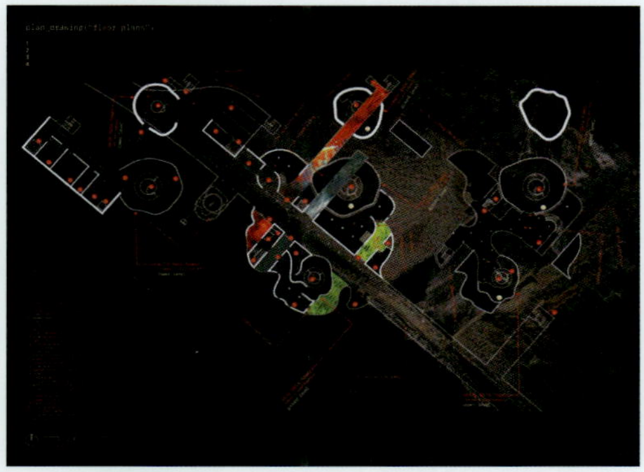

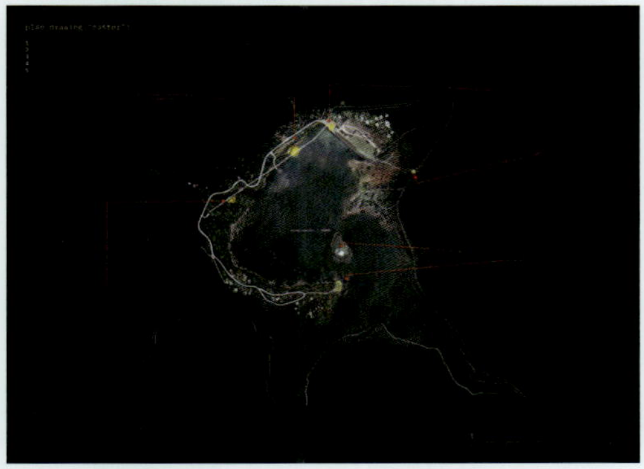

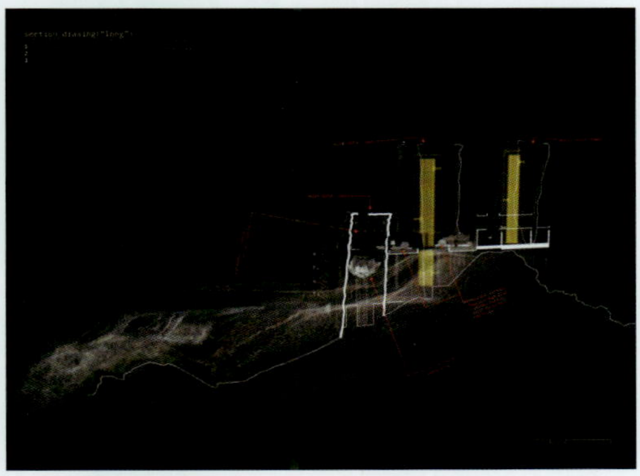

The exponential growth of the internet and all its sweeping infrastructural supports, geological hardware, and data waste, imparts a sense of ecological urgency but also a real creative opportunity within that immediacy for designers and practitioners of the built environment. How can we make visible and vital the material, infrastructural waste worlds of our digital lives? By raising questions and provocations, not only through critique but also through playful experimentation, we can begin to unpack the complex web of entangled information that not only surrounds us but piles up behind us.

2 Jacqui Durrant, "Mogullumbidj: First People of Mount Buffalo," *Victorian Historical Journal*, **Vol. 91, No. 1, June 2020.**

perspective_drawing ("a beacon on the way to the mountain caves")

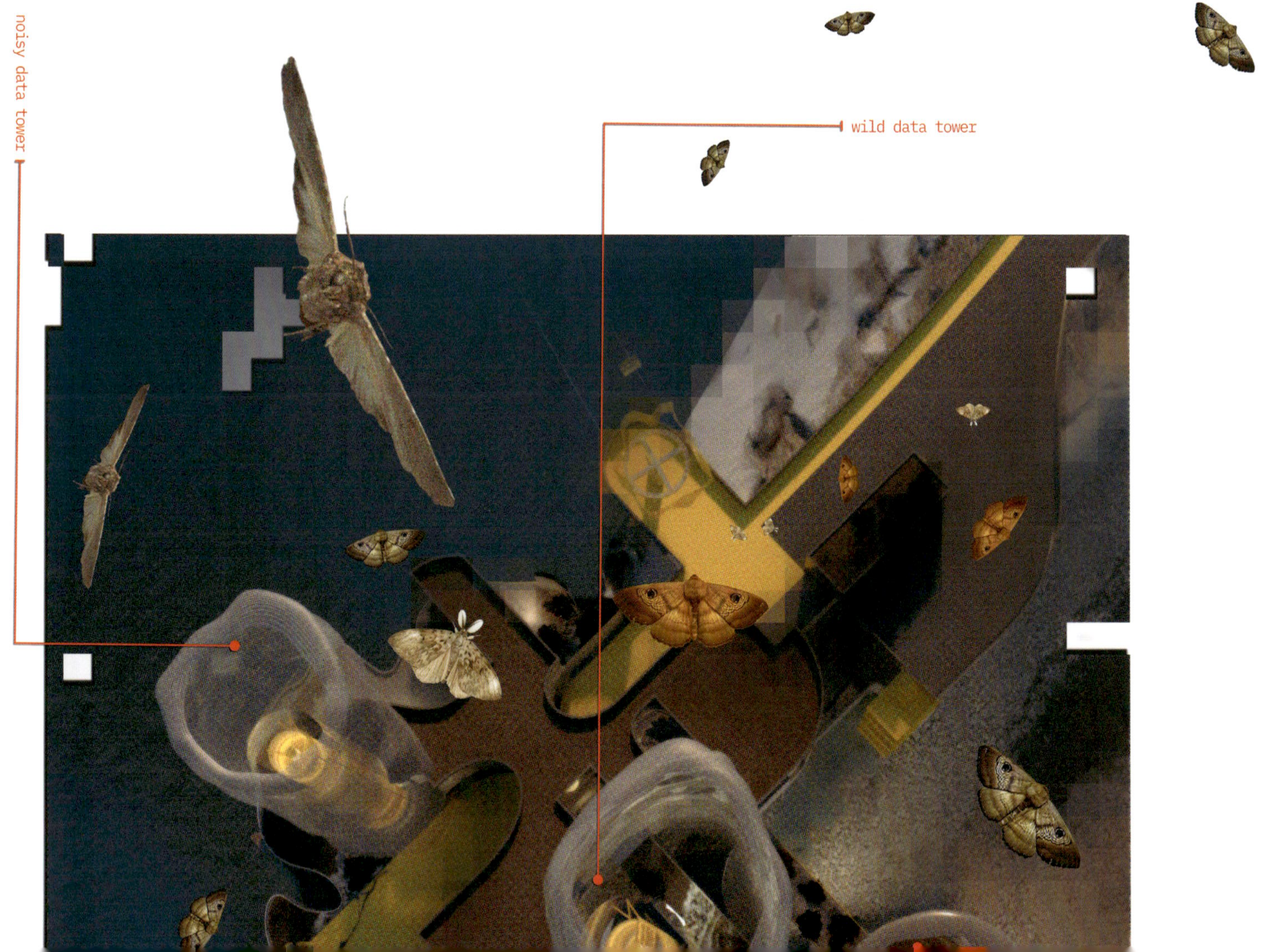

PLANTA
TIONOC
ENEPAR
ABLE

Chapter 10
Plantationocene Parable: Infrastructural Rhythms and After-Affects

Hélène Frichot

Siesta is drawing to a close. In the Seychelles archipelago, in the main settlement of Victoria, traffic revives around the central roundabout with its commemorative clock dedicated to the diamond jubilee of a dead queen. The faint sound of its 4 pm chime weaves its way along a coast laden with leaning coconut palms, up a driveway, past orange trees, to the concrete terrace of an old plantation house, its heavy Doric columns carved tree trunks. The plantation grounds take up some two hundred acres, terraced and planted up toward a prominent island peak called Signal Hill at an elevation of 436 meters. It is one of four such family properties spread across the main island of Mahé. Most have long since been requisitioned, parceled into smaller land holdings (although the driveway up to the old house survives), some of which were claimed by the hands once put to work on the plantation. There is tobacco, some of which is dried in the attic of the plantation house. The endemic coconuts grow wild across the estate and are harvested like manna from heaven. Each morning the working men with their hessian bags collect the fruit that has fallen during the night. Crack, one, two, three, they turn the fruit on the end of a stake to yield the nut inside. The introduced cinnamon trees are harvested in three yearly cycles following an elliptical loop up and across and down the slope of the property. The labor is divided: the women strip the leaves and cut the bark into quills with their small, curved knives; the men cut and collect the larger branches. Every part of the plant is used. (The aromatic timber makes an excellent stove fire in the old kitchen.) Balancing on their heads and strong necks the large bamboo and woven coconut palm leaf baskets that deft fingers have formed then cushioned with folded cloth, the women descend the slope with their bounty, while the men heave their gunnysacks of logs on bent shoulders. Once the leaves have been steamed in the four forty-foot vats in the l'usine, one of the plantation factories, and the thick essence collected in one-liter glass bottles—protected with straw, packaged in timber boxes, due to be exported by boat to India—the damp vegetable matter is spread across the grounds near the main house as mulch. The many sons of the plantation owner run like pups through the vegetable mess, rolling their bodies in it, smudging their white shorts and shirts to the daily horror of the plantation laundress. After the joys of shooting down birds with .22 rifles and catching rats with homemade bamboo traps to claim the price on their tails, their third favorite chore is undertaken on those mornings when the vanilla flowers are inseminated. They scamper from bush to bush with stolen stamens, inserting them into the yawning mouths of one pale waxy orchid after the next. Taken together this murder of sons is a constant blur of movement—one is barely distinguishable from the next—but when midday mealtime arrives, each is allotted a place in descending order, the eldest seated closest to the patriarch, the youngest at the matriarch's end of the long dining table, the supervisory end, closest to the servery, which leads to the kitchen, where the cook daily labors over her wood-fired stoves. Behind the kitchen, in the afternoon shade of a rear veranda, the cook, the nanny, the seamstress, and sometimes workers from other plantation estates gather to gossip.[1]

Ma Joie, Plantation House. Frichot Family Archive, c. 1955.

1 An earlier version of this ficto-critical scene is published in Hélène Frichot, "Decolonising Your Island Imaginary: Preparation for a Novella in Four Parts," in *WritingPlace: Journal for Architecture and Literature, Reading(s) and Writing(s): Unfolding Processes of Transversal Writing*, **ed. Catharina Gabrielsson, Hélène Frichot, Klaske Havik, and Marko Jobst, 99–109 (Rotterdam: nai010 Publishers, 2020). See also Hélène Frichot, "Seychelles Islands Idyll and the Planning of Eden: Speculating on Creative Ecologies," in** *Critical Care: Architecture and Urbanism for a Broken Planet*, **ed. Angelika Fitz and Elke Krasny, 44–52 (Vienna: Architekturzentrum Wien; Cambridge, MA: MIT Press, 2019).** **I extend my sincere thanks to my coeditors, who have all offered invaluable feedback on this chapter. I acknowledge the assistance offered by my father in situating some of the historical aspects of the Seychelles plantation. I thank Therese Keogh for reading an earlier**

Hints are offered in this opening scene of the support structures that render possible a colonial plantation infrastructure, including its local and global matrices of power relations, the supply lines it is hooked up to, and the communications systems upon which it depends, from boats to submarine telegraph cables, "communicating" resources as well as information. Less visible are the local, social, and material infrastructures at work: small kitchen gardens and provision gardens, embodied know-how, a feel for how things go together, where resources can be foraged and fished, and the quiet work of gossip, including the sharing of minor knowledge practices and the minor language that is creole. These less-visible structures, forming their own infrastructural relations of love and care raise important questions, intersecting with the kinds of urgent questions we are hearing more about in architectural discourse as a distinct shift is observed toward efforts to decolonize practices and habits of thought in the design disciplines. At the same time, given the discipline of architecture's historical propensity to support colonial ventures, aspirations to decolonize design curricula and research practices need to be treated with caution.[2] Roaming with an environmental eye across the composite plantation scene above, it is important to acknowledge such tensions and ask: Who are the laboring bodies? What "color lines" are being drawn here on the plantation? What social and material infrastructures are knotted into its ordinary architectural structures? What environmental relations are implicated, and how are they entangled with social relations? While offering little indication of the "ongoing great extinctions" that have been "unloosed" by what Donna Haraway and Anna Tsing call the

Less visible are the local, social, and material infrastructures at work: small kitchen gardens and provision gardens, embodied know-how, a feel for how things go together, where resources can be foraged and fished, and the quiet work of gossip, including the sharing of minor knowledge practices and the minor language that is creole.

version of this essay and offering invaluable feedback. I sincerely thank my co-editors for their close reading and advice on the text.

2 Eve Tuck and K. Wayne Yang, "Decolonization is not a Metaphor," *Decolonization: Indigeneity, Education & Society*, **vol. 1, no. 1 (2012): 1-40. I'm grateful to Therese Keogh for drawing my attention to this reference.**

"Plantationocene," this opening scene with its ambiguous historicity can nonetheless be situated in relation to today's planetary devastations.[3]

3 **Donna Haraway,** *Staying with the Trouble: Making Kin in the Chthulucene* **(Durham, NC: Duke University Press, 2016), 162.**

Here and now, scenes of planetary devastation flicker and disturb, contaminate imaginaries, and threaten the end of all things. The anthropogenic after-affects of the best laid infrastructural plans appear to have gone awry amid wild political mood swings. A planetary virus raises the temperature of a planetary collective body, circulating along routes of infrastructural communication, disproportionately impacting the aged, the vulnerable, the disenfranchised, and minoritized groups. Nature-culture entanglements have turned sour and weedy, supply chains have decoupled, support systems have fallen into disrepair. Just this week news emerged of the impact of dysfunctional supply chains holding up the global traffic in natural gas, a resource upon which industrialized agriculture—an early site of experimentation being the plantation—depends to produce fertilizer to stimulate growth to produce the monocultural crops that agribusiness sells to feed the world, in the process eradicating local diversity and creating chains of dependency. All of which leads us back to this scene and what it shelters in its shadows, an exemplary if idiosyncratic, specific, and partly fabulated site of the Plantationocene.

Vanguard Sedan at Pointe Conan House, Frichot Family Archive, c. 1955.

A planetary virus raises the temperature of a planetary collective body, circulating along routes of infrastructural communication, disproportionately impacting the aged, the vulnerable, the disenfranchised, and minoritized groups.

In the theoretical landscapes of concept-construction, where arguments are tended and problems articulated, not just "scenes" but "cenes" have been proliferating as rapidly as worldly ills. You will have heard them being rehearsed before. Their enunciation has become a refrain, a ritornello: Anthropocene, Capitalocene, Chthulucene, Wastocene, Plastocene, Plantationocene.[4] There is even a "Manthropocene."[5] These cenes are what feminist philosopher of science Donna Haraway calls systemic phenomena, where nothing acts alone, everything is knotted together, each one—human, nonhuman and more-than-human, biotic and abiotic, material-semiotic—is situated and affected.[6] Thinkers of the Plantationocene, for instance, assert that it has been a contributing factor in climate change, stirring environmental and social crises. A cene is a very long period of time—the Holocene, for instance, will have lasted around 11,650 years. Cene also designates an event, a rupture, a shift from difference in degree to difference in kind. Something decisive has occurred such that a transition from the Holocene to the Anthropocene can be decided upon by the privileged few who sit in scientific judgment. Elizabeth DeLoughrey points out that "discourses of the Plantationocene and Capitalocene may help raise questions of accountability for our Earth crisis, but they do not allow a "grounding" in the specificities of the soil."[7] *Scene* and *cene* are homonyms, yet they designate different scales, vast global networks apprehended abstractly at a distance as distinct from the small scenes that invite close-up vision and demand we pay attention to the details. The global scale of the cene that is the Plantationocene is composed of a multitude of minor, fleeting, affecting, and affected scenes that compose a life.

Haraway unpacks the concept of the Plantationocene in a footnote. The Plantationocene is a concept-tool generated collectively at a research event in Aarhus, Denmark, in October

> The Plantationocene designates "the devastating transformation of diverse kinds of human-tended farms, pastures, and forests into extractive and enclosed plantations, relying on slave labor and other forms of exploited, alienated, and usually spatially transported labor."

4 **In 2020, Porky Hefer exhibited** *Plastocene: Marine Mutants from a Disposable World* **at the NGV Triennial at NGV International (National Gallery of Victoria) in Melbourne, Australia. See https://southernguild.co.za/exhibition/plastocene-marine-mutants-from-a-disposable-world/.**

5 **Elizabeth DeLoughrey,** *Allegories of the Anthropocene* **(Durham, NC: Duke University Press, 2019) 62;**

6 **Donna Haraway, "Anthropocene, Capitalocene, Plantationocene, Chthulucene: Making Kin,"** *Environmental Humanities* **6, no. 1 (2015): 159–65 (here 159).**

7 **DeLoughrey,** *Allegories of the Anthropocene*, **44.**

2014, where Anna Tsing, known for her mushroom hunts and her collaborative work on feralatlas.org, was a key organizer. The Plantationocene designates "the devastating transformation of diverse kinds of human-tended farms, pastures, and forests into extractive and enclosed plantations, relying on slave labor and other forms of exploited, alienated, and usually spatially transported labor."[8] Haraway further notes how the slave plantation regime was the "model and motor for the carbon-greedy machine-based factory system" manifesting as an inflection point that erupts as the cene of the Anthropocene—an event of such significance it anticipates irreversible, likely irreparable planetary damage. Similarly, the Plantationocene is what Achille Mbembe calls the institutionalization of a plantation regime at a planetary scale.[9] In 1971, Sylvia Wynter talked of a "plantation system" and "plantation societies," associating these with the emergence of the novel and distinguishing the plantation from the plot.[10] In contrast to this planetary scale, Haraway pays attention to another kind of scene that is suggestive of more local, embodied, and specific practices and voices, the slave garden, Wynter's "plot," also known as the provision garden. The provision garden is discussed in DeLoughrey's *Allegories of the Anthropocene* and in the collaborative work of Janae Davis and her coauthors.[11] "Nurtured in even the harshest circumstances," Haraway explains, "slave gardens not only provided crucial human food, but also refuges for biodiverse plants, animals, fungi, and soils."[12] Disrupting the logic of the Plantationocene, minor life-sustaining and affective ecological practices such as these suggest a counterrhythm and other kinds of social and environmental practices and relations. One way to venture this other rhythm, a cross-weave that cuts in a direction counter to the global story of the Plantationocene, is through storytelling.

Mobilizing fiction as a method, in *Staying with the Trouble* Haraway "composts" a speculative story to think with the (s)cene that is the Plantationocene. She imagines a story dedicated to "Communities of Compost" and how they cope with what she calls "The Great Dithering" by building relations of kin and multispecies conviviality, attempting to live collectively and repair the dam-

8 Haraway, "Anthropocene, Capitalocene, Plantationocene, Chthulucene," 162. See also Janae Davis, Alex A. Moulton, Levi Van Sant, and Brian Williams, "Anthropocene, Capitalocene, … Plantationocene? A Manifesto for Ecological Justice in an Age of Global Crises," *Geography Compass* 13 (2019): 1–15.

9 Achille Mbembe, *Necropolitics* (Durham, NC: Duke University Press, 2019), 20.

10 Sylvia Wynter, "Novel and History, Plot and Plantation," *Savacou*, no. 5 (June 1971): 95–102 (here 96).

11 DeLoughrey, *Allegories of the Anthropocene*; Wynter, "Novel and History, Plot and Plantation"; Sylvia Wynter and Katherine McKittrick, "Unparalleled Catastrophe for Our Species? Or, to Give Humanness a Different Future: Conversations," in Sylvia Wynter: *On Being Human*

age of the world.[13] As human, nonhuman and more-than-human populations dwindle through future generations, Haraway imagines the task of the "children of compost" as one of healing in the aftermath of the "Great Catastrophes of the Plantationocene, the Anthropocene, Capitalocene."[14] For her, compost is a material-semiotic concept-tool, pointing at how thinking and materials are knotted together by working hands but also by hands in play; for instance, when engaged in the ancient game of string figures. With the right mix of vegetable refuse and leftovers from the kitchen, something heated can evolve, all the better to continue growing with. This hot, storied mix invites what Maria Puig de la Bellacasa identifies as "relations of care with the living soil," a material sensitivity that is involved in a present that is thick with multispecies timelines.[15] Care must be taken because things can get into a terrible mess, and the compost—the story it holds—can go off, begin to rot. It can be misconstrued or, worse, become co-opted. This is the cautionary note I repeat to myself as I proceed, handling my plantation story with care, trying to tie the knots just right.

The Plantation Regime

From the seventeenth century onward, the idea of the plantation was imagined as the ideal form of agriculture and became "fundamental to the rise of extractive global capitalism."[16] The plantation was imposed as an answer to existing tropical ecologies and predicated upon a presumed state of untrammeled wilderness and a landscape empty of people, ready and waiting to be transformed into resource. Tsing argues that the plantation operates according to a logic of scalability and "smooth expansion," obliterating the contingency of relations, and denying how site and material specificities might change things. In paying no attention, in refusing to listen, the knowledges that might be gleaned from the specificities of place fall on deaf ears. Instead, the project of the plantation follows an imperial logic: "exterminate local people and plants; prepare now-empty, unclaimed land; and bring in exotic and isolated

as Praxis, **ed. Katherine McKittrick (Durham, NC: Duke University Press, 2015), 9–89; Sylvia Wynter, "Unsettling the Coloniality of Being/Power/Truth/Freedom: Towards the Human, after Man, Its Overrepresentation—An Argument,"** *New Centennial Review* **3, no. 3 (Fall 2003): 257–331; and Davis, Moulton, Van Sant, and Williams, "Anthropocene, Capitalocene, … Plantationocene?"**

12 Haraway, "Anthropocene, Capitalocene, Plantationocene, Chthulucene," 162.

13 Haraway, *Staying with the Trouble*, **140–68.**

14 Haraway, *Staying with the Trouble*, **166.**

15 Maria Puig de la Bellacasa, *Matters of Care: Speculative Ethics in More Than Human Worlds* **(Minneapolis: University of Minnesota press, 2017), 203.**

16 Sophie Sapp Moore, "Plantationocene: When Trees Are Worth More Dead Than Alive," *Architectural Review*, **October 7, 2021, 6–12 (here 9).**

labor and crops for production."[17] Sugarcane proves to be an exemplary plantation crop. Cloned, self-contained, interchangeable, and "oblivious to encounter," it achieves the kind of biopolitical alienation upon which plantations depend to achieve the control of environments and the people who work there. Tsing describes an exemplary plantation assemblage as composed of the sugar cane (stick a cane into the ground and wait for it to sprout, as Tsing puts it) and the worker, who together become what she identifies as "self-contained interchangeable units."[18] Writing of Caribbean plantations, Wynter describes a similar transactional suite: "plantation societies ... came into being as adjuncts to the market system; their peoples came into being as an adjunct to the product, to the single crop commodity—the sugar cane—which they produced."[19] These qualities of scalability, interchangeability, and exchangeability—exchange value rather than use value—served well to shape capitalist modernization and later served as "the model for factories during industrialisation."[20] The Plantationocene is, as Elizabeth Dillon boldly states, "ground zero of the destruction of food sovereignty, ground zero of racial capitalism and the long history of uncommoning."[21] Dillon calls this the enclosure of the commons on a global scale, a repeated sociospatial act drawn along a color line and achieving the "racialized division of peoples."[22]

The "plantation regime," Mbembe asserts, is about "cutting down, burning, and routinely razing forests and trees; about replacing the natural vegetation with cotton and sugar cane; about remodeling ancient landscapes; about destroying the existing vegetal formations; and about replacing an ecosystem with an agrosystem."[23] Life on the plantation is shaped, he adds, according to a "racial principle."[24] In the reconfiguration of land and labor as resource to be extracted and exchanged, the "color line" forms part of the organizational complex of the Plantationocene.[25] My deceptively bucolic opening scene quietly draws attention to such a "color line," dividing the propertied class from those subaltern subjects historically categorized as property, many of whose forbears were enslaved. The color line draws a social infrastructural diagram by

17 Anna Tsing, *The Mushroom at the End of the World: On the Possibility of Life in Capitalist Ruins* **(Princeton, NJ: Princeton University Press, 2015), 39.**

18 Tsing, *The Mushroom at the End of the World*, **40.**

19 Wynter, "Novel and History, Plot and Plantation," 95.

20 Tsing, *The Mushroom at the End of the World*, **40, citing Sidney Mintz,** *Sweetness and Power: The Place of Sugar in Modern History* **(Harmondsworth, UK: Penguin, 1986).**

21 Elizabeth Maddock Dillon, "The Plantationocene and the Performative Commons," *Minnesota Review 93* **(2019): 83–93 (here 83).**

22 Dillon, "The Plantationocene and the Performative Commons," 85.

23 Mbembe, *Necropolitics*, **10.**

24 Mbembe, *Necropolitics*, **10.**

separating those who benefit from the bounty of the land from those whose labor is extracted. As Reinhold Martin writes, when it comes to our presumptions about the advancements of modernity, "we must come to terms with the conflicted preconditions of our own knowledge."[26] The color line, he explains, assists in the conversion of the particular and the environmental into the universal—scene is scaled up as cene—dividing not only master from slave but silence from voice, setting out the conditions for a combat between race and so-called civilization. In architecture, he argues, this line is what we call "modern."[27] Martin shows how processes of industrialization, including the development of technologies, are bound up in the category work of racialization, much as Haraway, Tsing, Mbembe, and Wynter have also argued

Kathryn Yusoff, who contributes to Anthropocene discourse—and by extension Plantationocene discourse—with a geological emphasis, or what she calls a "colonial earth-writing," argues that, "While Blackness is the energy and flesh of the Anthropocene, it is excluded from the wealth of its accumulation."[28] If the Plantationocene has an origin story, much as the Anthropocene does, then this story is "predicated on extraction and exploitation" and on the precondition of the deaths of black and brown bodies—bodies categorized as inhuman or subhuman subjects. Settler-colonialism undertakes this category work.[29] Yusoff sees geologic-material categories as a sliding scale and observes how the instability of the category of the inhuman and its "stickiness" subjugates the specificities of subjectivity.[30] She writes of geologic subjectivity and how the world is parceled out according to color lines. Blackness too easily gets collapsed into the "inhuman," becoming organized as so much matter, part and parcel of resources to be extracted (the "resources" here being both extracted materials and the extraction of labor from toiling bodies). What she means by this collapse is that scientific efforts to classify geological materials for extraction are similarly applied to the establishment of a color line that polices who is free and who is a mere resource to be managed.[31]

25 Reinhold Martin, "Drawing the Color Line: Silence and Civilization from Jefferson to Mumford," in *Race and Modern Architecture: A Critical History from the Enlightenment to the Present*, ed. Irene Cheng, Charles L. Davis II, and Mabel O. Wilson, 59–78 (Pittsburgh: University of Pittsburgh Press, 2020); and Kathryn Yusoff, *A Billion Black Anthropocenes or None* (Minneapolis: University of Minnesota Press). For a discussion of houses that can be associated with slave labor in the southern United States, see Jennifer Bloomer, who writes, "In the walls of these houses lies a powerful structure built of this and other more difficult relations of capital and culture. It is invisible, and never, ever, spoken about, but it is there, sinister and tragic." Jennifer Bloomer, "Pale Houses, Silenced Shadows," *Assemblage*, no. 37 (December 1998): 44–67 (here 48).

26 Martin, "Drawing the Color Line," 60.

27 Martin, "Drawing the Color Line," 77–78.

28 Yusoff, *A Billion Black Anthropocenes or None*, 2, 82.

29 **Yusoff,** *A Billion Black Anthropocenes or None*, **66.**

30 **Yusoff,** *A Billion Black Anthropocenes or None*, **72.**

31 **Yusoff,** *A Billion Black Anthropocenes or None*, **68.**

Outside the Path of Cyclones

The Seychelles is an archipelago of islands, numbering from 92 to 115 depending on who is counting and what is considered big enough to constitute an island. Ornamented by coralline outcroppings, they are the only mid-oceanic granite islands in the world.[32] Seemingly situated in serene isolation in the Indian Ocean, northeast of Madagascar, enjoying a tropical climate and outside the destructive path of cyclones, the leaning palms and crystalline waters of the Seychelles arouse visions of an easy-living bucolic idyll, but it must also be remembered that the main island, Mahé, once served as a convenient location for a slave depot. Visions of the island are complex, DeLoughrey warns: "The island, with its terrestrial boundedness, became foundational to figuring a newly encountered world."[33] The island readily lends itself to being an allegory of paradise, a plan for Utopia, much as Thomas More described. Yet such a pastoral idyll manufactures an image that represses the plantation's contributions to modernity and processes of industrialization.[34] Insofar as the figure of the island presents a quasi-fictional microcosm of the world, it renders invisible the structural racism, the color lines, upon which it is founded. In his history of the Seychelles as a slave and post-slavery society, Deryk Scarr notes the local insistence that the Seychelles never had a "color question," as though no such line organized a distinction between those who labored for little or nothing and those who owned estates.[35] Parcels of land, called *habitations*, were cut for the plantocracy, the *Grands Blancs*, each

Seemingly situated in serene isolation in the Indian Ocean, northeast of Madagascar, enjoying a tropical climate and outside the destructive path of cyclones, the leaning palms and crystalline waters of the Seychelles arouse visions of an easy-living bucolic idyll, but it must also be remembered that the main island, Mahé, once served as a convenient location for a slave depot.

32 **Deryk Scarr,** *Seychelles since 1770: History of a Slave and Post-slavery Society* **(London: First Africa World Press, C. Hurst, 1999), 1.**

33 **DeLoughrey,** *Allegories of the Anthropocene*, **35.**

34 **DeLoughrey,** *Allegories of the Anthropocene*, **38.**

35 **Scarr,** *Seychelles since 1770*, **4.**

concession organized as "a strip running to the mountains from a frontage on the sea," lengths of paradise originally distributed for the cultivation of crops destined for circulation in the global marketplace.[36] The island as idyll of serene isolation is, of course, a conceit, and the Seychelles is better situated as a strategic if distant node in a network of communications and trade. Writing of the exile's role in anti-colonial networks of resistance, Uma Kothari describes a Seychelles that has been composed from the beginning as an effect of global processes and flows: "Possessing no original population, it has been thoroughly shaped by various movements of people including French and British colonial administrators, traders, indentured laborers, slaves, plantation owners and exiles and thus has been very much constituted by a multiplicity of political, emotional, commercial, symbolic, cultural and familial connections."[37]

36 Scarr, *Seychelles since 1770*, **12.**

37 Uma Kothari, "Contesting Colonial Rule: Politics of Exile in the Indian Ocean," *Geoforum* **43 (2012): 697–706 (here 699).**

Sailing Boat, Seychelles. Frichot Family Archive, c. 1955.

The color line suggests a complex understanding of infrastructure as composed of people, places, things, and the specificity of their quotidian practices and relations, constrained by the insidious work of colonization and racialization.

The color line suggests a complex understanding of infrastructure as composed of people, places, things, and the specificity of their quotidian practices and relations, constrained by the insidious work of colonization and racialization. An understanding of infrastructure as pertaining to dynamic systems that work, but also fall apart and fail, that serve the powerful by oppressing the disenfranchised, and yet which might be flipped to produce other possibilities and opportunities for life, might nonetheless be hopefully ventured. Addressing the "African city," for instance, AbdouMaliq Simone looks specifically at Johannesburg and offers the conceptual construction of "people as infrastructure."[38] In his conceptual recalibration of infrastructures, Simone powerfully shifts the terms of reference of infrastructure—"commonly understood in physical terms, as reticulated systems of highways, pipes, wires, or cables"—and directs attention to multifarious combinatorials of objects, spaces, persons, and practices: "accelerated, extended, and intensified intersections of bodies, landscapes, objects, and technologies."[39] Simone is interested in how social power is channeled along vectors mixing forms of content and forms of expression and eventuating in the possibility of heady eruptions of collective enunciation. Less than fixing or concretizing practices and spaces, this formulation suggests the liberties of an unaccountable movement, a collective enunciation shot through with desire, even if at the brink of despair. Infrastructures, including those that support the Plantationocene, might be used otherwise or else disrupted and repurposed from within.

Expanding on this thought in a later article, where he reprises the concept of "people as infrastructure," Simone speaks of his desire to "consider urban collective life as something beyond notions of individuals, households, communities, and institutions."[40] He explains that he is searching for "an infrastructure generating possibilities of acting in concert."[41]

38 AbdouMaliq Simone, "People as Infrastructure: Intersecting Fragments in Johannesburg," *Public Culture* **16, no. 3 (2004): 407–29. The Seychelles, having claimed its independence from British colonial rule on June 29, 1976, can be considered as belonging to the African context.**

39 Simone, "People as Infrastructure," 407–8.

This notion of social infrastructure or how social life can be narrated in concert with material infrastructures is also discussed by urban theorist Ash Amin.[42] Infrastructure is conceptualized as a sociocultural assemblage, and in this thought-image Gilles Deleuze and Félix Guattari's definition of assemblage can be heard to reverberate: "a social machine, taking men and women into its gears, or, rather, having men and women as part of its gears along with things, structures, metals, materials."[43] This is what Amin identifies as the "liveliness of sociotechnical systems."[44] Likewise mixing the sociopolitical with the infrastructural, feminist philosopher Judith Butler argues that the "material conditions for speech and assembly are part of what we are speaking and assembling about. We have to assume the infrastructural goods for which we are fighting, but if the infrastructural conditions for politics are themselves decimated, so too are the assemblies that depend on them."[45] Even though infrastructures can prove oppressive and exclusionary, life depends on the stoppages and flows of infrastructures of one kind or another. Infrastructures can support the sustenance of facilitative environments. Even the oppressive plantation regime may give way to small ruptures of resistance, enough to pull it asunder when micro-acts of resistance are imposed over time and with enough persistence.

Simone, Amin, and Butler write about infrastructural opportunities and their entanglements with social relations—even infrastructure as inherently social—as well as the political claims that can be made to gain access to infrastructural goods. But the infrastructural rhythms of the plantation are controlled and constrained. To imagine a line of escape is difficult. The global impact of the plantation scaled up as the Plantationocene has been pronounced. Opportunities for collective enunciation and for infrastructural rhythms to be rerouted to produce a different pattern—that is, opportunities for leakage and rupture—are hard to see. Clyde Woods argues that the plantation has lent itself as a model to all manner of enclosures and reserves: "industrial estates and mill villages; free-trade and export zones; enterprise and empowerment zones; ghettos and gated communities; suburbanization and gentrification; game preserves and tourist resorts; pine plantations and mines; and migratory

40 AbdouMaliq Simone, "Ritornello: People as Infrastructure," *Urban Geography*, **March 5, 2021.**

41 Simone, "Ritornello," 1.

42 Ash Amin, "Lively Infrastructure," *Theory, Culture, and Society* **31, no. 7/8 (2014): 137–61.**

43 Gilles Deleuze and Félix Guattari, *Kafka: Towards a Minor Architecture* **(Minneapolis: University of Minnesota Press, 1986), 81.**

44 Amin, "Lively Infrastructure," 138.

45 Judith Butler, "Rethinking Vulnerability and Resistance," in *Vulnerability in Resistance*, **ed. Judith Butler, Z. Gambetti, and Leticia Sabsy, 12–27 (Durham, NC: Duke University Press, 2016), 13.**

and prison labor," all of which reproduce forms of plantation capitalism, in that they depend on "resource monopoly; extreme ethnic, class, racial, and gender polarization; an export orientation; and the intense regulation of work, family, speech, and thought."[46] Though, as Janae Davies and her coauthors explain, despite these conditions Woods finds a line of escape for African Americans; for instance, in the tradition of the blues, in the voice, in music ringing out to unsettle the spaces of confinement. Black life has the possibility of "refusals, ruptures, resistance, and openings."[47]

In their work on the Plantationocene, whose origin story they also sketch out, Davis and her coauthors Alex A. Moulton, Levi Van Sant, and Brian Williams have concerns about what they describe as Haraway's slight color blindness and attachment to a flat ontology of multispecies relations. They question her lack of references to Black ecologies and are concerned that "the matters of Black embodiment and the disciplinary regimes of the slave plantation remain obscured."[48] They argue that sustained attention to race in Plantationocene scholarship is crucial to socioecological justice and multispecies kinship, though at the same time they want to hold onto the multispecies relations that Haraway and Tsing have become famous for critically fostering. Tsing, for instance, continues to insist that, without meaning to, "most of us learn to ignore the multispecies worlds around us" and that, to counter this, projects for the rebuilding of curiosity are required.[49] Like Haraway and Tsing, Davis and her coauthors draw attention to provision grounds and slave gardens as a counterpractice that unsettles the will to universalization and global distribution of the cene that is the Plantationocene. Here a reading of the work of Jamaican author and critic Wynter becomes especially instructive. Reading Wynter, Davis and her coauthors tell how the small garden plot, where opportunities for sustenance were woven into the rhythms of plantation life, enabled the fostering of relations of care and creativity, resilience and sustainability, even offering sources of hope and suggesting visions of what life could be like otherwise.[50] Yusoff, also making reference to Wynter, writes of the "slave plot" where "the unsettled" (as distinct from the colonizing settlers) grew

46 Clyde Woods, (2007). "'Sittin' on TOP OF THE WORLD': The Challenges of Blues and Hip Hop Geography," in *Black Geographies and the Politics of Place*, **ed. K. McKittrick and C. A. Woods, 46–81 (Toronto: Between the Lines; Cambridge, MA: South End Press), 56, as cited in Davis, Moulton, Van Sant, and Williams, "Anthropocene, Capitalocene,… Plantationocene?," 6. See also Kris Manjapra, "Plantation Dispossessions: The Global Travel of Agricultural Racial Capitalism," in** *American Capitalism: New Histories*, **ed. Sven Beckert and Christine Desan, 361–87 (New York: Columbia University Press, 2018).**

47 Davis, Moulton, Van Sant, and Williams, "Anthropocene, Capitalocene,… Plantationocene?," 7.

things and thereby engaged in a biophysical and narrative act.[51] The provision garden is an infrastructure of love that is dedicated not toward exchange and market value but toward the sustenance of those who are most intimate: children and partners and parents, as well as kin. Kin relations, Haraway explains, are "enduring, mutual, obligatory, non-optional."[52] Beyond the nuclear family groupuscule, kin knot together the relations and sites of attachment upon which we depend for survival.

The provision garden is an infrastructure of love that is dedicated not toward exchange and market value but toward the sustenance of those who are most intimate: children and partners and parents, as well as kin.

Provision grounds, slave gardens, plots that produce a counter-rhythm to the daily toil of the plantation, situate a more complex affective weave than the Plantationocene can provide. DeLoughrey, who also cites Wynter's influential work on the slave garden, explains that the "provision grounds, with their diverse intercropping of Indigenous and African cultivars, are understood as the often unseen—but no less integral—voluntary cultivation of subsistence foods such as yams, cassava, and sweet potatoes that represent edible staples and the economically viable roots of the internal markets."[53] Yam was so important as an alternative to cereals such as wheat and barley—and, as DeLoughrey explains, less demanding on the soil—that provision grounds were often called "yam grounds."[54] What of such plots in the specific location that is the Seychelles? In a blogpost, Egla L. Rose, a Seychellois woman interested in cultural heritage, tells the story of the settlement of the Seychelles, the laying of the stone of possession by the French in 1744, and the establishment of slave gardens alongside the crops introduced by the white colonizers. She explains that, unless they wanted to survive off scraps, slaves were obliged to feed themselves and, in any case, found greater satisfaction and nutrition in the foods they cultivated, including cassava, yams, bananas, and plants, herbs, and spices used for medicinal purposes.[55]

Alongside the provision ground understood as a place of resistance or coun-

48 Davis, Moulton, Van Sant, and Williams, "Anthropocene, Capitalocene, . . . Plantationocene?," 5.

49 Tsing, *The Mushroom at the End of the World*, **281.**

50 Davis, Moulton, Van Sant, and Williams, "Anthropocene, Capitalocene, . . . Plantationocene?," 8, citing Wynter, "Novel and History, Plot and Plantation."

51 Yusoff, *A Billion Black Anthropocenes or None*, **65.**

52 Steve Pulson, "Making Kin: An Interview with Donna Haraway," *Los Angeles Review of Books*, **December 6, 2019, https://lareviewofbooks.org/article/making-kin-an-interview-with-donna-haraway/.**

53 DeLoughrey, *Allegories of the Anthropocene*, **39.**

terpractice—a place (as DeLoughrey, citing Wynter, notes) for the formation of refuges that foster the circulation of folk knowledge through oral histories, including the capacity for sustaining "African and Indigenous continuities"—is the role of the voice that speaks and sings, using creole as a minor language and a secret means of communication.[56] Martin talks of the color line being drawn between silence and the voice, but where such a binary is articulated it can also be resisted, challenged, and even undone. Woods, for his part, reclaims music and the voice through the blues. DeLoughrey finds in creole "a codified language that developed to be impermeable to plantation masters."[57] Citing Martinican poet and philosopher Édouard Glissant, Mairi O'Gorman describes the emergence of creole languages as bursting forth discontinuously in "snatches and fragments."[58] This was, she explains, a response to the "oppressive structures of the plantation and the necessity of communicating while leaving certain facts unspoken."[59] O'Gorman, whose PhD fieldwork enables an intimate encounter with the Seychelles, ties the shifting, hybrid properties of creole as language and identity to materials, including the soil, trees, and plants.[60] Creole for her is very much place-based, materially responsive, and situated. A minor language, stories told, oral histories shared—all are tied up with what it means to be involved in the care of the soil.

An infrastructure of love might be imagined flourishing in the provision garden, combining the voicing of shared stories with the tending of plants, the tying of knots to keep the vines in place, the tying of knots that once held together baskets balanced on heads, woven out of bamboo and coconut palm fronds. When Amin extends his argument on social infrastructures, he speaks of "Thoughts and feelings, along with social dispositions" and how these "appear as formed in the interactions of the sentient body and a sentient landscape with varying degrees of intelligence incorporated in its infrastructures."[61] The voice, the circulation of stories, the distribution of a shared language, care for the soil, and caring relations suggest another song here, a different direction to the rhythm and weave.

54 DeLoughrey, *Allegories of the Anthropocene*, 41.

55 Egla L. Rose, "Seychelles Traditional Creole Home Gardens," *The Seychelles and Me* [blog], April 16, 2018, https://theseychellesandme.com/seychelles-traditional-creole-home-gardens/. See also Scarr, *Seychelles since 1770*.

56 DeLoughrey, *Allegories of the Anthropocene*, 45.

57 DeLoughrey, *Allegories of the Anthropocene*, 50,

58 Mairi O'Gorman, "Tree of Knowledge, Tree of Life: Materials, Intimacy and Being Creole in London and Seychelles" (PhD diss, University of Edinburgh, 2019), 121, citing Édouard Glissant, *Poetics of Relation*, trans. by Betsy Wing (Ann Arbor: University of Michigan Press, 1997), 68–69.

59 O'Gorman, "Tree of Knowledge, Tree of Life," 121.

60 O'Gorman, "Tree of Knowledge, Tree of Life,"

Closing Scene: A Plantation House Slowly Falls Apart

61 Amin, "Lively Infrastructure," 140.

Once the family migrates, escaping what had become an increasingly untenable political situation for the plantocracy, the old plantation house is left in the hands of a caretaker. The doors and windows are shuttered, and over time the coconut palms grow wily. The introduced cinnamon trees continue to proliferate, as they have done since the botanist Pierre Poivre planned the first colonial garden on the Seychelles—a garden no doubt planted by subaltern hands.[62] Vanilla is lost somewhere up the slopes as the vines and undergrowth push in. The l'usine is eventually stripped of its vats and functioning parts. The drying shed where coconut was once transmogrified to copra for export had already been destroyed in a fire some years before the family migrated. The sweet, wet air gets into the grain of the timbers, and the house begins to rot and fall apart. Shutters hang dog-tailed off hinges. The old hewn granite blocks cut from the body of the island itself shed their whitewash. In time the old plantation will be subdivided, parceled off into smaller land holdings. Perhaps some of those who once labored on the land will now find a different kind of home here.

62 Scarr, *Seychelles since 1770*, 7. See also O'Gorman, "Tree of Knowledge, Tree of Life," 97.

> In time the old plantation will be subdivided, parceled off into smaller land holdings.

In the closing pages of *Poetics of Relation*, Glissant talks of the collapse of the plantation regime and describes an afterimage of plantations as "lonely places of isolation, unnatural enclosures."[63] He then takes this image and makes an association with ghettos and suburbs, abandoned villages, and fields given over to roads, "houses shut up against their surroundings."[64] He argues that a "second plantation matrix ends up in the shanty town."[65] These are sociospatial logics inspired by the plantation that Woods has likewise drawn attention to. Writing from the perspective of plantations in the American South, Bryan Norwood describes the "infrastructural scars" and material traces left in their aftermath.[66] "Behind the plantation house," he writes "lay the more explicit areas of enslavement—a factory town/

63 Glissant, *Poetics of Relation*, 209.

64 Glissant, *Poetics of Relation*, 209.

65 Glissant, *Poetics of Relation*, 73.

Two Women, Seychelles. Frichot Family Archive, c. 1955.

concentration camp operating through the violent expropriation of land and labor."[67] An afterimage persists in the ways that urban and rural enclosures continue to be planned and secured: the after-affects of the Plantationocene. Not one but a complex weave of infrastructures can be observed articulating and resisting the Plantationocene, producing concatenating, co-constitutive, sometimes mutually destructive effects—and sometimes openings, glimmers, and bursts of other possibilities. The space and time of the plantation comprises multilingual and multiracial relations, what Glissant describes as a "tangle of inextricable knots within the web of filiations," a tangle that breaks up any clear and linear Western notion of order.[68] Smudging color lines, taking up the threads of past violence that form this tangle, the challenge is how to compose—or perhaps compost—another weave and infrastructural rhythm that might lead toward the possibility of an infrastructural love. If infrastructure can be reconceptualized as infrastructural love, a final figure I offer is the knot and what relations it ties together. I offer the material thought-image of the knot, and, rather than getting caught up in the tangle as mess and nuisance, I direct attention to the entanglements that the knot participates in. Infrastructures are knotted and complex. They can be compared to Ursula Le Guin's and Haraway's deceptively simple material-semiotic figure of the carrier bag.[69] String carrier bags composed of knots tied alongside yet other knots serve the fundamental roles of carrying provisions and carrying stories. Rather than chains of dependence, relations of interdependence are tied into the carrier bag.[70] The knot that is tied, and tied again, creates in this multiplication, this embodied repetition, its own kind of rhythm. It is a material-semiotic knot: it might be tied to shape a string bag or basket or might be used to tie back a vine while a song is being sung or a story whispered. Each knot depends on the tensile and pliable strength of the material used and the knowledge of how best to secure the knot in place. Stories of small daily scenes, and material knowledge tacitly embodied in working hands, form part of a material-semiotics that entangles everyday ritual, the sacred and the profane, and that, in tying up, might just also take apart the imposed logic of the Plantationocene.

66 Bryan Norwood, "Museum, Refinery, Penitentiary," *Places Journal*, March 2021, https://placesjournal.org/article/museum-refinery-penitentiary/.

67 Norwood, "Museum, Refinery, Norwood, "Museum, Refinery, Penitentiary."

68 Glissant, *Poetics of Relation*, 71.

69 Ursula Le Guin, "The Carrier Bag Theory of Fiction," in *Dancing at the Edge of the World* (New York: St. Martin's Press, 1997); and Haraway, *Staying with the Trouble*, 39.

70 Isabelle Stengers, "Reclaiming Animism," *e-flux Journal*, no. 36 (July 2012), https://www.e-flux.com/journal/36/61245/reclaiming-animism/.

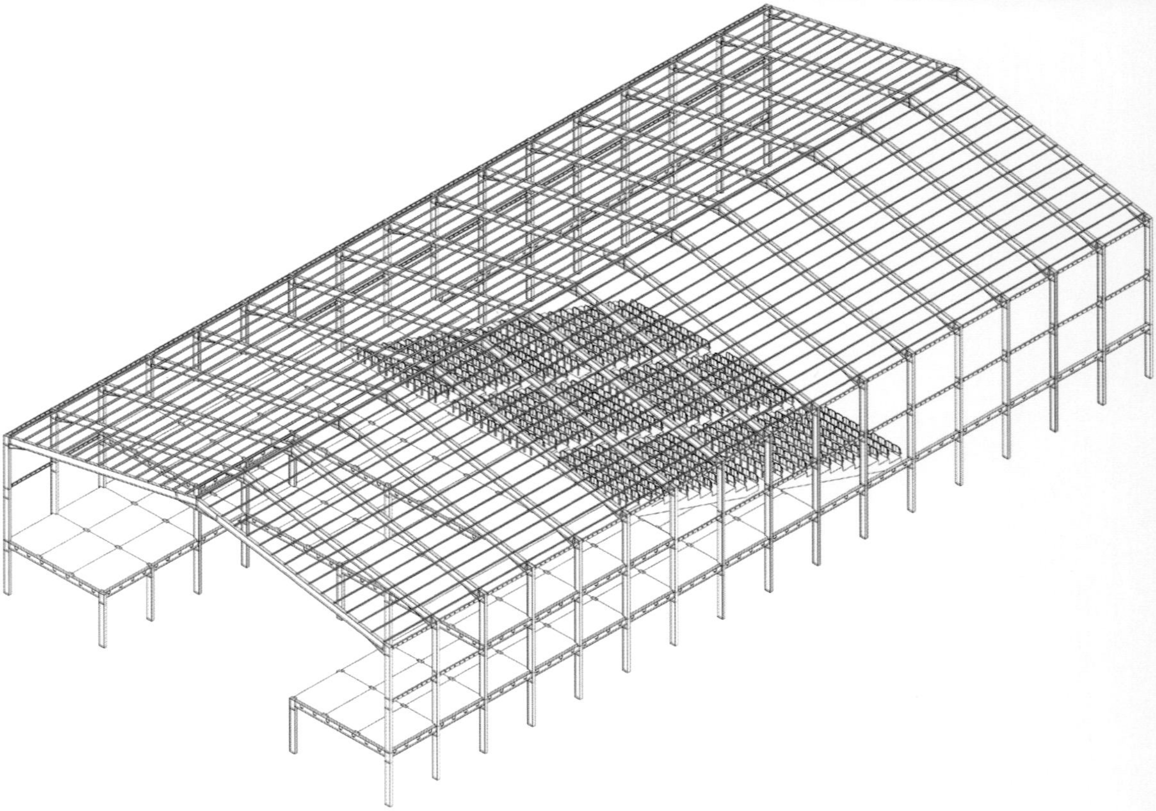

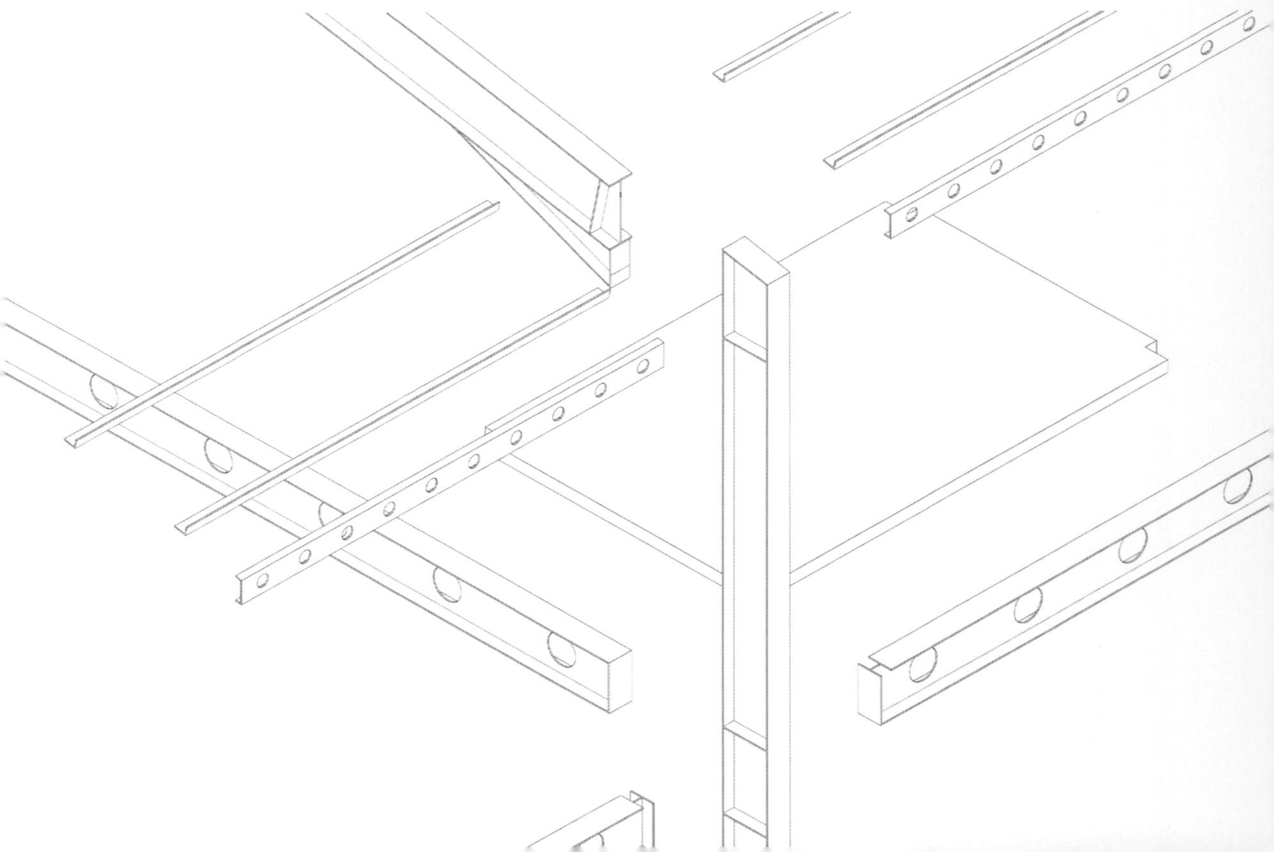

The Preemptive City

Richard Gray

The City

The current convention in development involves planning and designing a building, then completing construction as quickly as possible. A half-finished building, meanwhile, is considered to be a failure. The half-finished should instead be embraced and celebrated as a worthy part of the city.
Located around Stockholm's unfinished Kymlinge tunnelbanestation (subway station), this project envisages a "preemptive city." instead of planning rules written on paper, the envelope of the city is built in advance, forming a frame for the city to grow upon: streets waiting to be streets; buildings waiting to be buildings; and courtyards waiting to be courtyards. architecture that lives and mutates alongside its environmental context and sometimes escapes

The Preemptive

The preemptive city is not a city in the traditional sense. It is a city waiting to be a city, and in it are elements of the city waiting to be elements of the city. This gives them the ultimate potential, and the streets are no exception.
The city's streets are all fifteen meters in section. Beyond that they have no other set physical attributes but merely embody principles and will be allowed to grow and develop in time.

Between Rules and Walls

The planning system as it exists today is purely theoretical. It exists in legal texts and is supported in documents and drawings. While it may manifest in the buildings we build, the streets we lay, and the cities we spread, it does not exist in these, as these are simply reactions to rules.
In the preemptive city, these theoretical rules are usurped: the rules become concrete in every sense. As the walls go up, with their heights and openings, the rules become built realities.
But these walls are not buildings: they exist not to perform the materiality of a building envelope, nor to provide structural support for the buildings that will follow them. They exist to frame the city that will follow.
A set of principles will be composed supporting these built rules. A game-like logic, similar to that of games such as sudoku, will predetermine the choice of elements and how the city will grow. This puts growth out of the control of those who wish to use the city for personal gain. These principles allow the city to avoid having economic enclaves or land-use enclaves.

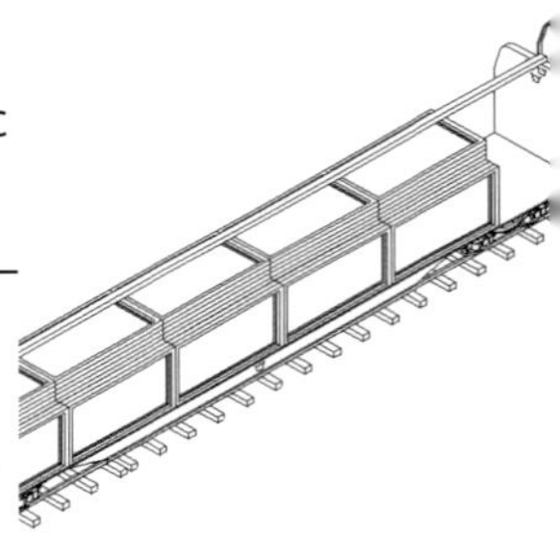

Buildings Waiting to be Buildings

The most eminent declaration of the existence of a city is the existence of its buildings. While the walls and openings of the Preemptive City provide a logic and framework for architecture and buildings, they are not meant to be architecture or buildings in themselves.
They await and they preempt. The act of turning the preemptive buildings into buildings is a job for many (autonomy should increase as scale decreases). This may be the job of masons, carpenters, architects, the clueless, the wise, opportunists, hedonists, or the dutiful, avoiding mutual exclusivity.

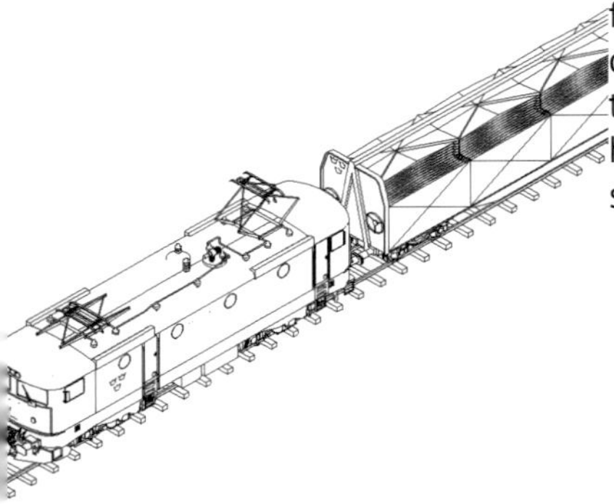

Endgame?

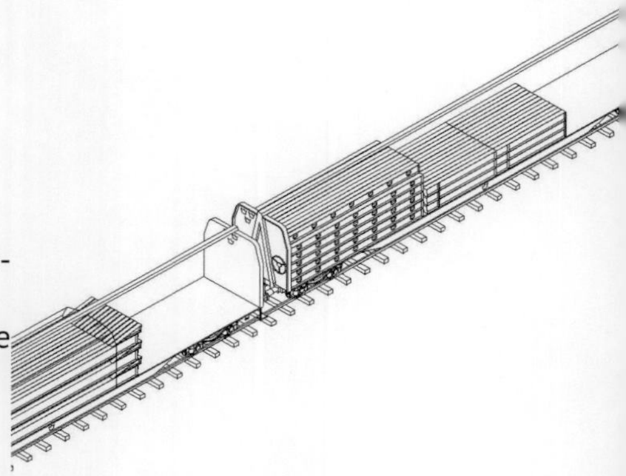

The Preemptive City forms a grid on which the puzzles and games of the city can be played; however, there is no prerequisite for answers, solutions, or conclusions. We must keep asking questions, as we can use them to preempt; however, we need not answer them, as to do so will inevitably lead to some wrong answers.
The questions we ask must also take aim at any external forces that may challenge the Preemptive City: climate, economy, sovereignty, the whims of politics, and the evolution of technology and culture. Questioning these must span time as a progressive action.
We cannot know our future, but in preempting it, we may gain the agency needed to change it—and, with this, guide life for the better. By forming this framework, we create the potential for a place that could be built well and could be lived in well. But it could also go terribly wrong.

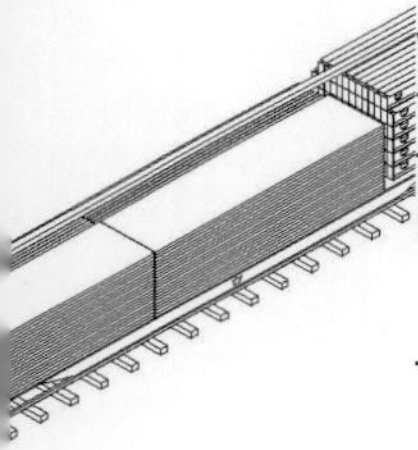

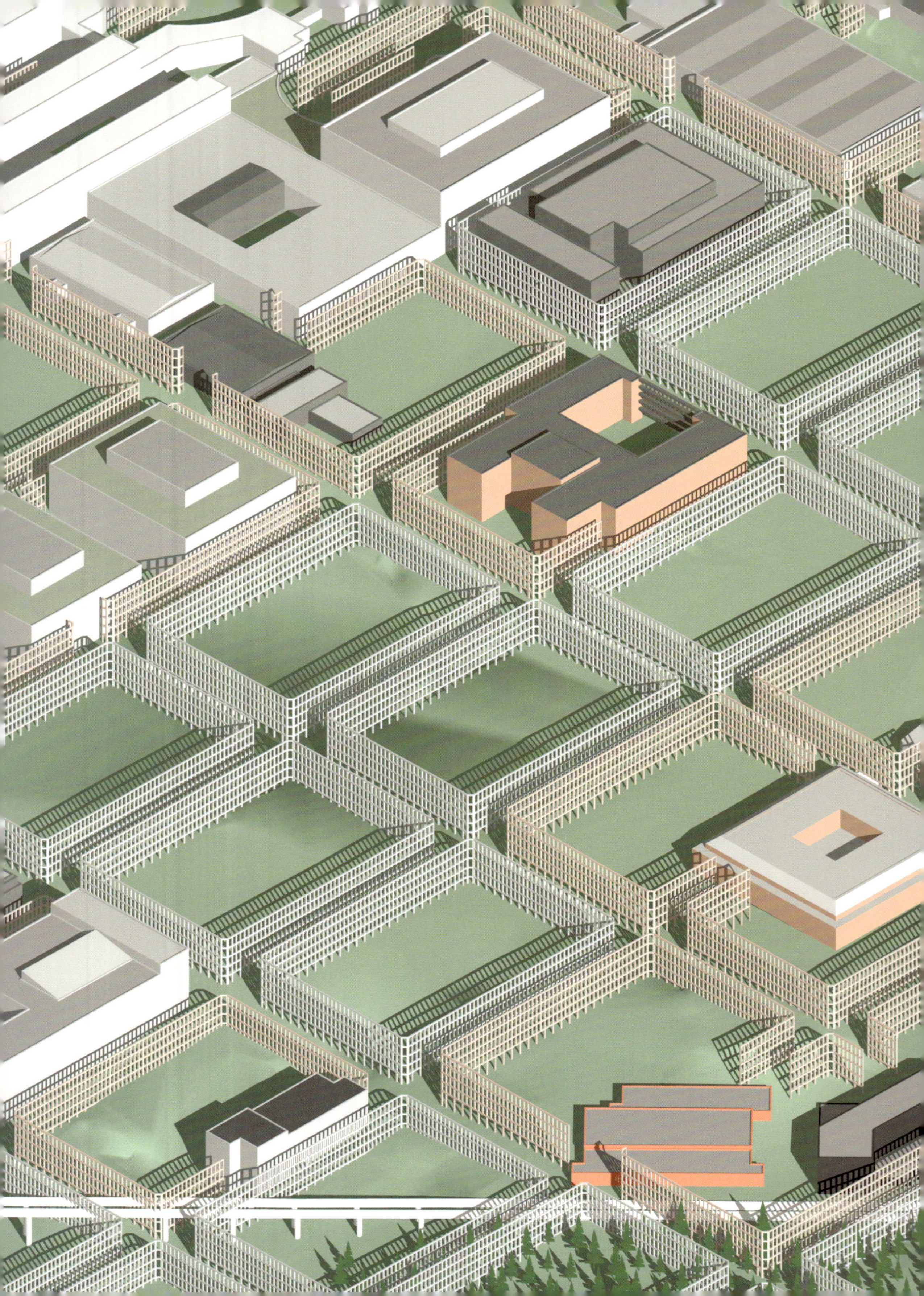

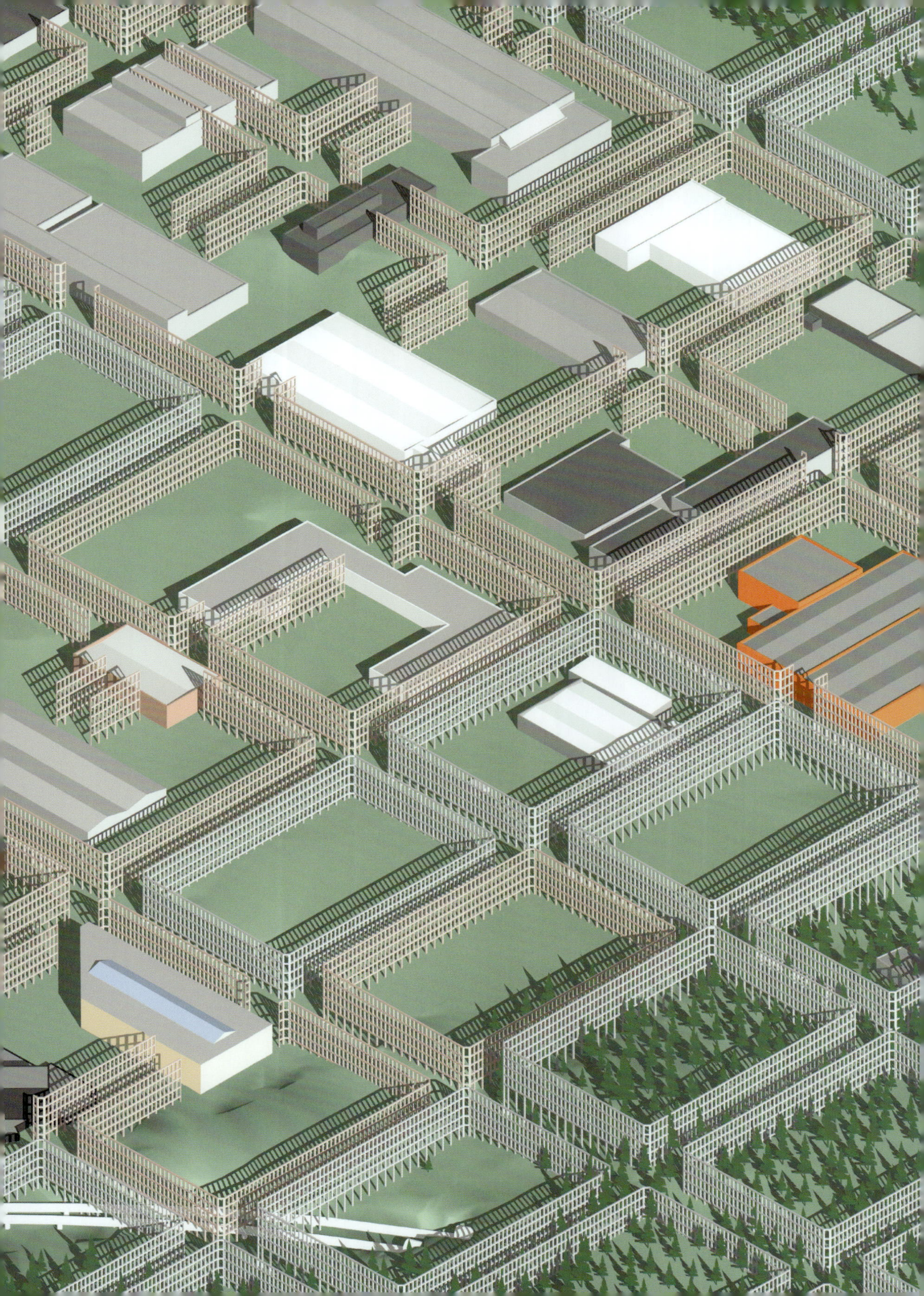

BORDERED IMAGINATION

Chapter II
Bordered Imagination

Shahram Khosravi

There was a wall. . . .
Like all walls it was ambiguous, two-faced. What was inside it and what was outside it depended upon which side of it you were on.

Ursula Le Guin[1]

The border is Janus-faced. Depending on which side of the border you stand, you see one of its two faces: one side hate, one side love. Love of the nation. Love of being in-walled. As Donald Trump stated in January 2019, building a wall along the U.S. border with Mexico was an "act of love."[2] From inside, borders are presented as infrastructures of care. On the other side of the border, you see hate. Border walls tend to be ugly. They are constructed with ugly designs and ugly materials. But they are also ugly because they indicate ugliness: fear, insecurity, distance, conflict, and hate. Both are sides of the same wall, although the hate side is older than the love side. Hatred of the Other goes further back in history than the love of country practiced in modern nation-states. If you fix your gaze on the hate side of the border, you will see that borders and border practices are in a sense colonial practices. In the walls you can see traces of the same materialities used against the colonized Other in the past and today: in unearthing and unsettling projects, invasions, and dispossession.[3] From the other side of the border, borders appear as the infrastructure of a durable racism. Those who wait at the border, those showing their faces at the door, those who are supposed to stay behind the wall, those who are supposed to be placed and not displaced, rooted and not en route, there and not here—they evoke historical uncanniness that arouses certain memories that are inscribed into the walls. The infrastructure of love/hate is based on the politics of visiblizing and invisiblizing, the seen and the unseen.

From inside, borders are presented as infrastructures of care. On the other side of the border, you see hate

1 **Ursula K. Le Guin,** *The dispossessed: an ambiguous Utopia* **(New York: Harper Prism, 1974).**

2 **"Trump Says Building Wall Would Be Act of Love," AP, January 8, 2019, https://apnews.com/article/93e8ede763f8408c-82c4e51baf132597.**

3 **Shahram Khosravi, "What Do We See if We Look at the Border from the Other Side?,"** *Social Anthropology 27*, **no. 3 (2019): 409–24.**

Roots vs Routes

Where are you from? This question, although asked with various intentions, is always enunciated in the same bordering and othering tone. It does not require an answer, because it is not really a question. Rather, it is a statement, a declaration; it is addressed to one who is already inside the border. Rather than a simple act of exclusion, it aims to keep the Other in their place in the social hierarchy. It excludes one who is already included. *Where are you from!* is posed as a statement to remind one that one's *foreignness* is neither forgotten nor forgiven, that coming from the hate side to the love side is not approved. It is a reminder that one will not be accommodated as just another citizen, a member of society, a loved one. The question, the statement, aims to measure the degree of foreignness—to evaluate, to calculate, to conclude. It targets those who will never elude being seen and treated as foreigners. It is as if the strangeness is carved on their bodies. The darker your skin, hair, eyes, the more often the question is asked. It is not an enquiry about geographical location but a declaration of race. As such, it has no expiration date. It lasts as long as your skin color.

Where are you from? is an interrogation, demanding confession: of the unforgivable sin of being on this side of the border. A*re you a refugee? Are you fleeing from the law?* The two words, *refugee* and *fugitive*, share the same root in Latin, fugere, which means "to flee."[4]

Those asked the question should also pose a question. *Where am I from? Or From which part of your fantasy and imagination do I come?*

The counterquestion discloses the fact that the stranger is always an extension of us. It unfolds the fact that *Where are you from?* is more about colonizing imagination than about satisfying the questioner's curiosity. Therefore, a politically and morally responsible answer to the question cannot be other than, "I am not from anywhere but you."

4 Angela Naimou, *Salvage Work: U.S. and Caribbean Literatures amid the Debris of Legal Personhood* **(New York: Fordham University, 2015)**

Face

Prosopagnosia is a Greek word, a combination of *prosopon,* which means "face," and agnosia, which means "not knowing." Prosopagnosia, also called face blindness, is a disorder that causes an inability to recognize faces, even familiar ones. Those who suffer from prosopagnosia look but cannot see the faces of people. I use prosopagnosia as a metaphor to assert that the gaze involves not an innocent act of seeing but a way of knowing that determines who is seen and who is unseen.

The visual field is not neutral. The gaze hierarchically interweaves gender, race, and class. One of the most notable aspects of seeing is racial. Those who suffer from face blindness may be able to recognize people based on other cues, such as clothing, hairstyle, skin color, or voice and accent—that is, based on types and stereotypes. A face-blind gaze exposes the Other to a gaze that does not see her as an individual but reads her as a type. A constant struggle is not to show who you are but to prove what you are not. A prosopagnosic gaze reduces a whole into parts. The Other is watched but unrecognized. The Other is actively unseen. Rather than being invisible, the Other is unseen: exposed to a conscious act of exclusion from the domain of recognition.

"I am invisible ... simply because people refuse to see me," Ralph Ellison writes in his classic *Invisible Man*, a testimony of African American experiences of being unseen, and thus unrecognized, as citizens.[5] In prosopagnosic American society, blackness signifies more as strangeness than familiarity. Active unseeing is also the underlying theme in China Miéville's novel *The City & the City*[6]. This science fiction novel depicts two cities that spatially overlap; they share the same geographical space, where citizens of one are disciplined to unsee the other. Each group is aware of the existence of the other in the city but consciously chooses not to *see* them. This is about politics. Making some people seen and others unseen has consequences for access to social and political rights and resources. As Socrates stated, "A thing is not seen because it

5 Ralph Ellison, *Invisible Man* **(New York: Random House, 1952).**

6 China Miéville, *The City & the City* **(London: Macmillan, 2009).**

> To see something is to make it visible. Accordingly, to unsee the Other means to invisibilize her so she is rendered faceless and unrecognized as a citizen; that is, disqualified from political membership.

is visible but on the contrary it is visible because it is seen."[7] Thus, to see something is to make it visible. Accordingly, to unsee the Other means to invisibilize her so she is rendered faceless and unrecognized as a citizen; that is, disqualified from political membership. Political invisibility induces denial of the right to participate and perform the act of citizenship.

7 **Quoted in David Kishik,** *Manhattan Project: A Theory of a City* **(Stanford, CA: Stanford University Press, 2015), 209.**

I use prosopagnosia metaphorically as a will to unsee. Exposed to the prosopagnosic gaze, the Other is made faceless; that is, denied an individual, personal, unique face. She is deprived of the right to singularity and the right to perform the act of citizenship. She and others like her are everywhere around us, but we unsee them: the homeless, the poor, the undocumented.

Reluctant to see, a prosopagnosic society uses other senses to diagnose and detect strangeness in people. Smell is commonly used as an indicator of otherness. Bong Joon-ho's *Parasite* (2019) depicts how class and smell interact. Class can be smelled. Hearing, too, is used to prove the strangeness of the unseen Other, or to distinguish between speech as human language and mere noise.

Several years ago, I was invited to give a lecture on migration to teachers in a school in a Stockholm neighborhood. After finishing my one-hour talk in Swedish, I asked the teachers about their thoughts on Swedishness. Suddenly, I was mentioned as an example of a non-Swede. I asked why they did not see me as a Swede. Many agreed with a middle-aged woman who said, "Because you don't speak Swedish." I had just given a one-hour talk in Swedish, and yet my speech did not qualify as a language. Those who do not want to recognize my face as familiar do not hear my words as familiar either. What were those words in their ears? If not Swedish, then they were just noise.

Once, on the bus, while I was speaking Persian on my mobile phone, an elderly man told me, "We speak Swedish here!" When speaking non-Swedish, I am considered awkward. When speaking Swedish, I am considered as unspeaking. Unlike Emmanuel Levinas, who believed that "speech cuts across vision," meaning that the face is always recognized through language, a Fanonian approach shows that the opposite applies in the context of race: "vision cuts across speech."[8] For Frantz Fanon, spoken words always are grounded historically and culturally, hence racially. Speech is not fixed and coherent but always dialectically in relation to the epidermal racial scheme. Bodies frame speech and affect how it is perceived.[9] If the Other's face is unseen, then her words are unheard. When one is deprived of speech, what will remain of one's place in the community and of one's citizenship? Racism is the continuum of vision cutting across speech. Perhaps the question, *Can the Other speak?* should be opposed with another: *Can we hear the Other?*

> For Frantz Fanon, spoken words always are grounded historically and culturally, hence racially.

8 **See Patrick Anderson, "Levinas and the Anticolonial,"** *Journal of French and Francophone Philosophy* *25*, **no. 1 (2017), DOI: 10.5195/jffp.2017.721.**

9 **Frantz Fanon,** *Black Skin, White Masks* **(New York: Grove Press, 1967).**

Prophets and philosophers claimed that the face of the Other engages and obliges. With face comes responsibility. The face of the Other calls for an ethical conversation, commanding not only "thou shalt not kill" but also "you should not let the Other die alone." Once a person is denied a face, her life can easily be turned into death. With no face, life is not counted, not considered lived. Not in Albert Camus's *The Stranger* nor in Ellison's *Invisible Man*. Nor in the case of border transgressors today.

The media representation of the so-called refugee crisis along European borders is based on face blindness. We usually see large crowds of people squeezed together in wagons, boats, or makeshift camps. The images show an incessant absence of visible faces and the constant presence of vehicles, tents, or boats packed with de-named and de-faced racialized bodies: a mass, a package of bodies, representing crises. Ironically, when the Other is dead, her face is revealed to us. Travelers without papers, robbed of their face while living, become visible to the rest of the world when dead. Death gives bodies washed up on the shores of Europe and of the suffocated men, women, old and young, in small shipping containers, a visibility they did not possess when alive. Death qualifies the unqualified. Death re-faces the de-faced.

10 Audre Lorde, "A Litany for Survival," in *The Black Unicorn*, 31–33 (New York: Norton, 1978).

What would be inexplicably strange is not if the Other died at the border but if she did not. To paraphrase Audre Lorde, she was never meant to survive.[10]

"But they did not kill you," said a British migration officer to an Ethiopian asylum seeker. The officer wondered why the Ethiopian authorities had not killed him when they had the opportunity. Not being killed indicated a lack of credibility. If they had killed the applicant, he would deserve asylum, but then he could not have been able come all the way to Europe to seek it. An Afghanistani asylum seeker received a similar comment from a Swedish migration officer when he described the torture he had been exposed to in prison: "But the torture apparently was not very severe, because you survived." And in an asylum interview in Denmark, an Iraqi woman who was talking about receiving death threats was told by the officer, "You are alive now. You have not yet died." The burden of proof lies with the asylum seeker, who should bring evidence to prove why she is still alive.

Tell us exactly why you are not dead?

Under-Standing

The Other is unseen while, paradoxically (or maybe not), being exposed to demands for total transparency and knowability. Strangers, be they border transgressors or racialized citizens, are deprived of a human face, while everything about them is screened, simplified, documented, and explained. So the Other's body is "hyper-visible and invisible at the same time."[11] A complex apparatus of illuminating otherness is at work, from bureaucratic paperwork in the form of a passport, visa application, or asylum process, to bodily visual documentation in the form of fingerprints, biometric data, and dental or bone X-rays (to assess

> So the Other's body is "hyper-visible and invisible at the same time."

11 Fanon, ***Black Skin, White Masks*****, 109.**

the age of asylum seekers). All to render the Other transparent and knowable. The answers to *Where are you from?* are thus crucial to the questioner's *under-standing*, albeit not in the sense of sympathizing but in the sense of grasping, getting hold of. The intent of the question is to dominate. The Other shall stand under. The violence embedded in the question Where are you from? lies precisely in the repressive demand for *under-standing*: the asylum seeker must be made to *stand under*. Racial privilege gives the questioner or interrogator the authority to command the Other to be knowable. This under-standing is a matter of police and policing.

Are you your fingerprint?

Are you your passport?

The desire for a standing above the Other requires visibility. A penetrataing gaze demands transparency and nakedness. The penetrating colonial gaze stretching over time and space—from the vertical gaz of American drones over the occupied lands in the Middle East, to surveillance by algorithm, to the European Union's asylum seeker fingerprint database (EURODAC)—all these eyes upon eyes enable the colonizer to penetrate into the lives, souls, and bodies of Others. This assemblage of eyes upon eyes creates a monster not unlike the Greek myth Argus Panoptes, a one-hundred-eyed monster, from whom the term panopticon is derived. It targets blacks, the poor, Jews (then), and Muslims (now). A racialized body should be easily distinguishable, observable, traceable. The regime of unseeing looking is an old technique to regulate the bodies of undesirable groups. From the Lantern Law in late-eighteenth-century New York, which required all slaves to carry a lighted candle when going out at night, to the red letter J on the passports of German Jews in the first half of the twentieth century, to screening every step taken by Muslims in the early twenty-first century—all are more than acts of control. These, to use Simone Browne's argument on racial aspects of surveillance methods, are techniques for illuminating otherness.[12]

The violence embedded in the demand for understanding is revealed in the terminology. To *understand* means "to comprehend," a verb that is synonymous with verbs such as to *apprehend*. The word *apprehension* also means "arrest"

12 Simone Browne, *Dark Matters: On the Surveillance of Blackness* **(Durham, NC: Duke University Press, 2015), 25.**

When Europe forces a Muslim woman to remove her veil, it is not an attempt to give her a face; on the contrary, it is to take her face away, to see her and to *under-stand* her on the colonizer's terms.

and "seizure." One meaning of to *comprehend* is "to realize," meaning to give form and to actualize something. The Other becomes *realized* in the process of the demand for understanding. That is, she becomes a reflection of the colonizer's own fantasy and imagination. When Europe forces a Muslim woman to remove her veil, it is not an attempt to give her a face; on the contrary, it is to take her face away, to see her and to *under-stand* her on the colonizer's terms. The forced unveiling of the Muslim woman is a projection of the European imagination about her onto her. She can be knowable only when her body is accessible in the colonizer's visual field.

Opacity

The Martinican cultural theorist Édouard Glissant identifies the demand for understanding as part of the colonial project for transparent universality.[13] For him, the ideal of transparency is a Western project rooted in modernity; it is to reduce, categorize, and hierarchize in order to understand and comprehend the Other. Against the colonizer's demand for knowability, Glissant claims opacity as the right to resist. The right to opacity is the right to refuse being understood on the colonizer's terms, To not *stand under.* Refusing to be under-stood and resisting the demand of transparency, remaining incomprehensible, entails possibilities for action and offers the potential emergence of subversive subjectivities. Opacity is the weapon of the subaltern. By not answering where I am from, by wearing veils, by keeping "unpronounceable" names and "incomprehensible" accents, by forging passports and visas, by destroying passports before arrival, by fabricating stories and lying about age or ethnicity to get asylum—all are forms of subaltern resistance through

The right to opacity is the right to refuse being understood on the colonizer's terms, to not stand under.

13 Édouard Glissant, *Poetics of Relations* **(Ann Arbor: University of Michigan Press, 1997).**

imperceptibility. Opacity and the refusal to satisfy the authorities' demands generates a sense of paranoia among the colonizers, who cannot under-stand and therefore keep asking.

If I forge a life, the border forges history

If I forge a journey, the border forges the earth

Prosopagnosia is not only a strategy for active unseeing but also for active unremembering. Not remembering faces that morally and ethically should be remembered is an evasion of responsibility and accountability. The presence of the Other on this side of the border evokes a sense of the uncanny. In his essay "The Uncanny" from 1919, Sigmund Freud used the German word *unheimlich*, which means both "uncanny" and "unhomely," to explore something that is strange and familiar at the same time.[14] The uncanniness of encountering the stranger comes from the fact that she is a part of the self that has been concealed and repressed. The presence of the Other at the door triggers uncanniness because she unearths and unmasks what has actively been unseen and unremembered.

Early in the afternoon of May 8, 2019, people who were in the departure area of the Budapest International Airport witnessed several police officers dragging a woman toward a gate to put her on an airplane for deportation to Kabul. She resisted and screamed words, which historicized a potential future for many of us: "One day you will be refugees, too, like me, and on that day you will remember this day."

The presence of the stranger reminds us of a past we do not want to remember and of a possible future we do not want to imagine. Facing the face of the Other, like the woman at the Budapest airport, makes us imagine a tomorrow that can come true. The unsettling uncanniness of interacting with the stranger is because we are then forced to confront the fact that the stranger is no one but us.

The border has two faces; one hate and one love. Those who are inside the border believe it is all about love—a love that lets us unsee the Other and disremember ourselves. Borders are infrastructures of blindness and oblivion, build with love.

14 Sigmund Freud, "The Uncanny," in *The Standard Edition of the Complete Psychological Works of Sigmund Freud, vol. 17, (1917–1919): An Infantile Neurosis and Other Works*, **ed. James Strachey, 217–56 (London: Hogarth Press, 1955).**

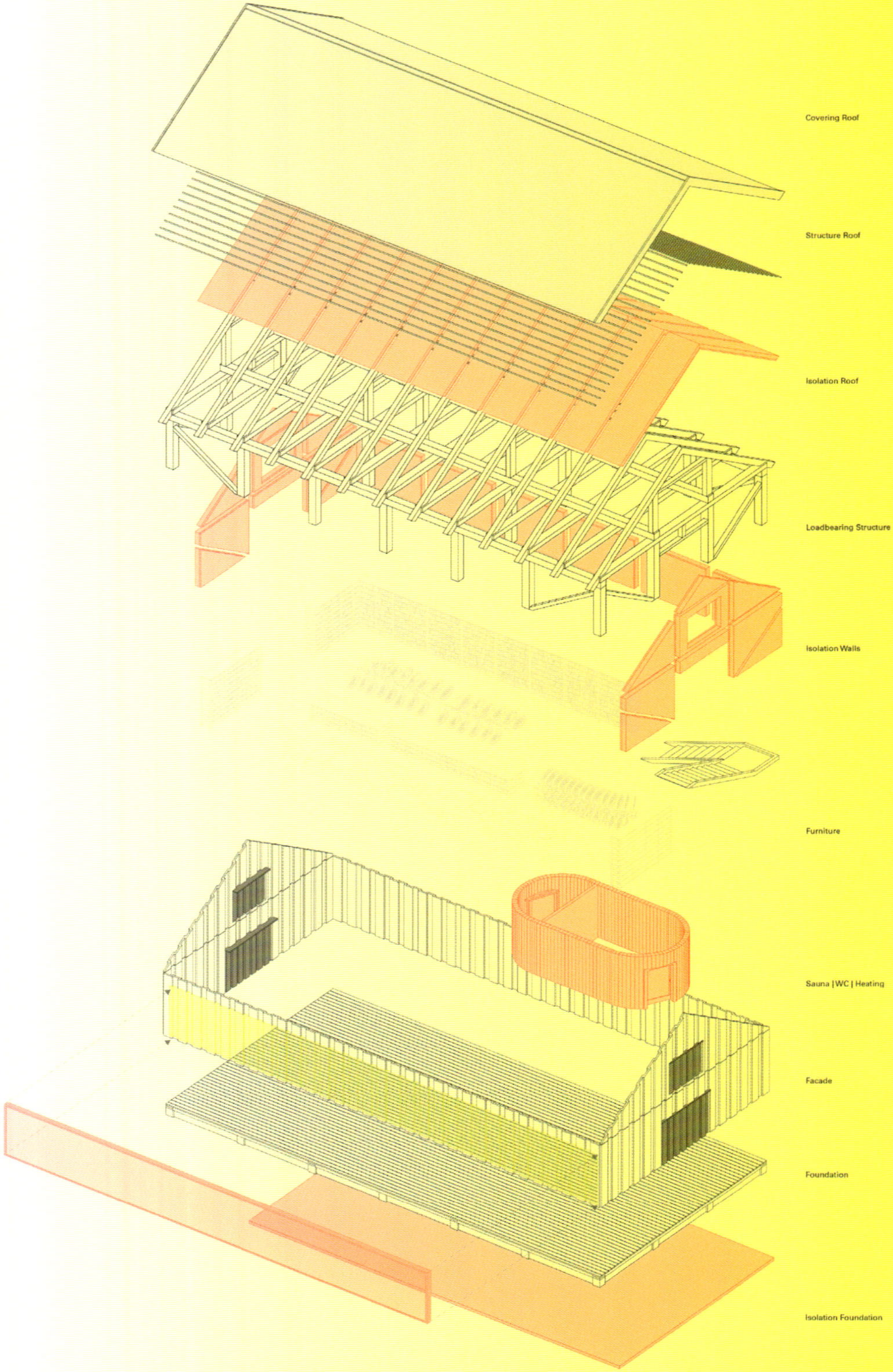

Covering Roof
Structure Roof
Isolation Roof
Loadbearing Structure
Isolation Walls
Furniture
Sauna | WC | Heating
Facade
Foundation
Isolation Foundation

Utö Campus: Student Housing Infrastructure

Marco Bruggmann

One of the main challenges for Utö, an island in the Stockholm archipelago, is its dependency on tourism, an industry that works within a small seasonal window from the end of April to the end of August. Once this four-to-five-month season is over, most of the tourism-related infrastructure remains unutilized. Whereas on Utö many buildings remain empty for at least seven months of the year, in Stockholm housing is in short supply, which leads to high market prices. This lack of access to affordable housing "closes" the city, as Richard Sennett would say. The "Utö Campus" project aims to bring students and their knowledge to Utö by developing a dynamic housing model, facilitating the occupation of housing on the island during the off-season.

An analysis of market prices and traveling distances compared student housing in Malvinas (6,800 Swedish kronor [SEK]), Björkästra (4,800 SEK), and at the Hostel Utö (2,100 SEK). The result of the analysis demonstrated that, if a student who lives at Malvinas Väg (student housing on campus at KTH Stockholm) instead lived half of the week in Stockholm and half of the week on Utö while renting out their apartment in Stockholm on Airbnb, that student could live for free and earn an additional 2,300 SEK per month to support living costs. Using this model, the more expensive apartments of Malvinas would become affordable for a student from Björksätra, while reducing their six-to-eight-hour weekly commute by one to three hours. Another model explored the benefits of sharing a room equally with another student, which would result in monthly costs of around 4,450 SEK per student.

The goal of both models is to avoid the unidirectional migration of "talented" young people from suburban and rural regions to the city by searching for models that would allow for knowledge to be brought back and forth. The tourist season on the island of Utö would be extended, which would also mean a greater range of labor possibilities on the island, with the further benefit of making living in Stockholm more affordable for students.

The design assumes that the hostel and the Utö-Stuga (Utö cottage) can shift their function from tourism to student accommodation. The hostel has two common kitchens, shared bathrooms, a shared balcony, a library, and a garden, and could support a community-orientated form of living. The Utö-Stuga could remain a studio. Within a short walking distance of five minutes, the students would find an ICA (grocery store), bakery, restaurant, bar, bistro, athletic field, tennis court, beach, kayaks, paddle boards, mini-golf, nature, and a free open-air gym. Adequate infrastructure to support students requires, as a minimum, a library, coworking spaces, and a video-conferencing room. The library could be installed in the bike-rental building that is run by the staff of the bistro at the harbor. In the short term this can generate synergies. The Societets-Hus has an existing infrastructure for conferences and meetings, which could be used as a coworking space located close to the Utö-Värdhus and its bar and restaurant.

As a designer and an exchange student (and thus a guest in a foreign country), my intent was not to show what the island of Utö needs. Instead, I wanted to show the qualities and potentials of the existing facilities. During final review, a key question was raised: Is it really architecture if a project simply shows how the use of existing infrastructures might be rethought? Just three months later COVID-19 emerged, which led to canceled bookings on the island and the closure of the university campus. I took the opportunity to contact the owner of the hostel and proposed that they invite fellow students to the island so we could continue studying without being a threat to those groups at risk of infection in the city. From the midst of a pandemic, the geography of the island presented itself as an ideal place to seek isolation.

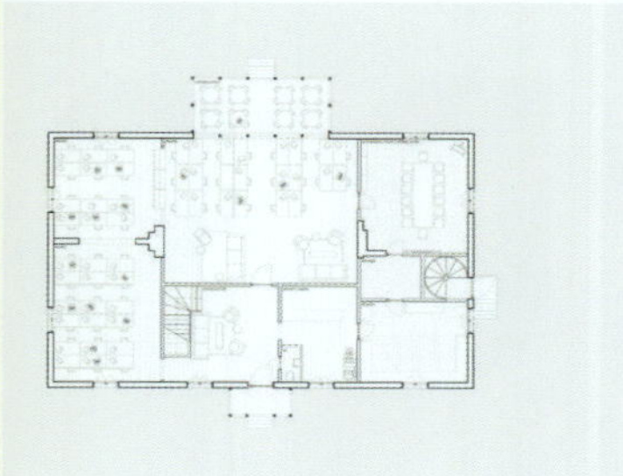

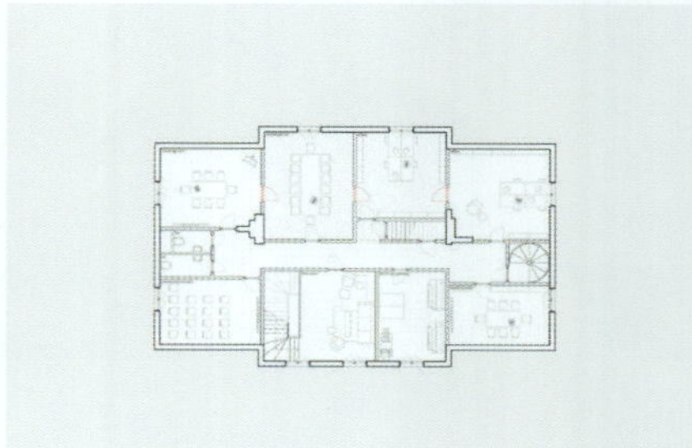

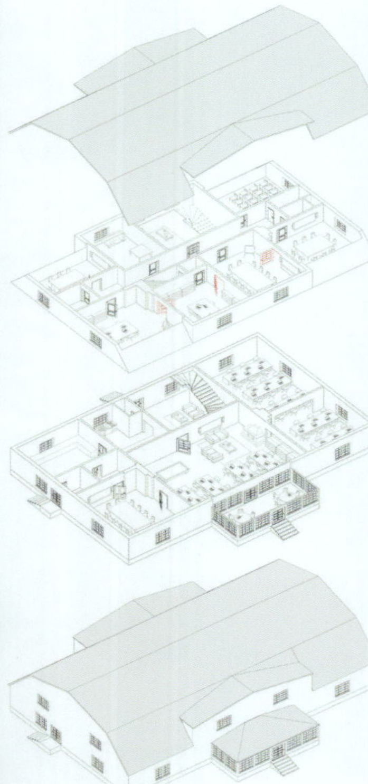

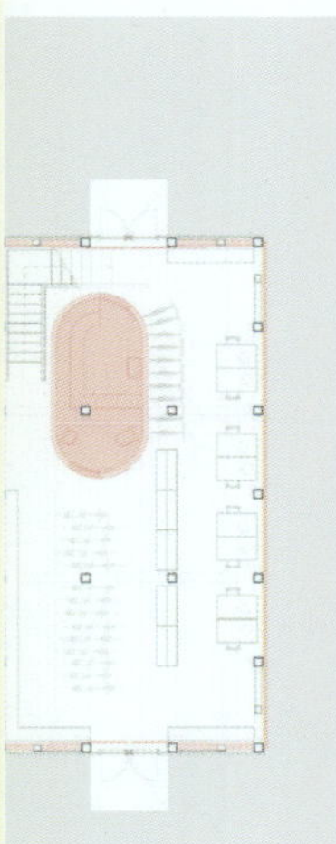

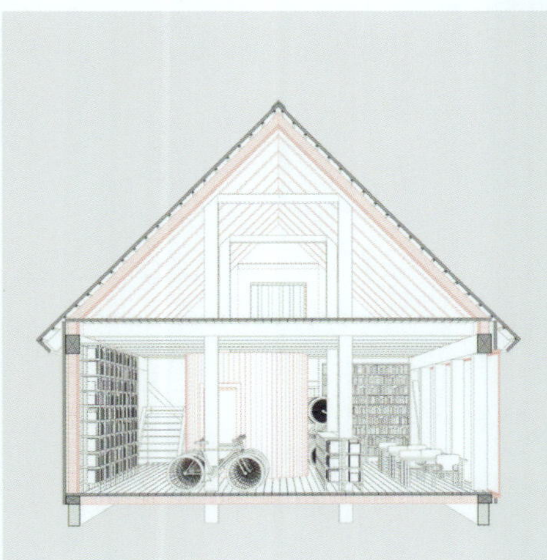

ALANDS
CAPEIN
VENTOR
Y

Chapter 12
A Landscape Inventory: Ulla Bodorff's Mapping of the Järva Field

Adrià Carbonell

Section A / 3 : 963 — Unsorted

Moving through the undulating landscape, Ulla Bodorff fixes her attention on a withered tree. Frost covers the bumpy slope, leaving glimpses of roots woven into the rocky ground. The sunlight slipping away behind the hill dyes the shady background black. Ulla carries a camera and a notebook, where she annotates a series of comments about the tree, its location, and its position within the surrounding topography. It is an old oak. Its chapped branches bend close to the ground; its fraying bark is beginning to rot. Ulla finishes the description, folds her notebook, frames a portrait view, and takes the last picture of the day. She has been repeating this operation over the last several weeks: she wanders through the Uppland territory, catches sight of a grass patch, readies her camera, and shoots the framed landscape. At most of her stops the targeted object is not sculptural like the free-standing oak tree but subtler, more diffuse aspects of the open field. After taking the photograph, she proceeds to annotate in her notebook information she thinks may be worth recording, not only to describe the actual object but the overall composition, the relative distances, the masses, the openings, the continuities and contrasts. She also writes down all facts and measures she is able to gather, such as biophysical descriptions of the surroundings, the biotopes and ecosystems, the qualities of the soil, and the types of vegetation. Although she planned her daily fieldwork well in advance, subdividing the landscape into walkable catchment areas, she tends to drift from the predetermined routes, distracted by unexpected thrills and waylaid by her untamable curiosity. In this mix of sensorial perception and methodical observation she finds the greatest pleasure. By carefully gathering this varied information, Ulla progressively assembles a landscape inventory of the Järvafältet area.[1]

Ulla Bodorff was a pioneering landscape architect in Sweden.[2] Returning from England after her education and a few study trips across Europe, she established her professional practice in Stockholm as early as 1937, then only

1 *Landskapsinventering och zonering av natursystem: Inom interkommunala friområdet av Norra Järvafältet – Bilagor L70* **(Stockholm: Friområdeskommittén för Järvafältet, 1970). Other bibliographical references to the same inventory I have come across include Ulla Bodorff,** *Landskapsinventering och zonering av naturtypsystem – L70* **(1969); and Ulla Bodorff,** *Landskapsinventering av Järvafältet* **(1967). However, I have been unable to locate any of these original publications in any library or archive in Sweden. The closest I have come was at the Stockholms Stadsarkiv (Stockholm City Archive), whose catalog lists an item corresponding to the 1970** *Landskapsinventering***, supposedly located on shelf 124:10:44. Mysteriously, the item is not in its place. Therefore, all references to Bodorff's inventory appearing in the text I have recreated or fictionalized based on secondary sources.**

twenty-five years old.[3] Alongside her successful career, Bodorff was actively involved in the formative years of her discipline and in promoting a landscape educational program in Sweden. Indeed, she had a leading role in the Swedish Association of Garden Architects and was also involved in the International Federation of Landscape Architects, of which she was Honorary Secretary of the Congress organized in Stockholm in 1952.[4] While Bodorff's most acclaimed projects were designs for gardens and parks, her work also played an influential role, albeit indirect and rarely acknowledged, in the formation of Norra Järvafältet, one of the most prominent Stockholm suburban areas developed within the Swedish Miljonprogram, an endeavor begun in 1965 to construct one million new homes in Sweden. Prior to the urban planning project, Bodorff produced a detailed landscape inventory upon which the subsequent planning process relied. The inventoried elements triggered the formalization of Järvakilen, a green wedge stretching from central Stockholm to its northwest territory and spanning several municipalities up to the town of Sigtuna. The Järva green wedge is today considered a regional green infrastructure containing within it several natural and cultural reserves, national parks, and large recreational areas.[5]

By tracing the process through which an inventory made its way into a planning document and, further, into an actual built environment, I highlight in this chapter Bodorff's original contribution of expanding design methodologies into mapping and landscape surveying. Although these are far older techniques, her detailed recognition of landscape elements and their inclusion in an urban planning process were precursors of today's transdisciplinary spatial practices and of contemporary notions such as ecological preservation and green heritage. Indeed, Bodorff's remarkable work anticipates the progressive integration of landscape and ecology in urban planning and design. Besides the historical interest in understanding the formation of green structures, Bodorff's landscape inventory contributes to a recognition of how significantly the landscape had been transformed and how, in fact, what today seems natural was the result of long processes of technical transformation of the

2 See Catharina Nolin, "From Gardening Manuals to Signum's Swedish Art History: Approaches to the Historiography of Swedish Landscape Architecture." *Konsthistorisk tidskrift / Journal of Art History* 85, no. 1 (2016): 126–40; Catharina Nolin, "International Training and National Ambitions: Female landscape architects in Sweden, 1900–1950," in *Women, Modernity and Landscape Architecture*, ed. Sonja Dümpelmann and John Beardsley, 38–59 (London and New York: Routledge, 2015).

3 Claus Nowotny and Bengt Persson, *Ulla Bodorff landskapsarkitekt 1913–1982* (Stockholm: ARKUS, 1988).

4 See Sidney N. Shurcliff, "International Conference at Stockholm," *Landscape Architecture Magazine* 42, no. 4 (1952): 174–75.

5 Länsstyrelsen i Stockholm, *Grön infrastruktur i Stockholms län: Bakgrund och tillstånd 2018*, Rapport 2019: 10.

land. The landscape inventory can be considered as a supporting document for the constitution of legal frameworks—plans, assessment reports, protected reserves—that ultimately determine *what-to-do-with-nature*. This recognition can help us reframe contemporary architecture and urban design as a set of practices invested in the making of human-mediated technical environments, and in the construction of new scales of territorial articulation that operate beyond nature-culture divides.

Section B / 6 : 1724—Infrastructure, Suburbanization, and the Modern Landscape

Järvafältet's landscape inventory is entrenched in the larger process of rapid suburbanization that Stockholm went through in the second half of the twentieth century. The area was developed in the 1960s and 1970s as a juxtaposition of neighborhood projects. Aiming to combine rapid connection to the city center with enjoyment of nature, the new districts were located along transport infrastructure and integrated within the landscape features. The process commenced in 1962, when the Swedish Crown, the property owner, expressed its desire to sell the land to neighboring municipalities interested in developing it for civil purposes. The first phase, covering 460 hectares and comprising the districts of Rinkeby and Tensta, was developed in 1964 following a partial land acquisition by the City of Stockholm.[6] To coordinate the much larger and more complex development of the second phase, which involved five municipalities, a cooperation group named the Järvafältets Committee was formed and given responsibility for planning and development. The general plan for Norra Järvafältet, covering about four thousand hectares and including the new districts of Husby, Kista, and Akalla, was approved in 1968.[7]

In the wake of the postwar welfare planning and absorbing a mix of doctrines from North American neighborhood unit, English garden cities, and CIAM functionalist models, the suburbanization of Stockholm was primarily driven by the construction of new transport infrastructures: two motorways (the E4 and the

6 Igor Dergalin and Josef M. Stäck, "Rinkeby, Spånga kyrka och Tensta," *Plan* **3 (1964): 101–7.**

7 Göran Sidenbladh, "Introduktion till dispositionsplan för Järvafältet," *Arkitektur* **1 (1969): 6–7.**

E16), a railway, and a subway line. Attached to the transport networks were demarcated zones categorized according to three land-use functions: residential, work, and services (*bostadsområde, arbetsområde and serviceområde*)[8]. Following the functionalist principles of urban design promoted by Sven Markelius, director of Stockholm's urban planning office from 1944 to 1954, the planning strategy tightly adhered to the ABC-*stad* model, the ambition of which was to create autonomous multifunctional nodes.[9] The ABC-city takes its name from the abbreviation of the Swedish words "arbete, bostad och centrum" (work, housing, and civic/commercial center), the three main urban functions that shape the satellite towns. The model's aims and diagrams were included in the general plan for Stockholm published in 1952. Thus, Stockholm's metropolitan expansion grew out of infrastructural connectivity and programmatic accumulation. The city went horizontal, motorway infrastructures flipped the congested urban centers into blankets spreading across the region. This is a vision that unfolds with strikingly clarity in Markelius' early sketches for the area as a series of meandering lines and bubbles traced over an otherwise blank topography. Hence, a system of converging green wedges, including the one along Järvafältet, was progressively formed as a negative space resulting from the linear and radial expansion led by infrastructural development.[10]

A dominant narrative today is that infrastructures were a major driver in modernist urban planning, particularly in the context of the welfare state project, as was the case of Sweden. The nationwide construction of railway infrastructure propelled not only a change in the relations between urban and rural areas but also in the understanding of nature-culture interplays. As Bodorff herself acknowl-

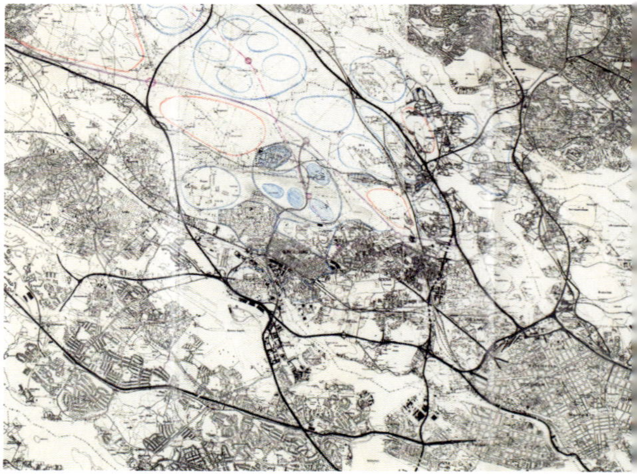

Early sketch for the suburban development over Järvafältet showing the decentralization of urban centers and the infrastructure led spatial pattern based on the ABC-Stad model. Drawing by Sven Markelius. Source: Arkdes Collections.

8 See the figure "Översiktsplan för Järvafältet enligt Dispositionsplanen 1968," in *Stockholm stad i utveckling 5, Järvastaden* **(Stockholm: Stockholms Informationsnämnd, 1979), 3.**

9 See Sven Markelius, *Framtida Stockholm: Riktlinjer för Stockholms Generalplan* **(Stockholm: Stockholms Stads Stadsplanekontor, 1946); and Stockholms Stads Stadsplanekontor,** *Stadeplanekontorets förslag till generalplan för Stockholm stad 1952* **(Stockholm: Stockholms Stads Stadsplanekontor, 1952).**

10 See Adrià Carbonell and Roi Salgueiro Barrio, "Reversing the Gaze: The Role of Metropolitan Voids as Structuring Elements of Stockholm's Territory," *ACE: Architecture, City and Environment* **16, no. 46 (2021).**

edged, the construction of infrastructures in remote rural areas was seen as a way of cultivating both nature and culture. According to her, "to all these people the railway carried a piece of culture in the form of gaily colored small gardens and parks which in our day surround and adorn even the smallest railway station."[11] However, the honorable egalitarian and redistributive function generally granted to social democratic projects deserves further scrutiny. The emphasis on the social democratic state as the main actor in the large-scale process of modernization eclipses the role played by industrial lobbies and the automobile sector. Indeed, the more nuanced reading offered by Helena Mattsson reveals the various forces at play in shaping a "Swedish corporatist policy that was striving toward a consensus between the state, the business world, and powerful interest groups."[12] Whether public or private, economic investments in infrastructure produce long-term dynamics that determine the evolution of urban growth as well as subsequent issues and contingent conflicts. Plainly put, infrastructures are the crucial generator of the urban system; however, they carry a disruptive capacity as they disentangle cities from their immediate surroundings in order to create a novel system of territorial relations. At its best, an infrastructure acts as a supporting and redistributive technology. At its worst, it performs as an exploitative and fracturing machine.

Within this context of infrastructural planning and functionalist rationality, Bodorff's inventory distinguishes itself as a game changer, inasmuch as it shifts the spatial focus and pays attention to the reversed spaces left between the lines and bubbles, between infrastructures, urban clusters, and neighborhood units, and constructs the scale of the *unbuilt*. This is not a task to be ignored. Thomas Atmer and Igor Dergalin, the main planners responsible for the overall scheme for the Järva North area, diligently noted, in an anecdotal aside, that "[a] detailed landscape inventory, carried out by garden architect Ulla Bodorff, has been used

11 Ulla Bodorff, "The Swedish Society of Landscape Architects: Brief Statement on Professional Practice in Sweden," ***Landscape Architecture*** **38, no. 3 (1948): 91–94 (here 94).**

12 Helena Mattsson, "Where the Motorways Meet: Architecture and Corporativism in Sweden 1968," in ***Architecture and the Welfare State*****, ed. Mark Swenarton, Tom Avermaete, and Dirk van den Heuvel, 155–75 (New York: Routledge, 2015), 156.**

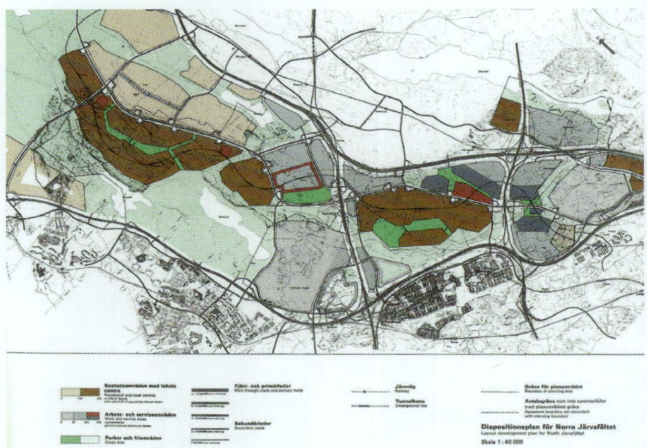

Development plan for Nörra Järvafeltet. The linear development along transport infrastructural networks leaves areas unplanned in between, thus forming what will become a "green wedge." Source: Arkitektur 1, 1969.

in the planning work."[13] They do not say in what way the inventory was used, nor what aspects or criteria were considered. A quick look at the *Dispositionsplan för Norra Järvafältet* may offer a reasonable interpretation: the inventory served as a technical basis to locate development areas, but also offered an opportunity to promote cultural-historical value, to consolidate and improve the environment, and to re-create the memory of the place. Besides the description of topographical and geological conditions, and a precise geotechnic map annexed to the written documentation, the general plan included a map of the area marking twelve "cultural sites and ancient monuments."[14] Some—if not all—of the elements highlighted in the plan were also inventoried by Bodorff, who, in her explorative walks a couple of years earlier, had recorded many architectural objects such as farms, villas, fences, and old timber sheds. Alongside landscape types, ancient remains and traditional buildings with remarkable historical value were preserved so that antiquities of various kinds became historical sites and monuments, thus resignifying the Järva territory. The plan also aimed to regulate access to generous green recreational areas, in which the inventory served as the basis to both classify and qualify the land. Planning for the so-called free areas (*friområdet*) was a growing issue that eventually emerged as a new field of spatial and landscape planning in Sweden. Unbuilt spaces played a crucial role in the suburbanization of Stockholm and were an essential component of the urban models developed within the social-democratic project of the welfare state in the Nordic countries, where, as Ellen Braae suggests, "the landscape both frames and forms the center of the planned micro-society."[15] The welfare landscape embodies a sense of morality in modern life and a progressive understanding that land is not only a resource for productive exploitation but a ground for leisure and free time activities. As Bodorff wrote in describing the tasks of the incipient landscape architect, "our work consists mostly of the laying out of gardens, playgrounds, and recreation spaces around the modern housing developments, the design of the park systems of different towns, and the planning

13 **Thomas Atmer and Igor Dergalin, "Dispositionsplanen för Norra Järvafältet,"** *Arkitektur 1* **(1969): 8–19.**

14 *Dispositionsplan för Norra Järvafältet* **(Stockholm, 1968), 33.**

15 **Ellen Braae, "Welfare Landscapes and Communities," in** *Forming Welfare*, **ed. Katrine Lotz, Deane Simpson, Kirsten Marie Raahauge, Kjeld Vindum, Mette Jerl Jensen, and Jannie Rosenberg Bendsen, 34–49 (Copenhagen: Danish Architectural Press, 2017), 48.**

of cemeteries."[16] Landscape became an essential component of what came to be called "welfare planning," in which a new ideal of modern urbanity was shaped by the juxtaposition of transport infrastructure, suburban housing, and "natural" landscape. Nature was made accessible and enjoyable. Its experience, a condition for social wellbeing. As Paul N. Edwards notes, infrastructures "simultaneously constitute our experience of the natural environment, as commodity, object of romantic or pastoral emotions and aesthetic sensibilities, or occasional impediment. They also structure nature as a resource, fuel, or 'raw material,' which must be shaped and processed by technological means to satisfy human ends."[17]

16 Bodorff, "The Swedish Society of Landscape Architects," 94.

17 Paul N. Edwards, "Infrastructure and Modernity: Force, Time, and Social Organization in the History of Sociotechnical Systems," in *Modernity and Technology*, ed. Thomas J. Misa, Philip Brey, and Andrew Feenberg, 185–225 (Cambridge, MA: MIT Press, 2003), 189.

Subway viaduct in the suburb of Farsta conveying the new urbanity of suburban life shape by the harmonic integration of infrastructure, landscape and housing. Drawing by John Goorland, 1959. Source: Stockholms stadsarkiv.

All of these being true, infrastructures may also support other ways of living and help shape new imaginaries. We tend to think of infrastructures as material networks that enable particular types of circulation, from people and goods, to matter and energy, to waste and data. Expanding the notion of infrastructure, we can think about these systems together with the sets of objects, devices, and spaces we find associated with them and which are required for their smooth operation. These are the support systems, facilities, and services necessary for a given society or community to function. The role that infrastructures have played in the making of metropolitan regions and in the engineering of the modern landscape has been widely studied, but what if we attempt to flip our point of view on infrastructures by looking instead at the spaces that separate them? What if we pay attention to the gaps that allow for breathing, to the minimum distances that activate movement, to the flattened topographies that enable crops to grow and rivers to flow? Qualities such as these may well be the items listed in Ulla Bodorff's landscape inventory.

Section C / 9 : 2003 — Mapping the Järva Field: Inventorying Landscape, Surveying Nature

It is autumn and a golden glimmer bounces off the ground. A bulky layer of colorful leaves covers the plain, making Ulla's pace difficult, yet joyful too. Stepping out of the weeds, feeling the weight of her muddy boots, Ulla loads her camera and shoots the path in front of her. Roads and trails and earthy ways slice through the valley's soft terrain, while Ulla pictures in her head the crossing lines they draw in the ground. "Where do they lead?," she might have wondered. "How were they formed?," she may have queried. And what will they become, once they have been swallowed by oil and asphalt? Should they resist, or should they give up?

Ulla might have been concerned about what natural landscapes do in an urban setting and, conversely, about what relationships her city was in the midst of establishing with its former countryside. Although the early modernists had a clear answer—largely seeing urban hinterlands as spaces to urbanize through industrialized mechanical technologies—the question was trickier in the late 1960s, when environmental concerns were on the rise and claims to restrain rapid urbanization and to reconstruct city centers gained traction. The key question that had to be asked was how to negotiate the need for urban expansion into large tracts of natural landscape that had been, until then, left untouched.

Untouched is used here with intended imprecision, or rather as a provocation. Although *untouched landscape* ("orörda" landskap) is an expression used by the Free Areas Committee and by Bodorff herself when classifying landscape types,[18] the green spaces left between infrastructural networks and multifunctional city nodes are anything but untouched. Even if, in our urban imaginary, they persist as *natural environments*. A condition that is by no means exclusive to the Järva field. "There is little left of original, untouched nature,"[19] Sabine Höhler writes in her work on Sweden's first Phytotron, a climate laboratory for plant research established in Stockholm in the 1960s. Along the same lines, the Global Human Modification of Terrestrial Systems research project estimated that around 95% of the Earth's terrestrial land has been modified by human action, [20] hence providing empirical evidence to the prediction made by Karl Marx, as early as 1866, when asserting that "the nature that preceded human history, ... is nature which today no longer exists anywhere."[21] Through human labor and production, Marx argued, human beings had erased any categorical distinction with an external "nature."

The Järva field is a phenomenal example that helps unpack the question of how natural, or unaltered, a "natural" environment actually is. Currently publicized as the longest of the ten green wedges infiltrating Stockholm's metropolitan area, stretching more than thirty kilometers from the center of the royal park of Djurgården into the northwest nature reserve, the Järva corridor is the outcome of multiple long-lasting actions into the city's surrounding lands. It is a fabricated terrain. Rather than empty or untouched, Järvafältet's open valleys, bounded by sparse forest masses and sprinkled with lakes and

18 See annexes and reports published by the Free Areas Committee, for instance *Olika Parkanläggningar* **(Stockholm: Friområdeskommittén för Järvafältet, 1970).**

19 Sabine Höhler, "Earth, a Technogarden: Planting for the Planet in Sweden's First Phytotron, 1950–1970," *Geschichte und Gesellschaft* **46, no 4 (2020): 706–28 (here 706).**

20 C. M. Kennedy, J. R. Oakleaf, D. M. Theobald, S. Baruch-Mordo, and J. Kiesecker, "Global Human Modification of Terrestrial Systems," NASA Socioeconomic Data and Applications Center (SEDAC), 2020. Accessed March 7, 2022.

21 Karl Marx, *The German Ideology* **(New York: Prometheus Books, 1998), 46.**

streams, have been inhabited since ancient times. Buried in the memory of the soils lie carved rune stones and human remains.[22] During archaeological excavations performed in the 1960 and 1970s, burial sites with around one thousand graves were found, suggesting that the Järva area has been inhabited since the Iron Age.[23] More recent studies estimate that less than 10 percent of the open space in Järvafältet is composed of natural indigenous vegetation.[24] Today's highly protected Igelbäcken, a stream running through the wedge, has been remade, redirected, even repopulated with new species to preserve, paradoxically, its *natural-ecological* value.

Anticipating the increasing interaction between the disciplines of landscape ecology and urban planning, Bodorff's careful study and recording of the Järva landscape set in motion a negotiation between ecological values and urban demands. As a result, the practice of urban planning incorporates not only the design of the unbuilt but the preservation of its "exteriority." The later emergence of landscape urbanism (together with its former and subsequent ramifications, from infrastructural urbanism to ecological urbanism) emphasized the key role of open spaces in the contemporary urban condition. In turn, metabolic urbanism has broadened the frame and scope of design practices by focusing on processes of extraction, circulation, and accumulation from the regional scale to the planetary. Urban agglomerations have been reconceptualized as dissipative structures dependent on the import of energy and matter from their host environments, thus highligthing the socioecological interdependencies and uneven relations characteristic of recent decades of rampant urbanization. Alongside this, the focus of architecture and urban design has also gravitated from the built environment to so-called *unbuilt* areas: landscapes, ecologies, infrastructures, and so forth. By doing so, they have signaled the vital importance of integrating urban thinking in the analysis of new forms and scales of territorial restructuring. That is, they have revealed that the

22 Archaeologist Solbritt Benneth, former director of the Medeltidsmuseet (Medieval Museum) in Stockholm, wrote about an eleven-hundred-year-old woman from Järvafältet in "En 1100 år gammal dam från Järvafältet," in *Stadsvandringar 2* **(Stockholm: Stockholms Stadsmuseum, 1978), 5–9.**

23 Anita Biuw, *Norra Spånga: Bebyggelse och samhälle under järnåldern* **(Stockholm: Kommittén för Stockholmsforskning, 1992).**

24 Clas Florgård and Oskar Forsberg, "Residents' Use of Remnant Natural Vegetation in the Residential Area of Järvafältet, Stockholm," *Urban Forestry and Urban Greening* **5, no. 2 (2006): 83–92.**

functional landscapes of cities and their increasingly globalized hinterlands, spaces so often considered *external* to the urban, have been internalized by expansive and globalized contemporary urbanization.

Here, let us return to Bodorff's fieldwork. Gathered in contact sheet number 17, at the bottom-right corner next to a bucolic set of pictures is an intriguing photograph of Akalla storgård, taken on her walk to Sollentuna. The caption suggests it is a picture of Akalla's old farmhouse, built at the end of the seventeenth century. However, what the picture shows is a steep ditch with a red tractor in a steady position. In the background, next to an electrical post, is a pitched roof with three chimneys. Because of the unsettling composition, one could easily mistake the image as depicting an industrial landfill. A misreading that is not that far from reality. Today, within the space tagged as "green wedge," industrial areas can be found next to nature schools, agricultural fields, animal farms, and sports and recreation facilities. Among the "non-green" activities are a cement factory, aggregate extraction sites, dumping and recycling stations, golf courts, motor circuits, bunkers, and an airfield. The list invites the very questions posed earlier, questions Bodorff might have asked when figuring out what was in fact "valuable," "natural," or "urban" in the Järva landscape.

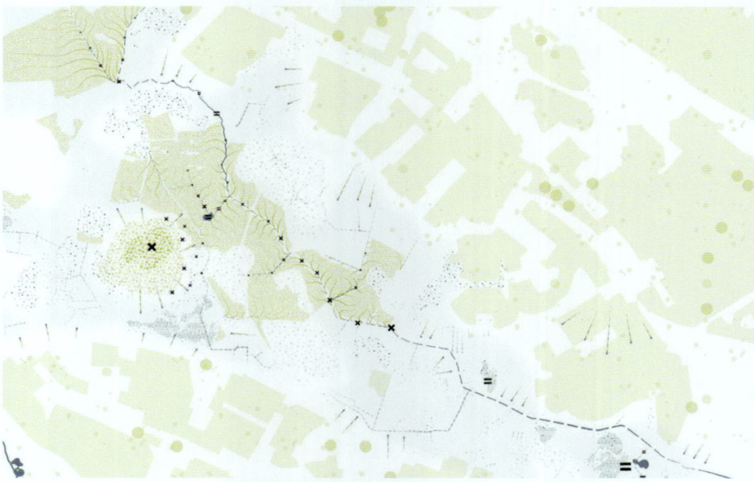

Invisible Disease Inventory: Diagnosis for Järvafältets Blue System. Project developed in the Urban Ecologies design studio – Fall 2021, SUPD program, KTH School of Architecture. Authors Gloria Annunziata, Sofia Lichvarova and Sophie Spanlang.

The tradition of natural inventories in Sweden goes back to the renowned taxonomy of Carl von Linné and his *Systema Naturæ*, first published in 1735. To the early practices of methodological classification of natural types followed, as Sabine Höhler explains, efforts in nineteenth-century Europe to inventory the entire planet, leading to the formation of the earth sciences: meteorology, geomagnetism, geography, and oceanography.[25] Nonetheless, a substantial difference arises between the scientific classification of biological and mineral species carried out by Linné and others, and the work initiated by Bodorff. If early natural scientists were preoccupied with the recording of exact measurements in the study of geophysical and climatic phenomena, more recent landscape classifications have also included assessments of "values." Landscape types are classified not only by their common features but by how human beings perceive them, how valuable they are inherently, and in terms of human appreciation. As Region Stockholm acknowledged in a report from 2013, the green wedges "are invaluable for human well-being, . . . very important for biodiversity and have great cultural-historical values."[26]

Different from technical assessments and reports, the landscape inventory contains an embedded judgment and incorporates a course of action oriented toward the remaking of the studied grounds. Inventories have historically been used for purposes of material or economic evaluation. An inventory of a warehouse, or of an archive, must be exhaustive and rigorous: it should list each stocked item forming part of a collection, whether the objects listed are books or metal hardware. To properly create a comprehensive inventory record, a suitable coding system is needed to count and enumerate the objects, their placement and, if necessary, the movements of those objects. An adequate system of classification, one entailing a taxonomic logic, would have to be chosen, or created. However, the modern landscape inventory has become an essential first element of spatial analysis, one that in turn constitutes the ground for further design actions. This approach to landscape inventories was picked up on by Hans-Rudolf Heyer about a decade after Bodorff's work:

25 Sabine Höhler, "Inventorier la Terre," in *Histoire des sciences et des savoirs: 2 Modernité et globalisation*, **167–81 (Paris: Seuil, 2015).**

26 "Gröna kilar," *Region Stockholm*, **accessed February 8, 2022, http://www.rufs.se/sakomraden/gronstruktur/grona-kilar.**

"the inventory has to make recommendations concerning methods of more detailed inventory, the actual state of the garden, its real value and its importance to the landscape, settlement or building."[27] The inventory is a material and spatial register but also a working tool with a projective potential. Mapping and cartographic documents, through their power of definition, frame our image of the world.[28] As representations shaped by a particular interpretation of reality, maps propose a partial, specific and concrete reading of the object described.[29] Any act of selection, however, implies an even bigger exclusion. Precisely in the process of rejection or exclusion that is contained in any active choice, knowledge is produced. The landscape inventory presents what is apprehended and valued. It is presented before the committee, the planner, the politician, the researcher, or any reader. The partial reality that Bodorff captured can be considered and qualified.

The practice of mapping has long been linked to landscape and territory. Every time a map is drawn, an image of a landscape is created and a political stand on a territory projected. Yet, beyond representation, cartographic documents also have a projective potential. In this way mapping, as a creative practice, "precipitates its most productive effects through a finding that is also a founding; its agency lies in neither reproduction nor imposition but rather in uncovering realities previously unseen or unimagined, even across seemingly exhausted grounds. Thus, mapping unfolds potential; it re-makes territory over and over again, each time with new and diverse consequences."[30] In this sense, the practice of recording and writing carried out by Bodorff ressembles that of mapping, yet its content and level of resolution varies. It constitutes a "projective inventory," inasmuch the items and types listed exceed the mere enumeration and description, while becoming the support of normative frameworks. As mapping practices have recently expanded into a broad register of formats and modes of representation, Bodorff's inventory innovatively combined photographic surveys, map-like drawings, landscape sections describing topographical features and ecological cycles, heritage catalog, and technical descriptions of flora and fauna. The inventory as a form of classification becomes,

27 Hans-Rudolf Heyer, "Shifting Meanings in a Garden Landscape," *Landscape Architecture* **66, no. 3 (1976): 240–47 (here 247).**

28 Manuel de Solà-Morales, "The Culture of Description," *Perspecta* **25 (1989): 16–25 (here 16).**

29 Roger Paez, *Operative Mapping: Maps as Design Tools* **(New York: Actar Publishers, 2019).**

30 James Corner, "The Agency of Mapping: Speculation, Critique and Invention," in *Mappings*, **ed. Denis Cosgrove, 213–52 (London: Reaktion Books, 1999).**

in this case, a propositional document. The traces of Bodorff's inventory have been lost in the midst of the archive's bureaucracy. Fortunately, the impact it made on the landscape has remained to this day.

Section D / 7 : 1875 — Technical Lands: The Remaking of Nature's Ground

Ulla wrote the following passage in the section that introduces her inventory: "According to the shooting map of 1924, combat shooting took place on the entire Järva field with bullet-filled tree trunks as a result. With the exception of the shooting range areas, however, the terrain on Södra Järvafältet is strikingly unaffected by previous field shots."[31] Or so it seemed. While passing close to the tall spruce trees in a dense forest zone through which she could glimpse Lake Säby down the hill, Ulla noticed an unfamiliar mark on a trunk. As she got closer, she wondered what could have caused the scratches. Her first thought was a wild animal. Perhaps a bear or the horn of a moose? Such explanations did not make sense, however. The grooves were horizontal and too linear. Her second thought was that the lines might be signs of a disease. She discarded this thought immediately. Finally, after finding a few tiny holes in a nearby tree and feeling in one of the cavities, she discovered a squashed metal object and connected the dots.

After mapping the shooting area, extraction of soil samples and further analysis of possible metal leakages would follow. As Ulla expected, the ammunition had become sedimented and consequently contaminated the grounds. Regardless of the obvious explanation—a shooting range was located a few hundred meters away—and logical aftermath of the lead and copper disseminated across the area, Ulla could not help but feel unease about the persistence of a harm caused several decades earlier. Her unease grew when explosive sites were found in the adjoining hills of Lilla and Stora Björn. From 1905 until the 1960s, Järvafältet had been used as a military training zone. Shooting ranges were used, among other things, for artillery and machine gun exercises.[32] The

31 Cited in Tiina Laantee and Thomas Strid, *Igelbäcken: Järvafältets pulsåder,* **Rapport 1992:12 (Stockholm: Länsstyrelsen i Stockholms Län, 1991), 42.**

32 Mats Brunberg, *Järvafältet* **(Sollentuna: Sollentuna hembygdsfören, 1979).**

young members of a legion would line up in the Ärving area and shoot north toward targets in Djupanbackarna and the heights.[33] In a nearby area, the terrain was flattened to accommodate a military airfield that has remained until today, squeezed between the new districts of Barkarby and Akalla. The Kungliga Svea Flygflottilj (Royal Air Squadron) ran its operations in the Barkarby airfield from 1938 until 1974, although the first reported military flight dates from 1913. The history of military activities knots together the interwoven layers that make up the Järva field. Rather than natural ground, the green wedge can be regarded as technical land. In addition to material traces of earlier activities and old structures absorbed by the wedge, fundamental to its spatial configuration are the overlapping stories that have been litigated in the area. Today's green wedge is the result of a long process of political negotiation over ownership and control of its territory. The land has been leased to farmers for cultivation, to the military for its reserve zone, and classified as having recreational and cultural value warranting various levels of "protection." Agreements and tensions can be found between the various levels of administration involved—municipal, regional, and national. These technical operations and their institutional involvements are conflated with the land, producing and regulating the landscapes of today. Technical lands are an essential and substantial part of contemporary processes of extended urbanization, informing our understanding and experience of the urban condition. These spaces are the product of long processes of land management and exploitation that, with the rise of new understandings of city-nature relations, have become constitutive parts of urban spaces.

Besides the technical craft involved in shaping such landscapes, often they sustain productive activities too. Not only because they produce food, energy, or metabolic material processes (from the extraction of raw materials to waste dumps) but because they are shaped by a myriad of environment-making technologies. Technical landscapes, as opposed to natural landscapes, are the result of the terraforming effect of what Sverker Sörlin and Nina Wormbs call "environing technologies," which are responsible for creating and mediating

33 Cited in Laantee and Strid, *Igelbäcken.*

Photographic survey of Järvafältet by Ulla Bodorff. Source: Stockholms Stadsmuseet.

Järvafältet
I
Medeltidsvägen från tingsplatsen mot Husby.
Foto trädgårdsarkitekt Ulla Bodorf
Medeltidsvägen från tingsplatsen mot Kista.
Ravalens Fornborg. Vårdträd. Sedd mot öster.
Foto trädgårdsarkitekt Ulla Bodorf
Ravalens Fornborg sedd mot väster
51
tuna leden i passet mellan Solhylls och Älgkärrsberget.
Läge för blivande Järvastadens Centrum.
Foto trädgårdsarkitekt Ulla Bodorf
Bodorf
till Kista. I bak-
Flygfält.
stuga i hagmark.
17
Översjön, utsikt från östra stranden mot Getholmen
Foto trädgårdsarkitekt Ulla Bodorf
Fa 45544
Nedanför Bögs Gård.
Akalla Storgård
Kista. Till höger
ädgårds arkitekt Ulla Bodorf.

environments that are simultaneously natural and technical.[34] Sörlin and Wormbs further propose a subset of three types of environing technologies: *writing, sensing,* and *shaping*. While all three types are interconnected, shaping implies direct transformation of the physical environment, whereas sensing and writing suggest the capacity to act indirectly by provoking alterations in nature. The impact on nature that projective inventories have lies precisely in their capacity to co-work with shaping.

Reframing a green wedge as technical land foregrounds the process through which a terrain is activated for a particular purpose by technical means. However, technical expertise in no way excludes cultural values. Together with Bodorff, Lars Forsby, an architect appointed as a member of the "Free Areas Committee" wrote in an appendix to the general layout plan that the open spaces surrounding the housing estates "can be regarded as fairly spacious walking areas and treated as such, which of course also makes the landscape type natural."[35] How does a landscape look *natural*? Forsby seems to believe that a more "natural" landscape can be planned, hence implying that there are "natural" experiences of the landscape and some that are less. The most hilarious moment in the phenomenological reconstruction of Järvafältet can be found in a report published by Stockholm's regional authority in 2004, in which the experience of walking through a dense, deep forest was defined as providing "a sense of eternity"![36] Eternity, that is. Nothing less.

In fairness, that should come as no surprise, because nature has long been used to project an endless range of values and aesthetic judgments. As Lorraine Daston reminds us, "people have linked the natural and moral orders—and disorders."[37] "Nature" has been historically used to underpin and justify ideologies of many kinds. As Daston further argues, "like all truly interesting words, 'nature' is a mille-feuille of meanings."[38] It is a polymorphous notion that has exercised different and distinct forms of authority, also in urban planning and design. The urban expansion commencing at the turn of the century transformed not only the geography of the city but the very substance

34 Sverker Sörlin and Nina Wormbs, "Environing Technologies: A Theory of Making Environment," *History and Technology* **34, no. 2 (2018): 101–25.**

35 Lars Forsby, "Bilaga 1: P.M. Beträffande förslag till generalplan för Kista, Husby och Akalla inom stadsdelen Järvafältet i Stockholm Pl. 7160" (1970), 1,044.

36 Regionplane- och trafikkontoret, *Järvakilen: Upplevelsevärden i Stockholmsregionens gröna kilar* **(Stockholm: Regionplane- och trafikkontoret, 2004). I am grateful to Erik Lokrantz for drawing my attention to this document.**

37 Lorraine Daston, *Against Nature* **(Cambridge, MA: MIT Press, 2019), 3.**

38 Lorraine Daston, "The Naturalistic Fallacy Is Modern," *Isis* **105, no. 3 (September 2014): 579–87 (here 582, 587).**

of its so-called nature. A rising awareness of the implications and interdependencies between urban and ecological systems has motivated the reconceptualization of natural systems as infrastructures. The emergence of new categories, such as green and ecological infrastructures, relies on the "alliance between landscape ecology and infrastructure design, as it is believed to produce complex adaptive systems able to both integrate and materialize myriad interactions between the 'social' and 'natural' realm."[39] Where in all of this does nature reside? In these unsettling times of the Anthropocene, whether the focus is on the *Anthropos*, on industrialism, capitalism, colonialism, or on any other ism, the cosmological tension between what constitutes nature and what constitutes culture has again flourished. On the one hand, nature and culture have collapsed into each other; on the other hand, maintaining separate categories for social and natural processes seems to be advantageous when deciding on who or what should be held accountable and how we might get out of the multiple and overlapping planetary crises we got ourselves into. To illuminate ways forward, philosopher Yuk Hui argues for the reopening of the question of technology in the era of the Anthropocene, "where the earth *and* the cosmos have been transformed into a gigantic technological system."[40] Hui argues it is necessary to elucidate the meaning of *nature* before embarking on further discussion of the relation it may have with technology. And he is not alone. After a few mil-

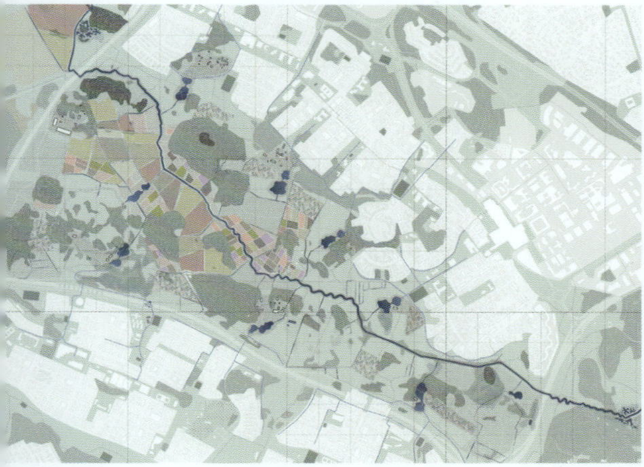

Visible Interventions and their Implications on Järvafältets Blue System. A landscape inventory served as a base to recognize the elements and systems on which the proposal intervenes. Project developed in the Urban Ecologies design studio – Fall 2021, SUPD program, KTH School of Architecture. Authors Gloria Annunziata, Sofia Lichvarova and Sophie Spanlang.

39 Greet De Block, "Ecological Infrastructure in a Critical-Historical Perspective: From Engineering 'Social' Territory to Encoding 'Natural' Topography," *Environment and Planning A: Economy and Space* **48, no. 2 (2016): 367–90.**

40 Yuk Hui, "Cosmotechnics as Cosmopolitcs," *e-flux Journal*, **no. 86 (November 2017): 2, https://www.e-flux.com/journal/86/161887/cosmotechnics-as-cosmopolitics/; emphasis in original.**

lennia discussing the nature of nature, we are still entrenched in an ideological battle to define what nature *is*, or *ought* to be. To overcome the pitfall of an external nature, and "to avoid indulging in an illusion of a pure and innocent *first nature*, as well as to avoid imprisoning ourselves in a pure technological rationality," Hui proposes to speak of a *second nature* no longer independent from humans.[41] This idea of nature stems from particular world views and is co-constructed by the uniting of cosmos and technics.

41 **Yuk Hui, "On Cosmotechnics: For a Renewed Relation between Technology and Nature in the Anthropocene,"** *Techné: Research in Philosophy and Technology* **21, no. 2/3 (2017): 319–41.**

Equally, the advantage of considering land as technical ground is that romanticized ideals of nature can be disregarded as unhelpful. Our task remains to imagine what supporting devices and systems will be required to reconstruct the missing link between nature and technology, the absence of which led industrial societies astray. If we are to act against the massive global challenges lying ahead, recomposing that link will be critical. We may engage in a full inventory of the land, understanding that a survey is as an act of design, one that can motivate the preservation, the restitution, or the transformation of urban landscapes. This is what can be learned from Ulla's rambles through Järvafältet. By bringing ecological systems alongside traditional "urban" elements, the practice of architecture and urbanism is expanded, not only in its multiscalar dimension but, most important, in the inclusion of earth systems. Biophysical cycles, cultivated lands, and functions typically associated with rurality can be brought together into a reshaped notion of urbanity that takes responsibility for its outsourced peripheries. In doing so, a path can be opened that can absorb contemporary critiques of modernity and nature/culture divides, enabling a more flexible but grounded spatial practice while avoiding the naivete of pastoral narratives that claim a return to a pristine nature. Understanding that city-territory relations are inextricably linked can twist the false premise that the space exterior to the city is unbuilt. That landscapes are unbuilt. That green wedges, green belts and green corridors are unbuilt. That the natural ecosystems interwoven with urban systems are not built. And acknowledge that hinterlands and natural landscapes are deeply determined by human action. In this, landscape inventories can be instrumental in fostering the co-working of urban planning and landscape ecology. As environing technologies, they can help imagine new patterns of urbanization that are not constrained by boundary demarcation. Nature has been, and still is, a great source of legitimization. Let us use it to reframe urban design as a practice of re-articulation rather than growth and development.

Connecting Infrastructure

Raphael Marius Schall

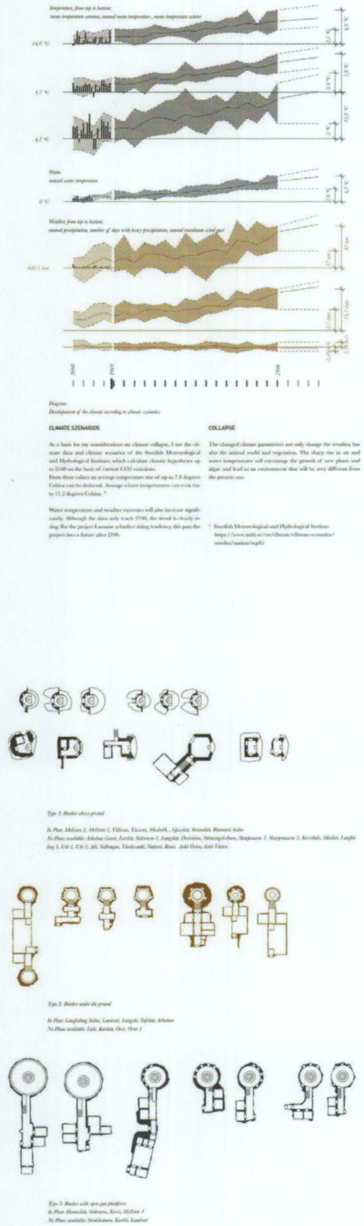

The island of Utö, part of the southern Stockholm archipelago, is located on Sweden's eastern coast facing the open sea. Three major actors with clearly defined areas occupy Utö. They account for economic, environmental, and social aspects of the island in its relation to the archipelago. The first actor is the Skärgårdsstiftelsen (Archipelago Foundation), which takes care of the environment by developing and operating preservation areas throughout the archipelago. Additionally, it connects tourism with nature reserves, resulting in campsite structures, accommodation, and outdoor activities, all of which are framed under the concept of sustainability. The second actor, and the institution that claims the largest area of the archipelago, is the Försvarsmakten (Swedish Military Corps), which occupies half of Utö as exercise terrain for its troops. Using a system of towers and ships, they control the surrounding areas while practicing their shooting. The local population constitutes the third actor. Areas claimed by local residents are not limited to existing settlements but are more clearly defined in the territorial claims made by individuals doing various activities outside their properties.

The problems that arise in connecting these programs and their stakeholders on Utö are evident in the presence of borderlines, restricted access to certain parts of the island, and a missing connection between environmentally protected areas and areas used by tourists and local residents.
Considering the larger context and the understanding of Utö as not only an individual island but as part of the Stockholm archipelago, the lack of connectivity is limited not only to Utö but to the whole archipelago itself. To redefine the interconnection of the separated areas and to strengthen affiliation as a unified region, my design project proposes an infrastructural support element to bring together the currently separated parts of the island and to unify the archipelago. Although the design primarily focuses on developing a single intervention on the island of Utö, the prospect of adapting and reproducing the infrastructural element on different islands creates an additional value for the archipelago.
Among the possible sites and extant or transformable infrastructures, the ruins of former World War II bunkers along the defensive coastline of the Baltic Sea provided an opportune system. In the late 1930s and early 1940s around forty bunkers and shooting ranges were constructed on strategic island positions to overlook, control, and connect the archipelago. Even though only ruins remain today, this strategic system fits with the concept of connecting the archipelago's islands.
To create visibility and connection among the existing, albeit largely invisible infrastructure of the bunkers and shooting ranges, the design calls for the addition of towers, which would become landmarks along the coast. These structural elements, prefabricated on the mainland and placed atop the bunkers, would provide self-sufficient technologies such as water collection, fresh air, and electricity for the underground structures, which could be used as shelter and storage spaces for tourists and travelers. Appearing all along the coastline and connected by piers, these elements would narrate the use and purpose of the archipelago as a whole.

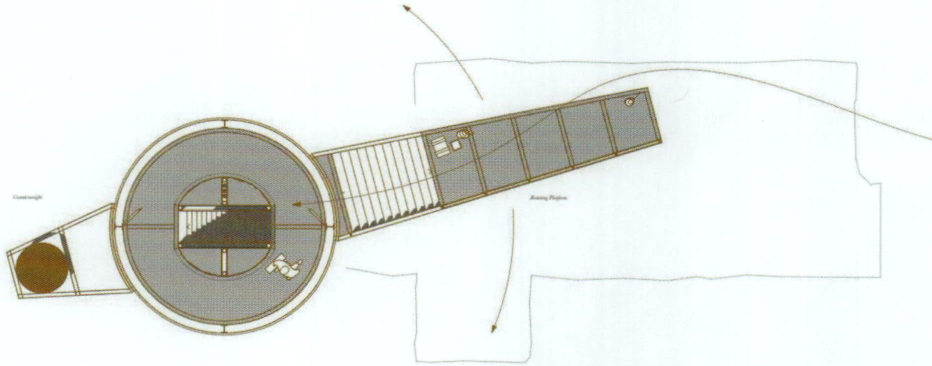

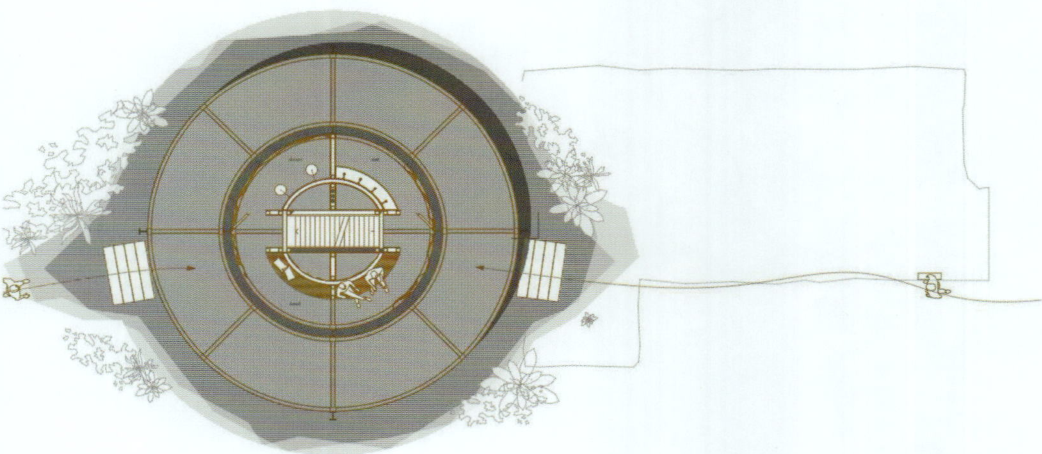

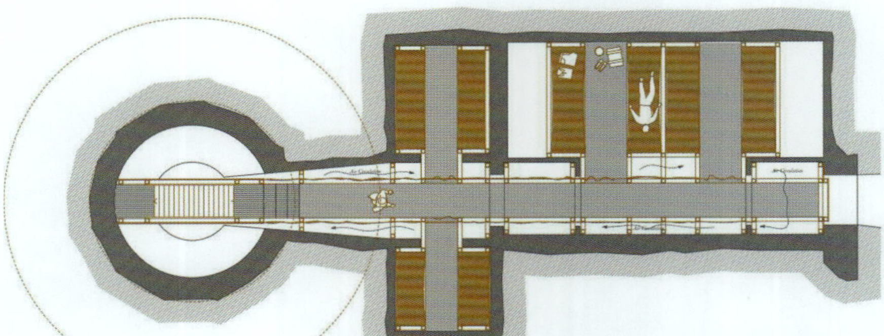

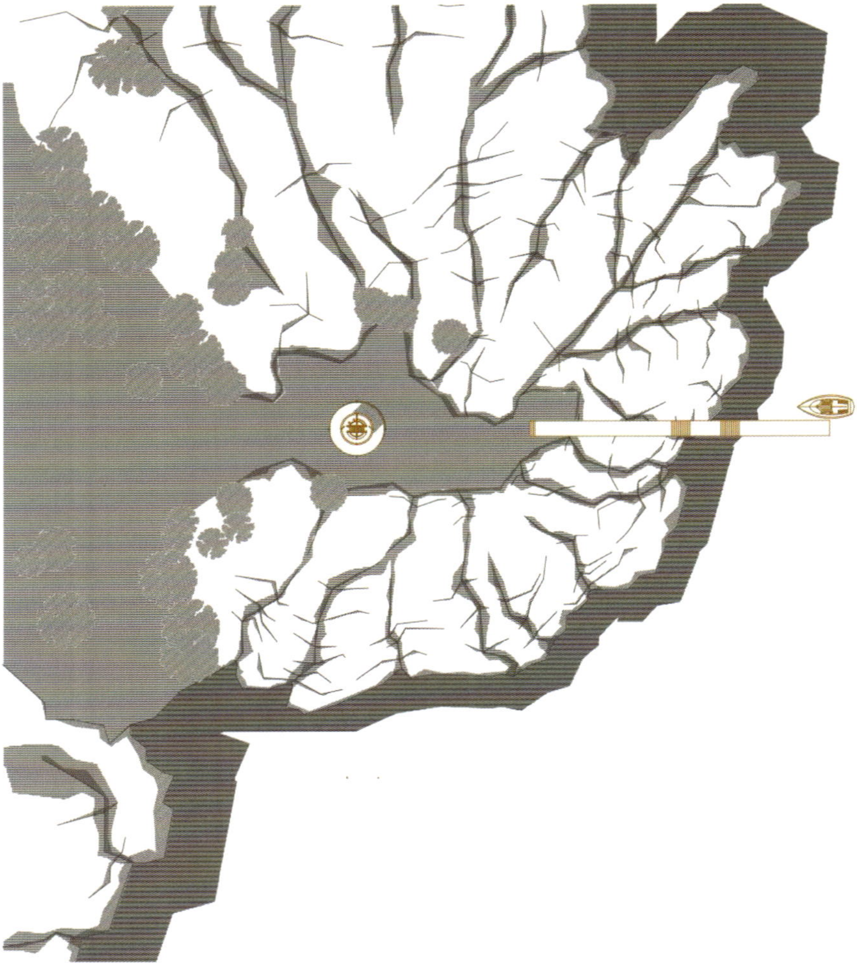

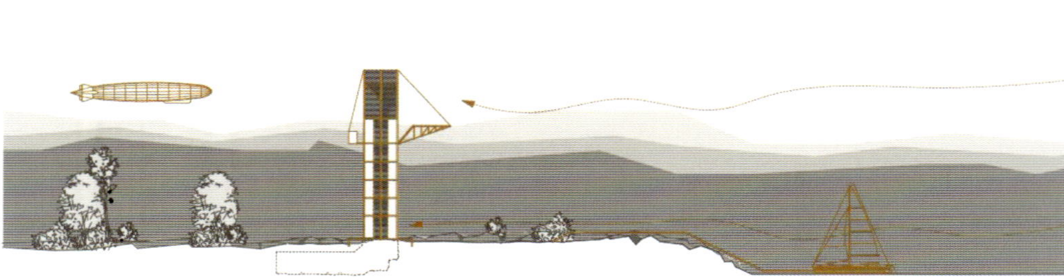

DRAI N ONTO LOGY

Chapater 13
Drain Ontology

Yaseera Moosa

We have many names for urban water:

rainwater
stormwater
gray water
black water

All of it is drained.

The British invasion of Australia brought with it a culture of hydrophobia. Rerouted, dislocated, dammed, and damned, ancient flows of water were abruptly altered by a *drain ontology*. Through the mechanism of drainage, a sludgy, muddy, murky, oozing earth—teeming with beings and becomings—was dehydrated, cultivated, "civilized." Land and water were separated and relegated to the quantifiable realm of "resource." To consider an ontology of draining—as both "causing liquid to run out" and "depriving of life or vitality"—offers a framework to understand the dominant relations of our variously named epoch: Anthropocene, Capitalocene, Chthulucene, Drainocene(?). In her essay "All the World's a Drain," Jennifer Mae Hamilton writes, "Drains are both metaphor and metonymy for this mess we're in. Drains offer a way of conceptualizing the contemporary political economy of toxic and anoxic planetary flows.
In the creation of surplus for the wealthy, capitalism loves externalizations; drains make such externalizations seem materially possible."[1]
A drain ontology is predicated on the mythical land of "*Away*."[2] It imagines a world where the wastes and murky waters of industrial capitalism can be piped away and sealed off, in denial of the basic reality that water—and the world that contains it—is a closed loop. The functional reverberation of draining is not merely the ridding of

> The functional reverberation of draining is not merely the ridding of that which is deemed abject but an illusion of disappearance—an intimation that it was never there at all.

1 Jennifer Mae Hamilton, "All the World's a Drain," *Sydney Review of Books*, **November 15, 2017, https://sydneyreviewofbooks.com/review/bodies-of-water-by-astrida-neimanis/.**

2 Timothy Morton, *Hyperobjects: Philosophy and Ecology after the End of the World* **(Minneapolis: University of Minnesota Press, 2013).**

that which is deemed abject but an illusion of disappearance—an intimation that it was never there at all.

Drain ontology is materialized through the entwined capitalist-colonial regimes of property and infrastructure, imposed in the name of "development." In delineating boundaries, colonialism is inscribed into the earth, making material the imposed figments of property. To legitimize this inscription, and flush any lingering residues of its preceding violence, the land within its bounds is declared "empty." This emptiness is in fact an active and ongoing process of "emptying-out."[3]

3 Andrew Herscher and Ana M. León, "At the Border of Decolonization," in "At the Border," special project, ed. Nick Axel, Jan Boelen, Charlotte Dumoncel d'Argence, and Nikolaus Hirsch, *e-flux Architecture*, May 2020, https://www.e-flux.com/architecture/at-the-border/325762/at-the-border-of-decolonization/.

As Brenna Bandhar identifies in *Colonial Lives of Property*, dispossession is "both a prerequisite and a consequence of the coproduction of racial value and property ownership, rendered possible by a logic of abstraction that was central to emergent capitalist forms of property and the racial subjugation of Indigenous peoples and their lands and resources."[4] Through the denial of preceding worlds and the reproduction of colonial ideals, dispossession extends beyond land and resources; it is "the dispossession of difference itself."[5] Drain ontology can thus be understood as the colonial "ordering" of the world through dissection, taxonomy, and hierarchy: land and water, past and present, civilized and savage. It seeks to flatten complex, fluctuating systems that flow within and throughout one another into purportedly rational, static entities that can be measured by the standardized logic of capitalist value production. Following this atomization, it seeks to erase all specters of connection. While resource is siphoned off the wastes of development are flushed into the sewers of settler amnesia, spectrally surfacing as the effluvia of *elsewhere*. As Ghassan Hage suggests, "the more a colonizing nation can shield its citizens from realities, carving out spaces where they are not exposed to the colonial conditions of their good life, the more civilized it

Through the denial of preceding worlds and the reproduction of colonial ideals, dispossession extends beyond land and resources; it is "the dispossession of difference itself."

4 Brenna Bhandar, *Colonial Lives of Property: Law, Land, and Racial Regimes of Ownership* (Durham, NC: Duke University Press, 2018), 102.

5 Vivian Ziherl, "On the Frontier, Again," *e-flux Journal* 73 (May 2016), https://www.e-flux.com/journal/73/52560/on-the-frontier-again/.

appears."[6] In its fixation with progress, drain ontology imagines the pipelines of time and transfer as both linear and one-directional, marching toward an endless horizon of extraction, accumulation, and "development."

On the eastern edge of Whadjuk Country the relationship between draining, development, and dispossession unfolds, as Perth's double-brick suburban fringe inches toward the ephemeral clay wetlands of the Swan Coastal Plain. It is a peculiar meeting of clay forms: the infant and the ancient, the baked and the bogged. For millennia, the drying region of what is now known as Perth was a fluid landscape of fluctuating hydrology. A chain of wetlands, interwoven by rivers and streams, connected the vast surface to a deep network of aquifers. In *Swamp*, Nandi Chinna describes the relational condition of this landscape: "Wetlands are neither water nor earth but exist in the meeting of these two, changing seasonally to become more or less of each element and blending the two elements to form mud. Perth's wetlands directly or indirectly support most of its wildlife."[7] This shifting hydrological condition supports a heterogenous range of life-forms, both aquatic and terrestrial, hosting extraordinary biological and ecological diversity.

> It is a peculiar meeting of clay forms: the infant and the ancient, the baked and the bogged. For millennia, the drying region of what is now known as Perth was a fluid landscape of fluctuating hydrology.

Within two hundred years, the hydrological condition of Whadjuk Country has been rendered unrecognizable. The ephemeral ground condition, in constant hydrological flux, was beyond settler comprehension. Shallow, seasonal lakes and swamps did not fit the European understanding of water bodies, presenting a taxonomic anomaly in classificatory orders that sought to distinguish land and water, time, and space.[8] Many of the wetlands were swiftly drained, cultivated, developed, or filled. Flushed of their history, only the aseptic surface of terra nullius remained. The process of draining wetlands for development—a practice that continues today—has left less than 10 percent of

6 Ghassan Hage, *Is Racism an Environmental Threat?* **Polity Press Cambridge, UK; Malden, MA 2017**

7 Nandi Chinna, "Swamp," *Griffith Review*, **no. 47 (January 2015), https://www.griffithreview.com/articles/swamp/.**

8 Western Australian Museum, "Postmodern Wetlands," in "Reimagining Perth's Lost Wetlands," *Western Australian Museum*, **https://museum.wa.gov.au/explore/wetlands/city-development/postmodern-wetlands.**

9 Chinna, "Swamp."

10 Chinna, "Swamp."

the precolonial wetland extents intact, and all are at risk.[9] Declining rainfall along with groundwater overextraction to support increasing urbanization has limited the few remaining wetlands' ability to replenish, and many of these seasonal swamplands and damplands will soon become dryland areas.[10] The wetlands function as a filtration system for the aquifers below that provide much of the city's potable water. Both surface and groundwater are increasingly under strain. In examining the drying of Perth, the fluid, entangled, and multidirectional implications of drain ontology begin to surface.

The terrain of the Swan Coastal Plain is a negotiation between the Indian Ocean and the Yilgarn Craton, the earth's oldest geological block. Over time, this granite landscape has been weathered down by water, forming clay minerals that have been carried toward the coast. Sandy deposits from the lapping ocean and clayey deposits washed down from the Yilgarn have formed a complex sedimentary profile, holding ancient bodies of water deep within its structure.[11] Viewed in deep time, the plain comes to life, transformed from a singular mass into a complex network of relationships in a constant state of becoming. Through the Yilgarn's natural drainage network, the movement of water creates and carries clay, and in turn the accumulation of clay captures and redirects the movement of water. The earth is neither inert nor inanimate but a network of complex interdependencies.

Over time, this granite landscape has been weathered down by water, forming clay minerals that have been carried toward the coast

11 Daniel J. Martin and Geoffrey London, "The Deep Waters of Perth," in In *Time with Water: Design Studies of Three Australian Cities*, 157–65 (UWA Publishing, 2019).

While this may be regarded as a "new materialist" perspective, it has been understood by Indigenous Noongar peoples for tens of thousands of years. As the cracks and leaks in the drain ontology of capitalist colonialism threaten the impending burst of climate catastrophe, the emerging framework of new materialism in Western philosophy seeks to unsettle the Enlightenment humanism and nature-culture dualism that undergirds this precipice. A significant catalyst to this movement is Karen Barad's concept of "agential realism," which posits agency as a quality not limited to human capacity but manifest in all aspects of reality.[12] Through this lens, the futility of drain ontology is elucidated—the lively, agential, more-than-human world cannot be dismembered into the inert, standardized logic of "resource" and "waste." Métis scholar Zoe Todd points out that, while the Western canon's "ontological turn" presents an opportunity to recognize our "common cosmopolitical concerns," non-Indigenous scholars too often fail to recognize or cite the Indigenous philosophy and scholarship that has understood nonhuman agency and more-than-human reciprocity for millennia longer.[13] This recurring epistemic erasure renders much of the scholarship of the ontological turn as a perpetuation of drain ontology, rather than the disruption it holds potential for. When writing from a settler perspective, it is critical to acknowledge that, while Indigenous epistemologies share commonalities with the ontological turn they predate, they are distinct, place-specific systems of knowledge that cannot be compartmentalized and reappropriated; they are inextricably tied to Indigenous self-determination and sovereignty.[14]

For Noongar peoples, the ecological and cosmological significances of the wetland landscape are entwined, as Noongar elder Cedric Jacob explains:

> It is through the lake system. There is a water serpent down there below which is extremely important and the water on the surface is really the marks where the Waugyl wound his way through and came up after making the streams and the waterways. It's all part of the ecological system to purify the land and the family. Once it was surrounded by waterways and if they fill them up with rubbish then the land begins to die.[15]

Noongar epistemologies are grounded in deep interdependencies between ecological, social, and spiritual worlds, at odds with humanist separations of nature and culture, spirit and matter.[16] In contrast to the English notion of "nature," which implies the existence of dualistic nonnatural, culturally constructed matter that is distinct from its surroundings, the Noongar notion of boodjar, often translated as "Country," comprises holistic place-relationships that encompass land, people, law, narratives, spirits, and more-than-human

12 **Karen Barad,** *Meeting the Universe Halfway: Quantum Physics and the Entanglement of Matter and Meaning* **(Durham, NC: Duke University Press, 2007); and Jerry L. Rosieck, Jimmy Snyder, and Scott L. Pratt, "The New Materialisms and Indigenous Theories of Non-human Agency: Making the Case for Respectful Anti-colonial Engagement,"** *Qualitative Inquiry* **26, no. 3–4 (2020): 331–46.**

13 **Zoe Todd, "An Indigenous Feminist's Take on the Ontological Turn: 'Ontology' Is Just Another Word for Colonialism,"** *Journal of Historical Sociology* **29, no. 1 (2016): 4–22.**

14 **Todd, "An Indigenous Feminist's Take on the Ontological Turn."**

15 **Western Australian Museum, "Reimagining Perth's Lost Wetlands,"** *Western Australian Museum*, **2014, https://museum.wa.gov.au/explore/wetlands/aboriginal-context/noongar.**

16 **Sandra Wooltorton, Len Collard, and Pierre Horwitz, "Living Water: Groundwater and Wetlands in Gnangara, Noongar Boodjar,"** *PAN: Philosophy, Activism, Nature* **14 (2019): 5–23.**

17 Wooltorton, Collard, and Horwitz, "Living Water."

beings.[17] Noongar knowledge advances beyond the mere recognition of agential realism that new materialism is concerned with, revealing systems of reciprocity that govern the particularities of more-than-human relations.[18]

Through an infrastructure of kinship, which extends to more-than-human beings, different groups have reciprocal responsibilities to distinct totemic ancestors, but all are understood to be interrelated.

18 Rosieck, Snyder, and Pratt, "The New Materialisms and Indigenous Theories of Non-human Agency."

19 Eve Tuck and K. Wayne Yang, "Decolonization Is Not a Metaphor," *Decolonization: Indigeneity, Education and Society* 1, no. 1 (2012): 1–40.

Through an infrastructure of kinship, which extends to more-than-human beings, different groups have reciprocal responsibilities to distinct totemic ancestors, but all are understood to be interrelated. The Noongar word for totemic ancestor, borungur, also translates to "in relation to" or "second brother," expressing the familial nature of kinship ties. The displacement of Noongar peoples and the ongoing drainage and dispossession of the land, water, and all it holds can thus be understood not only as physical violence but as "a profound epistemic, ontological and cosmological violence."[19]

From the establishment of Perth's settlement, colonial understandings of the land were characterized by ignorance and arrogance in equal supply (an unfathomable abundance). The premise for settlement was rooted in a misreading of the land by James Stirling, who spent twelve days sailing along the river, venturing no further than the alluvial soils of its banks. This was sufficient basis to return home with a glowing review of the agricultural potential of the land, convincing the British government to establish a settlement across the Indian Ocean. The first fleet of settlers arrived in June 1829 to a sandy shore on a largely sandy plain.[20]

20 Pamela Statham, *The Origins of Australia's Capital Cities* (Cambridge, UK: Cambridge University Press, 1990).

The first suburb of Perth was built on the edge of a wetland now known as Lake Claremont, sheltered under a canopy of swamp paperbarks. Upon arrival, colonists commenced the clearing of large trees and shrub-dominated native vegetation for the purpose of construction, agriculture, and timber export. The combination of clearing and increased runoff from impermeable urban surfaces resulted in a significant rise in groundwater. The bed of Lake Claremont was permanently flooded from 1918 to 1920, with the water body eventually covering twice the area of the original wetland. Permanent inundation killed the swamp paperbark woodland and removed the protective canopy that shaded the lake.[21]

Concurrent with the flooding of the lake was eutrophication. The wetland was inundated with agricultural waste and human "night soil" from the rapidly urbanizing city of Perth. The increase in sunlight and nutrients facilitated a flourishing of the bulrush weed, which encouraged rapid breeding of mosquitoes, causing concern about disease in the colony. The subsequent "War on Mosquitoes" saw the introduction of the eastern mosquitofish (*Gambusia holbrooki*), which ironically preferred native mosquito-eating fish and frogs to mosquitoes. As a result, the colony faced a significant depletion in edible fish stocks and a triumphant mosquito population. Colonists attributed the depletion in fish to thousands of cormorants who roosted and bred in the wetlands. Shooting programs were run to reduce the number of birds, whose carcasses were left to decay in the wetlands. By this point, the amount of rotting organic material exceeded the natural filtration processes of the lake ecosystem, resulting in botulism, which caused several mass die-offs of birds, exacerbating the problem further and producing noxious odors.[22]

By this point, the amount of rotting organic material exceeded the natural filtration processes of the lake ecosystem, resulting in botulism, which caused several mass die-offs of birds, exacerbating the problem further and producing noxious odors.

Orthodox miasma theory of the time declared that disease was transmitted through odors, often linking the foul smells of the city to the swamps. The chief authority on matters of miasma was the "Inspector of Nuisance," whose job was to sniff the streets in search of malodorous problems. The official qualification for the job was a "good nose."[23] The lake, deemed a nuisance, a cesspit of decay, was eventually converted to landfill.[24]

The feral entanglements of Lake Claremont pertain to many wetlands across Perth. The site of present-day Queen's Gardens, for instance, was once a

21 Greg Simpson and David Newsome, "Environmental History of an Urban Wetland: From Degraded Colonial Resource to Nature Conservation Area," *Geo: Geography and Environment* **4, no. 1 (2017): 1–13.**

22 Simpson and Newsome, "Environmental History of an Urban Wetland."

23 Western Australian Museum, "Reimagining Perth's Lost Wetlands."

24 Simpson, "Environmental History of an Urban Wetland."

wetland, later refashioned into a brickworks known as East Perth Clayfields. Convicts put to work in the claypit were plagued by poor working conditions and infestations of mosquitoes. Toward the end of the nineteenth century, protests mounted against the clayfields, citing the importance of the city's "beautification."[25] The land has been repeatedly drained, but the residues of the past persist in the bricks. Perth Town Hall, built from the clays of Queen's Gardens, is an agglomeration of the earth's oldest crustal crumblings, made sludgy by rains and remains of the vast fauna and flora that lived and died in its fertile fragments, molded and baked by convict hands. We live, quite literally, in the enmeshed artifacts of natural and social history. The brick provides us with a humbled sense of the earth, as "inextricably bound to human endeavor yet profoundly disinterested in it."[26] Today, the distinguishing feature of the English-style garden is a replica statue of Peter Pan, its murky and mucky histories traded in Never Never Land.

The establishment of urban settlements and their associated infrastructure projects tend to be synonymous with "progress"—an exercise in civilizing land and people through property. Despite the violent and contested means to its existence, property is typically accepted as natural and inevitable or celebrated as an inalienable right.[27] While Karl Marx cites "primitive accumulation"—the enclosure of common land in sixteenth-century Europe to create private property—as the origins of industrial capitalism and inequality, critical Indigenous theorist Glen Coultard expands the term, reconstructing dispossession not as a historic backdrop but "as an ongoing feature of the reproduction of colonial and capitalist social relations in our present."[28]

This notion is particularly evident in the ever-expanding landscape of suburban settlement, when considering Vivian Ziherl's concept of the "axiomatic order" of the frontier: "Once the proprietorial line in the sand is enclosed in a circle, the imperative is to expand. The modus for doing so is the axiomatic, a reproduction of the same. The frontier anticipates an order governed through calculable—i.e., endlessly exchangeable, and hence indifferent—relations."[29] The suburbs of Australian cities share a common urban logic with several

25 "Deep Drainage and East-End Park for Perth," *Daily News*, **February 23, 1894, 2.**

26 Saskia Beudel, "Fossils in the City," in *Open Spatial Workshop: Converging in Time*, **exh. cat., 25–38 (Melbourne: Monash University Museum of Art, 2017), 28.**

27 Malini Ranganathan, "Property, Pipes, and Improvement," in "Liquid Utility," special project, ed. Nick Axel, Nikolaus Hirsch, Reinhold Martin, Jacob R. Moore, and Jordan Steingard, *e-flux Architecture*, **July 2019, https://www.e-flux.com/architecture/liquid-utility/259669/property-pipes-and-improvement/.**

28 Karl Marx, *Capital: A Critique of Political Economy*, **vol. 1 (1887; Moscow: Progress Publishers, 1977); and Glen Coulthard, "The Colonialism of the Present,"** *Jacobin*, **January 13, 2015, https://www.jacobinmag.com/2015/01/indigenous-left-glen-coulthard-interview/. nous-left-glen-coulthard-interview/.**

The suburbs of Australian cities share a common urban logic with several settler-colonial states: New Zealand, Canada, the United States, and South Africa. Despite distinct terrains, a common morphology prevails.

settler-colonial states: New Zealand, Canada, the United States, and South Africa. Despite distinct terrains, a common morphology prevails. It is predicated on the flattening of complex intermingling worlds into plots of land to be bought, sold, and registered. As Lorenzo Veracinci aptly identifies, “suburbia re-enacts settlement.” Like the settler colony, the suburb is predicated on tabula rasa, terra nullius. It is established both in fear and denial of its surroundings, constructed as a “fortressed frontier” against the ecosocial worlds it inhabits.[30]

29 Ziherl, “On the Frontier, Again.”

30 Ziherl, “On the Frontier, Again.”

Urban development in Perth has largely occurred on sandy soils, resulting in a building culture characterized by concrete slabs on benched sites and heavy double-brick construction. As much of the sandy low-groundwater sites have now been built upon, suburban development is projected toward the few remaining claypans at the foothills of the Swan Coastal Plain. Construction in this high-groundwater region will rely on draining, clearing, and deep infill, which will further exacerbate the declining water table. Drain ontology is authoritative and imposing; it controls and directs flows, rather than adapting to them. It persists in its pursuit of Technocratic and infrastructural solutionism continues to enable this socioecological alienation and hydrological erasure.

Drain ontology is authoritative and imposing; it controls and directs flows, rather than adapting to them.

Despite decreasing rainfall and a dramatically overexerted groundwater table, Perth maintains the highest level of water consumption per capita in the country.[31] Over 50 percent of this is provided through desalination, which has increased the energy intensity of supply more than tenfold.[32] The Water Corporation declares this a “climate independent” water source.[33] The wetlands and claypans have been drained, filled, and flattened into brick suburbs, leaving

31 Jo Lindsay and Sian Supski, “Changing Household Water Consumption Practices after Drought in Three Australian Cities,” *Geoforum* 84 (2017): 51–58.

only seawater to be siphoned and purified by coal. The wastes have not merely been piped away (coal-purified water relies on extraction and combustion that will severely deplete the water table of an ignorable elsewhere) but deemed nonexistent, "climate independent." Through these abstractions, drain ontology offers both an elusion of responsibility and the illusion of purity.

The toxic flows of drain ontology are multidirectional, and the impacts of hydrological erasure that have always been known by Indigenous peoples are trickling into settler worlds. Our discourse around water is characterized by paradoxical anxieties of absence and excess, prolonged drought and rising sea levels. We are caught in a cascade of concurrent crises, ironically caused by the colonial desire for "order."

To move beyond drain ontology is to consider a form of existence that is contingent, adaptive, and fluid. It is to recognize the uninterruptable flows between land, water, human beings, and more-than-human beings. While the complex systems of place-relations evidenced in Indigenous culture present a sophisticated form of such an existence, Tony Birch preempts potential appropriation, cautioning against "Indigenous ecological knowledge being branded and packaged as a quick fix solution to climate change by retro-fitting it to suit Western society."[34] To move beyond a drain ontology is to recognize not only the reality of relationality but the toxic currents of dispossession, extraction, and violence that undergird our "development" to this point. Settlers might locate our relational responsibilities using Eve Tuck and Marcia McKenzie's notion of "turning toward place": "Turning toward place necessitates acknowledgment and reparations based on these histories: of settler colonialism, capitalism, and of Cartesian and (post)modern separations of mind from body, body from land."[35] Seeking a meaningful "ontological turn" demands dredging up the sewers of settler amnesia, not merely for recognition, but for repair and reparation.

32 S.J. Kenway, A. Priestley, S. Cook, S. Seo, M. Inman, A. Gregory, and M. Hall, *Energy Use in the Provision and Consumption of Urban Water in Australia and New Zealand* **(Canberra: CSIRO, 2008), https://publications.csiro.au/rpr/download?pid=csiro:EP116078&dsid=DS1.**

33 Water Corporation, "Securing Supply," *Water Corporation*, **https://www.watercorporation.com.au/Our-water/Climate-change-and-WA/Climate-and-Perth/Securing-supply.**

34 Tony Birch, "Climate Change, Recognition and Social Place-Making," *Sydney Review of Books*, **March 3, 2017, https://sydneyreviewofbooks.com/essay/climate-change-recognition-and-caring-for-country/.**

35 Eve Tuck and Marcia McKenzie, "Relational Validity and the 'Where' of Inquiry: Place and Land in Qualitative Research," *Qualitative Inquiry* **21, no. 7 (March 2015): 633–38.**

Acknowledgments

I acknowledge and pay my respects to the First Peoples of the Melbourne region, the Woi Wurrung and Boon Wurrung language groups of the Kulin Nation, upon whose unceded lands I live, work, and study. I acknowledge and pay my respects to the First Peoples of the Perth region, the Whadjuk language group of the Noongar Nation, upon whose unceded lands this chapter is situated. Thanks to my dear friend Thandi Paterson for reading and editing earlier drafts of the chapter.

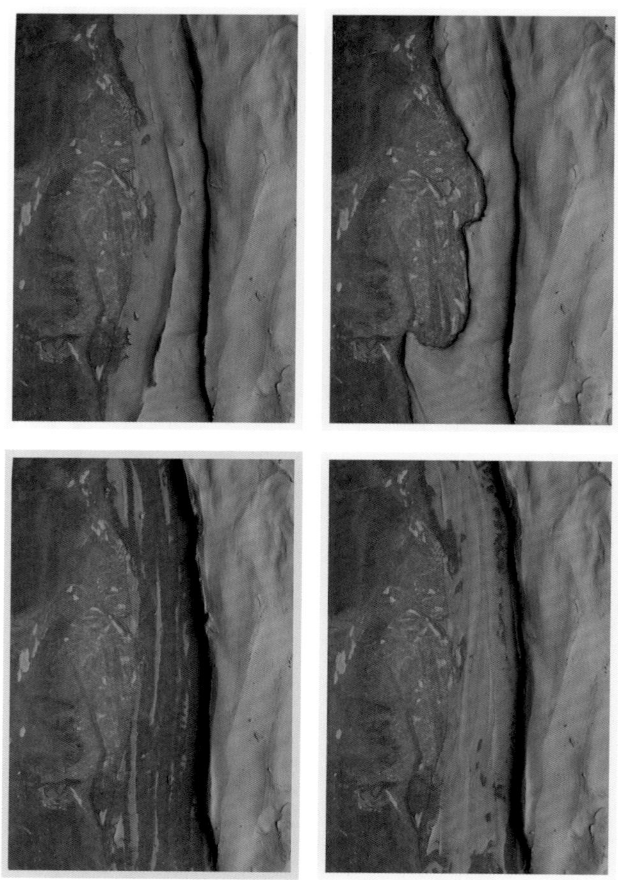

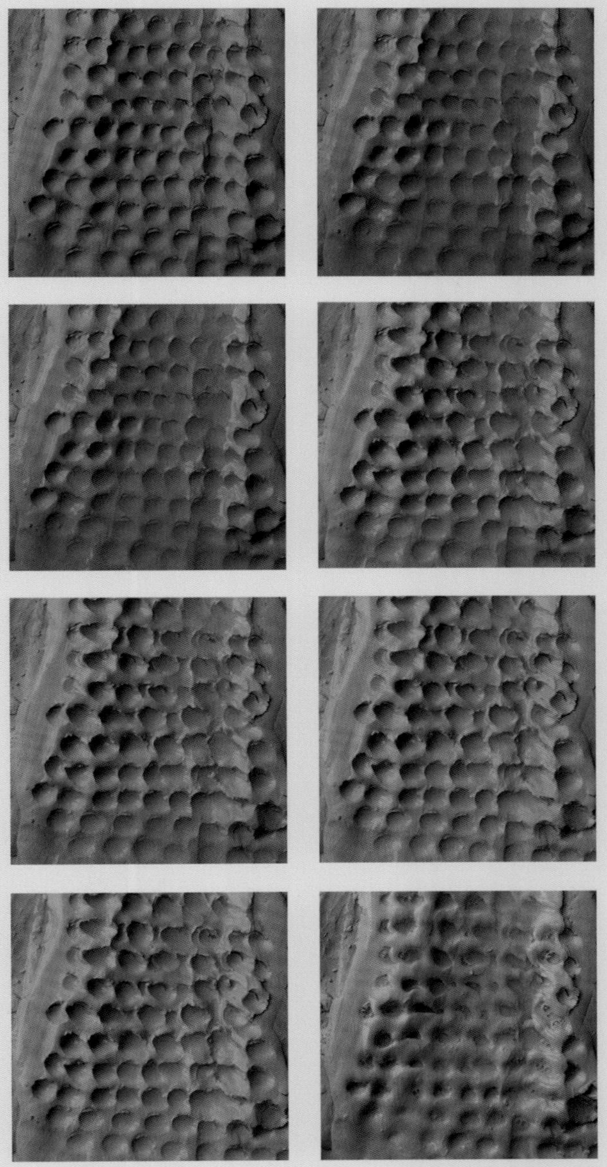

Conversion of a Military Base: Reuse of Infrastructural Left-overs

Leonie Hartung

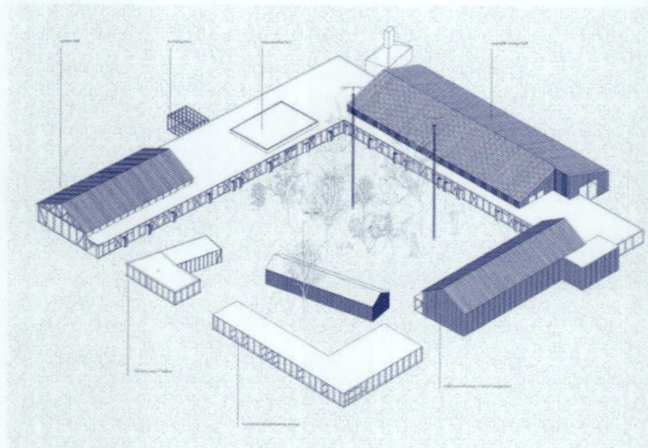

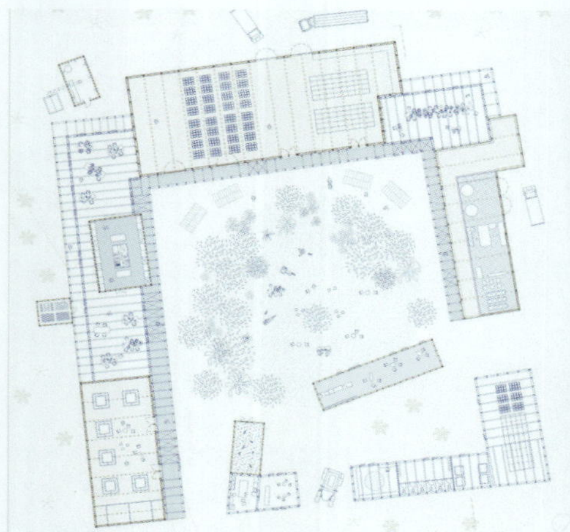

The main industries on the island of Utö—from settlement until the island's occupation by the military—were originally livestock, fishing, agriculture, and mining. This project addresses the challenges of food supply and food production on the island today and aims to revive public space on the island by reintroducing a local food production system that has been almost entirely lost. Analysis of the island's import and export infrastructures shows that nearly all food is delivered to the local ICA (grocery store) by boat from the Swedish mainland, which sources its food from across Europe. The potential exists to return to local food production to reduce import requirements, thereby providing a more ecological, sustainable, and resource-friendly way of providing nourishment to the island's residents. Fostering local production can raise environmental awareness of the impact of consuming imported goods and reduce the energy consumption required to support import infrastructures. The loss of the island's original marketplace, which was replaced by a supermarket that ships all its goods from the mainland, also meant the loss of a public space. The military, which owns more than 50 percent of the island, is one of the main employers on Utö. While providing economic stability it has not meaningfully sought local engagement or facilitated interaction between locals and employees. Furthermore, while Utö once claimed a strategic position within the Stockholm archipelago, the threat of foreign invasion is no longer as urgent as it was once perceived to be, raising the question of what might happen to the island should the military eventually leave?

An analysis of an agricultural map from 1951 shows that the military shooting ranges were once pastures for livestock. These pastures could be reactivated for ecologically responsible farming of dairy cows, sheep, and goats, as well as for growing crops such as potatoes, beans, and leafy vegetables. The existing forests could be used for foraging mushrooms and berries that could be stored in the former bunkers. The military base and its facilities are located along the main road that connects the northern, touristic part of the island with the local village and with the residents living at the southern end of the island. The base could be repurposed to handle all of the logistical processes associated with food production, including a marketplace, restaurant, and facilities for small-scale food production. The four key components of food production—production, processing, retail, and consumption—could be united in one place to raise awareness about the necessary relations among the different procedures.

The project focuses on the military base camp's industrial storage halls, which could warehouse food produced on the island before it is sold at the market to both tourists and residents. Loosely arranged, the timbered base-camp buildings enclose an open space that forms a garden where visitors could gather and rest. A basic timber-frame construction could be added to the existing facade and function as a public walkway connecting the existing structures and protecting the courtyard. Folding doors could be opened during the summer for ventilation, creating a pleasant indoor climate. The low threshold increases accessibility for visitors. Within the new structure a restaurant could serve food produced on Utö, using traditional Swedish methods of cooking and preserving (e.g., smoking, fermenting, storing) combined with modern digital technologies of harvesting. The project offers a critique of current food industries and their rush to satisfy customer demand, their marketing of cheap, low-quality products no matter the long-term impacts on the environment, climate, health, and the living conditions of animals. The aim is to raise awareness of infrastructural systems of supply, delivery, and consumption and shift the food industry's emphasis toward more local, ecological, and environmentally friendly approaches to food production and consumption.

THECRI
TICALZ
ONE

Chapter 14
The Critical Zone: Observatory Space

Alexandra Arènes

Earth's "critical zone" is the thin surface layer of the planet that extends from the tree canopy to deep rock. It is where water, soil, and organisms interact to make the planet habitable. The zone is threatened by what has come to be called the "Anthropocene." To monitor landscapes undergoing severe environmental disturbance and to better understand how they behave and what threatens their habitability, a network of earth scientists established critical zone observatories (CZOs) around the world.[1] Observatories are not physical buildings but areas of physical space (watershed, forest, field, mountain, etc.) monitored for scientific study. And scientists from several earth science disciplines are developing instruments to understand how Gaia (to use Bruno Latour's and Isabelle Stengers's preferred term for the planet and its entanglements) responds to human activities.[2]

1 There are international and national networks. For more information: https://www.czen.org/about, https://www.ozcar-ri.org

2 Bruno Latour, *Facing Gaia: Eight Lectures on the New Climatic Regime* **(Cambridge, UK: Polity, 2017); and Isabelle Stengers,** *In Catastrophic Times: The Coming Barbarism* **(Ann Arbor, MI: Open Humanities Press and Meson Press, 2015), DOI: 10.14619/016.**

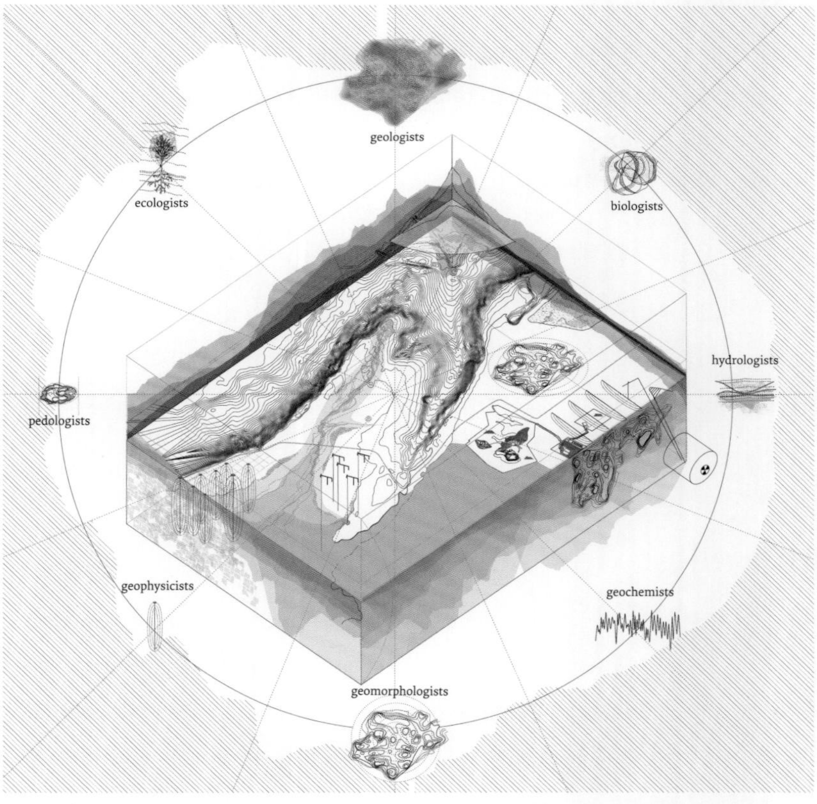

Axonometric diagram showing the locations of various observatories and the scientific disciplines studying the compartments of the critical zone. Drawing by the author based on fieldwork.

An installation by Alexandra Arènes and Soheil Hajmirbaba, Atelier SOC (Société d'Objets Cartographiques), in the exhibition *Critical Zones: Observatories for Earthly Politics*, 2020/2021, ZKM | Center for Art and Media Karlsruhe, Germany, curated by Peter Weibel and Bruno Latour.

In 2020, for the exhibition *Critical Zones: Observatories for Earthly Politics*, the Atelier SOC (Société d'Objets Cartographiques) reconstructed a watershed inside the ZKM | Zentrum für Kunst und Medien (Center for Art and Media) in Karlsruhe, Germany. After a long investigation of the Strengbach observatory in the Vosges forest—located in eastern France on the border with Germany and comprising eighty hectares of steep slopes assailed by acid rain and forest death—we redesigned the components of the observatory in the atrium of the museum. None of the traditional features of a landscape—trees, slopes, topography, river—were represented. Instead, we reconstructed the network of instruments that scientists use to understand the responses of this specific watershed to environmental disturbances. Thanks to this infrastructure of instruments, the landscape appears in a different way. The trees, river, and soil examined by the scientists' instruments, both high-tech and low-tech, in the critical zone challenge traditional scales, agencies, and temporalities. The research infrastructure of the CZOs, which locates laboratories in vulnerable landscapes, troubles our understanding of the earth. Our installation aimed to give the public an opportunity to experience an encounter with these new technologically advanced optical instruments by navigating from one instrument station to another, following rivers, soils, and trees with a new gaze. Artistic mediation and documenta-

The trees, river, and soil examined by the scientists' instruments, both high-tech and low-tech, in the critical zone challenge traditional scales, agencies, and temporalities. The research infrastructure of the CZOs, which locates laboratories in vulnerable landscapes, troubles our understanding of the earth.

tion are mixed with the images produced by scientists to develop a dialogue that fosters ways of becoming sensitive to the movements of the earth. The installation is conceived as a model of the watershed brought back into an architectural space. On the occasion of this exhibition, a series of micro-architectures spatialized a landscape populated by instruments. This chapter offers a photographic tour through the installation, providing insights into this new way of observing and mapping landscapes.

When entering the museum hall, you discover scattered objects hanging from beams, fixed to posts, on the ground or above your head. Covering the surface of the hall, an articulated steel structure levitates between two and four meters off the ground. You are invited to wander beneath the structure. At the entrance to the installation, a massive sand and concrete model reproduces the topography of the observatory's watershed. From the vantage of the entrance, you can see the reduced model of the watershed in the foreground and the suspended structure in the background. They have the same shape and follow the same landscape undulations. The two models represent the topography of the watershed in two different ways. The first, made of concrete, corresponds to the classic topographical model. The second, composed of suspended lines, reconstructs the topography revealed by the geophones that scientists use to probe the ground. The technical instrument cuts sections through the watershed from one side to the other, following lines called "geophones." These record the propagation of vibrations in the ground at depth and thus allow scientists to "see" the subsurface, its porosity, its granularity, its humidity, its fractures. The soil contains a deep and rich world. But the soil is not a solid mass; it is full of holes, voids that allow for the passage of life. Like a scientist, you are invited to probe the depths of the watershed by collecting stories as you move from one station to the next, reconstructing the landscape of the critical zone.

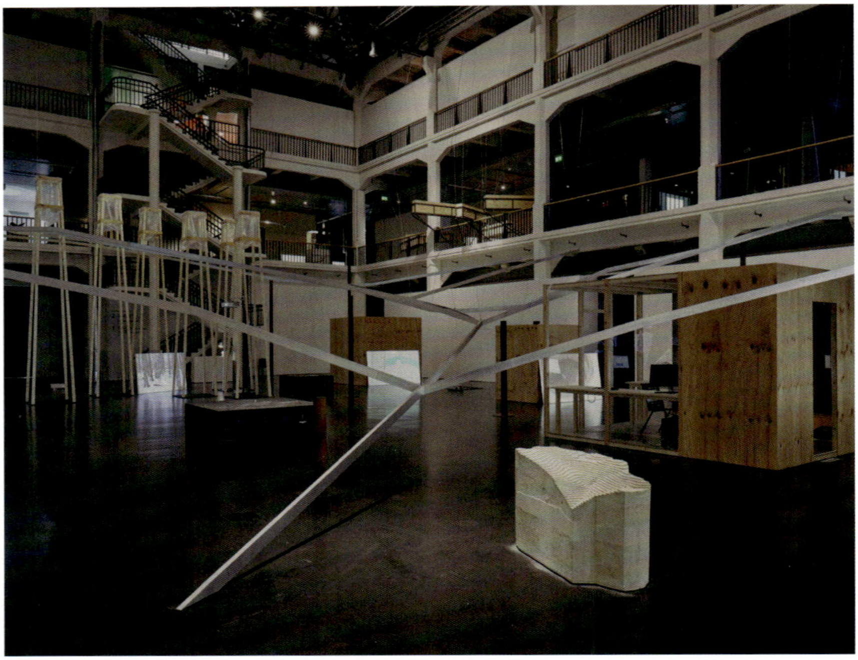

The entrance showing the concrete model and the hanging structure. Installation view of *Critical Zones: Observatories for Earthly Politics*, 2020/2021, © ZKM | Zentrum für Kunst und Medien Karlsruhe

Photograph: Tobias Wootton.

Critical Zone Observatory Space
Location: ZKM, Karlsruhe, Germany

Watershed scale: 1:40

Altitude: from 0 to 5 meters

Instrument stations: 8; geophysics

profiles: 6

Monitoring: atmosphere, trees, soil, rocks, groundwater

The geophysics station (station 05). Left image: reconstitution of the depth of the watershed with geophysics technique. Image: Sylvain Pasquet, scientist at the Institut de Physique du Globe de Paris (Paris Institute of Earth Physics). Right image: reconstitution of the geophysics lines in the space of the museum.

Drawing: SOC.

Critical Zone Observatory

Location: Strengbach, Vosges forest, France

Watershed scale: 1:1 = 80 hectares

Altitude: from 880 to 1,080 meters

Instrument stations: 8; geophysics

profiles: 6

Monitoring: atmosphere, trees, soil, rocks, groundwater

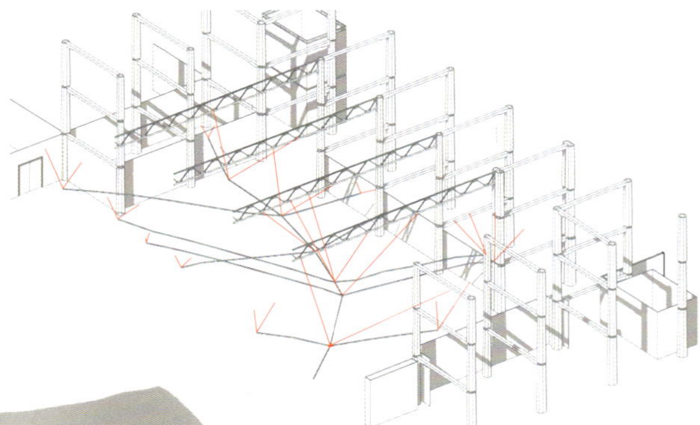

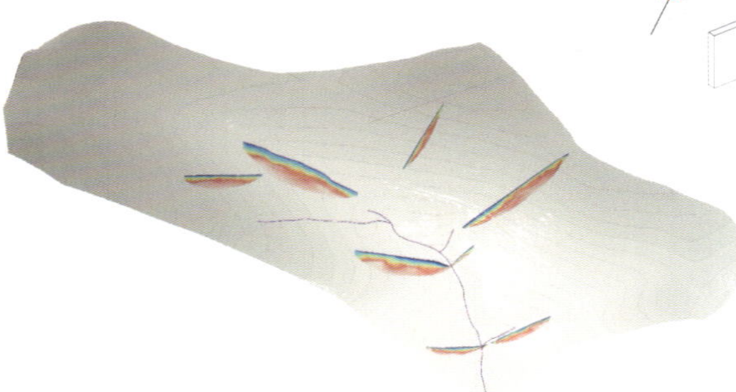

Moving through the exhibition, you traverse a model of the watershed of the Vosges forest observatory. The watershed is scaled down to a factor of forty so that it can be accommodated by the museum and on the atrium levels. Respecting this scale, each station is placed at the same altitude and longitude as its actual observatory in the forest. In contrast, the instruments on display maintain their original scale. In effect, different spatial and temporal scales are presented simultaneously, from instruments showing geological events over millions of years to instruments showing chemical events taking place in a river every twenty minutes.

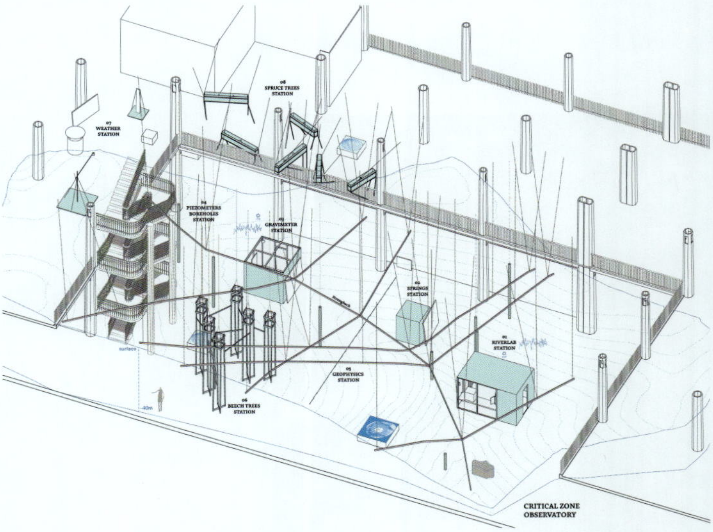

Axonometric drawing of the installation showing the stations. Drawing: SOC.

Grasping the Incommensurability of the Earth

Equipped with a field guide, which reports the data collected by each station, and a map, you can experience a field visit to a CZO, passing from one instrument station to another, observing the work of the scientists through short films projected onto the architecture of the stations. Each station reveals a hidden aspect of the landscape, thanks to the specific instruments imported into the museum.

Riverlab (Station 01)

Listening to the chemical symphony of the river (the microscale composition of the river).

The Riverlab is a tiny field laboratory. Inside, a machine records the chemical variations of the river as river water passes over its circuits in real time. The ten chemical elements measured by the station exhibit different behaviors depending on the time of day, the season, and whether the river is flooding. Using data gathered from the site, a composer generated music that can be listened to in the "potamosensory"[3] space of the museum. Each chemical element becomes a musical instrument that plays its own score and whose rhythm may or may not match that of the other elements.

3 Potamosensory is a term invented by the geochemists I have interviewed. Potamology means the study of rivers. Potamosensory means to become sensitive to a river's behavior. A specific space in the installation has been designed where visitors can hear and feel the variations of the chemical contents of the Strengbach river through a musical composition specifically created with data derived from the river.

Inside the installation, ground floor, Riverlab on the left (station 01). Photograph: Tobias Wootton.

Gravimetry (Station 03)

Echoing the coastal tides (macroscale of the earth).

This machine records the signal from the water table at depth, but it is so sensitive that it also records other signals, such as the force of gravity of the tides breaking on the sea coast hundreds of miles away, like echoes rippling through the continental forest.

Piezometers and Core Samples (Station 04)

Archiving the weathering of rocks.

Columns extract soil from deep underground, exposing previously unsuspected pockets of water at depths of nearly 120 meters. The water triggers chemical reactions in the rocks, perhaps even enabling the presence of organisms. The boundaries of the critical zone extend intensively into the depths.

Geoseismic (Station 05)

Probing the depths.

Lines of geophones placed momentarily on the surface of the watershed probe the composition of the ground up to 150 meters. Vibrations are triggered on the soil, and their propagation is monitored, allowing the rock's qualities to be assessed.

Beech Trees (Station 06)

Cosmic beings.

Trees are sentinels of the environment. Large parts of the forest are monitored to understand whether they exhibit resilience after storms, acid rain, parasite invasions, and the impacts of the forest industry.

Inside the installation, ground floor, the beech trees station (06). Photograph: Tobias Wootton.

Weather Station (Station 07)

Tracing connectedness.

Multiple devices record variations in the lower atmosphere, the direction of the winds, and the components they transport. Sulfur emissions from industrial activity in Asia can reach the Vosges forest in less than twenty days.

Inside the installation, first floor, the weather station (07). Photograph: Tobias Wootton.

Spruce Trees (Station 08)

Harvesting pollutants from the rain.

Large rectangular gutters placed under the trees collect rainwater to analyze its pollutants, including sulfur, which acidifies the soil and is responsible for the death of trees.

Inside the installation, first floor, the spruce trees station (08). Photograph: Tobias Wootton.

The spaces between the CZO's stations invite you to reconstruct the shape of the forest—its trees, its water, its soil—in a complex way, where imagination mixes with scientific data and where micro- and macro-worlds intertwine to create a living environment. The space between the stations is left open to the affordances of exploration. "Staying with the trouble" is a prerequisite to approaching the complexity of the earth, because "all knowledge, human and non-human, is now stammering, and the question asked in each zone is how to share a concerned perplexity, how to not dream of a solution but to learn, as Donna Haraway puts, to stay with the trouble."[4] You must physically pass and repass the various mediums, arts, and scientific demonstrations, which are sometimes so intermixed it is hard to discern the influence of the one or the other, artistic practice or scientific practice. You must venture questions, suffer disorientation, and get lost while searching for signs and traces if you are to cultivate a curiosity toward the earth. Indeed, "the answer of what earthly sciences could be has nothing to do with a conversion, a new general understanding of what the Earth demands from us. This is also not a new perspective, because the Earth won't let itself be watched. It is there, folded many ways, entangling all scales not only space but also of time. And efforts to simplify it have further increased complications."[5]

You must venture questions, suffer disorientation, and get lost while searching for signs and traces if you are to cultivate a curiosity toward the earth.

The installation is an artifact, so we are not really in the territory itself alongside its problems, its inhabitants, and its political complexities. What we can grasp in a museum are fragments that come from the territory; fragments of practices; fragments of time, of live data, of live movements, or of something that has already happened; fragments of instruments that are here at the same scale as there, questioning the scalability of laboratory instruments and of the entities that they record and that they cannot render totally generic. This is also why critical-zone science cannot be practiced exclusively in the

4 Isabelle Stengers, "The Earth Won't Let Itself Be Watched," in *Critical Zones: The Science and Politics of Landing on Earth*, **ed. Bruno Latour and Peter Weibel, 228–35 (Cambridge, MA: MIT Press, 2020), 233.**

5 Stengers, "The Earth Won't Let Itself Be Watched," 232.

laboratory; it must be performed in the field because the earth is not scalable. The installation stages this tension between the possibility and impossibility of scalability. The geography is scaled, but the instruments are not, and these instruments in turn magnify tiny elements.

The CZO is a device that plays with measures, models, and scales without announcing the rules or fixing them once and for all. It is somewhat like the fable of Alice in Wonderland. As in the depths of the critical zone, Alice falls into an underworld full of surprising effects, including strange scaling phenomena that are beyond her control and that dramatically alter her body. In the same way, the Anthropocene and the COVID-19 virus cause our bodies to change scale in unexpected ways that are, to say the least, elusive, since we cannot control them. Every time Alice wants to regain control of her scale (by trying to scale herself to the world around her), she fails, and, more dramatically, she makes the situation worse. You will find yourself, like Alice, in a kind of underworld called the "critical zone." You must not try to control the scales but let yourself be guided, dive into the folds of the earth. Test an instrument (or a potion?) so that your mind becomes tiny and can explore the microcosm. A few minutes later, expand again to grasp the terrestrial scale of human habitation. As in Alice's adventure, we do not move from one scale to another smoothly, as in Charles Eames and Ray Eames's short film *The Power of Ten*, but we are projected into each world, each scale of the entity we follow, grasping a fragment of each terrestrial monad through the scope of a chthonic hole.

It is somewhat like the fable of Alice in Wonderland. As in the depths of the critical zone, Alice falls into an underworld full of surprising effects, including strange scaling phenomena that are beyond her control and that dramatically alter her body.

Soil Map, Down to Earth

View of the installation from the first floor. Photograph: Tobias Wootton.

You can also explore a map of the observatory in the middle of the installation. The map is a kind of toposcope (orientation map) that produces an inversion of the conventional repertoire of cartography. It has no north, no latitude or longitude references, and no scales. Or rather, different scales coexist on the map. The map directs us to the ground. The gaze is reversed: we do not map the surface of the earth from above (i.e., from a vantage point) but instead map the depth of the ground from below (i.e., from the inside). The map is a cross-section of the critical zone—a circular cross-section where the depths of the rocks encompass the thin, fragile layers of fertile soil and its organisms. In the center, the sulfur-laden atmosphere threatens the soil with acid rain. What is released into the atmosphere on the other side of the world does not escape into infinite space (the universe) but is trapped in the protective layer of the earth and thus falls back down upon us. Pollution remains in the atmosphere. The blue elements denote the instruments of the observatory. The map visualizes what we see through their lenses: the composition of the soil, the movements of water, the turbulence of the atmosphere, the microscopic world, and so on. The soil map shows that even the soil is not stable but composed of a watery and viscous consistency. The depths are not a solid infrastructure; there is no stable surface on which we can unquestionably build more and more. If we can no longer consider the depths as a guarantee of stability, then the idea that the ground is a fixed surface (covered by roads, squares, building slabs) disappears like a modernist infrastructural chimera. What, then, is infrastructure?

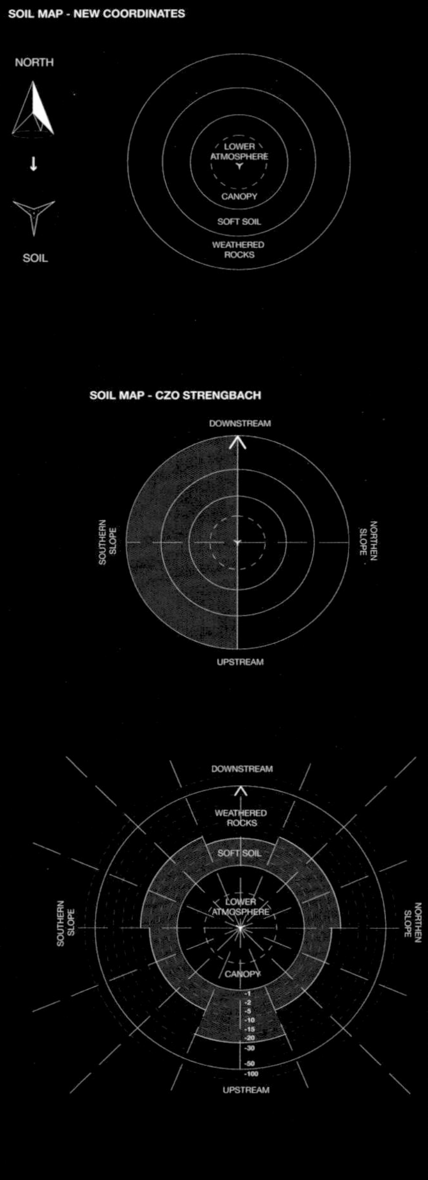

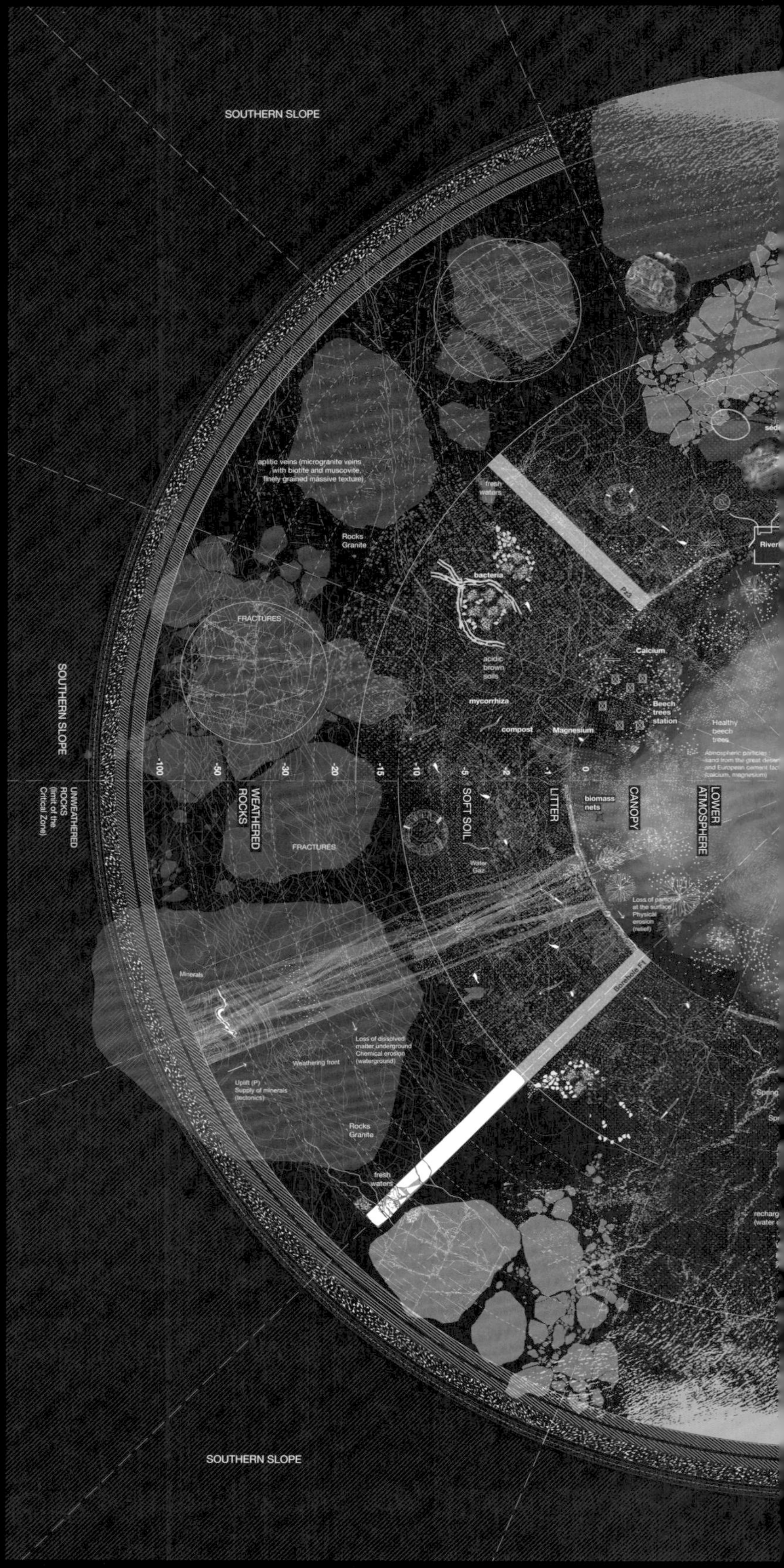

Soil map of the Strengbach Critical Zone Observatory. By the author.

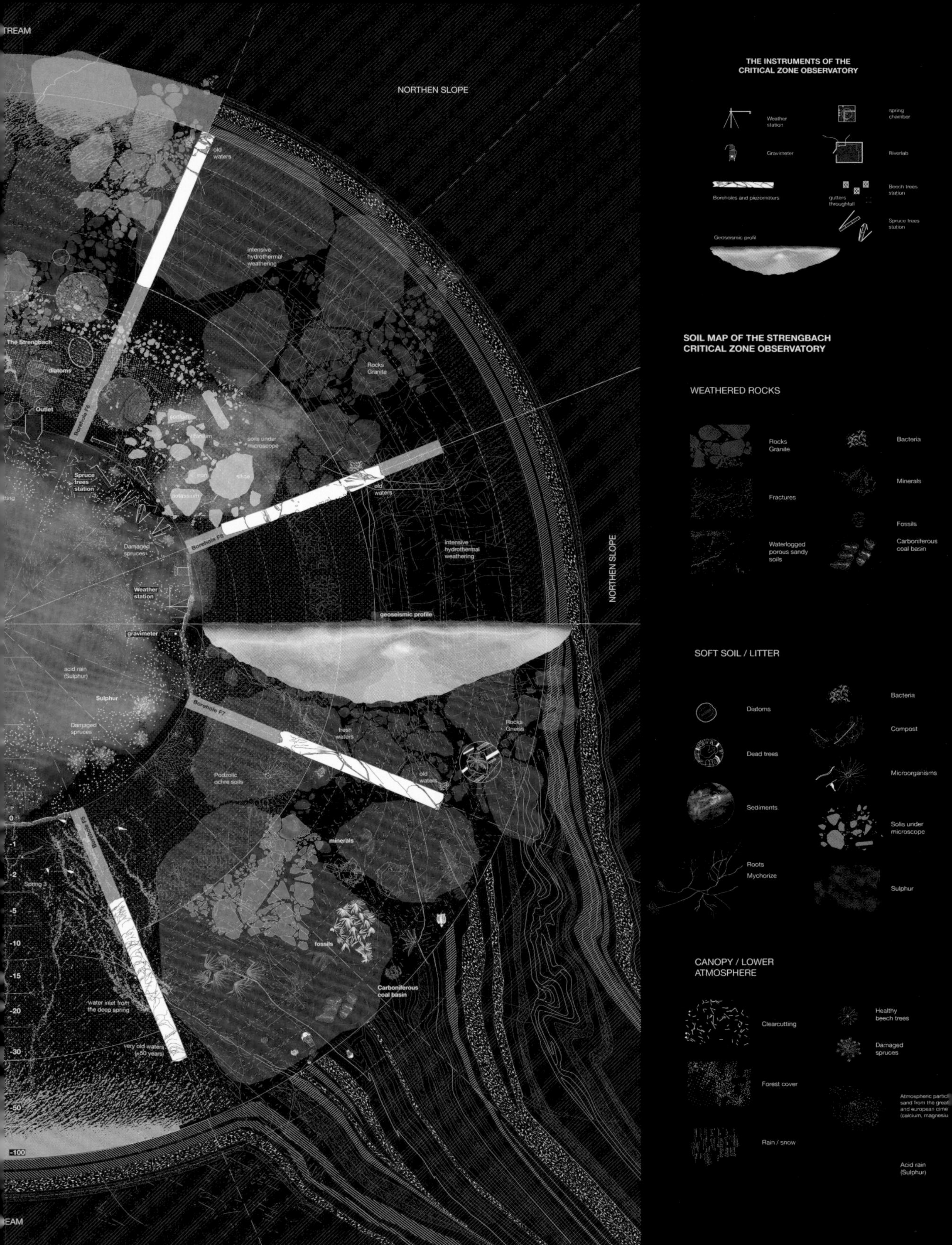

TREAM
NORTHEN SLOPE
THE INSTRUMENTS OF THE CRITICAL ZONE OBSERVATORY
Weather station
spring chamber
Gravimeter
Riverlab
Boreholes and piezometers
gutters throughfall
Beech trees station
Spruce trees station
Geoseismic profil
SOIL MAP OF THE STRENGBACH CRITICAL ZONE OBSERVATORY
WEATHERED ROCKS
Rocks Granite
Bacteria
Fractures
Minerals
Fossils
Waterlogged porous sandy soils
Carboniferous coal basin
SOFT SOIL / LITTER
Diatoms
Bacteria
Compost
Dead trees
Microorganisms
Sediments
Soils under microscope
Roots
Mychorize
Sulphur
CANOPY / LOWER ATMOSPHERE
Clearcutting
Healthy beech trees
Damaged spruces
Forest cover
Rain / snow
Acid rain (Sulphur)
old waters
intensive hydrothermal weathering
The Strengbach
diatoms
Outlet
Borehole F6
Rocks Granite
soils under microscope
Spruce trees station
old waters
Borehole F8
Damaged spruces
intensive hydrothermal weathering
NORTHEN SLOPE
Weather station
geoseismic profile
gravimeter
acid rain (Sulphur)
Sulphur
Damaged spruces
Borehole F7
fresh waters
Rocks Gneiss
Podzolic ochre soils
old waters
minerals
Spring 3
fossils
Carboniferous coal basin
water inlet from the deep spring
very old waters (+50 years)
0
-1
-2
-5
-10
-15
-20
-30
-50
-100
EAM

After the Human: Monument to the Anthropocene

Changhyun Ahn

Reaching back into the history of Kymlinge, an underground rail station and infrastructural system that was never opened, it is easy to see how the conflicts associated with the site and its development led to the station being abandoned. The land around the station contains not only rare natural species but also traces of human beings from the Neolithic era. If we zoom out and consider the site from a larger time scale, we see that thousands of years ago, before the Baltic Sea had connected to the Atlantic Ocean, the entire Stockholm area was submerged. Today, following the onset of the Anthropocene and failures of natural systems, the sea level is again rising, rendering the effects of environmental change visible.

For my project, I proposed a new infrastructure based on the imaginary scenario of a climate dystopia, a future of rising sea levels that forces the migration of human beings away from the site. In my imaginary scenario, a last community of human beings decides to build an archive to store their remaining knowledge and memories. Inspired by the U.S. National Aeronautics and Space Administration's "golden record" project (which sent two gold phonograph records into space aboard the Voyager 1 and 2 spacecraft) and the underground nuclear waste disposal project in Finland, the project focused on how remnants of human knowledge could be left behind as a message to a sentient being thousands of years in the future. Thinking at the vast scale of geological periods required that the structure and its materials be durable. Stories of human lives and their accumulated knowledge would be engraved into the surface of a thick column composed of a series of sections. The column would be stored at the center of a new infrastructure under the ground. Hard disks and other data storage devices would quickly become defunct or degrade over the planned time period. Paper, while in many ways more durable, is fragile, and ink fades away. The only medium capable of recording history for thousands of years is rock. Consider, for example, Sumerian stone artifacts that are thousands of years old. I imagined support structures that would enable access so that stone columns could be engraved before being stacked in place. Underground earth works at the Kymlinge site would create a secure space for the storage of the archival columns and a main infrastructure to load each column into place. Much of the design was conceived in section, due to the vertical nature of the archival column. Visualizing each step helped me to develop each stage of the scenario. After thousands of years have passed and the land has been erased by rising sea levels, the water pressure will push the massive compound column slowly upward, revealing its archival message to the future beings who are so often imagined in Anthropocene discourse.

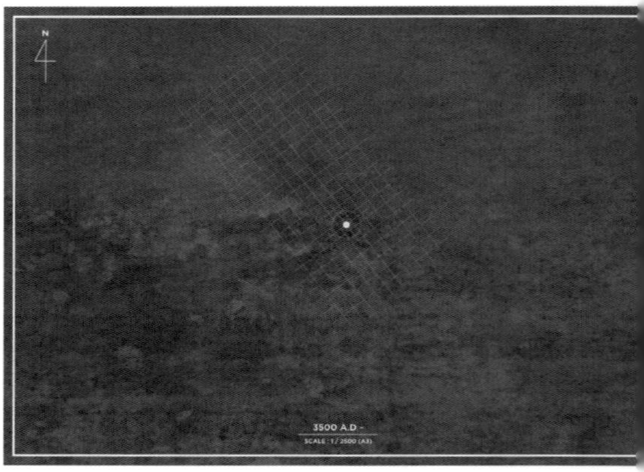

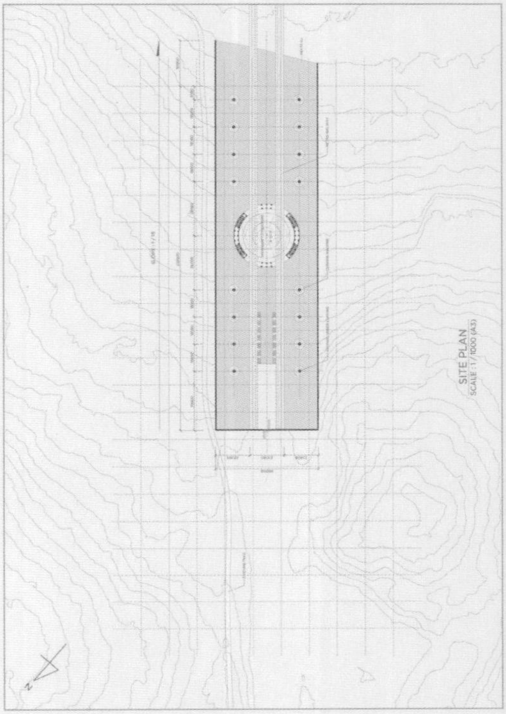
SITE PLAN
SCALE 1 / 1000 (A3)

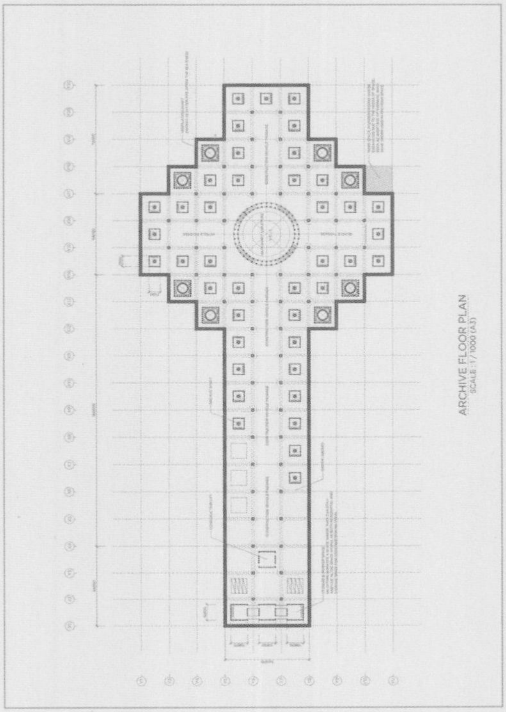
ARCHIVE FLOOR PLAN
SCALE 1 / 1000 (A3)

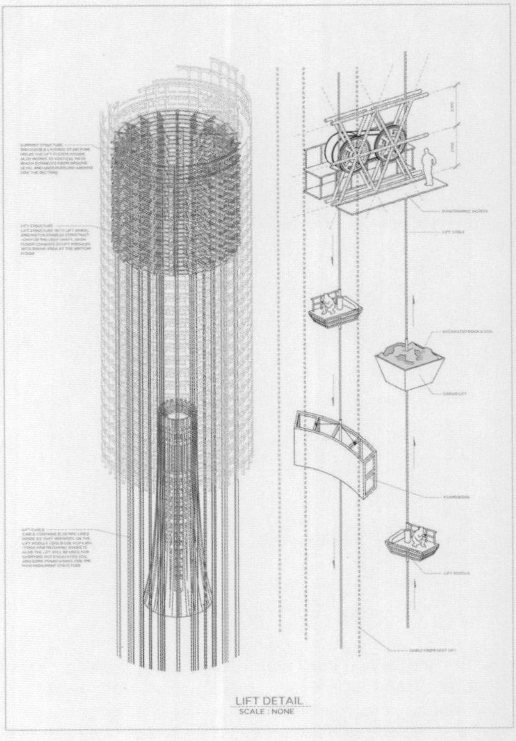
LIFT DETAIL
SCALE : NONE

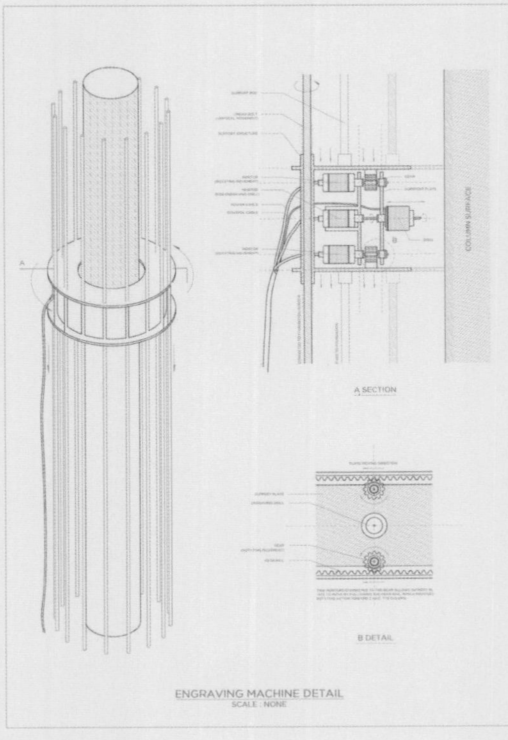
A SECTION
B DETAIL
COLUMN SURFACE
ENGRAVING MACHINE DETAIL
SCALE : NONE

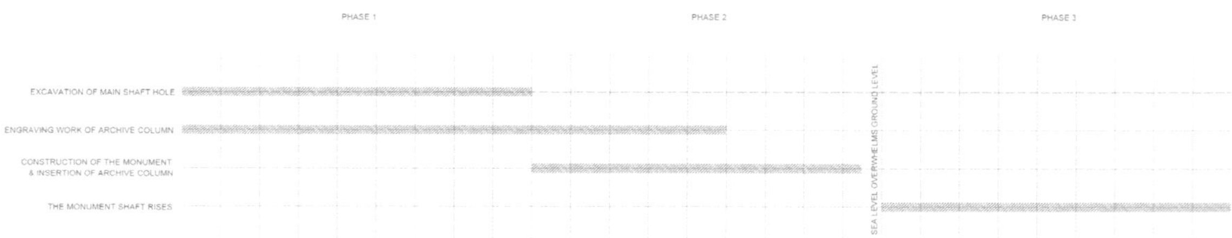

From construction to rising up against the sea, the project is devided into three phases. In the first phase, excavation of ground for securing the space, used for the construction of monument shaft, will be held. Engraving work for the archive column will be also continues at the same time. After the excavation of shaft hole is finished, actual construction of monument shaft and insertion of archive column start, which is phase two. When the sea level rises over the ground level of the site, phase three, the monument shaft start rising against the water level.

Deeply excavated hole will hold the monument shaft. Inside of the shaft structure, jointed archive columns will be stored vertically. Every floor is connected with staircase and tutorial monument, holding tutorial information of reading the binary code with all kind of language and existing symbol, is located on the top floor that has bigger opennings compare to others. This differenciated size of openings will attract the future intellectual beings by stimulating their curiosity. On the other hand, smaller openings will work as water drainage against an accidental invasion of the water and will work as entrances of the shaft structure.

Multi-layered structure of the shaft not only allows more durability, but also less density, which makes top part of the structure to float on the water. On the surface of the outer layer of structure, rough texture will be formed so that future beings can climb up with it, in the case the estimated exposed line of shaft structure is higher than actual water & ground level.

ASYNT
HETIC
UNIVE
RSE

Chapter 15
A Synthetic Universe: An Underground Network of Sensing Infrastructures

Blanca Pujals

About one hundred trillion neutrinos pass through your body each second.[1]

Since the end of the Second World War, new architectures and infrastructures for containing and artificially reproducing the conditions present at the beginning of the universe have surfaced across the world: a synthetic replica of the early universe on Earth.

These sophisticated technospaces are composed of sealed chambers that recreate specific and non-existent physical conditions on Earth to reveal the origin of matter. Spread throughout a subterranean global chamber system, they constitute an invisible underground network.

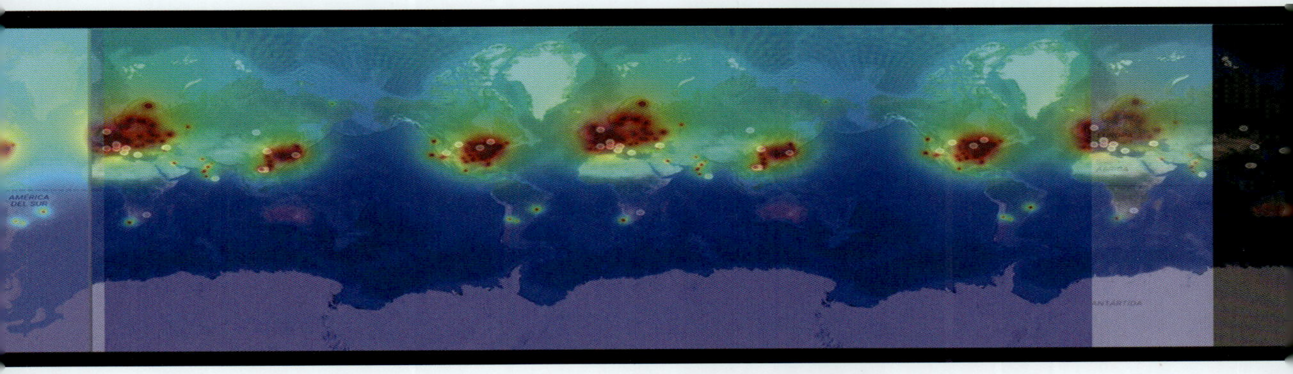

Blanca Pujals, A Synthetic Universe. The Unmaking of Microscopic Bonds in Transnational Space, 2016. This map shows elementary particle colliders and neutrino observatories merged with the Antineutrino Global Map 2015, which documents human-made synthetic antineutrino emissions from nuclear test sites and nuclear power plants. The Antineutrino Global Map was created in 2015 using data from two neutrino detectors—Borexino in Italy and Kamiokande in Japan—and from the International Atomic Energy Agency.

The world's largest and most complex scientific instrument, the Large Hadron Collider (LHC) at the European Organization for Nuclear Research (CERN) in Geneva, is a ring twenty-seven kilometers in diameter buried one hundred meters under the Franco-Swiss border. At the Sudbury Neutrino Observatory (SNO) in Ontario, Canada, a twelve-meter-diameter acrylic sphere detector is located two kilometers below the surface in Vale Limited's Creighton nickel

1 Neutrino is a particle that carries energy and information. The singularity of neutrinos is that they are the weakest, the smallest, the most abundant, and the most elusive of all the particles in the Cosmos. Neutrinos are mainly described as elusive because they have no mass or electric charge. Since they do not interact with matter, as we know it, they are classified as potentially the dark matter of the Universe. The Neutrino is impossible to contain, we cannot stop it or shield it. We can only see its traces and how it mutates. It is an unstable particle that defies the Standard model and intercepts a predictable way of understanding our environment.

mine. The IceCube Neutrino Observatory at the Amundsen-Scott South Pole Station is a one-cubic-kilometer array of sensors at depths between 1,450 and 2,450 meters beneath the Antarctic ice. Particle physics experiments require highly specific and controlled conditions, since the production of elementary particles is extremely difficult and their detection requires extremely sensitive equipment. Any small interference can skew the results.[2] The sensors used for this scientific work need to be placed deep underground, either in massive new holes, in old mines, in deep-sea waters, or under the Antarctic or Siberian ice to avoid the cosmic radiation that would interfere with the results. These laboratories are creating a new subterranean infrastructure—a material, epistemological, and ontological layer of contemporary science.

12,000 trillion neutrinos have just passed through you.

The tiny monastic laboratory of the seventeenth century has been replaced by a global technoscientific infrastructure spread across the planet. These major scientific spaces and networks have expanded the idea of the lone scientist's lab to large cities of scientists working on the same dilemmas. Experiments for studying the smallest particles of matter and their phenomena now involve massive urban complexes, buildings, and chambers designed to host the invisible. These hybrid urban environments comprise scientists, particles, liquids, data, politics, and technologies working together for the production of knowledge and to translate a world not directly perceptible to humans. As Donna Haraway states, the human body is the prosthetic body par excellence. It relies on tools to evolve.[3] Scientific infrastructures became architectures of hybrid systems of transnational and more-than-human collaborations.

The notion of infrastructure acts as a revelatory of the "working" quality of this universe, opening into the perception of a whole world of invisible labours that are more than human. —Maria Puig de la Bellacasa[4]

2 Some neutrino detectors, such as the the SNO in Canada or Super-Kamiokande built inside the closed Kamioka mine in Japan, have reused existing extractivist infrastructures. The overlapping of infrastructural layers reveals the changes in economy and labor structures and the social problematic surrounding these specific sites when the mine closes. The substitution of a mine for a highly sophisticated scientific facility does not repair the social fabric of the surrounding villages, struggling with unemployment and its economic dependency on the extraction of minerals.

3 Donna J. Haraway, "A Cyborg Manifesto: Science, Technology, and Socialist-Feminism in the Late Twentieth Century," in *Simians, Cyborgs, and Women: The Reinvention of Nature***, 149–82 (London: Free Association Books, 1991).**

4 Maria Puig de la Bellacasa, "Encountering Bioinfrastructure: Ecological Struggles and the Sciences of Soil," *Social Epistemology* **28, no. 1 (2014): 26–40 (here 27).**

Blanca Pujals, *A Synthetic Universe: The Unmaking of Microscopic Bonds in Transnational Space*, **2016. Three-channel video installation, color, stereo, HDV. 18' 44". (Images in the picture are from CERN's historical archive, ©CERN).**

Contemporary laboratories are an assembly of parts: multiple teams, disciplines, and countries. Their machines are built and designed around the world, and scientific teams comprise large global collaborations of experts. These teams not only study phenomena at the smallest of scales but also look at large-scale phenomena, in the process participating in synchronized global networks supported by complex infrastructures. The data collected from the rare collision of neutrinos in detectors is also shared among neutrino infrastructures spread across the world, which, by observing the trace of the same neutrino, unveil the almost silent infrastructure of subatomic particles that are relentlessly trespassing us.

As a large techno-organism, this transnational laboratory of observatories and colliders is simultaneously storing and processing the data it collects. It is an architecture of wire and sensor networks enlarging the physical space to an infrastructure of worldwide interconnections. The massive amount of information collected during the experiments requires an international computing collaboration for its storage and processing. Both the computers and communications need increased capacity and speed to store, analyze, and share results with the full community of scientists and experts around the world. It is no coincidence that Tim Berners-Lee—who created the World Wide

Web in 1989 to allow researchers to share and update information—was, at the time, a computer scientist at CERN.[5] Scientific infrastructures around the world are sensing and collecting data uninterruptedly. Earth itself has become a planetary laboratory, endlessly monitoring and being monitored by scientific infrastructures that are largely invisible.

5 **"The Birth of the Web,"** *CERN*, **https://home.cern/science/computing/birth-web.**

24,000 trillion neutrinos have just passed through you.

Blanca Pujals, *A Synthetic Universe: The Unmaking of Microscopic Bonds in Transnational Space*, **2016. Three-channel video installation, color, stereo, HDV. 18' 44". (Images in the picture are from CERN's historical archive, © CERN).**

Infra- means "below," an underlying and invisible structure, a substrate to events. Following Karl Marx, changes in the *superstructure* depend on changes in the infrastructure.[6]

In W*e Have Never Been Modern*, Bruno Latour, following a discussion advanced by Steven Shapin in *Leviathan and the Air Pump*, expands on the notion of the laboratory as a seventeenth-century space of concealment for independent scientific opinion beyond state control.[7] Thus, "the Modern Constitution invents a separation between the scientific power charged with representing things and political power responsible for representing subjects."[8] Science and politics became "a public space with restricted access."[9]

6 According to Marx, infrastructure supports the social structure and the superstructure, which includes culture, institutions, political power structures, roles, rituals, religion, media and state.

7 Bruno Latour, *We Have Never Been Modern* **(Cambridge, MA: Harvard University Press, 1993); and Steven Shapin and**

However, the dimensions and sophistication of these new scientific laboratories increasingly require an excess of financial resources from the participating countries, with costs exceeding most national budgets—even more so if the countries are small—so fundamental science experiments are planned and sustained with shared public resources. Treaties, alliances, joint ventures, and collaborations through scientific infrastructures and knowledge are made on a planetary scale. They have generated a new infrastructure combining political pacts with developments made in the scientific field. Science is participating actively in political treaties and agreements in the name of peace and scientific knowledge, playing a key role in countries' foreign relations, where scientific collaborations are used as a source of soft power which, in contrast to hard power, is the ability to attract co-opt rather than coerce.

33,600 trillion neutrinos have just passed through you.

In 1949, shortly after the Second World War, a group of scientists conceived the idea of a European atomic physics laboratory to avoid resource competition and war in Europe. It was the first postwar proposal for scientific collaboration among European countries.[10] The European physicists Niels Bohr, Edoardo Amaldi, Pierre Auger, Lew Kowarski, and the engineer and politician Raoul Dautry imagined the creation of a future physics laboratory to host the new fundamental physics knowledge, an architecture where physicists from different nations would work together to produce future facts across multiple generations. Eight years later, the European Atomic Energy Community was created at the same time as the European Economic Community (EEC). The Euratom Treaty was signed for the coordination of research in atomic energy and the creation of CERN in Geneva.[11] That Geneva was chosen to host CERN, despite Switzerland not being a member of the EEC, was not by chance. The reasons were geological and political. The Swiss Confederation had maintained neutrality and remained a stable state during both world wars, and

Simon Schaffer, *Leviathan and the Air Pump* **(Princeton, NJ: Princeton University Press, 1985).**

8 Latour, *We Have Never Been Modern*, **28.**

9 Shapin and Schaffer, *Leviathan and the Air Pump*, **336.**

10 The first signed treaty, the European Coal and Steel Community (ECSC), was proposed by French foreign minister Robert Schuman on May 9, 1950. It was formally established in 1951 by the Treaty of Paris, signed by Belgium, France, Italy, Luxembourg, the Netherlands, and West Germany.

11 The 'Euratom Treaty' was not included in the general ECC treaty due to the disapproval of the word 'atomic' within the civil society for its connotations after the War and the raising menace of nuclear weapons. In order that the collaboration in the research of atomic energy would not create suspicion about the European Economic Community, it was written in a separate document under its own conditions and still has a separate legal form.

science, although is historically involved in military development, and after the wars in Europe, scientific experiments, national defenses and energy resources increasingly merged, paradoxically needs long-term stable conditions to carry out experiments over long periods. CERN, an interstate organization that is not administratively linked to either country within which it is sited, became a surrounded/enclosed space with particular, controlled conditions. France and Switzerland are the "host countries" but do not exercise sovereignty over CERN. A fence with checkpoints surrounds the laboratory, and one must be accredited to pass through. In the name of scientific knowledge and peace, the Euratom Treaty built a new architecture of the territory—a new political entity

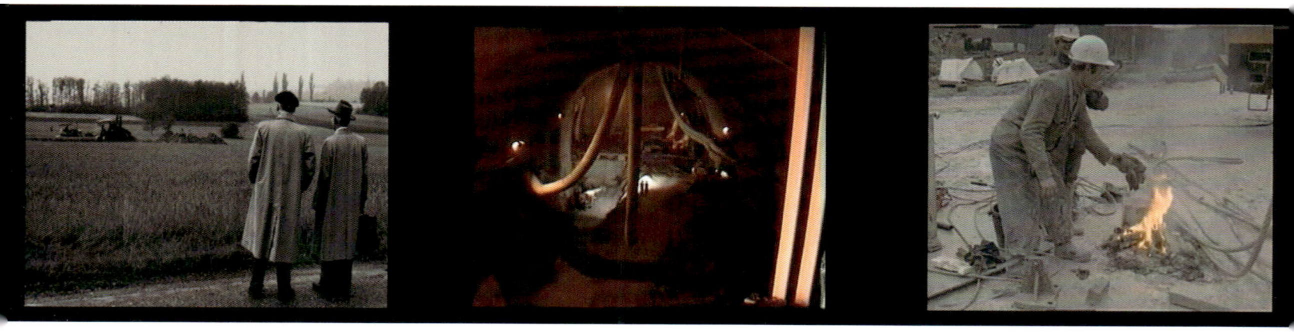

Blanca Pujals, *A Synthetic Universe: The Unmaking of Microscopic Bonds in Transnational Space*, **2016. Three-channel video installation, color, stereo, HDV. 18' 44''. (Images in the picture are from CERN's historical archive, © CERN).**

based on a multinational political union, a supranational political form with negotiated power.

Although the LHC at CERN is imperceptible from the surface, it also organizes the land above it. Billions of subatomic particles cross the French-Swiss border about eleven thousand times every second. Twenty years after the first ground works started in Geneva, the construction of the first large accelerator, the Super Proton Synchrotron, crossed underneath the Franco-Swiss border, entering French territory, trespassing across the threshold of the nation-state. The free circulation of the elementary particles in 1983 predated by twelve years the Schengen agreement abolishing internal border controls in Europe (implemented in 1995) and predated Switzerland's incorporation to that agreement by twenty-six years. During the construction of CERN, not only was the horizontal nation-state border surpassed, but it also challenged vertical private property laws. Although the experimental machine was built deep underground to avoid radiation and damage to the properties and land existing along the tunnel's path, in France a landowner's property rights extend from the surface to the earth's center. Therefore, French authorities had to declare the land occupied by the future collider a public good and turn the underlying rock, down to the earth's nucleus, into "public property."

New supranational laboratories like CERN transformed physics into a force within politics, creating new spaces of negotiation and agreement.

49,700 trillion neutrinos have just passed through you.

Although political alliances made on the scientific field demand territories and transnational collaborations based on science for peace, bodies in some of these countries are still and increasingly locked within a regime of violence and systemic discrimination, which reveal different forms of structural differences, rights, and conflicts.

"Science is a natural way to build bridges between cultures and nations, because of its common language."[12] This claim, made by theoretical physicist Eliezer Rabinovici, celebrates a new elementary particle laboratory in the Middle East set up on the model of CERN. First proposed in 1993 following the Oslo Accords and the Israeli–Palestinian peace process, the Synchrotron-Light for Experimental Science Applications in the Middle East (SESAME) was inaugurated in May 2017. The new laboratory is based on the claim that regional peace can be achieved through science. Located in Jordan, SESAME aims to build "scientific and cultural bridges between neighbouring countries, promoting mutual understanding and tolerance through international cooperation, and fostering a regional community of scientific users who will

12 Eliezer Rabinovici quoted in Dennis Overbye, "A Light for Science, and Cooperation, in the Middle East," *New York Times*, **May 8, 2017, https://www.nytimes.com/2017/05/08/science/sesame-institute-jordan-synchrotron.html.**

13 "SESAME," *UNESCO*, **http://www.unesco.org/new/en/natural-sciences/science-technology/basic-sciences/international-basic-sciences-program/sesame/.**

work together."[13] The founding members are Bahrain (not currently a member), Cyprus, Egypt, Iran, Israel, Jordan, Pakistan, the Palestinian Authority, and Turkey. "I don't know how many places there are where all these governments have representatives who have the opportunity to come and talk to each other," said Giorgio Paolucci, the scientific director of SESAME.[14]

This collaboration, made possible by scientific soft power, reveals an inevitable paradox, however. Israel supports transnational research with the State of Palestine, a state it does not recognize, and agrees to cooperate for research in subjects ranging from medicine and biology, through to basic properties of materials science, physics and chemistry to healthcare, the environment and archaeology, while it erases the traces of abandoned Palestinian villages to erase their right on the land, and bombs Palestinian cities and its social and medical research institutions. Transnational collaborations to enable world-class research in the scientific field are built, but fundamental social structures are endlessly destroyed.

14 Kareem Shaheen, "Open SESAME: Particle Accelerator Project Brings Middle East Together," ***The Guardian*****, August 30, 2016, https://www.theguardian.com/world/2016/aug/30/sesame-particle-accelerator-project-middle-east-jordan.**

58,700 trillion neutrinos have just passed through you.

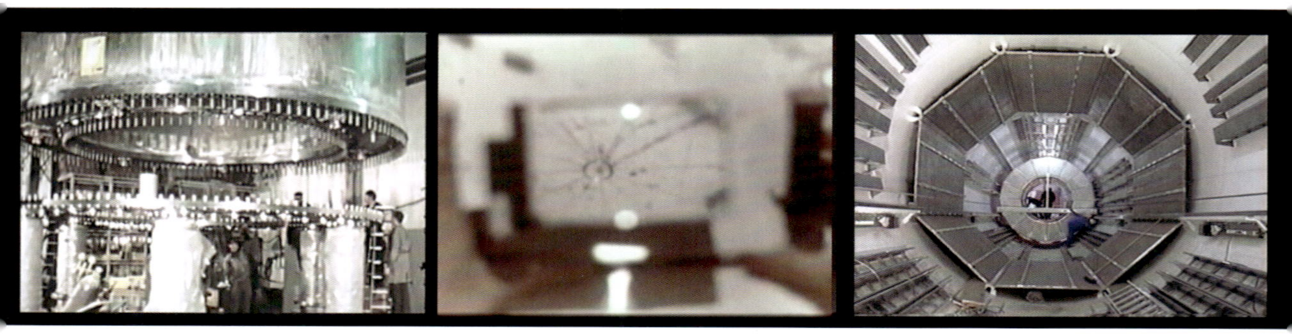

Blanca Pujals, *A Synthetic Universe: The Unmaking of Microscopic Bonds in Transnational Space*, **2016. Three-channel video installation, color, stereo, HDV. 18' 44''. (Images in the picture are from CERN's historical archive, © CERN).**

Elementary particles reconfigure a net of frictions full of paradoxes and unstable propositions that are constantly changing. Subatomic particles question the Standard Model of Particle Physics, while scientific infrastructures simultaneously challenge previous geopolitical models determining new political and social structures, especially on a micropolitical and microsocial level. Quantum Physics is not detached from our social and political structures; it is entangled with its spatial, territorial and material interactions and interferences, although it remains as an invisible infrastructure.

With the rise of a new scientific era, a parallel need to develop new political architectures that surpass the nation state in order to build transnational agreements has emerged. Is it possible that scientific architecture can be a potential driver of political progress? Science struggles against ideology in a very particular way. Science often destroys existing models to create new provisional ones. It refutes logic through experimentation. Scientific laboratories very often produce the conditions for future transformations of socio-political models.

While historical layers of political power and scientific sovereignty overlap, the new historical layer now emerging—informed by new understandings of materiality and related to astronomy, meteorology, and ecological processes—is creating collisions and transformations. In this picture, matter moves increasingly toward a hybrid, ungraspable state. However, although liminal matter problematizes the matter of facts, and political agreements are becoming hybrid, bodies are still trapped in a regime of modernity and borders. Imposed official landscapes and bodies disregard the intra-actions, a neologism introduced by physicist Karen Barad, which "understands agency as not an inherent property of an individual or human to be exercised, but as a dynamism of forces in which all designated 'things' are constantly exchanging and diffracting, influencing and working inseparably."[15]

15 Karen Barad, *Meeting the Universe Half Way* **(Durham: Duke University Press, 2007).**

The quantum infrastructure of matter profoundly defies the systems that emerged with the modern project. New results from quantum physics concerning the origin of matter can lead us to reconsider old categories. The uncertainty principle, which disrupts cause-effect determinism, and the entanglement phenomenon, which blurs the notion of borders and separability, can provide us with new generative possibilities of social imagination and politics, offering entangled and generative, vulnerable and intra-dependant forms of sociality.

The transnational network of particle physics underground laboratories is constructing a new scientific architecture around the world: a sensing infrastructure, which amplifies new political and material interactions. Paraphrasing Isabelle Stengers, "every new machine is a new époque."[16] We might also say that every new scientific experimental chamber is the architecture of a new époque of hybrid systems of transnational and more-than-human collaborations.

A hybrid human-machine-electron-organism, a planetary/time-space where cables, rare earth, bodies, soil, entities, liquids, particles, atmosphere and outer space are increasingly interconnected in a techno-organism that is speedily evolving and relentlessly intra-acting from the very base of the quantum infrastructure of matter.

72,000 trillion neutrinos have just passed through you.[17]

16 "The Insistence of the Possible: Symposium with Isabelle Stengers," Goldsmiths, 18 May 2016.

17 Joanna Rose: What are Neutrinos, then?
Olga Botner: Oh! I wish we knew what Neutrinos are! ... Neutrinossss aaaareeee amongggg these few fundamental particles which make up matter. And we know them from radioactive decaysssss, but what they really are, no one knows, no one has ever seen a Neutrino. Neutrinos have no electric charge, and we can only detect particles, which carry electric charge, and so we can only discover Neutrinos when they interact with something and produce charge particles. And this is how we know three kinds of Neutrinos but no one has ever seen the Neutrino itself.

Professor Olga Botner, Member of the Nobel Committee for Physics, was interviewed by freelance journalist Joanna Rose regarding the 2015 Nobel Prize in Physics.

Contributors

Changhyun Ahn is a designer working for Gusang Group Architects, Seoul. He received a master's degree in architecture from the KTH Royal Institute of Technology, earning honorable mention for his thesis, "Leftovers." Interested in mega-scale projects, Chang currently works mainly on cultural projects such as memorials and art spaces.

Rouzbeh Akhbari is an artist working in video installation and film. His practice is research-driven and usually exists at the intersections of storytelling, critical architecture and human geography. Through a delicate examination of the violences and intimacies that can occur at the boundaries of lived experience and constructed histories, Akhbari uncovers the minutiae of power that regiments the world around us. He holds a BFA in sculpture and installation from Ontario College of Art and Design University and a masters of visual studies from the University of Toronto School of Architecture, Landscape and Design. He has authored and co-authored peer-reviewed articles in *Projections 13* (a journal of the MIT Department of Urban Studies), *Funambulist*, *Scapegoat Journal*, *Society + Space*, and *C-Magazine*, and contributed book chapters to *The Work of Wind: Land* (K-Verlag, 2018), *Unsettling Colonial Modernity in Islamicate Contexts* (Cambridge Scholars, 2017), and *Shift* (Sugar Contemporary, 2019). His first long-format story titled *Prizes from Fairyland* was released in 2018, and his most recent ficto-critical novella *Perturbation: A Speculative History of Future(s) Past* was launched in the summer of 2021 in collaboration with Universidade Católica Portuguesa. Akhbari is currently a Ph.D. student at University of Toronto's school of Geography and Planning.

Malin Bergman is an architect practicing in London. An attentive listener, she is devoted to tuning in to silenced narratives through caring spatial explorations, an approach she developed as a student in the Infrastructural Love design studio. She holds a master's degree in architecture from the KTH Royal Institute of Technology, where she completed her thesis, "Residual Care—Stories from an Extractive Landscape."

Marco Bruggmann studied architecture at ETH Zurich and did his exchange semester at the KTH Royal Institute of Technology in autumn 2019. He graduated at the chair of Anne Lacaton and received his master's degree in architecture from ETH in 2020. Since graduation he has been working as project manager of spatial and urban planning in his hometown of Uzwil, Switzerland.

Adrià Carbonell is an architect and urbanist. He is a lecturer in architecture at KTH Royal Institute of Technology. He has held teaching positions at KU Leuven Sint-Lucas, Tallinn University of Technology, Umeå Universitet, and the American University of Sharjah. He is cofounder of the research collaborative Aside, where he writes on the interplay between architecture, territory, politics, and the environment. His writings have been published in *PLAN*, *ACE: Architecture, City and Environment*, *ZARCH Journal of Interdisciplinary Studies in Architecture and Urbanism*, *San Rocco*, *MONU*, *Cartha*, among others. His current research addresses two guiding questions: how to reframe cosmopolitical spatial practices and how to challenge existing urban inequalities through processes of territorial redistribution.

Céline Condorelli is a London- and Lisbon-based artist and one of the founding directors of Eastside Projects in Birmingham. She is the author and editor of *Support Structures* (Sternberg Press, 2009). Her work combines multiple approaches, from developing structures for "supporting" (the work of others, forms of political imaginary, existing and fictional realities) to broader enquiries into forms of commonality and discursive sites. Her work has been exhibited international at group and solo shows in France, Spain, Austria, Portugal, Italy, and Australia. In 2017 she was awarded the Australian Institute of Architects Art and Architecture Prize. Her first monograph, *bau bau*, was published by Mousse in 2017.

Danika Cooper is Assistant Professor of Landscape Architecture and Environmental Planning at the University of California, Berkeley, where the core of her research centers on the geopolitics of scarcity, alternative water ontologies, and designs for resiliency in the world's arid regions. Her work incorporates historiographical research methods, data visualizations, and theories of urban infrastructure to evaluate and design for environmental and social justice. Specifically, Cooper is focused on emphasizing alternatives to the prevailing nineteenth-century conceptions that the aridlands should be overturned through technocratic solutions and neoliberal politics. Her work has been published and exhibited around the world, and she has practiced architecture and landscape architecture in both the United States and in India.

Isabelle Doucet is Professor of Theory and History of Architecture at the Department of Architecture and Civil Engineering at Chalmers University of Technology. Her research focuses on the relationship between architecture, (urban) politics, and social/environmental responsibility, which she examines through both conceptual-methodological inquiries and historical and contemporary cases. Ongoing research focuses on women in architecture after 1968. She is the author of *The Practice Turn in Architecture. Brussels after 1968* (2015). Recent editorial projects include the edited volume *Activism at Home. Architects Dwelling between Politics, Aesthetics, and Resistance*, coedited with Janina Gosseye (2021), and the thematic issue "Resist Reclaim Speculate: Situated Perspectives on Architecture and the City," coedited with Hélène Frichot, in *Architectural Theory Review* (2018).

Emilie Evans is an architectural graduate from the University of Melbourne and holds a BA (Honours) in interior architecture from Monash University, where she teaches history and theory in the architecture faculty. Her teaching engages with ideas of architecture and the urban on a planetary scale. She is also a research assistant at the University of Melbourne and a practicing architectural graduate specializing in the residential sector. Her independent thesis project "Infrastructural Remains: Caring for Anthropogenic Ruins" was nominated for a Royal Institute of British Architects Silver Medal Award and an Australian Institute of Architects Victorian Chapter Graduate Prize. Her research interests lie in speculative architectural fictions, more-than-human agency, and multispecies relations.

Hélène Frichot is professor of architecture and philosophy and director of the Bachelor of Design Program in the Faculty of Architecture, Building and Planning at the University of Melbourne. She is the former director of the Critical Studies in Architecture program at the School of Architecture, KTH Royal Institute of Technology, where she was based from 2012 to 2019. Drawing on the two disciplines in which she is trained, architecture and philosophy, her research fosters creative practice methodologies and develops concept-tools and theories that draw on feminist new materialism, the posthumanities, environmental humanities, and affect theory. She is the author of *Creative Ecologies: Theorizing the Practice of Architecture* (Bloomsbury, 2018), *How to Make Yourself a Feminist Design Power Tool* (AADR, 2016), and *Dirty Theory: Troubling Architecture* (AADR, 2019). She has collaborated on numerous collections, including, as a coeditor with Catharina Gabrielsson and Helen Runting, *Architecture and Feminisms: Ecologies, Economies, Technologies* (Routledge, 2017); with Naomi Stead, *Writing Architectures: Ficto-critical Approaches* (Bloomsbury, 2020); and with Marco Jobst, *Architectural Affects after Deleuze and Guattari* (Routledge, 2021).

Hannes Frykholm is an architect, educator, researcher, and currently the Rothwell Chair Postdoctoral Associate at the University of Sydney, School of Architecture, Design and Planning. He holds a PhD in architecture from the KTH Royal Institute of Technology, where he has been teaching the master's degree studio Infrastructural Love. His doctoral thesis, "Building the City from the Inside," considers entrance situations that occur between buildings and cities in order to develop new ways of investigating architecture and urban transformation. The thesis points to the threshold of three buildings as sites of a transformational relationship between architecture and capitalism, whereby the city is reconfigured through the extension of interiors onto sidewalks and squares. He is a member of FyR Architects, a Stockholm- and Madrid-based practice exploring the relationship between architecture and infrastructure.

Richard Gray is an architect based in Stockholm. He holds a BSc (First Class Honours) in architecture from Queen's University Belfast and an MSc in architecture from the KTH Royal Institute of Technology. His master's thesis, "A Design for Decline," researched and proposed solutions for architecture in shrinking cities. He is employed at UrbanWorks, an architecture and urban development office in Stockholm.

Leonie Hartung is an architecture master's degree student at Berlin University of the Arts and a bachelor of philosophy student at HU Berlin. She has worked and studied in Stockholm, Brussels, and Basel. A recent fellow with the editorial team of *ARCH+ Journal for Architecture and Urbanism*, she currently assists at the Chair of Urban Design and Urbanization at TU Berlin.

Isak Hellström is an architect (SAR/MSA) and artist at Respons Arkitekter, where he mainly works on reconstructing existing housing units in central Stockholm. He graduated from the KTH School of Architecture in 2019 and from the art school Nyckelviksskolan in 2013. As an artist he works with figurative painting to describe the urban landscape, in-between places, and the infrastructure of everyday life.

Sepideh Karami is a writer, architect, teacher, and researcher and currently a Lecturer in Architecture at the University of Edinburgh, School of Architecture and Landscape Architecture (ESALA). She holds a PhD in architecture and critical studies from the KTH School of Architecture, where she also held a lecturer position until 2020. She developed her thesis *Interruption: Writing a Dissident Architecture*, through writing practices and critical fiction as political practices of making architectural spaces. She completed her architecture education at Iran University of Science and Technology (MA, 2002) and Chalmers University (MSc, 2010). Since completing her first degree in architecture, she has been committed to teaching, research, and practice in various international contexts and has developed her work through artistic research and interdisciplinary approaches at the intersection of architecture, performing arts, literature and geology, with the ethos of decolonization, minor politics and criticality from within. She has presented, performd, and exhibited her work at international conferences and platforms, and is published in peer reviewed journals.

Shahram Khosravi is professor in anthropology at Stockholms Universitet (Stockholm University). He is the author of *Young and Defiant in Tehran* (University of Pennsylvania Press, 2009) and *"Illegal" Traveller: An Auto-ethnography of Borders* (Palgrave Macmillan, 2010). He has also contributed to publications such as the *New York Times* and *Red Pepper*. His research interests include anthropology of Iran and the Middle East, migration, human rights, and forced displacement.

Elke Krasny is professor for art and education at the Academy of Fine Arts Vienna. She is a feminist cultural theorist, urban researcher, curator, and author. With colleagues at the Acadmemy of Fine Arts Vienna and the University of Applied Arts Vienna she initiated the Alliance Art and Education against Racism and Fascism. Her scholarship addresses epistemic violence and memory politics, matters of care and social reproduction, and ecosocial justice at the present historical conjuncture, with a focus on emancipatory practices in architecture, urbanism, and contemporary art. She was advisor for the exhibition *Un paradiso amaro / Bitter Paradise* (2021) dedicated to remembering the erasure of the Jewish sculptor Teresa Feodorowna Ries. Together with Angelika Fitz, she edited *Critical Care: Architecture and Urbanism for a Broken Planet together* (MIT Press, 2019). Her forthcoming book, *Living with an Infected Planet: Covid-19 Feminism and the Global Frontline of Care* (transcript Verlag, 2022), develops a feminist perspective on imaginaries of war and the realities of care in pandemic times.

Erik Lokrantz is a graduate of the School of Architecture, KTH Royal Institute of Technology, where he also participated in an exchange at the Berlin University of the Arts. His interests include fashion, film, liberatory politics, and sci-fi. These interests lay the groundwork for his practice, which reflects on multispecies relations, property, violence, and the performed dichotomies of nature/civilization, human/nonhuman.

Shannon Mattern is a professor of anthropology at The New School for Social Research in New York. Her writing and teaching focus on archives, libraries, and other media spaces; media infrastructures; spatial epistemologies; and mediated sensation and exhibition. She is the author of *The New Downtown Library: Designing with Communities* (University of Minnesota Press, 2007), *Deep Mapping the Media City* (University of Minnesota Press, 2015), *Code and Clay, Data and Dirt: Five Thousand Years of Urban Media* (University of Minnesota Press, 2017), and *A City Is Not a Computer* (Princeton University Press, 2021). She also contributes a regular long-form column about urban data and mediated infrastructures to Places, a journal focusing on architecture, urbanism, and landscape, and she collaborates on public design and interactive projects and exhibitions. She can be found online at wordsinspace.net.

Yaseera Moosa is a photographer and architecture student at the University of Melbourne on unceded Wurundjeri Country. Through design, image-making and writing, she is interested in unearthing material-embodied narratives and interdependencies, as well as critically examining constructs of nature and infrastructure, in an effort to unsettle and enrich understandings of place.

Thandi Lane is a quietly passionate Master of Architecture student at the Melbourne School of Design, University of Melbourne, who deeply values architecture's potential for boundless curiosity and lateral inquiry. She applauds the discipline's innate reliance upon a collaborative spirit and sees endless possibilities for the interweaving of architecture within a rich tapestry of creative, interdisciplinary expression. Establishing her own meandering desire lines, Thandi earnestly pursues inventive, thoughtful, playful, and kind communications and storytelling within everything she does.

Marie Le Rouzic, a creative designer and researcher with an education in applied arts and architecture, is a graduate of École Boulle (Paris), Central Saint Martins (London), and the KTH Royal Institute of Technology. Her work explores perspectives that defy the anthropocentric model and enable collaborations within our ecosystems. As an advocate for ecofeminism, she values fair and sustainable approaches and emphasizes the design of innovative, ecologically conscious living environments mindful of their contexts and users.

Blanca Pujals is an architect, spatial researcher, and critical writer. Her cross-disciplinary practice uses spatial research and critical analysis to engage with questions around the geographies of power on bodies and territories, policies of scientific and technological knowledge production, as well as transnational politics, developing tools for undertaking analysis through different visual and sonic devices. Her work encompasses film, architecture, lecturing, curatorial projects, teaching, and critical writing. She received her BA in architecture from UIC Barcelona School of Architecture. She completed her studies with an MA in critical theory from the Independent Studies Program of the Museu d'Art Contemporani de Barcelona (Barcelona Museum of Contemporary Art), tutored by the philosopher Paul B. Preciado. She was recently a postgraduate at the Centre for Research Architecture (Visual Cultures Department) at Goldsmiths University of London, directed by Susan Schuppli and Eyal Weizman. She is currently developing her practice-led PhD in arts and sciences, focusing on the geopolitics and spatial articulations of particle physics infrastructures. She can be found online at www.blancapujals.com.

Raphael Marius Schall is a graduate of the Technical University of Munich, where he focused on history, theory, and built heritage conservation. For his master's thesis, he investigated the potential and possible constructions of design-build within existing building structures as an interim use strategy. After finishing his bachelor's degree at the Leibniz University Hannover in 2017, he gained work experience in the field of architecture in Zurich before starting his master's studies in Munich in 2018. As part of the master's program, he studied at KTH Royal Institute of Technology for a year and was part of the Infrastructure Cares studio. Since 2021, he has been working as a junior architect in Munich.

S.O.C. (Société d'Objets Cartographiques) is a France-based studio of three architect-artists (http://s-o-c.fr). The studio's main objective is to help foster exchanges among the arts, sciences, and architecture with long inquiries emerging from field practices and involving a network of actors from various disciplines. The S.O.C.'s current inquiries—*Terra Forma, Où atterrir?*, and *Critical Zones*—will be represented by various multimedia objects (e.g., books, workshops, installations, cartographies). The studio designed the installation CZO space at the ZKM | Center for Art and Media Karlsruhe, for the exhibition *Critical Zones: Observatories for Earthly Politics* (2020–2022), curated by Bruno Latour. Alexandra Arènes cofounded S.O.C. in 2016 after years of practice in a landscape architecture firm. She is a doctoral researcher at the University of Manchester. Her research interests include the impact of the Anthropocene on landscape studies and visualizations. She is the author of *Terra Forma: Manuel de cartographies potentielles* (B42, 2019).

Helen Stratford is an artist with a background in architecture. Located between art, performance, architecture, and writing, her practice and research embrace site-specific live events, video works, and speculative writing that search for modalities to expand architectural conventions. Currently a lecturer in architecture at Sheffield Hallam University, she completed her PhD, "Feminist Performative Architectures: Making Place in and with Public Space," at Sheffield University in 2021. She has held residencies at Yorkshire Sculpture Park, Wysing Arts Centre, METAL, g39, Oriel Davies, Akademie Schloss Solitude, and the Center for Contemporary Arts Celje. A member of the Taking Place feminist architecture collective, her research has been presented at the Oslo Architecture Triennale, Floating University Berlin, KTH Royal Institute of Technology, National Theatre, Royal Institute of British Architects, Tate Modern, Institute of Contemporary Arts London, Škuc Gallery, and P74. She has published in peer-reviewed journals and in the edited volumes *Material Matters: Architecture and Material Practice* (Routledge, 2007) and *Altering Practices: Feminist Politics and Poetics of Space* (Routledge, 2007). Her artist's books include *The Day of the Duck* (Marmalade Publishers of Visual Theory, 2018) and *Mechanical Operations in Cambourne* (Marmalade Publishers of Visual Theory, 2009). She can be found online at www.helenstratford.co.uk.

Hélène Frichot, Adrià Carbonell, Hannes Frykholm, Sepideh Karami (Eds.)

Bettina Schwalm (Designer)

Printed with the financial support of School of Architecture, KTH (Royal Institute of Technology) Stockholm, Sweden with a contribution from the Professor of Architecture and Philosophy research fund, Melbourne School of Design, Faculty of Architecture, Building and Planning, University of Melbourne, Australia.

Acquisitions Editor: David Marold, Birkhäuser Verlag, Vienna, Austria
Content and Production Editor: Katharina Holas, Birkhäuser Verlag, Vienna, Austria
Proofreading/Copyediting: Christopher Davey, Bolton, Connecticut, USA,
Ada St. Laurent, Vienna, Austria
Layout, cover design, and typography: Bettina Schwalm, Stockholm, Sweden
Image editing: Bettina Schwalm, the Editors, and the Authors
Printing: Beltz Grafische Betriebe GmbH, Bad Langensalza, Germany
Paper: Condat matt Périgord 135 gsm, Offset 350 gsm
Typeface: Two Points Stulle, Didot, PT Sans,

Library of Congress Control Number: 2021951465

Bibliographic information published by the German National Library
The German National Library lists this publication in the Deutsche Nationalbibliografie; detailed bibliographic data are available on the Internet at http://dnb.dnb.de.

ISBN 978-3-0356-2519-6
e-ISBN (PDF) 978-3-0356-2520-2

P.O. Box 44, 4009 Basel, Switzerland
Part of Walter de Gruyter GmbH, Berlin/Boston

9 8 7 6 5 4 3 2 1 www.birkhauser.com